MY LIFE AND TIMES
OCTAVE NINE
1946-1953

BY COMPTON MACKENZIE

Novels and Romances

SINISTER STREET
SYLVIA SCARLETT
GUY AND PAULINE
CARNIVAL
FIGURE OF EIGHT
CORAL
THE VANITY GIRL
ROGUES AND VAGABONDS
THE ALTAR STEPS
THE PARSON'S PROGRESS
THE HEAVENLY LADDER
HUNTING THE FAIRIES
WHISKY GALORE
KEEP THE HOME GUARD TURNING
THE MONARCH OF THE GLEN
THE RIVAL MONSTER
BEN NEVIS GOES EAST
THE RED TAPEWORM
PAPER LIVES
ROCKETS GALORE
THE STOLEN SOPRANO
THE LUNATIC REPUBLIC
POOR RELATIONS
APRIL FOOLS
RICH RELATIVES
BUTTERCUPS AND DAISIES
WATER ON THE BRAIN
VESTAL FIRE
EXTRAORDINARY WOMEN
THIN ICE
EXTREMES MEET
THE THREE COURIERS
OUR STREET
THE DARKENING GREEN
THE PASSIONATE ELOPEMENT
FAIRY GOLD
THE SEVEN AGES OF WOMAN
PARADISE FOR SALE
MEZZOTINT
THE FOUR WINDS OF LOVE:
    THE EAST WIND
    THE SOUTH WIND
    THE WEST WIND
    THE NORTH WIND

Play

THE LOST CAUSE

Verse

POEMS 1907
KENSINGTON RHYMES

History and Biography

EASTERN EPIC. VOL. I
ALL OVER THE PLACE
GALLIPOLI MEMORIES
ATHENIAN MEMORIES
GREEK MEMORIES
AEGEAN MEMORIES
WIND OF FREEDOM
MR ROOSEVELT
DR BENES
PRINCE CHARLIE
PRINCE CHARLIE AND HIS LADIES
CATHOLICISM AND SCOTLAND
MARATHON AND SALAMIS
PERICLES
THE WINDSOR TAPESTRY
THE VITAL FLAME
I TOOK A JOURNEY
COALPORT
REALMS OF SILVER
THE QUEEN'S HOUSE
MY RECORD OF MUSIC
SUBLIME TOBACCO
GREECE IN MY LIFE
CATS' COMPANY
CATMINT
LOOK-AT CATS

Essays and Criticism

ECHOES
A MUSICAL CHAIR
UNCONSIDERED TRIFLES
REAPED AND BOUND
LITERATURE IN MY TIME
ON MORAL COURAGE

Children's Stories

LITTLE CAT LOST
SANTA CLAUS IN SUMMER
TOLD
MABEL IN QUEER STREET
THE UNPLEASANT VISITORS
THE CONCEITED DOLL
THE ENCHANTED BLANKET
THE DINING-ROOM BATTLE
THE ADVENTURES OF TWO CHAIRS
THE ENCHANTED ISLAND
THE NAUGHTYMOBILE
THE FAIRY IN THE WINDOW BOX
THE STAIRS THAT KEPT ON GOING
    DOWN
THE STRONGEST MAN ON EARTH
THE SECRET ISLAND
BUTTERFLY HILL

Autobiography

MY LIFE AND TIMES: OCTAVE ONE;
OCTAVE TWO; OCTAVE THREE;
OCTAVE FOUR; OCTAVE FIVE;
OCTAVE SIX; OCTAVE SEVEN;
OCTAVE EIGHT

MY LIFE
AND TIMES

OCTAVE NINE

1946-1953

Compton Mackenzie

1970
CHATTO & WINDUS
LONDON

Published by
Chatto & Windus Ltd
42 William IV Street
London, W.C.2

★

Clarke, Irwin & Co. Ltd
Toronto

SBN 7011 1577 7

137253

Printed in Great Britain by
T. & A. Constable Ltd
Hopetoun Street, Edinburgh

To

GILBERT and IDA MacNAUGHTAN
with gratitude and affection

CONTENTS

*

ACKNOWLEDGMENTS

My grateful thanks for permission to quote letters are due to the following: Field-Marshal Sir Claude Auchinleck, Sir Michael Balcon, Mr Richard Church, Brigadier-General Sir Harold Hartley, Mr Denys Kilham Roberts, Mrs Rosamond Lehmann, General Sir Rob Lockhart, Mr Bernard Miles, Admiral of the Fleet Earl Mountbatten of Burma, Mr Ian Parsons, Mr and Mrs Harold Raymond, Mrs Norah Smallwood, Lord Snow, General Sir Montagu Stopford, Mr P. G. Wodehouse; and to Lord Birdwood for the late Field-Marshal Lord Birdwood of Anzac and Totnes, Mrs Brett-Young for Francis Brett-Young, Lady Mairi Bury for Lady Londonderry and to Mr J. C. Medley for Charles Morgan.

I would like to offer my apologies to those literary heirs whom I have been unable to trace. I hope they will accept this general acknowledgement for material I have quoted.

C.M.

LIST OF ILLUSTRATIONS

FOREWORD

On July 21st 1947 I wound up my diary with these words:

"Since October 1st 1946, I have travelled over 8,000 miles by sea, made over sixty flights totalling about 30,000 miles, driven over 9,000 miles by road and travelled over 3,000 miles by train, over 50,000 miles in all and 101 different beds. I look back at those ten months and wonder if I have dreamed them."

Extracts from the diary I kept of that Odyssey were published in 1948 under the title *All Over The Place*. These extracts amounted to some 130,000 words, and *All Over The Place* has long been out of print. It was published at a time when the public was tired of hearing about the war and was still bewitched by the prospect of the Welfare State. What was more the public had been persuaded by Whitehall to believe that the commanders and troops on the spot were responsible for the victories of the Japanese in Malaya, Burma and Hong Kong. Even the Fourteenth Army whose achievement in defeating the Japanese in Burma was the greatest military achievement of the Second World War was played down by Whitehall. Well was the Fourteenth Army called the Forgotten Army.

In *Eastern Epic* I wrote:

"It has been a melancholy task to relate the story of Hong Kong, Borneo, Malaya and Burma, and the melancholy is not lightened by the knowledge that these bitter tragedies were caused by lack of trained troops, lack of proper material of war, lack of air support, lack of medical supplies, lack, indeed, of everything that would have enabled those men, sacrificed to pusillanimous economy and besotted unreadiness, to defend themselves against the superior forces of a highly trained, a well prepared and a dauntless enemy.

"There were some, indeed there were too many, who dared to wonder at the time why the white flag was hoisted so soon (at Hong Kong). The answer is because the white flag had been flapping from every flagstaff in Whitehall and from Parliament itself for eight years before war came."

Only last year there was a preposterously ill-informed account of the surrender of Singapore in *All Our Yesterdays* of Granada television.

I hope that the extracts from my diary which I am including in this Octave will interest those who never read *All Over The Place* and I apologize to those who have already read them for a twice told tale.

STILL SIXTY-THREE YEARS OLD: 1946

—————————⊶◦⊰◦⊷—————————

BRIGADIER W. E. Condon, the Director of the Historical Section at Simla, with Major John Shaw were down at the harbour to meet us when the *Lancashire* docked. 'Bill' Condon had secured for me a Dogra bearer, Gulaba Ram, and never did anybody have a better bearer. He was to give Chrissie MacSween and myself devoted service for the next fifteen months. I remember Gulaba with gratitude and affection.

Condon and Shaw were taking our heavy baggage with them up to Simla as we were due to leave Bombay for Poona after two nights at Government House.

I met at Gun House Douglas Gracey[1] who had commanded the 20th Indian Division in Burma and would not so long hence be Commander-in-Chief of the Army of Pakistan. Douglas Gracey and his wife Cecil, who had been with us in the *Lancashire*, would become intimate friends. I recall his saying that we had lost India because we had never learned to say 'please' or 'thank you' at the right moment. At this date it had been settled that we should abdicate from our Indian Empire in June 1948.

From Poona with Major-General Maurice Chambers, who had commanded the 25th Indian Division at the capture of Rangoon, as our guide we drove inland through the fascinating Mahratta country with a night at Kolhapur to Belgaum where we stayed with Colonel Ralph Isaacs, Commandant of the Mahratta Regimental Centre. At Belgaum I was privileged to witness the last Retreat which, as I look back to it, seems like a Requiem for the old Indian Army.

The Parade Ground was laterite almost as deep in colour as red Devonian sandstone. On the far side from the pavilion was a screen of trellis work from behind which emerged the drums, bugles and band of the Fifth Mahratta Light Infantry, dressed in khaki with black and blue striped *pagris*. The big drum was played by an Anglo-Indian, the son of a drummer in a Highland regiment. A ceremonial fanfare was blown, and the rain which had been threatening cleared away at the sound of the bugles. The band retired, and after a display of physical training, sixty-four dancers, wearing a skilful arrangement of coloured turbans and coats but all in white trousers, performed the Lezim dance. Each dancer held a curved piece of wood from which was suspended a series of heavy metal discus-like miniature cymbals but shaken like

[1] The late General Sir Douglas Gracey, K.C.B., K.C.I.E., C.B.E., M.C.

bells. The performers danced in four sets of sixteen. Two men stood in the middle, one of them sounding at intervals a weird note on a large, slim, circular brass horn round his shoulder and the other beating a drum. From time to time the war cry of the Mahrattas was chanted in honour of their great leader Shivaji whose fort we had visited the day before. The rhythm and colour of that wonderful Lezim dance will be forever memorable. I was sad when it finished and the dancers retired to sit under the trees on the side of the parade ground and watch the Malkhamb which is the recognised recreation of every Mahratta village. Three great poles with a gilded knob at the top of each and greased with castor-oil were set up by orderlies. Then about three dozen magnificent figures of men wearing nothing but orange-buff loin-cloths performed a series of bewildering acrobatics which included revolving, outstretched on the gilded knob, merely by movement of the stomach muscles. The Malkhamb was followed by a display of massed P.T. by the Boys' Company (ages 15 to 17) perfectly carried out.

When the boys had retired behind the screen three sentinels emerged dressed in the scarlet and white uniform of the Regiment more than a century ago and remained absolutely motionless for about twenty minutes while the drums, bugles and band marched and counter-marched, playing among other tunes *John Peel*. This was followed by a beautifully executed slow march, with dusk turning the men's *pagris* to violet. The sound and the scene were almost unbearably poignant. I had a lump in my throat, and I knew that Maurice Chambers and Ralph Isaacs had the same, for to both of them this show was seeming the end of an old song.

The bugles sounded the Retreat. The drums, bugles and band vanished behind the screen. The three motionless sentinels came to life and vanished too. It was now the edge of night. One of the most moving ceremonies I have ever witnessed was over.

The Mess dinner was impressive, about forty officers sitting at the long silver-gleaming board. I sat between the Colonel and the handsome young Raja of Savantvadi who was a Captain in the Regiment. Opposite the Colonel's chair was an alcove beyond the table in which were the drums and colours guarded by a sentry with fixed bayonet, dressed in the scarlet of pre-war days, who never batted an eyelid or twitched a muscle all through dinner. Round the walls were photographs of successive Commandants of the Regimental Centre, a hirsute frieze from the Dundrearies of the 'fifties, through the smaller whiskers of the 'sixties, the beards of the 'seventies, the mutton-chops of the 'eighties, the heavy moustaches of the 'nineties, down to the toothbrushes of today. Field-Marshal Montgomery's grandfather was among them. The band played a selection of Scottish tunes, and after dinner we were joined by the ladies who listened to the band in scarlet playing melodious old musical-comedy selections in an open pavilion in the garden of the Mess. I felt I was in a scene of some Drury Lane drama of 1895.

Next morning we left Belgaum by the narrow-gauge train for Bangalore whence we drove by car to Mysore. Our guide was Major Philip Poonoose, a Syriac Christian from Travancore. We reached Seringapatam about lunch-time, and walked round the fort to see the breach made upon that fourth of May in 1799. We also visited the dungeons where Tippu Sultan kept the British officers he had captured earlier chained to the walls. The niches for their elbows were still to be seen. Highlanders and Madrassis were most prominent in the storming of Seringapatam and in reading through the names in the memorial to the fallen I realized the extent to which England drew upon the Highlands during the first century of aggressive imperialism. In the Napoleonic Wars 10,000 officers and men went to fight from Skye alone.

We stayed at Mysore in the luxuriously equipped Government Guest House. The Maharaja expressed a desire to see me, and at half-past five I drove to the Palace which looked like the largest wedding cake in the world.

In the entrance hall stood half a dozen tigers and three enormous bison shot by His Highness, and on the walls hung the head of a rogue elephant whose tusks reposed on the floor underneath while false ones were set in the head because the weight of the original was too much for the wall to stand. I also had a look at the armoury and saw some of Tippu Sultan's tiger-fanged knuckledusters, and what looked like a large pair of scissors eighteen inches long which when opened became three separate daggers. I also had a glimpse of the Durbar Hall and noticed the blue-glass-lined gallery in which the *purdah* ladies could watch the ceremonies without being seen. H.H. received me in the music room, the end of which was taken up by a large electric organ. He was dressed in white with a turban of bluish-grey, silver and gold. He was wearing some rich jewelled rings. He had a pleasant, quiet, precise way of talking, and he much surprised me by saying that he had been taking in *The Gramophone* ever since 1932 when he was thirteen years old. He had secured all the earlier numbers since, and told me that the intimacy of the paper had been one of his great pleasures and that my own writing about music had meant much to him.

We were driving to Ootacamund on All Saints' Day and I went to Mass at St Philomena's Cathedral before we left. The Cathedral was full of birds whose presence added much to the light and airy space of the graceful Gothic building which had been built and endowed by the late Maharaja.

We emerged from thick jungle to make the spectacular ascent to

Ooty, a rolling downland to which gorse and broom had been intro-duced. Had we been a month earlier we should have seen the Nilgiris (Blue Hills) covered with *strobolanthes*, which is a kind of blue Canter-bury bell, and although this happens only every six years it gave the hills their name. We stayed the night at Winchcombe with Lt.-Colonel Phythian-Adams. I spent a memorable evening with that famous hunter, hearing tales of the tigers he had shot and of the exploits of the old Madrassi Army before its famous regiments were turned into the Punjabis who inherited their honours. I see still our host's sitting-room hung with tiger-skins and many heads of deer and bison. The chairs were covered with leopard skins and the stools were elephants' feet. From time to time we could hear the chanting at some tribal ceremony of the Todas, handsome aborigines, few in number by now, with large beards and aquiline features.

When we were leaving to lunch in Ooty our host gave me a tin of tiger's grease which was considered a great help to rheumatism. The ointment had a rather disagreeable smell and Chrissie managed to mislay it as soon as she could.

I was gratified to find that my article in the *Billiards Player* about the origin of Snooker in the Ooty Club on a rainy afternoon in 1886 had been framed and hung. I wonder if it is still there today.

The next night we spent in the train on the way to Madras where we stayed with Sir Archibald Nye[1]. I had two crowded days in Madras which we left by the night train for Bangalore.

Lady Nye told me a good war story of Winston's successfully dodging a tête-à-tête with the Editor of *Time*, all through the day at Chequers and of Henry Luce's getting more and more annoyed. When she went to say good night to the 'Old Man', she noticed that Luce was sitting with him in a corner at last and supposed that Winston had been defeated. Not at all. He was moving ash-trays and matches about the table and talking to Luce about the Battle of Omdurman!

I am resisting the temptation to quote too much from my diary but I cannot resist a few words about Hyderabad which we reached after a rich two days in Bangalore.

The drive around the great city was absorbing. We went up to see the late Nizam's Palace, Heaven's View, which was only used now when the Viceroy visited Hyderabad. The top of the morning's interest was our visit to the Golconda Fort which we entered by the Fath Dowaza (Gate of Victory), heavily spiked to protect it against the battering of elephants. Beside it was an old cauldron which once upon a time held the boiling oil used in defence. The Kohinoor Hill lies

---

[1] The late Lt.-General Sir Archibald Nye, G.C.S.I., G.C.I.E., K.C.B., K.B.E.

outside the Golconda Fort, which formerly was the diamond market of the East. The small rocky hill where the great diamond was found looked like an abandoned Cornish tin mine. The Hall of Privacy is a dream of oriental architecture. The four houses of a bygone Sultan's four wives stand in each corner and his own house stands in the centre. A sort of shrubby white verbena and an orange-buff bougainvillea were in prodigal bloom among the fretted woodwork and sculptured marble of one lonely silent courtyard after another.

We lunched with Brigadier and Mrs Gilbert in a picturesque house which had been the old Residency. Dr M. G. Naidu and Mrs Sarojini Naidu were guests and I had the pleasure of sitting next to Mrs Naidu at a superlative lunch which included a masterpiece of a curry. Mrs Naidu was in glorious form and we had a great time recalling the figures of the late 'nineties when she was a young poetess in London. She was equally amusing about contemporary figures. I recall her saying of a young A.D.C. who had been given an administrative job that it was like making a duster out of a piece of chiffon. I happened to mention that all the Hindus I had met had spoken to me with indignation about Beverley Nichols' book *Verdict on India* which had extolled what was to be Pakistan at their expense.

"Oh, they should not be taking it so seriously," Mrs Naidu laughed. "One must not be too angry if one is scratched by a little pussy cat. He did not mean to hurt our feelings."

We flew from Hyderabad to New Delhi. Some idea of the difference air had made to travel in India may be gathered from the fact that Gulaba had to leave Bangalore on November 7th in order to meet us in Delhi four days later. There we stayed with the Commander-in-Chief. On the second night we dined with the Viceroy whom I had not met since 1916 when he was a Major in the Black Watch. 'Guinea a word' Archie who had been as much of a chatterbox as myself once upon a time was sitting silently at dinner when suddenly he asked me if I had ever heard the story of the sergeant and the private at the First Battle of Ypres. I shook my head.

"Well, a sergeant and a private were walking along through the mud and rain and wind toward the front line. At last the private asked if he couldn't sit down and rest for a minute or two. 'Rest', exclaimed the sergeant. 'What do you want to rest for now? You'll be dead in half an hour'."

I told Wavell that most of Whitehall had notified Chatto's that they expected to see *Indian Epic* (as it was still called) before publication.

"Don't let anyone tinker with your work," he said. "It has nothing to do with Whitehall."

I asked him if a speech of Winston just reported was going to make things difficult. In this speech he had talked as if the Mutiny was at its most menacing. There was something about our women and children being escorted across India to safety by British troops.

"I don't think so," said Wavell, "though I must admit I do wish sometimes that Winston would not look at India through the eyes of a subaltern at Bangalore fifty years ago."

I have always thought that the fundamental cause of the different approach to every problem which made it difficult for Wavell and Churchill to appreciate the other's point of view was that the former was in College at Winchester and the latter an Old Harrovian. 'Wykeham's adamantine mould' as I wrote of it in *Sinister Street* is no longer adamantine today but it moulded Archie Wavell once upon a time. His first cousin, Raymond Wavell, was in Houses at the same time and one of my most intimate friends at Magdalen. A few days after meeting Wavell again after many years, I met his son, Archie John. He was a Major in the Black Watch as his father had been in 1916 when that only son was six months old. Archie Wavell had just lost an eye in France; Archie John had lost a hand in Burma. He was doing Army Education work at Simla. He told me of his father's hairbreadth escapes in planes during the war. I noted in my diary that he was 'a most attractive young man—sensitive, humorous, completely natural, and an obvious artist.' After Lord Wavell's death he used to come and see me occasionally at Denchworth and I was more and more impressed by the prospect of his future. Then he insisted on rejoining his regiment when the Black Watch were dealing with Mau Mau in Kenya and to his country's loss was killed in 1953.

My first impression of Simla was 'as if a giant jigsaw puzzle with a view of Grindelwald on one side and of Golder's Green on the other had been upset over a jumble of mountains'. I had a busy three days working at the details of our forthcoming tour in the Near and Middle East and Eritrea. Back in Delhi we stayed at Viceroy's House.

I dined with Pandit Nehru. Mrs Naidu was there with an attractive and witty daughter who lived in Hyderabad. There were no Europeans except myself, and before dinner people kept coming in and going out of the house in an agreeable Bohemian atmosphere. Nehru was a man of altogether unusual charm. I had a longish talk with him alone after dinner and I offered to hand over all my material to an Indian if one could be found to write *Indian Epic*. Questions were continually being asked in the Assembly about my qualifications and why an Indian author had not been chosen. Nehru said that the country had had to be 'infected' with Nationalism, and that I would understand why that had been necessary in order to make it nation-conscious. He thought I should pay no attention to the sharpshooting in the Assembly.

I had been reading his last book *Discovery of India* on the voyage out and I told him how much I was in agreement with his philosophic outlook. This seemed to please him, and he went on to talk much more frankly about the Indian situation. He repeated several times that India would never accept partition and I could feel how profoundly anxious he was about what might happen when Great Britain abdicated from her Indian Empire in June 1948. When I was leaving what for me was a memorable evening Mrs Sarojini Naidu came to the door with me to say,

"Do not worry about your book. He is pleased you will write it. He thinks you are very understanding."

From Delhi we went on by the Frontier Mail to Lahore where I had a crowded two days. I quote:

"I went on to visit the Regimental Centre of the 8th Punjab Regiment. Colonel Scotland the Commandant, a large genial man, showed me round with an infectious enthusiasm. He rivals Colonel Isaacs at Belgaum with the farm he is running, and showed me a patch of sugar cane from which he expected to make Rs. 3,000 clear profit. I was shown a real beauty of a model house for ex-soldiers costing Rs. 2,500. I feel it is impertinent to praise the devoted work done by the Commandants of these Regimental Centres, but I must set on record my deep appreciation of what they have done and what they are doing. Where the idea originated that Indian Army officers are particularly prone to blimpery I do not know, but it's bad biology."

From Lahore we drove the 160 miles to Dharmsala. After we crossed the dusty Punjab plain the road grew more and more beautiful all the time and the last sixty miles ran through as lovely a country as ever I saw. It was like the Highlands on a much larger scale. The Himalayan peaks run right along the northern horizon, rising to about 17,000 feet. There was not much in the way of wild life except an occasional monkey and lots of green parrakeets. I saw a blue jay which is supposed to be lucky.

From Dharmsala we drove 182 miles to Jullundur where I visited the Dogra Regimental Centre, to watch a display of jungle warfare arranged by Colonel Bristowe. Once again I was impressed by the complete competence of those British officers in command of Regimental Centres and of the affection in which they were held. We drove back to Lahore and next day flew to Karachi, whence after another two crowded days we started on our flight to Bahrein. With us was Major Peter Petit who was to be my conductor for the next three weeks.

The flying-boat *Castor* was airborne by 10.15 but after flying over the sea for an hour and a half one of her engines went wrong and we had to return to Karachi. Next morning it was a long dark bumpy drive in the bus to the airport where the custom formalities gone through the day before had to be repeated. When we reached Bahrein we were

told that another engine had gone wrong and that we were likely to be
there for at least four hours. So we were driven in a hard-seated
transport bus along a bad road to see a pool among the date groves, full
of large stately fish and small turtles. On the way back to the Rest
House we passed a gathering of wild dancers bare to the waist, with a
band and three banners. They were practising with noisy groans for
Mohamar, the Muslim day of mourning on December 5th. When we
got back to the Rest House we found we should have to stay there for
the night because the engine was not ready. It was a poor dinner and
the place was black with flies. I was given a bedroom to myself and I
was so tired that I fell asleep before I had finished undressing.

We were called at 4.30 a.m. I was the first down in the dark to find
the eating-room black with flies, and at 6 when we were due to start
for Habbaniya we were warned of heavy fog at Basra. However,
Captain Blackaller decided to leave half an hour after sunrise and hope
that the fog would have lifted. All was clear at Basra and we were
grateful for the half-hour wait to sit by a cheerful fire and drink
coffee.

We came down on the lake at Habbaniya expecting to hear that a
plane would take us on to Damascus. However (I am afraid I must say
as usual) the R.A.F. were completely vague about everything when
Peter Petit rang up to inquire about the prospects of getting on. We
decided it would be best to continue our journey in the *Castor* as far as
Cairo, but meanwhile some other passengers had gone aboard and with
the conked-out engine he was carrying the Captain wouldn't take the
risk of a bigger load. Peter Petit, Chrissie and myself hung about the
embarkation office and filled up forms to say we had nothing dutiable
in Iraq until Wing-Commander Fraser, the Intelligence officer, came
along in a car, drove us to the Cantonment, and gave us a capital lunch
in the Officers' Club. After a lot of telephoning it was finally decided
that the only possible way of getting anywhere was to take the Service
Dakota to Lydda in Palestine.

It had been arranged for me to visit the battlefield of Rashid Ali's
coup d'état in April 1941. Before catching the Service Dakota I was
up and dressed early, but the heavy downpour of rain turned into a
mist and there was no visibility for visiting a battlefield. Wing-Commander Fraser came along to say that the Dakota had broken down at
Shaiba and would not be leaving until the afternoon. Squadron-Leader
Stapleton came along to say it would not leave before 19 o'clock, which
meant landing in the dark at Lydda and did not sound too good a
prospect. The whole business was a muddle and Habbaniya was like
an enormous lunatic asylum. It was built before the war at a cost of
£7,000,000 and the lease with the Iraqi Government had to be renewed
in 1948. There was no training school here now and only four planes.

So the ground staff of 2,000 had nothing to do. Beside the ground staff there were 5,000 civilians occupied in maintaining the station. Ten years before the whole place had been desert; now it was beautifully planted with avenues of gum trees already 30 feet high. There were yachts on the lake, squash courts, cricket and football fields, a race course, cinema theatres, everything to keep people amused except the female form for the absence of which pin-up girls were not perfect compensation. Women were not allowed on the station because the thermometer goes up too high in the summer. So the atmosphere was unhappy. I doubted if the training of the R.A.F. was capable yet of turning out men to run a station like this properly. It was a sad contrast to the Regimental Centres in India.

After hurrying down to the aerodrome to be there by seven o'clock, we finally got off at half-past nine. The Dakota was draughty, ramshackle, foully uncomfortable, and frightfully cold because we had to fly at 10,000 feet to get out of bad weather, and the heating didn't work. The machine was full of Erks and a couple of Waafs. At 1 a.m. after three and a half hours of misery we landed at Lydda on one wheel and put up at the Transit Rest House.

The Rest House at Lydda was uncomfortable and the toilet arrangements squalid. The Group-Captain finally managed to secure an Anson in which we could fly to Heliopolis. While we were waiting for the plane there was a big explosion. A few miles away Jewish terrorists from Tel Aviv had driven a lorry laden with explosives into the camp at Sarafand.

We had a noisy and very expensive two days at Shepheard's Hotel in the detestable city of Cairo for 24 hours of which I was laid low with the only really bad go of pain I was to have in ten months. However, I slept nearly all the way in the flying-boat to find myself quite fit again when we reached Khartoum.

Next day we drove to Omdurman, which was all *café au lait* and neat compared with Indian towns of the same kind. They were shooting a couple of mad dogs as we passed. The florid cemetery of those who fell in the battle is on the outskirts of the town. We drove on across the desert to the site of the battle. It's an arid and desolate spot. We saw a couple of sand devils—the equivalent of a water spout in sand.

At 8 o'clock I went off to supper with the Governor—Major-General Sir Hubert Huddleston. He was still at church when I arrived at the Palace, and I found Lady Huddleston watching a total eclipse of the moon with a pair of opera glasses. The whole disc turned to an unnatural greenish-red colour. We had been told that the natives would start beating drums to frighten away the rat that was supposed to be eating the moon, but sophistication had evidently set in here, for no one seemed to pay much attention to it. Sir Hubert came back from a

long sermon by a Church of Scotland minister and we went out in
the Palace launch to eat supper in the middle of the Nile under the
emerging moon.

Huddleston was the only Governor, Admiral or General I met who
was older than myself and moreover a senior much to be admired. He
was Colonel-in-Chief of the Dorset Regiment and had been proud to
find his name next to Thomas Hardy in the roll of the freemen of
Dorchester.

Next morning we took off in a Wellington to Asmara. At first, the
ground below was amber and ochre with occasional splashes of raw
sienna. Then the whole desert became a kind of greenish-yellow tabbied
silk over which we flew at about 10,000 feet. When we drew near to
Kassala we came down to less than 500 feet for Peter Petit to take some
photographs; this caused a good deal of alarm to the goats and camels,
and to the human beings living in clusters of beehive huts, or rather
haycock huts for that was what they resembled more. Extravagant
rocky shapes rose up from the desert, which as we flew on increased in
size to become isolated mountains and reminded me of the scattered
bens of Sutherland. For a while the pilot was uncertain of his way and
was looking for a telephone wire to guide him out of the fantastic gorges
and ravines through which we were roaring into as much space as
would give him a chance of gaining the height to fly over the 8,000-ft
barrier of mountains. It made us a little anxiously pensive until we
reached the air over the high plateau round Asmara, from which after
circling round two or three times we landed safely on the small Asmara
aerodrome. There was the usual fuss about passports and as we got out
of the plane we were solemnly flitted. This was a zone of British
Military Administration, and a customs examination for a party like
ours seemed otiose.

The sixty-mile drive down to Keren was along a continuously well
engineered and occasionally spectacular road between great candelabra
cactus trees and giant spurges. Every few hundred yards there was a
signpost painted with a skull and crossbones to record a fatal accident
at that spot and urge other drivers to be careful. These were the result
of our passion for making drivers keep to the left. It was the first thing
we did after entering Asmara, and the Italian lorry-drivers were baffled
by it because the road had been constructed for keeping to the right.
At the end of the descent the road ran for a few miles down a fertile
valley, and shortly before reaching Keren we drove between hedges of
bougainvillea which seemed to burn like a furnace of magenta. I never
saw such a solid mass of hot colour.

After a night in the Grand Hotel, which had formerly been the
bordello di lusso of the Italian officers, we set out to survey the incredible
battlefield of Keren. My leg was still inclined to protest and I shirked

going up to Fort Dologorodoc on the mules which had been provided. From where we stood the view of the battlefield was clear enough. The more one looked at it the more amazing did the achievement of the 4th and 5th Indian Divisions seem. No description I had read of the surroundings of Keren had prepared me for the nightmare scene.

The barren mountains heaped with greyish-green boulders and the serrated peaks were what you would expect to find if you landed upon the moon. Granite predominated but there were a good many smooth rounded boulders. We paused for a few minutes to look at the site of the road block made by the Italians in the ravine through which the road curved down to the wide strath ironically called Happy Valley, where so many of our soldiers died. A troop of great baboons with preposterous carmine bottoms and what looked like heavy fur capes gathered on the slope above and barked angrily at us. If we had got out of the car they would have pelted us with stones. The wide level Happy Valley was dotted with thorny *zizyphus cristospina* and acacias whose thin spreading foliage cast a pale shade. Here and there among them were ancient baobab trees whose massive trunks with a tuft of twiggy growth on top seemed like browsing pachyderms. Small pied goats with wagging greedy tails and wanton eyes were all over the place, and from time to time hornbills in plumage of rusty black and off-white, some with red, some with yellow beaks, would alight to peck about in the stony soil.

I should write of the Battle of Keren in *Eastern Epic*:

"The decision of General Wavell on that December night (in 1940) to withdraw the 4th Indian Division from the triumph of Sidi Barrani and send it to wage an offensive campaign in East Africa must rank with any major military decisions which have set the course of history. Such a decision required imagination, faith and a plenitude of moral courage. He dreamed of the impossible: his dream was fulfilled by men who achieved the impossible.

"And what men they were! . . .

"The unfortunate licence of wartime propaganda allowed the British Press to represent the Italians almost as comic warriors; but except for the German parachute division in Italy and the Japanese in Burma no enemy with whom the British and Indian troops were matched put up a finer fight than those Savoia battalions at Keren. . . .

"It must be stressed that the Indian and British soldiers who won that tremendous victory against odds won it at a period in the war when equipment was at its lowest, and if the difficulties of the attackers are added to the vital results achieved by overcoming those difficulties at that date, the fall of Keren can claim to be one of the truly decisive battles of the world. . . .

"The fall of Keren followed almost immediately by the capture of

Massowa freed the Red Sea for the American ships bringing the precious munitions of war to aid the struggle in North Africa. . . .

" 'If' is an arid conjecture and the speculation it prompts is usually fruitless. Nevertheless, one can affirm that if Keren had held out our position in 1941, desperate enough, would have been disastrous, and the sane world owes an inestimable debt to the men who thwarted that ominous contingency. When Field-Marshal Viscount Wavell of Cyrenaica and of Winchester was created an Earl he chose for his second title the viscountcy of Keren and Winchester, and by doing so came as near to wearing his heart upon his sleeve as he ever came except in some anthology of well-loved poetry."

Two days later we were back for the night in Cairo and up before dawn to catch the Anson for Tobruk. We flew over El Alamein which seen from above was a vast monotone of sand on which the military operations were still intagliated—gun pits, shell craters, slit trenches, wire entanglements, tank traps, and even the tracks of lorries. I say 'even', but considering that the tracks of the Roman chariot wheels are still to be seen in the crusted Libyan soil it is not so remarkable.

The harbour at Tobruk was full of sunken ships; there were 132 of every nationality. The whole area was a scene of utter desolation covered with smashed aeroplanes, tanks, lorries, petrol tins, guns and endless heaps of barbed wire. I was immensely struck by the happy atmosphere in Tobruk. Everybody seemed to be pulling well with everybody else, an agreeable contrast to Habbaniya. The German prisoners-of-war of whom there were still 4,000 had decorated the whole place.

After dinner in Colonel Guy's Mess, sitting round a huge log fire I heard a desert story in which Boccacio himself would have rejoiced. An officer called X was caught with his own and the other armoured cars in one of our minefields during the retreat from Bir Hakeim. They tried to clear a way through, but night fell and in the morning they were overtaken by the German tanks and shot to pieces. X lay down, pretending to be dead, and managed to escape being made prisoner. The retreat had long swept past, when he wandered on across the desert for many weary days and finally reached Buq Buq. Here he undressed on the beach and enjoyed a good swim, after which he lay sunbathing on the warm sand and fell fast asleep.

When he woke he found himself in the middle of a Boche bathing party. Nobody had paid any attention to his sleeping form and perhaps if he had not grabbed his clothes and tried to make off he might have bluffed it out. However, he was caught and taken along with other prisoners to the cage. He was the last man in the line and, noticing an empty cookhouse by the gate, slipped aside into it. Here he pulled a blanket over himself and lay down in a corner. Unluckily when night fell a guard party came into the cookhouse for a game of cards. One of the players, feeling chilly in the course of the game, spotted the blanket in the corner and X was revealed. He was hauled up before the commandant and told that if he tried to escape again he would be shot. Back he was put in the cage and in a thoroughly depressed mood started fiddling with the padlock of the gate when the sentry had passed by. It was not that he expected any result; it was nervous fidgets. To his amazement the padlock opened. The hook had not caught when the key was turned. He slipped out quickly, and this time he managed to reach our lines.

X was given an M.C. for the two escapes and sent to recuperate at a rest camp near Suez. Here there was a number of Wrens who slept in tents in a wired-in enclosure, which of course was known as the Aviary. One night, coming back from a party and being well ginned up, the companions of X challenged him to demonstrate his skill at escaping by getting in and out of the Aviary. He took on the bet and when he got over the wire he saw a Wren sitting outside her tent in the moonlight. She had been to a party and she was thinking about love, a Jessica without a Lorenzo. And suddenly Lorenzo appeared. They talked for some time and then she invited him into the tent she shared with fourteen other Wrens, all of them respectably fast asleep. When the time came for X to leave his Wren and make his way carefully out of the tent, one of the sleepers woke up and seeing a male shape profaning the sanctity of the tent screamed a shrill alarm. X dashed out and hid in a slit trench, but here he was discovered and barely escaped a court martial. However, X was let off with a reprimand.

Two days after leaving Tobruk we were in Beirut where prices at this date were higher than anywhere in the world. My most vivid memory is of driving out to the River of the Dog which runs down a narrow gorge to the sea about seventeen miles north of the town. A series of inscribed stone plaques beginning with Nebuchadnezzar and going on through Assyrians, Greeks, Romans, French and finally Australians in the last war commemorate among the rocks the various armies that had passed this way. Caracalla with the Third Gallic Legion, Napoleon III, Gouraud and Allenby in the First World War and the Australian advance against the Vichy French in the Second World War are among them.

We walked up the gorge and found a few cyclamens in blossom, also *iris sisyrhinchium*. The cyclamen was the arrow-leaved type, pink with a red nose. We were just going to walk up a path to look at the Assyrian steles when a tremendous thunderstorm began, which lasted for the rest of the afternoon and a good deal of the night. The road back to Beirut reminded me of the road through Piano di Sorrento with sugar cane and bananas added to the oranges.

I was hoping to see the cedars of Lebanon when we drove to Damascus. We were only able to admire the mighty stone-pines and terraced vineyards above Beirut before the weather cheated us of beauty; most of the ascent of the Lebanon was shrouded in thick mist, and at 5,500 ft the car had to crawl at a snail's pace through sleet and slush past dimly seen slopes of snow. When we descended to the wide valley of the Anti-Lebanon the sun came out. We passed grove after exquisite grove of poplars with slim silver trunks and the golden leaves of autumn not even yet fallen from their filigree of boughs. Concrete dragon's teeth had been sown by the Vichy French in the pass before Damascus. When Mahomet drew near to Damascus from the desert east of it, he turned aside from the city because he did not wish to anticipate Paradise by entering it. I can understand his impulse. As we drove into Damascus by the wide road from the west beside that clear bottle-green river which flows through the heart of the city, I thought I had never come to a place which so completely satisfied every dream of what it should be. Those three lovely words 'damson', 'damask', and 'damascene' have stirred the imagination with such colour from earliest youth that one might well expect to be disappointed. So far from being disappointed I was enraptured.

After lunch, defying the rain which by now had reached Damascus we drove out to study the advance of the 5th Indian Brigade against the Vichy French, and ended up by going to see the house in Mezze where the 3/1st Punjabis had to surrender after 30 hours without food or ammunition. That pinkish house in a high-walled garden will always be haunted. Peter Petit who was taken prisoner from here was able to give me a vivid picture of those hours. We went up the hillside toward the old French barracks and had a superb view of Damascus under a luminous blue and white sky, fruitful Damascus with its golden poplars and fountains and cypresses, its domes and minarets and orchards. Mount Hermon crowned with snow rose from the southern horizon. We then drove across a sandy track to the British cemetery which lies surrounded by cypresses in the middle of large plantations of prickly pears. The graves of the First World War had stone headstones and the cypresses were already tall, but the additional space taken in for the graves of the Second World War had only white wooden crosses as yet and the young cypresses swung in the light breeze. The paths in the first graveyard were edged with rosemary, cut square and as thick as box. Both graveyards were covered with pinkish-mauve chrysanthemums. It was a melancholy thought that the most beautiful war cemetery I had seen should have watched men advancing along the edge of it who would presently rest within it. Some, indeed, must have walked over their own graves.

Later we drove down the Street called Straight and had the good fortune to be almost the first to see a 3,000-year-old gate which they had just excavated in the middle of it, showing that the level was originally at least twenty feet below where it is now. Five thousand years of continuous city life! Can any other city in the world compete with this? We went on to the Jerusalem Gate on the south side of the city and saw the window through which St Paul was let down in a basket.

Our next visit was to the Tomb of Saladin and his Grand Vizier, Aladin. We crossed a courtyard with a fountain and some orange trees and were admitted by a heavily veiled old woman. The tombs were surmounted by triangular cubes covered with ancient green silk at one end of which were the green turbans of Saladin and Aladin. The walls were covered with blue and green tiles with a design of grapes, and all round were chairs and divans of crimson velvet on which the faithful might sit in contemplation. The Kaiser paid for the renovation of the tomb when he visited the place.

The souks of Damascus were completely Arabian Nights. One crawled down a narrow alley in a car, being bumped by a loaded camel on one side and an Arab on a donkey on the other. Marvellous brocades at £5 a yard made us covetous.

I was interviewed by eight representatives of the Damascus Press. I told them that it had been long my ambition to write a history of the Crusades and that in a couple of years' time I should like to have a house in the middle of Damascus near the Arab University with a courtyard, a fountain and four orange trees from which I would explore the great castles of the Crusaders—Krak des Chevaliers, Chastel Rouge, Chastel Blanche, and the rest of them. They all applauded this idea and were sure I should be given every facility.

We left Beirut next morning in a Beechcraft plane called Cleopatra. Some of our luggage was put in her mouth. When we reached Cairo we had to spend three-quarters of an hour with the complications of a transit visa. I hope that one day before I depart from this world the Sudanese will sack Cairo, and then occupy it permanently.

Next morning was spent in the formalities of transit visas for our flight back to Karachi. I wrote in my diary:

"This damned business of passports and visas and customs has been the only wearisome part of our tour. I little thought what a Franken-stein I was creating when I originated the present passport system at Athens in 1916. I shall shake the sand of Cairo from my feet with zest tomorrow morning after another 5.30 a.m. breakfast and the boring rigmarole of customs, passports, and health certificates at the Nile seaplane base. Cairo was a detestable place in the last war and it is twice as detestable now. Obviously Lawrence's passion for Arabian adventure was sustained by a horror of being caught in Cairo. My adventures in Greece were originally inspired by a dread of finding myself in a Cairo office when Gallipoli was evacuated."

On December 22nd Peter and Rachel Petit came to bid us good-bye at the Nile port. We were travelling in *Champion*, which was the first flying-boat to cross the Atlantic and was to be broken up at Durban when she got back there at the end of the month. I have never been able to understand the folly of giving up flying-boats in order to concentrate on super-jets and finally upon those infernal machines flying faster than sound. If statesmen, politicians and business men would fly a little more slowly they would not arrive at their destination in advance of their brains, with the consequent mess they have made of the world at the moment when I am writing these words.

Our first stop was Kallia at the end of the Dead Sea. I asked what a patch of green was on the hillside to be told it was Jericho. We reached Basra in time for dinner; although the hotel was equipped with aqua-marine baths and basins and comfortable beds, good food was sadly lacking.

We were called at 3.45 and went on to Bahrein at five o'clock. There was a superb scarlet, gold and green dawn over a deep steel-blue sea. At Bahrein we took on a very old Arab, two middle-aged ones, and two women heavily veiled in black. The two women and one of the men sat on the seat near us and chattered incessantly for an hour. Then they all covered themselves with blankets and slept until the steward brought a large basket of cakes, biscuits and sandwiches which they devoured *in toto*, a complicated business under a veil. It was interesting to notice how naturally the Arabs had taken to flying. The same thing happened in the Hebrides. Old people who shuddered at the notion of a sea-voyage hopped into a plane like grigs. We reached Karachi at six that evening and as a welcome change from Cairo the medical and customs examinations were expeditiously and pleasantly carried through.

When I was in Delhi I had met the Jam Saheb of Nawanagar[1] whom I had last met in Dublin as long ago as 1924 when he was a quiet solemn young man obviously in awe of his uncle the great Ranji; he was now a magnificent Rabelaisian figure. He invited Chrissie and myself to spend Christmas with him at Jamnagar. I had told him regretfully that I did not think it could be managed but by great good luck Claude Auchinleck was going there himself for a brief holiday and so we were able to accept the invitation.

We flew to Jamnagar on Christmas Eve in two and a half hours on a journey that took two and a half days by train. Twenty-two people sat down to dinner at about ten o'clock, with as much champagne as they could drink after many champagne cocktails beforehand, and some

----

[1] The late Maharaja Jam Saheb of Nawanagar, G.C.S.I., G.C.I.E.

marvellous '35 brandy. One was back in 1911, and could imagine that Nijinsky and Karsavina would be dancing *The Spectre of the Rose* at Covent Garden after dinner. I sat next to the beautiful Maharani of Jaipur.

His Highness arrived on Christmas morning to drive Chrissie and myself round Jamnagar. It was a fascinating walled city, full of temples and mosques, the temples all flying red and white flags. Goats and pigeons were everywhere and green parrakeets wheeled screaming round the heavily carved fort. A great flight of demoiselle cranes had arrived the previous evening and we saw them standing about in the estuary. They had come there from Siberia.

I was much impressed by the evidence on all sides of the affectionate regard in which His Highness's people held him. Nawanagar was a happy state and Jamnagar a happy city. This was an oriental Dingley Dell and Mr Wardle wore a black silk coat with jewelled buttons. When we got back to the Palace the Jam Saheb sat in the drawing-room to receive Christmas greetings. Among those who came was a Polish woman who had been there since she escaped from Russian imprisonment seven years before. Her face was tragic, and there were ashes among her fair hair. She had just received a photograph of her grownup daughter whom she had not seen since she was a little girl.

When the guests were gathered for lunch, His Highness went round with his presents. He gave me a pair of enamel and gold links which was just what I wanted and to Chrissie and the other women he gave a dozen handkerchiefs and two scarves of gold tissue made in Jamnagar. We had some wonderful '27 hock at lunch which to a palate denied good hock for five years tasted rather better than nectar.

I was roused at five-thirty from what was more like a stupor than a siesta with news that His Highness was waiting to drive us out to the game preserve on the island in the estuary. There hares, guinea-fowl, partridges and quail were on all sides of us, but to His Highness's disappointment we did not get a glimpse of the cheetal deer. It was flat country with many thickets of low trees and here and there dense bushes of cactus. Indian warblers, bulbuls and rosy doves were the most frequent birds. Sometimes we would pass a tree from which the body of a hawk or jackal or jungle-cat or iguana would be suspended as a warning to the rest, but I doubted if the iguana's cold eye would be sufficiently impressed by his brother's bad end to abstain from poaching. When we got back to the Palace in a grey and crimson sunset, I saw the new moon over my right shoulder, an auspicious end to a delightful drive.

Sixty-six of us sat down to Christmas dinner in the banqueting-hall at half-past ten, with gold plate and cutlery and great boxes of crackers that Titans might have pulled with one another. After a dinner of

Dickensian prodigality, with turkey and one of the best plum puddings I ever ate, I recall as if it were yesterday the Jam Saheb rising to propose the loyal toast and hear the very tone of his voice as he says 'Ladies and gentlemen, the King-Emperor'. After dinner there was dancing till 5 a.m.; Boxing Day was a prolonged siesta.

Next day after an early lunch we drove to a range of low hills where marble was quarried, some thirty miles south of Jamnagar. Here two panthers had been ringed by beaters. We stood on a stone platform facing a glade out through scrub, forbidden to talk above a whisper. His Highness made me take off my white cap and gave me his own topee to wear. The Maharani of Jaipur, who had a new Holland and Holland rifle brought back from England by her husband, was given first shot. After a quarter of an hour of unearthly noises by two hundred beaters the female panther broke from the scrub and seemed to be ambling across the glade. Actually she was moving at a very fast pace and after the Maharani had missed with both barrels there was no time for the Jam Saheb to get in his shot. About five minutes later the male panther came across and was also missed. So we drove on about a quarter of a mile and took up a fresh position above a nullah. This time it was the male panther who broke first, but in such a way that it was impossible for anybody to get a shot at him. We waited a long time until the ring of beaters closed in at last without a sign of the female. We now moved on to a tower up which we climbed by wooden steps, and the beating began again. The three motor-cars had been parked in the sunlight up the slope to discourage the panther from turning away from the tower as he crossed the open ground in front. Finally he broke cover and this time the Maharani hit him and Colonel Himatsinhji, the Jam Saheb's brother, followed up with a shot through the head. The panther measured seven feet five inches over all.

His Highness told me afterwards that he never expected to see the female panther again and that the beaters had no doubt deliberately let her through because they liked having panthers about, which at the cost of an occasional goat kept the woodland free from poaching woodcutters.

We drove on to a miniature shooting-box beside a stream running through a rocky gorge overhung with trees, and there under the shade of a huge banyan covered with red fruit we sat down on a red carpet to a picnic tea, all of us unaware that two panthers were watching us. The head shikari dressed in green was a most distinguished-looking Rajput Major, seventy years old, without a tooth in his head and still able to run uphill as fast as a young man. At dinner His Highness related how in 1918 175 Punjabi Mussulmans had expelled two complete Egyptian Divisions from their Cairo barracks at the point of the bayonet. Later on, I told the Maharani of Jaipur how much I had sympathized with her over that first miss and she said how thankful she had been that her husband wasn't there. She thought that the desire to kill was leaving her. Indeed, she had made up her mind to give up shooting, but the new rifle had been irresistible. She was a really enchanting young woman and the nearest thing to a fairy princess the material world has shown me. I told her that I had come to the conclusion—regretfully— that I must have been up at Oxford with her grandfather, the Maharaja of Cooch Behar.

Claude Auchinleck arrived and also Bill Condon but I must refrain from writing any more about that superlative week.

Loaded with garlands of chrysanthemums and marigolds heavy with morning dew, Bill Condon, Chrissie and myself flew from Jamnager the last day of 1946 to reach Ahmedabad a couple of hours later. We were met by Lt.-Colonel Houghton of the 2/7th Gurkhas. He drove Condon and myself round the Cantonments and I had an interesting picture of a Kipling set-up of once upon a time, for nothing had been changed except that electric light had been put in and the stables had been turned into stores. The huge banyan trees offered shade to the pipe-clayed ghost of that great man Thomas Atkins who had laid down his life at Mons and Ypres and on the beaches of Gallipoli. We could still see where the punkahs used to hang in the dormitory of the British N.C.O.'s, the old magazines, the gun park, and all the rest of it.

After lunch Mrs Houghton, a charming Australian woman (I don't know why I add the epithet because Australian women, thanks to their naturalness, always are charming), drove us and her 16-month old son into Ahmedabad, after we had visited her clinic and school for wives. I was entranced by the spectacle of a dozen wives being instructed with unbroken high-pitched eloquence by a young pundit of eleven armed with chalk and a blackboard. When the women turned away from their slates to look at the visitors they were sharply rebuked by their young schoolmaster and bidden to pay attention to the blackboard on which he was demonstrating how to write 'yours' in Gurkhali.

We were in Delhi for New Year's Day and went to a cocktail party where several of those who had figured in the Birthday Honours were being toasted. One of the new Ladies asked me what had impressed me most in the tour so far, and I said "Keren". "Oh, yes?" she went on in a puzzled voice, "and where and what is Keren?"

Brigadier Kenneth Bayley[1] arrived from Meerut, where he was commanding a British Brigade, to be my conducting officer as far as the Chindwin. I earned his respect by alluding to his regiment as the 52nd not as the 2nd Oxford and Bucks Light Infantry. The 1st bat-

---

[1] The late Major-General Kenneth Bayley, C.B., C.B.E.

talion, the old Oxford Light Infantry, liked to be known as the 43rd. We flew next day to Calcutta on the maiden flight of the *Indus*, a new Vickers-Viking plane. There was a lot of experimental adjustment of the seating in the aircraft to get the best balance for taking off and coming down. I must say I felt more at ease in Dakotas whose virginity was years old.

We stayed with Major-General Roy Bucher[1] in historic Fort William. Bayley and I flew in a jolly little four-seater plane to Jamshedpur, which is a fantastic romance of industry. In 1907 it had been a haunt of tigers; it was now a garden city of 150,000, with the largest steel works in the Empire. Yet only a mile or two away from the five square miles of steel works one might pass on the road dark aborigines who still used bows and arrows.

Lt.-Colonel J. G. Thomson, I.A.M.C., who was doing a survey of the medical side of the war, had joined us for the next expedition. He was soon to become an intimate and much valued friend to whom, and his wife Alice, I should one day dedicate Octave Three.

We had a long and tiring railway journey on our way to Digboi, and reached the Brahmaputra ferry eighteen hours after leaving Calcutta. The view of that mighty river as we crossed it to Pandu inspired awe. I still see the Brahmaputra with the mind's eye flowing between huge cliffs in the pearly morning mist and it remains in my memory as a symbol of the mysterious East. We reached Digboi about three in the morning and woke to find our coach had been put into a siding. I was up first, and noted in my diary 'I am amazed at my anxiety to get up in the morning nowadays.'

Jim Thomson after putting us all on mepacrine, including Gulaba, left us for a day or two. We were to spend the night with Mr and Mrs Valentine. He was the General Manager of Assam Oil and an Aberdonian; she was a Glaswegian; it was a combination after my own heart.

Bayley and I drove to visit various people. Among them was Vernon Brown, one of those Assam tea-planters who made such a superb patriotic effort in the war. He showed me some of the leaflets which the Japs dropped over Panitola. They had ridiculous pictures of scarlet-clad Tommies with big teeth such as one used to see in French comic rags during the Boer War. He also showed me a leaflet which *we* dropped on the Japanese. This was a picture of a naked woman bound to a post and a Jap soldier leering at her. And this was the legend underneath: 'The Japanese are rapping (*sic*) your women and robbing your homes." Could anything have been more fatuous than printing that in English in the hope of impressing the local inhabitants?

[1] General Sir Roy Bucher, K.B.E., C.B.

We drove from Digboi to the Ledo Road in jeeps. After a few miles of shocking road we came to Margarita, so named by an Italian who discovered coal there. The coal was fetching 30 rupees a ton at the pit head. The oil here was discovered by one of the elephants who were turned loose at night. On arriving back to work one morning its legs were covered with black oil ooze. A little way outside Ledo stood a big white signpost about eight feet square, right across the top of which was painted in large letters STILWELL ROAD. Underneath were the names of more than a dozen places and their distances. I noted 'Myitkyina 275 miles' and at the bottom of the table 'Kuomting 1078 miles'.

The splendour of the natural scene made the worst bumps a jeep can give hardly noticeable. We drove on and on, penetrating the wildest jungle, but every mile or so passing the remains of camps either of workmen or of refugees. There was a Chinese cemetery where the soldiers of the Far East lay under heavy tombstones and headstones covered with Chinese ideographs. In the middle of the cemetery was a tall monolith on which a rising sun was painted. I was puzzled to see this political emblem of Japan.

When we alighted from the jeep to stretch our legs by a particularly grand sweep of the road, the jungle just beyond was loud with the eldrich ululations of black gibbons, but these apes are shy and we did not catch a glimpse of them. I was told that the females are in labour for three days with their young, and that when the Naga women are near childbirth it is the custom to drive away all the gibbons in the neighbourhood so that the evil influence of their slow parturition may be avoided.

At one point the road ran beside the loop of a sinister rifle-green river called Namchik over which the oil pipe line was carried like a suspension bridge. On the far side rose a steep conical jungle-clad hill. It was down a bridle track on this hill that the stream of refugees slithered in exhaustion after the deathly trail from Myitkyina up the pestilential Hukawng Valley in that tragic Burma spring of 1942, to cross the river and make for Lagopani. That, of course, was long before the road or pipe line was made. By this path, too, came footsore Gloucesters and K.O.Y.L.I.'s—stragglers from Alexander's retreat.

It was interesting to see how the jungle was advancing on the road. First, like 'recce' parties, convolvulus, purple and white and mauve, threw out its long tendrils, young tufts of elephant grass had established themselves, and behind them the bamboos had consolidated the jungle's gain. Creepers were climbing up all the telephone poles and festooned the wires where they remained. I doubted if the road would even be jeepable after another monsoon.

We stopped for lunch at the cleared site of an old camp, a few hun-

c

dred yards before Hell Gate, which marked the frontier accepted at that time between India and Burma. I found a plantain with a bunch of bright carmine bananas smelling of cucumber. The inside was full of very astringent seeds. Beyond Hell Gate the road rose 3,500 feet in three miles, and God knows how it was ever made in the time. Bayley and I kept looking round after we had negotiated a curve through thick yellow mud, with a wall of rock on one side and a thousand feet sheer drop on the other, to see that the jeep behind had not gone hurtling down. Once or twice there was a hole in the road at the bottom of which the jungle was visible; that was a bit alarming. Nevertheless, it was impossible to feel nervous in a scene of such staggering beauty and grandeur. By great good fortune the day was clear, which is very rare at that time of the year and when we came to the top of the Pangsau Pass we could see across three or four green ranges stained with blue air the Himalayan snows for mile upon mile, ten days' march away and about a hundred miles as the eagle flies. This was the famous hump over which the American airmen flew, day in day out, with supplies for China. It was a hazardous task. In one day 32 planes were lost in an electrical storm. At that moment two Americans were jeeping down right through Burma to obtain information about lost aircraft and if possible rescue the bones for burial across the Atlantic.

We went on for about a quarter of a mile round the head of the Pass to look down at the Forbidden Lakes which lie in a vast marsh where there were neither birds nor beasts and where any aircraft that crashed would never be found. Until the Ledo Road was made nobody had seen those Lakes since 1885 when an American Baptist missionary called Elliot reached them by paddling up the Namchik in a Rob Roy canoe.

I should write in *Eastern Epic*:

"The view from the top of the Pangsau Pass, over green ranges stained with blue air to the Himalayan snows a hundred miles away and down upon that wide expanse of grey-green marsh through which flow those deathly rivers, can vie with any on earth. Yet he who stands there, awed by the beauty and vastness of the scene, is haunted by the memory of those nameless, numberless dead—Indian men and women and children of every caste and province, British men, women and children of all classes, Anglo-Indians, Anglo-Burmans, British, Indian, Gurkha, and Chinese soldiers, their bones soon to mingle with those of American airmen lost in flying over the Hump of those sublime Himalayan snows to take supplies to China. Agony, terror, bravery, cowardice, squalor, starvation and disease may be at one now for ever with beauty, but the silence of the Pangsau Pass is the voice of Death himself."

After that memorable day we travelled all night from Margarita to

Dimapur, or as it was known during the campaign, Manipur Road. Brigadier Michael Roberts, the Sub-Area Commander at Shillong, who had commanded 114 Brigade of the 7th Indian Division in Arakan, was going to be of the greatest help to me now and later. Jim Thomson joined us bringing a supply of atebrinum, a variant of mepacrine. The Kabaw Valley, down a part of which we should be driving in due course, produces the worst malaria in the world, but at this time of the year it is less vicious.

We drove round what was left by the relentless jungle of the huge Manipur Dump, eleven miles long and never less than a mile wide. We saw the curious remains of an ancient fort near which were a group of stones like enormous button mushrooms. There were at least two dozen of them and they were obviously of phallic significance. Thomas Atkins used to call this place P— Park. They were carved with various animals and hieroglyphics and were about eight feet high.

After Nichuguard the scenery became magnificent. It was rather like the Wye Valley carried to a nth degree. We drove slowly up through a superb gorge with a prodigal vegetation on either side and a river below. Higher up, an immense view of dense jungle was unfolded to lose itself in a blue haze miles away. In that level tract of country there were said to be more elephants than in the rest of India put together. Tigers abounded and there were both buffalo and bison. The pick of the fauna was the great Indian rhinoceros, the remnants of which were protected in a reservation. This was the only part where they were still found.

Just beyond the 32nd of the 46 milestones to Kohima the road ran across the low Zubza ridge which marked for a few days the farthest advance any Japanese troops had made into India. They were soon turned out by the advance of the 7th Indian Division and on the right hand side of the road Frank Messervy[1] had had his H.Q. We walked up the bank to have a look at the bamboo beside which his caravan stood. A leopard had left his card close by after a good meal of dog.

We reached Kohima about five o'clock and were met by C. R. Pawsey,[2] the Deputy Commissioner. It was a bit of luck that I was able to meet this remarkable man to whose devoted service among the Nagas we owed the marvellous loyalty they displayed during the Japanese invasion. The Commissioner's bungalow had been destroyed, and he was living in a tiny improvised cottage. Chrissie and I were housed in what amounted to a shack of two rooms made of sheets of corrugated iron full of bullet holes.

[1] General Sir Frank Messervy, K.C.S.I., K.B.E., C.B., D.S.O.
[2] The late Sir Charles Pawsey, C.S.I., C.I.E.

Charles Pawsey, driving me in his own jeep, led the way up to the top of the Naga village on the crown of the hill some 500 feet above what was called the Treasury, the office of the Deputy Commissioner. The road wound round and round and was swarming with small pigs and minute piglets, mostly black and white. A full-sized pig was no bigger than a large cocker spaniel. To one part of Assam a pigmy wild hog eighteen inches long was indigenous. The Naga village was entirely destroyed by the various British and Jap bombardments and had been rebuilt with corrugated iron. This was painted a dull maroon, and the houses had managed to preserve a much better shape than the average tin shack in England. I noticed that two or three of them had what looked like large wings of corrugated iron with two big round holes through them at the gable end of the roof. These were the horns that a Naga who has given a feast of a cow to his neighbours was allowed to put up as a decoration. The Nagas in Government service wore bright red blankets. One of them who took us round the village spoke good English and Hindustani. He told Chrissie he had himself killed six or seven Japs, but added with a smile that he had not taken their heads.

The language was difficult. A lot of words as in Chinese depend entirely on intonation. Thus the word *dzu* with one intonation means water, with another egg, and with a third intonation something which made the women laugh inordinately when asked if they had any eggs. Not only was the language difficult, but there were twenty different languages. One village not far from Kohima had a language entirely its own. The vocabularies, too, were fairly large.

Chrissie's stockings caused a good deal of mirth among the women. They could not make out whether her face and her legs were a different colour. They felt them, but they were so thin that they couldn't believe they were stockings until she pulled up her skirt and showed them where her legs began. This had a great comic success. They really were delightful people. The young girls' heads were cropped until marriage, and the men grew a sort of small top knot into which they put ornaments and flowers. I saw two boys with marigolds in their hair. Some of the women wore brass earrings four inches across; the girls wore thick brass bracelets. We watched them doing some wonderful weaving with cotton. We also watched the hulling of rice by a woman and her daughter, the daughter working with a pestle and the mother shaking the rice rhythmically in a large flat basket sieve with a most graceful action.

At the very top of the highest peak of the village called Hunter's Hill we came upon a memorial to the men of the First Camerons killed there. It consisted of a plaque with their names above which was engraved LOCHABER NO MORE. Yet I can say to any Highland wife or mother who laments a loved one lying eight thousand miles and more away from the braes of home that this Naga village was far nearer in spirit to Lochaber than almost any place in between. We came down from Hunter's Hill just before dusk. It had been a wonderful experience. I wished I could have spent a long time with those lovable people. It was evident that Pawsey was heartbroken to be leaving them in two or three months. His three servants had been with him twenty years.

We were introduced to *zyu* or rice beer; it tasted rather like fermented coconut milk. The Nagas will not drink cow's milk; they think the idea disgusting. We enjoyed more the spirituous *zyu* which is very potent. Bayley and I voted it to be a good apéritif.

Next day after breakfast we jeeped and walked round various parts of the battlefields. The cemetery with 1,100 British dead had been constructed in terraces on the site of what was once the Deputy Commissioner's garden and bungalow. His tennis court was No Man's Land, and the remains of it, even the white markings, were still to be seen. The crown of the hill constituted the Kohima Box which was held through that desperate fortnight in April 1944. On the edge of the perimeter was the Royal Berkshires' Memorial where the Chinese dragon of the regimental badge looked northward away across the Himalayas to China. Just above and close by was the Memorial to the Durham Light Infantry with, as I think a misplaced facetiousness or sentimentality in the circumstances, a signpost inscribed 'New Gateshead'. On the knoll beyond, called Kuki Picket, was the Memorial to the Royal West Kents—the old Dirty Half Hundred—who were flown in from Arakan with 161st Brigade of the 5th Indian Division and fought superbly. The Memorial to the Royal Welch Fusiliers was inscribed *Ond Nid Ym Ofer*, and the famous black flash, a yard high, was painted on the tablet. This, too, was on Kuki Picket. The Memorials to the 4/15 Punjabis, the 4/1 Gurkhas and the 77th Indian Field Company overlooked that fatal cut in the road where so many lives were lost.

I walked round nearly all the various ridges and hills which had seen fighting as desperate as any recorded in history. On the east side of he cemetery where the ground was held by the Japanese a stone slab was inscribed "At Kohima in April 1944 the Japanese invasion of India was halted". Beyond this stood the most impressive of the War Memorials. A great rough block of stone bore a copper plate with the names of those who died in 161st Brigade of the 5th Indian Division. At either end of the small semi-circular terrace in which the block was set was the Divisional badge—a ball of fire in red stone and black marble.

Farther along, I was surprised to find a Memorial going back to 1879 to two British Officers and a Subedar-Major of the 44th Native Infantry (afterwards 8th Gurkhas) who were killed on November 22nd of that year. They were killed not at Kohima but at Konoma, a village some six miles away, between which and Kohima existed an old blood-feud likely to break out at any time if Deputy Commissioners like Pawsey were no longer available. Then I came across a Memorial to a Manipur Raja who burnt Kohima about 1820. This consisted of an inscribed headstone with a cow and a dragon and on the horizontal stone slab in front the imprint of the Raja's two bare feet.

I have seldom said goodbye to a man with more regret than when we left Pawsey in Kohima to drive on to Imphal. I felt more indignant than ever with the cowardly way the Ministry of Information and the B.B.C. had blanketed that heroic struggle in April 1944, though in justice to them the General Staff in Whitehall was the inspiration of that cowardice and the boosting of the American effort at Myitkyina which was comparatively minute.

I recall from that enthralling drive to Imphal a spot where the road ran above a rich green river, impassable in the monsoon. Round one corner a rusty car was standing on end festooned with convolvulus and decorated with a notice: "This might happen to you!" The trees on either side of the road were full of what looked like mistletoe.

When we reached the Residency at Imphal we were greeted by the Political Agent and his wife, Mr and Mrs Gerald Stewart. Stewart was captured by a German raider in the Indian Ocean and finally after spending a fortnight in a supply ship was taken to Japan and interned. The Residency was a fantastic house, and it had been made more fantastic by the twenty-five bombs which were dropped all round it. The house was full of stucco Corinthian columns inside and out. The plaster was half down in most of the rooms and the tiled roof which was knocked to pieces had been temporarily replaced by corrugated iron.

Christopher Gimson, the late Political Agent, who had been there for many years, had a passion for lawns. He was a champion tennis player and there were five grass courts of the finest quality. He was a great gramophone fan, and on top of the wardrobe in my room stood an E. M. Ginn horn which he had not taken back with him with his collection of gramophone records. He also left behind all his copies of *The Gramophone*. It had been his custom to give a concert of good music every Sunday evening. I need hardly add that he was a bachelor. After the Residency had been knocked about and nearly every pane in the windows had been broken he continued to live in it quite happily and, though it was cold there at night during the winter, he was unperturbed. The garden, much of it planned by Gimson, with advice from Kingdon Ward, was beautiful, and as I sat on the west veranda looking across a wide green lawn to majestic trees I might have been in Devon, except for the sound of the drums being beaten by the Nagas at their ten days' harvest festival.

After tea we walked along with the Stewarts and Thomson to the market where at least 500 women were sitting on the ground displaying their wares. The Manipuri women ruled the roost. The market could not open until they had done their day's work because they insisted on selling the stuff themselves. They could be pretty tough, too. About twenty years before, the President of the Durbar, who was the British Political Adviser to the Maharaja, annoyed the women about something. So they debagged him and threw him into a pond. On another occasion a predecessor of Stewart's (not Gimson) who had promised to telegraph to the Government about some matter connected with the price of rice was shut up in the post office by a crowd of 4,000 women. The President of the Durbar went to his rescue, and he too was shut up. Finally the Commandant of the Assam Rifles went along and he in turn was shut up. All three had to remain until the telegram came from Calcutta, but the women allowed them to have refreshments brought.

Imphal was the capital of Manipur State, the massive Maharaja of which drove about in a jeep. He was away at this moment. In the garden of the Residency there was a memorial to the five military and civil officers who were beheaded by an usurping Maharaja as lately as 1891.

The next three days were taken up with making myself familiar with the sometimes complicated topography of that great struggle by Fourth Indian Corps under the able command of Sir Geoffry Scoones.[1] I was grateful for the clarity with which Bayley expounded the significance of various sites of action. Not for nothing was he known affectionately as the Professor when he was B.G.S. to 4th Corps, for the foresight of whose commander he had great admiration.

When we got back to the Residency on the second day we went along to the Naga village to see the dancing on the last day of the harvest festival. The men were wearing horns tipped with a bunch of white bunting and a bunch of peacock feathers at the back of the head. They wore sashes in the style of a sergeant-major sewn with large sequins and most of them wore a kind of crimson kilt, though some were wearing shorts and gym shoes. There were many women and girls dancing, and there were boys down to a child of about five in a yellow shirt. They danced round a maypole decked with banana leaves and bougainvillea. At the moment of our arrival they were all seated and beating time with knives to a lament for members of the tribe who had died during that year. All the men, and even the smallest of the boys, carried knives. There was one dance in which the performers were presented with rice balls and oranges by women in the audience. There was also a band which from time to time played *For He's a Jolly Good Fellow*, regardless

---

[1] General Sir Geoffry Scoones, K.C.B., K.B.E., C.I.E., D.S.O.

of the ceremonial chanting and the two ceremonial drummers. We sat
there sipping our *zyu* until it was dark.

That evening Major Hulme (1/7 Gurkhas) came along with Wynd-
ham Robinson, who had been sketching his way up from Rangoon.
Hulme, who was to take us to Kalewa and Schwebo, was not encourag-
ing about the state of the roads on which we should travel and warned
us that we should have at least one night's camping in the jungle.
Hulme insisted it was imperative for me to see the Chin Hills and
Tiddim, which could be reached from Kalewa. So it was decided that
Chrissie should stay on at the Residency for three days and join us at
Kalewa, escorted there by Major Cassels of the Assam Regiment, while
Bayley, Jim Thomson and myself would tackle the Chin Hills. The
Chin tribesmen sounded tough. When the fight with Nippon was at
its height, one of them came down to Imphal with a bag in his hand
and asked for his reward. When the British officer asked him 'What for?'
the tribesman offered him the bag. The officer dipped his hand in and
hastily had to extricate it from six decomposing Japanese heads.

On our last day we drove to see the sites of the fighting by Douglas
Gracey and the 20th Indian Division. Not far outside Imphal a great
peepul tree stood in the middle of the road and traffic had to pass on
either side. A peepul tree is sacred both for Hindus and Buddhists
and must never be cut down. A large aloe beside the road was covered
with a silver network of dewy gossamer, and the telegraph lines at
intervals were festooned with it. Brigadier Roberts told us that one of
the most shuddery experiences in the Arakan jungle was to walk in the
dark into the cobweb of a very large black, white and green spider.

The scenery when we left the plain behind and went sweeping up
toward the Shenam Saddle was sublime. There was one point where
the road ran into the cold shadow of a northerly aspect, when I had to
alight from the car and gaze entranced at the view of wooded gorges
and ravines and jagged ridges, beyond which the plain of Imphal lay
like a pale green lake in the sunlight, bounded along the horizon by
grey-blue mountains. This view was framed by a couple of 20 ft high
peach trees in full rosy blossom; they were growing above the 2,000-ft
wooded precipice along which the road had been driven. Behind, the
same wooded precipice towered above us and cut off the sun, so that
the peach blossom seemed a frozen blush, the beauty of which almost
hurt.

As we were looking round the various sites on the Saddle we heard
the crackle of a fire, where the hillmen were burning the jungle to clear
a space for cultivation; the crackle sounded like small arms and one
could have fancied it was an echo of that desperate battle three years
before. The holding of this vital bastion by Douglas Gracey and the
Silver Sword Division cut many petals from the chrysanthemum.

From where we were standing we could look down to the old road along which Alexander's men came wearily out of Burma in '42. This terrace was ablaze with what we call African marigolds, and I was told that these maroon and golden flowers are always found where Gurkhas have been. I was also told that the Japs used to fling their dead over the precipices from which they fought in order that as much as a finger could be burnt and the ashes sent home to Japan. In the troopships the Japs used to keep the trimmings from their fingernails and burn these to send home in advance for burial when news of their death should reach home.

When we got back to the Residency we found Chrissie seemingly threatened with jaundice. Brigadier Roberts told Jim Thomson that he would arrange to get her into hospital at Shillong if she became worse. However, she was definitely better before we set off for Kalewa next morning and we could feel reasonably sure that she would be able to meet us in Kalewa. Hulme's Dodge had got into trouble on the way up to Imphal and was in hospital: it was hoped that it would be well enough for Cassels to drive Chrissie.

Bayley, Jim Thomson and I said goodbye to our kind hosts and were southward bound with Hulme, two jeeps, two 15-cwt trucks, and a small Gurkha escort. Brigadier Roberts who had arranged everything so splendidly for our Assam tour lent his staff car to take us as far as the road was tolerably good. From the Shenam Saddle it ran down in great sweeps through majestic scenery and glorious vegetation. As we came round one of the curves a troop of rhesus monkeys crossed the road in front of the car, a baby monkey bringing up the rear. Later on they must have crossed the road back to the other side, for the baby monkey was killed by a lorryful of Manipuri black-marketeers just behind us. One of our jeeps found it.

About two miles before Tamu we sent back the staff car and ate an agreeable lunch beside a dry waterfall. We were slightly shaded by slim trees growing up the bank; when the faint breeze blew, their leaves came whirling down as upon an autumn day at home, but instead of reaching the ground silently their fall was as audible as a sliver of tin. Just past milestone 28 from Tamu we turned left along a track through the jungle by a notice-board with 'H.Q. Elephant Company' on it. This was a relic of Lt.-Colonel J. H. Williams, the famous 'Elephant Bill'. After a mile or so of jungle we came to the bungalow of the Bombay-Burma Trading Corporation. It was built on piles with a teak frame, unceiled rooms and walls of split bamboo. The roof was shingled with teak tiles. Sam Cope the boss gave us a warm welcome. He had a remarkable war career, having spent much of his time with Force 136 which was the organization for dropping men behind the Japanese lines, where indeed Cope had spent most of his time. I found he was a devotee of my comic books. It is extraordinarily gratifying to find that one's work has diverted somebody like Sam Cope. I never expect to hear it and that makes it all the more pleasant to hear.

The view at twilight across the Kabaw valley to the blue misty bluffs of the Chindwin seemed rather sinister, probably because I had been told about the blackwater fever for which this hollow land is notorious. However, the melancholy dusk was brief. A huge log fire had been lighted outside the bungalow—one could not have a fire inside such an inflammable structure—and we sat down to dinner beside it. After dinner we sat round the fire and it was 2 a.m. before I went to the camp-bed Hulme had lent me after a grand evening. We were told that a thick mist would rise and envelop us before dawn, but although it was very damp the mist was not too formidable. As there was no glass in the windows of these Burmese bungalows and the walls admitted as much light and air as they excluded, the mist penetrated everywhere. I had had rheumatism in Imphal; in this damp place I was without a twinge.

The teak trunks—a teak tree is in prime condition when 150 years old—were dragged by elephants to the Yu whence they floated down into the Chindwin. They were then collected into rafts and by way of the Irrawaddy finally reached Rangoon, at least 600 miles away. I can imagine nothing more remote than that bungalow. The last papers they had had from Calcutta had been just after Christmas.

Just before I fell into a sound sleep that night I thought how much younger I should feel when I woke up tomorrow to be 64 than I had felt last year when I woke up to be 63.

HULME gave me a bamboo pipe from Moulmein as a present for my 64th birthday. The bowl had two small excrescences which looked like ears and were excellent guards for the fingers against a hot bowl. We left Htinzin just before ten, the hour at which I was born, for the 72-mile journey to Kalewa. This may not sound far, but as our average progress was twelve miles an hour it was a tiring trip. Once again 50 yards of Western Avenue and then 200 yards of ruts, potholes and bent P.S.P. (Perforated Steel Planking) which made a noise like a train when we drove over it. We crossed 150 bridges between Tamu and Kalewa, each one over a stream which, shallow enough at that moment, could be 12-feet deep and more in the monsoon. I hope this suggests the kind of country through which the Fourteenth Army had to fight its way. The girders of some of the bridges were now festooned with creepers. On one of them was painted 'Battersea Bridge'. We passed a dropping place for supplies where Bayley remembered standing once at dusk and seeing the trees all round hung with parachutes like ghosts.

At last we emerged from the jungle and had a view of the Chin Hills we should be tackling next day. Birds were now more frequent. A large kingfisher was perched on the rail of one bridge and we stopped to admire its azure-flashing plumage. Doves kept fluttering in front of the jeep. The people on the road were unresponsive in contrast to the jolly Nagas. Just before Kalewa I saw my first pagoda, on a bluff above the river.

We reached Kalewa at half-past four and found that the rest house was without furniture except for four chairs and a table. The only decoration was a parachute which draped the inside of the roof. Every plank in the floor was loose and one could see through to the ground. We had only one lamp—a dim and dirty hurricane. There was a moment of great beauty after sunset when I went out on the west balcony and saw a tree in the foreground such as you see in Chinese paintings, black against a luminous green sky in the dip between two ranges of hills.

I had started to write up my diary, when I was interrupted by a visit from Kwan Lone, the District Supply Officer, a Chinese speaking perfect English. He had been taken by the Japs and tortured, but on the day he was to be executed he 'played a trump card' by appealing to a Japanese professor he had known and instead of being executed was released, after which he spent two years in a hill village. He vowed he had read many of my books, but I did not think he had. He said his memory had been affected by the hammering the Japs had given his head.

A troop of strolling players had reached Kalewa, and at nine o'clock Hulme, Thomson and myself went along to the theatre with Kwan Lone who had set a bench for us at the back of the audience. There were well over six hundred spectators, all sitting on the sloping ground, men, women, and children, most of them (children included) smoking what looked like Roman candles but were in fact tobacco wrapped in maize. The performers consisted of four 'clowns' and three women in long tight pink skirts and white 'boleros'. They danced beautifully, sometimes turning deliciously discreet somersaults, and when a whistle blew they instantly remained motionless in a stylized pose like figures on a Chinese screen. Their faces were white with rice powder, and how they managed that acrobatic dancing in those tight long skirts was a mystery. The orchestra was a medley of queer instruments, but we could not get near enough to see what they were. For our benefit there were several gags in English. We left at ten after which there was to be a play, the performance of which would last till dawn. Outside the theatre vendors of food sat at their candlelit stalls, ready to sustain the audience during the nine hours' show. A good birthday, and it was a relief to hear from Imphal that Chrissie was better and would arrive at Kalewa on the date fixed.

When we were setting out from Kalewa for Tiddim I decided to leave Gulaba to help Chrissie and Cassels when they should arrive and commended both of them to the good services of Kwan Lone. We had to drive back through the Myittha Gorge to take the turning to Kalemyo. The river was beautiful in the glitter of the morning and I had the thrill of seeing the flight of a scarlet minivet dipping bright as a firework against the jungle. Just after that we met a Dodge truck with a solemn white man under an outsize topee beside the driver. We decided he must be an American Baptist missionary. These American Baptists had a strong hold on the hill tribes, and their influence over their way of life had not always been beneficial. One would have thought that they would all have stuck to their posts when war came to Burma and Assam, but most of them cleared off.

From Kalemyo, where the villagers stared at us with obvious dislike, we drove along an avenue of various trees which must have been left when the ground on either side was cleared for cultivation. We admired particularly a tall acacia-like tree with large glittering pods the colour of rose-madder. We stopped to look at a minute cemetery on the left of the road. There were four white crosses without names and a wooden headstone inscribed Sapper Iruchan, Q.V.O.M.S.M. (Queen Victoria's Own Madras Sappers and Miners) 5.12.44. I recalled the Mess in

Bangalore and the silver mule upon the table and the dark merry faces of the boys training for what might be a lonely grave like this.

"The avenue now entered a grove of magnificent trees and began to climb, narrowing to barely enough width for one way traffic by trucks. The surface was slimy and damp and often fairly deep in mud, which made the turns tricky for a jeep with a trailer. Up and up through a gothic landscape of craggy water courses and huge trees, the land rising steeply to the left of us and dipping down on the other side to a green sea of jungle below. Up and up, occasionally passing parties of Chins who with their heavy packs looked like gnomes. We reached a superb punchbowl of foliage. Up and up until we were in the clouds, though never dense enough to create an awkward fog. Sometimes the sun, striking the mist aslant, turned it into a ladder with silver rungs. Up and up, until we were above the clouds, which now became a sea of milky billows in which was set an archipelago of mountain tops like dark pyramids. Up and up, corkscrewing up the slimy ochreous road, I suddenly saw my first *rhododendron arboreum* and nearly bounced out of the jeep; I was back in Cornwall forty years ago. The rhododendrons became more plentiful, some of them with hoary trunks at least a yard round and thirty feet of blossoming rubies, but mostly they did not exceed fifteen feet. We turned left to run along a level ridge. A foot or two beyond the jeep on the left there was an almost sheer drop of 3,000 feet to a wild glen, but the sides being covered with trees it was easy to gaze down unperturbed. From time to time we passed an abandoned lorry rusting away, and once we saw a Jap tank. It was down this road that 5th Indian Division marched through the monsoon to victory.

"The air began to be really cold as we came to a country of what looked like dark holm-oaks. Birds of every kind were now numerous, but for the first time the ubiquitous wagtail did not go dipping along the road ahead of us. We saw two or three large trees with silver trunks and a spreading head of grey-green poplar-like leaves. We passed the Third Stockade, which our forces held in 1890, and reached Fort White, where down below the small village we could see the cemetery of those who fell then. Presently Hill 52 (8,198 ft) rolled up skyward before us— an eagle soaring above its bald top. We found a spot where the wind was not too shrewd and settled down to tiffin. The lower slopes of Hill 52 were sprinkled with the debris of war—the quick release buckles of parachute containers and many empty cartridges. I saw to my joy my first primula. It was the colour of *P. denticulata* but grew with a looser head of flowers and was perhaps a shade rosier. I ached for a Flora. With the primulas were growing what resembled an *androsace* of exactly the same shade of rosy-mauve. They both bloomed above the short brownish grass on which the cattle of the Chins seemed to thrive. These were being driven to their grazing—bells tinkling from their tawny necks.

"After lunch we drove on round to Kennedy Peak (8,876) on the forward slope of which Hulme and his Seventh Gurkhas used to watch with mixed feelings a bunch of red tabs observing their bitter and bloody struggle for Hill 52. The road ran into light jungle. We saw a large civet cat with a dark bristling tail as bushy as a fox's go bounding along a tree-trunk above the road. After rounding Kennedy Peak we passed Vital Corner after which the road ran gradually down into a country full of pines and at about half-past four we reached Tiddim (5,500 ft) at the end of the most wonderful drive I had had in all my life, the beauty and grandeur of which evaporate in these feeble words of mine."

Tiddim was completely destroyed, but the village had been rebuilt with corrugated iron. We were being housed by Lt.-Colonel West of the 1st Chin Battalion, Burmese Frontier Force. Unfortunately he was away on a month's tour of his 3,000-odd square miles of territory. The walls of the Assistant Resident's house remained and a new roof had been made of corrugated iron which was like a starry sky from within on account of the many holes. I slept in his room, the furniture of which consisted of a wire-bed without a mattress, a mosquito net held up by four slivers of split saplings, and improvised low wardrobe with two shelves and no doors, a rough table, and a deep low cupboard with a small battered mirror. The planks of the floor clattered and were sometimes an inch apart. There was no glass in any of the windows, which were closed with wooden shutters at night. There was another bedroom on the other side in which Bayley, Hulme and Thomson slept. Between was the living-room which had a splendid fireplace for logs, a coconut-fibre mat, two wooden-seated chairs and two canvas-seated chairs both shrinking fast and one without a back. In a corner stood a wireless set with signal batteries on which we listened to Australia. For this palace West was charged 90 rupees a month by the Government. I will add that the privy followed the Burmese fashion of an inverted ace of spades for the seat and was covered by tattered netting.

West had already made quite a garden. Hemerocallis was in bloom, peas were podding, and a bed of strawberries showed promise of fruit. There were also some pink Wichuriana roses, a young bougainvillea, nasturtiums, a small plum-tree, a sizeable lemon-tree and two clumps of hippeastrum, pale pink with a pale green stripe—an attractive medley.

An earthenware pot of the local zyu was brought in by a Chin boy. This was filled with fermenting millet in water and everybody was supposed to suck through a bamboo in turn. However, Hulme syphoned some into bottles. Bayley and I demanded the strong stuff at 2 rupees a bottle, but it was not nearly as good as the Kohima brew from rice. It tasted like methylated spirits which had been filtered through mildew. I went to bed at a quarter to eleven after a supper of tinned salmon and soup, and read a chapter of a tattered Western blood called *Singing Guns* which I found in the bungalow. An agreeable feature of the night was the striking of the hour on a sweet-sounding bell at the Police Station.

Next morning we started off at ten in two jeeps without trailers, Bayley driving me and Hulme driving Thomson to descend the Chocolate Staircase which zigzagged down to the Beltang Lui, a swift flowing mountain stream, glaucous but clear. The Chocolate Staircase still looked like chocolate here and there, but mostly the rich brown soil down which it had been cut was green again. We crossed the wide stream by an improvised bridge and ascended the opposite slope through groves of large-leaved trees as fine a crimson for that brief autumn of theirs as the vegetation along the Palisades of the Hudson seen from Riverside Drive in October. Here and there among the prevailing crimson were trees with foliage turned to gold or amber. We emerged from the woodland, and the road narrowed to run parallel with the Manipur River flowing at the bottom of a shaly precipice, without a tree to break one's fall. One bridge over a deep burn was tricky. Only two of the girders were left, luckily at the right interval to take the wheels of a jeep. The Chauffeur Brigadier and the Chauffeur Major both did their stuff well. We went up a steep rise as far as Milestone 139 and looked at the Tuitum Saddle which was finally captured by 48th Brigade after severe fighting. We could go no farther because the headman of Tongzang had diverted the road into his own village and put up a barrier. While we were looking across at the Saddle we heard, far above, the drone of a Dakota. I could have fancied it was the ghost of one of those Dakotas whose ability to supply our troops during those critical months was a major factor in the defeat of the Japanese.

In an angle of the road where we got out to study the terrain a large group of Chins were sitting round a memorial stone to a Subedar-Major of the Burma Rifles who was a native of Tongzang. When we examined it we found a superbly executed bas relief on a plaque of reddish slate. If Cyril Connolly could have secured a good reproduction of this for *Horizon* it would have created a sensation in advanced aesthetic circles. It was done by a Chin artist and measured 24 inches by 18. The upper half commemorated events in the life of Subedar-Major Pau Za Gin and his father. The lower half depicted the animals he had killed during his life—monkeys, a hornbill, an owl, three other birds, a sambur, a porcupine, a bear savaging a wild pig, a rhinoceros, a tiger on top of a buffalo, and an elephant. The killing of that elephant had called for a big feast, and the lower half showed Pau Za Gin with a glass of *zyu* in his hand and his wife handing the jar round to the assembled guests. One would have said it was of Egyptian or Assyrian workmanship. It was an unique work of art perfect in composition and execution. The inscription above said:

PA THUAL KHAM A KHAN LAM A GALL MAT VAI TUN
LIM MI
Sub-Maj. PAU ZA GIN.
Burma Rifles
1.8.45

[He was killed in South Burma far from his native village.] There was a longer inscription above, but as there was nobody at Tiddim, West being away, to translate it I did not copy that out. Most of the Chins were primitive animists, but we were informed that he belonged to a family of hereditary gravers.

We drove back to Milestone 144 and ate tiffin beside a brawling stream that leapt down to join the greenish-yellow Manipur which had already been joined by the glaucous Beltang Lui. It was a perfect site for a picnic. We raced some twigs and bits of bamboo down the little waterfalls. A bird of wagtail size with white cap, dark back, and a ruddy chestnut breast flitted from stone to stone. I found out later that it was a redstart of sorts.

I was tired by the time we got back to Tiddim after sneezing my way up the Chocolate Staircase with a sudden cold in the head. Three hot whiskies and orange juice brewed by Jim Thomson revived me and I was up next morning, when Bayley drove me to the cemetery which lay a few paces below the road. It was almost an exact square surrounded on two sides by pines and looked up a slope covered by a shrub with scarlet tubular flowers round the branches. Three bushes of cherry-red roses were growing among the graves, and those were the only flowers. Seventy-four British soldiers, many of them Borders, lay there. On one side of the square were seven unpainted crosses to eight "unidentified R.A.F. Soldiers (*sic*) who crashed near here 12.9.45." In the other half of the square lay sixty-six Mussulman soldiers. There were the graves of an Unknown British Major and an Unknown British Captain, and in the Mussulman half the grave of an Unknown Major. I did not understand how any of these could be unknown if their rank was ascertainable. The bodies in that cemetery were to be taken to Imphal so that the graves might be better cared for, but surely with a little trouble the War Graves Commission could have secured their being cared for in the beautiful spot where they lay.

When I was walking through West's garden a little Gurkha girl with a ring through her nose smiled at me and I presented her with an orange sweet with which she walked away in her cupped hands as if it were a precious stone. After the annexation the British Government settled a number of Gurkhas in north-east Burma like the military colonists of Greece and Rome. Finally the Maharaja of Nepal objected and insisted that all Gurkhas must receive their pensions in Nepal. Nevertheless, many of those Gurkha colonists remained.

Hulme told me a story about a concert party of six called the Roosters which was the only one that reached up here. One night at a concert on Kennedy Peak, a Rooster was singing 'You'll never know just how much I love you', when a Gunner officer put his head in and shouted, 'All men to the guns.' 63rd Brigade had asked for a 'crump'. Seven-eighths of the audience vanished, but the singer (a Blackpool Folly) stuck to the stage and tried to make his voice heard above the noise of the guns. When the crump was finished the audience came back to hear the rest of the performance. Hulme spoke highly of the work that concert party did. He also paid a tribute to Noel Coward for giving a show in Bishenpur when the Japs were still in Potsangbum two miles away.

We were hoping that the rain would hold off when we left Tiddim next morning. It was going down day according to schedule, but just before we started the head of the police in Tiddim told Hulme that the order had been changed. He probably had a friend who wanted to come up from Kalewa. We were now faced with the problem of twelve lorries coming up a road where passing places were scarce; it is not easy to back up a greasy corkscrew. Bayley drove one jeep and trailer with Thomson and myself. Hulme and his Gurkhas were in the other; the two 15-cwts followed with the baggage and rations. Two golden orioles flew across a background of dark oaks just before we stopped for a while to discuss the importance of Vital Corner. Our road ran on round Kennedy Peak where Hulme pointed out Bare Patch, the scene of such bitter fighting. We stopped where we had lunched on our way up, and jeeped up the hillside in a perishing wind from the west. The brownish herbage was starred with primulas and a small aster which would be a cinch in rock gardens.

In a hollow just below a strong Jap bunker we saw the bones of the 1/7th Gurkhas who had advanced to within a few yards of it. A dozen tin helmets lay around, most of them pierced by bullets. There were boots with shinbones sticking out of them from decayed clothing. Thigh bones, skulls, and vertebrae were scattered all around. Only the primulas spoke of life in that haunted hollow above which a grove of blasted trees wrote their grim hieroglyphics on the grey skyline. Some of the bones were charred as if an attempt had been made to cremate them, but Hulme thought that was probably the result of a scrub fire. The three Gurkhas of our escort wandered about among those relics of their comrades while the icy wind swirled among the white bones like the

D

wings of Death himself. The very bells of the cows grazing at the foot of the hill were made out of shell cases. We were glad to leave that stricken spot and escape from that wind.

Hulme went ahead to intercept the ascending lorries and presently we found three of them waiting for us by a wider stretch of road. We heard that one of the twelve had not left Kalewa and that two had broken down on the way up. Hulme went on again and we passed two more. There were only four ahead of us now. The 3,000-ft drop was an immense cauldron of seething grey cloud beyond which the sun shone on the low land. In spite of the clouds the actual road was free of mist the whole way. We reached Number Three Stockade of 1890 and passed two more lorries decked with rhododendron flowers, and then to our great relief the last of them was met and safely passed.

Down and down, with the sun behind us painting the vegetation in the punchbowls and gorges with every shade of green imaginable, while the shadows of the clouds in dragon shapes or like fantastic sea-monsters moved slowly across the mountains. Down and down round hairpin after hairpin. A lilac creeper, *congea tomentosa*, festooned some of the trees. A pigeon with iridescent emerald back and dark breast flew over. At last we came to level ground below Number Two Stockade where beside the rapids of the Kwe Lui we sat down to eat our lunch to the accompaniment of the river's music. A Public Works Department *chokidar* with hardly a tooth left came out from the bamboo basha where he lived to show us a battered Jap rifle and a clip of cartridges. It was idyllic there in the afternoon, but dusk could be lethal, for this was one of the worst spots for blackwater fever.

When we reached Kalewa at half-past five Chrissie was having a bath, having arrived an hour earlier and seeming quite well again, though she had had a pretty poor time. The immediate problem was light. We had only the glimmer of one battered hurricane-lantern. So we hired for five rupees a Petromax which lasted only two hours in spite of repeated pumping. Gulaba had made a dressing-table for me of the two green trunks and Bayley generously sacrificed his own comfort by lending me his camp-bed. I slept well in spite of the noise of chattering from the village, and the crowing of the cocks at dawn.

I woke quite rested after the arduous driving of the last three days out of four. It's amazing what one can stand when one is interested. I sat lazing on the balcony while Chrissie was busy typing the 17 pages I had written somehow during the Tiddim expedition. At midday I watched the children come fluttering out of school like gay butterflies. One boy in pale blue shorts was wearing a topee painted a vivid orange which the other children kept knocking off.

Kwan Lone came round in the afternoon and told me a strange story. The image of Buddha in the monastery on the little hill opposite was of great antiquity. When the British were trying to subdue the Chins and finding it a bit of a job, one of the monks told a British Major to carry the image before him, when resistance would cease. In due course resistance did cease, and the Major took the Buddha back with him to England. In 1939 some Burman students asked the officials of the British Museum to be allowed on religious grounds to take it back. This request was granted. When its Buddha came back to Kalewa an ancient monk said that this return would bring bad luck to the British and by astrology he calculated that they would be out of Burma within three years. The Buddha had been a free gift, and they should have kept it in England. When the Japanese arrived, the Buddha was hidden and Kwan Lone discovered it finally in a small jungle village on the other side of the Myittha. He brought it back to Kalewa where it now stood in its immemorial place. It was inscribed *Bilat Pyan Paya*—the God that came back from the British.

Before we crossed the Chindwin ferry to Shwegyin next day Bayley left us for the journey back to his Brigade in Meerut. We knew how much we should miss the Professor. Besides being a perfect exponent of military matters he had been an ideal travelling companion, and I was truly grateful to Scoones for suggesting him. Bayley had shown me a copy of Scoones' appreciation of the situation, written in February 1944, which was uncanny in its forecast of what the Japs would probably do. Cassels who had been another good companion went off with the Brigadier.

We walked down to the ferry at half-past nine of a misty morning to find Kwan Lone waiting to say goodbye. He shook me warmly by the hand and wished Heaven would grant us a safe journey. He was nervous about dacoits past Pyingaing (Pink Gin to the troops) and begged us to cut the linesman's wire there which was a source of communication with them. X—, a former British officer with a lorryload of smuggled goods, had been murdered only three weeks before some miles past Pink Gin. I heard later that he himself had not been murdered but some of those with him were.

By ten o'clock the mist was lifting and the ferry started. It was delicious gliding along for eight miles farther down this stately river. Fishermen in dug-outs were pulling up the long lines set from bamboo poles in mid stream. The morning light emerging from the fast-fading mist had a kind of virginal quality. The sun scattered diamonds upon the water ahead. Our progress was strangely serene. It was hard to evoke the confusion of that army crossing in retreat five years before. Above the ferry at Shwegyin we saw remains of the motor transport. It could not be got across because the Japs were already on a hill overlooking the river, luckily without enough guns to wreak destruction on the troops scrambling over in every kind of craft and plunging into the jungle on the other side to find the road north to Assam. One Stewart tank got across—God knows how—and reached Imphal. Not only that, but it actually went back to Rangoon in 1945. Its name was 'The Curse of Scotland'.

To the right was a large semicircle of scrub with a few trees surrounded by a line of switchback cliffs. This was the Basin. Here we saw the mass of tanks, trucks, armoured cars and guns left behind on that sweltering day just before the monsoon broke, and the slit trench dug to protect from Japanese bombing those who were putting them out of action.

When we were on the move again, Thomson driving me in one of the jeeps and Hulme driving Chrissie in the Dodge, we passed vehicle after vehicle on either side of the road, the bonnets of them all pointing north. There was one group of six tanks in perfect alignment which recalled the 7th Armoured Brigade, who had brought them all the way up through Burma. Those tanks were painted yellow; they had been intended for the desert not the jungle. Then about eight miles along the road I noticed an abandoned staff car the bonnet of which was pointed south. I realized with a thrill that this was an early casualty of the advance of the Fourteenth Army in January, 1945. I felt inclined to dejeep and pat that bonnet, but enjeeping and dejeeping were a strain on the legs and I sacrificed sentimental elation to sciatic prudence.

The road to Pyingaing lay through extremely beautiful jungle. We crossed one or two streams with water in them, but mostly the beds were dry stretches of what looked like sea sand above high water mark. An extravagant zigzag of sheer sandstone cliffs suddenly slashed the jungle, in one of which the water of a stream had gouged out a great round dark cave. I saw giant ant-hills for the first time since the jungle of Mysore, and tall trees smeared with mud for some way up which was a sign that the termites were at their deadly work. Green parakeets were frequent, Cycads occurred from time to time. Those primeval palms look ugly and artificial in a suburban front garden but here they had a tree-fern effect. We lunched under the shade of high trees. I fired at the bone-grey trunk of one fifty yards away with a carbine and to my satisfaction hit it. We had eleven rifles in the party. When we were driving on after lunch I was on the point of telling Jim Thomson about a wild cat in Glen Affric I had once seen cross in front of the car and go bounding up the brae beside the road when a leopardess with her cub crossed the road and plunged up the slope of the jungle on the right.

We reached Pyingaing at four o'clock and found that the rest house was just a large waste-paper-basket on bamboo piles. The floor was bamboo slivers and one was liable to put a foot through it if one stepped off the rush mats. It was like walking about on a wire mattress. There were three rooms. The ground was reached from the balcony by steps of single bamboo canes.

Just before dusk we explored the abandoned temple near by. The pagoda had been badly knocked about, but the gilded Buddha in the small dark sanctuary below was not much damaged. Three alabaster Buddhas had had their heads knocked off by the Japanese. A gilded papier mâché Buddha had nothing left but the trunk. The guardian *chinthis*—lions with a bit of griffin about them—on either side of the sanctuary were undamaged. From the wall of the roofless fane a clump of cockscomb was glowing red above the painted blue and pink of the decoration. The drooping white bells of a datura clinging round a slim tree scented the evening air. A wrecked Bofors gun was standing beside the entrance. In the gloom beyond was the ruined monastic dormitory on high teak poles. A large red and green woodpecker flew chuckling to a tall palm and played peep-bo with us from the other side of the bare trunk. The scene was a symbolic picture of Burma 1942-45. The plaster walls inside were scribbled over with the names of Indian and British troops.

A log fire had been kindled when we returned to the basha, a noble fire which lasted all night in spite of showers of rain. We sat round our dining table, which was a drum of wire—no wire left of course—I in a crazy deck-chair, the others on two wooden chairs and a stool. We retired to bed early. I heard a rat exploring the basha and one of our fowls for tomorrow's lunch clucking uneasily on the ground underneath. In the morning we found the rat had nibbled a hole in Chrissie's slacks, gnawed my bananas, and gone off with Hulme's toothbrush.

When I woke at seven I saw a large black and chestnut shrike sitting on a pole opposite the window-door. The sky was grey and a drizzle of rain was falling when we left our paper-basket lodging. Thomson and I with Gulaba led the convoy. Hulme and Chrissie were in the Dodge. The two 15-cwts followed, and the other jeep brought up the rear. The rain became heavier but I was glad to see the jungle in rain. Not having to make my way through it on foot I could admire the heightened colour of the various greens. Presently our jeep, which had been making a noise like an outboard motor puffing along on one cylinder, conked out just before it reached a bridge over a wide sandy *chaung* (watercourse) bounded on the opposite side by a fifty-foot cliff of sandstone. Thomson and Gulaba tried to start the jeep by pushing it downhill, but to no purpose; when it reached the bridge it stuck there. We expected every minute to hear the rest of the transport, because we had not been driving fast. There was no sign of the others and the silence was eerie. There was nothing but the whisper of a fine rain and the occasional husky rattle of a big dead leaf as it reached the ground from one of the tall trees that enclosed us. After waiting half an hour

Thomson and I began to wonder if we could possibly have taken the wrong road, but we decided against the possibility of error because Milestone 60 of the Fourteenth Army's advance was visible on the tawny slope up from the dry watercourse. We were about eight miles from Pyingaing—in fact just about where the people had been murdered by dacoits three weeks before. An hour passed. Neither Jim Thomson nor I was armed. We walked back round the next bend but there was still nothing except the whisper of the rain and the fall of leaves. At last we told Gulaba to walk back for half an hour in the hope of finding the rest of the transport. Thomson strolled up the road ahead to see if he could get a view. I settled down in the jeep to finish my diary of January 22nd. Half an hour later the other jeep arrived with Chrissie, one of the Gurkhas, and an R.I.A.S.C. driver. Some five miles behind the Dodge had also seized. It had been towed by one of the 15-cwts, but the latter had skidded on a slope and gone off the road, mercifully being stopped from plunging down into a deep gully by a fallen tree.

Jim Thomson superintended the clearing of three of the plugs of our jeep, working himself twice as hard as the driver. One plug was broken. While they worked hard to get them right, Chrissie wandered off along the *chaung* and discovered a Japanese inscription cut in the sandstone cliff. At last Thomson got the jeep going, and we all returned to the scene of the Dodge disaster. We found Hulme on his back under the 15-cwt lorry, which was hanging over the gully, and finally by some miracle of determination he managed to get it back on the road.

At two o'clock we lunched where the ground on either side of the road was clear of dense jungle for two hundred yards and dacoits would have had difficulty in making a surprise attack. As we finished lunch Hulme arrived with the convoy. A quarter of an hour later the jeeps went on. The jungle then turned to thinnish teak forest. A hoopoe kept flying in front of the jeeps and alighting on the road from time to time, until it tired of this fidgety progress and disappeared in the woodland.

We reached Milestone 90 after thirty miles of fairly good road (or rather not *very* bad road) about five o'clock and were puzzling which turning to take for Shwebo when Hulme and his convoy overtook us, having made wonderful time in the circumstances. The next fifteen miles were terrible. Heavy rain had fallen and the road was a quagmire in which the jeeps seemed to be on roller skates. Luckily the road was wide and there was plenty of room to skate from side to side, but the bridges were nasty. Thomson and I reached the outskirts of Ye-U at last, and there we had to wait anxiously for Jeep Two which we had last seen successfully crossing a brute of a bridge. Dusk was falling fast when Jeep Two reached us with the news that it could go no farther without oil. We managed to get some oil from a near by rice mill, but it was too late to repair the damage, and Jeep Two conked out. We were on the extreme outskirts of Ye-U, a mile from any telephone, and at least twenty-five miles from Shwebo. Even if we could have started Jeep One to which Chrissie had been transferred we had no lights because the battery had run out, and the prospect of walking into Ye-U in the dark through mud above the ankles was grim. At that moment, when I was wondering if we should have to spend the night in a jeep, I saw the new moon above a dull red scar in the clouds where the sun had set. I felt completely at ease and began to meditate on the beauty of the drive.

Even when slithering about during those last fifteen miles we had been enchanted by the pagodas along the road. I don't know why people call pagodas monotonous. They are all different and not a bit more monotonous than the towers or steeples of our own village churches. Apropos of steeples and towers, we passed a large Catholic church with a steeple on a tower. It had been burnt out by the Japs, but we were told that some ten miles away at the end of a bullock track there was another church completely undamaged, with French and Karen priests, an English Mother Superior, and nuns of various nationalities. The Japs had interned them. They suffered much and six died, but the rest of the Community was back. It is to be noted that with rare exceptions Catholic missions flourish where Buddhism prevails.

At last one of the 15-cwt trucks arrived, and with it Hulme. The battery was transferred from Jeep Two to Jeep One, and Jeep Two was taken in tow by the truck. We started on again, everybody and everything caked in mud. In Ye-U Jim Thomson went along to the police station to telephone Shwebo for a truck to be sent to meet us in case we broke down on the twenty-five miles that still lay between us and Shwebo. While we waited for him to come back a train of 50 bullock-carts passed, every wheel squeaking. It sounded like a movement from a contemporary symphony. It was close on eight o'clock when we moved on again. We had a tricky bamboo bridge over the Mu to negotiate and the roads out of Ye-U seemed alarmingly complicated in the darkness. At last, two miles out, we reached the metalled road to Shwebo, along which we were able to drive at 15 miles an hour, which seemed a breakneck speed after what we had been doing.

Finally just after half-past nine we reached the Mess of the Assam Rifles where the 1st Chin Regiment was stationed. Lt-Colonel Sullivan gave us a cordial reception. They had been telephoning along the road without getting any news and had expected us by half-past four. A farewell party to the Chins, who had been transferred to Rangoon, was in progress, and fortified by strong whiskies we joined it. Our host and hostess, Mr and Mrs Trevor Hay, were marvellous. After a buffet supper Mrs Hay drove Chrissie round to their house, and she was in bed by eleven o'clock. I sat on at the party to watch an amusing substitute for musical chairs in which the couples had to reach and then hook their arms round the poles of the tent. As there were only three poles the process of elimination was much more rapid than at musical chairs. Hulme arrived after a hot bath and performed doughtily for a man who had had such a harrowing day. Dear Hulme, I shall never forget his coming up to me, that chin of his jutting out like a cow-catcher, and inviting me in deep solemn tones to shake hands.

"I just want to thank you," he said.

"What for?"

"For never fussing once."

It was an hour after midnight before that merry evening broke up.

St Paul's Day came with a flawless and serene morning, which is a good omen for 1947. I sat talking to our hostess who was a niece of David Seth-Smith, sometime Curator of the Mammals and Birds at the Zoo, and beloved by innumerable children (and grown ups) as the Zoo Man of the B.B.C. Trevor Hay himself was a New Zealander, and he was in charge of the Irrigation Department. The Hays had been lucky to find their own house not too badly damaged by the Jap occupation, but of course they had lost most of their furniture and personal belongings. The only visible sign of the departed enemy was an inscription in Japanese on one of the bricks and the Hays were hoping to find somebody who could read it for them. They had been most ingenious at improvising domestic necessities. For instance, cocktail glasses had been made by cutting off the tops of beer bottles with oil and a red-hot poker. Then the top was recorked and after being fixed with sealing wax was set in the upturned lid of a cigarette tin covered with aluminium paint, and Betty Hay painted little decorations on the glass. Tumblers were cut from the bottom halves of the bottles.

The sunset was exquisite—a luminous pale blue-green sky deepening to orange-gold behind a filigree of small trees and in the level distance a pagoda dark against one slim rosy cloud, above which the young moon was sailing on her back like a boat. Lt.-Colonel C. C. Dykes of the 1/6th Gurkhas, known as 'Sailor' Dykes because he had been a Marine for nine years before he became a Gurkha, arrived before dinner. He was to conduct us as far as Mandalay and went over with me on a map the country road round 19th Indian Division's bridgehead for the first crossing of the Irrawaddy, which we were to see next day. We persuaded Betty Hay to come with us, but Trevor Hay insisted on staying behind to superintend the erection of a theatre in the garden for the puppet-show they had planned for our entertainment the next evening.

Kyaukmyaung (pronounced 'Chawk'—'Ky' is always 'Ch') was a fascinating riverside village with a good pagoda destroyed by an earthquake the previous September being repaired. We had plenty of time to look around because the motor-boat was behaving in a Hebridean way and could not be found. A pole with white flags had just been put up in front of a big bamboo basha. Betty Hay thought it was probably for the funeral feast of a *hpoongyi* (priest). Apparently when a *hpoongyi* died it was customary to pickle the body in honey until the feast was over, at which the dead man presided. It was another aspect of the wake. The dead were carried round the village on the beds on which they died, and were always gaily decorated. The shops were rich studies in still life with lovely coloured patterns of fruit and grain and other comestibles.

At last the boat, which was a pontoon with an outboard engine, was found. Deck chairs were put in and we set off up the noble river to see the cove two miles from Kyaukmyaung where the first crossing was made by the 4/15th Punjabis. We turned back downstream, passing the long strand which received the greater part of the 19th Division. At first the mules had to be swum across six on a stick and the least vigorous of them were drowned. We stopped below Pear Hill, the scene of much desperate fighting when held by the 5/10th Baluchis against suicide Japanese attacks. The last time Dykes had seen it the supply parachutes made it look like a laundry's drying ground. We landed below a steep stairway of 302 wide steps and walked to the top, from which I had a wide view of the surrounding country, and was able to follow all the details of the fighting. The story of the crossing of the Irrawaddy by Major-General 'Pete' Rees and the 19th Indian Dagger Division is a highlight even in the bright epic of the Indian Army's defeat of Nippon.

We came down the 302 steps of Pear Hill to picnic under a tree beside the silver river. Chrissie sat on an abode of some red ants, and for two or three minutes gave a realistic performance of ants in pants. The weather was like a perfect midsummer's day at home. The Irrawaddy varies from half a mile in width to nearly a mile at that spot, and everybody was unmistakably aware of its being one of the great rivers of the world.

When we were back in Schwebo Ba Kyi (Ba Chee) a charming Burman with a scholar's distinction, who kept the records, came along to take us over the great Pagoda, but first to see in a stone alcove beside the road statues of the three contractors and the works manager who built it about four hundred years before. Those long vanished worthies of the building trade had slipped from their pedestals and were lolling against one another with ludicrous effect. The Pagoda itself was covered with scaffolding. We drove round it and heard the nuns chanting their evening prayers. Then we went to see a modern stucco tomb commemorating some king, which was almost as ugly as the Albert Memorial.

When we got back to the Hays bungalow the orchestra was rehearsing for the puppet-show on their strange instruments. Normally the puppet-play would have lasted all night, but we were only to see the dancing items. Even those lasted two hours because there was a lot of dialogue. The back cloth was painted in four panels—a throne room with a vermilion rug, a house and garden, a moat with a red wall and mountain in the distance, and a woodland lake. The performance began with the entrance of a marionette dressed in rose du Barri who offered bananas to the *nat* or spirit who presided over the play. Then a monkey did a dance while two parrakeets flew around him all the time. A hermit followed this with a lively dance for his age, the only evidence of which was the stick he held over his head. The hermit vanished. A white horse then pranced about the stage. Then a golden throne was brought on and put against the throne-room panel, after which the Queen, with white face and silver dress, entered and sat on the step of the throne to hear the reports of three ministers and a provincial governor. The handling of those puppets was astonishing. They were utterly alive; their painted faces seemed to change expression to suit the dialogue.

After this the throne was removed, and a Prince and Princess danced, supported by two clowns who cracked jokes and did some good slapstick. Then a red throne was put up against the throne-room panel on which the King sat in majestic tranquillity while a fantastic dance was performed by nine dancers, a dragon-spirit like a scarlet snake, and a white rabbit. In the end the fast and furious dancing became too much for the King's composure, and he began to dance upon his throne. With this finale the curtain came down.

The dolls were brought out to show me, and not one of them was more than eighteen inches high. Yet on the stage they seemed life-size. The greatest compliment one can pay a live Burmese dancer is to say that he or she dances as well as a marionette.

We went forward on our travels at nine o'clock next morning after most regretfully taking leave of our host and hostess whose kindness had been outstanding even on that tour when everybody had been so kind. The road was dull and much corrugated.

"We killed a lot of Japs here" said Sailor Dykes in the tone of a village blacksmith who had earned a night's repose. This contented ejaculation was uttered when we were crossing a small bridge.

As we crossed the Irrawaddy past the great Ava bridge, the two central spans of which had been blown up by us in the retreat, I saw a wonderful composition. The pillars of the bridge were terra-cotta and

grey-brown. The girders were red. Framed in the gap was the grey-
brown hill on which Sagaing is built. Red brick and white pagodas
were everywhere. Just before we reached the opposite bank a Catholic
nun surrounded by singing children under bright parasols in one of the
small gondola-like craft glided past the ferry-boat. The twelve miles to
Mandalay, whose hill had been visible from the ferry engraved upon
the sky like an aquatint, were full of bustle and traffic.

We drove round with U Lu Pe Win, the Superintendent of the
Archaeological Department of the Burma Government in Mandalay,
to be shown what was left of worthwhile buildings, and that was almost
nothing. The King's palace of teak was burnt out by an incendiary;
nothing of it was left except the steps up and the two old guns on either
side. Afterwards we went to see the Arakan Pagoda which lying away
on the extreme outskirt of the city had escaped damage. That Pagoda,
reputed to be 1,500 years old, was originally in Arakan whence it was
removed by some King to Mandalay and there re-erected. The task of
transporting it over the mountains, through the jungle, and down the
river must have been formidable indeed.

In the middle of the Pagoda was a large Buddha with golden gates
round the four aspects. Those were sometimes opened to give the faithful a better view. The Buddha itself faced East, and here worshippers
were kneeling in prayer, some holding bunches of blue lotus flowers.
Although the arcade leading to the shrine was used as a bazaar, the
ground was too sacred for shoes. So Dykes, Thomson and myself
ambled along between the shops in our socks. In one of the courtyards
was a three-headed elephant in bronze and a bronze statue of a warrior,
with a hole in his navel which I was told was illuminated occasionally
and with the help of contemplation would cure anything. The whole
place was full of Eastern magic.

Next morning we drove off to the far side of Mandalay Hill in order
to make the ascent from the northern side. U Hla-Aung, the Secretary
of His Holiness the Venerable U Khanti, was waiting for us. There
were 737 steps to the top. The shrines on Mandalay Hill had been built
through the efforts of a humble village priest, who in the year 1907 at
the age of forty was inspired to begin collecting money to fulfil his
dream. He was now eighty, and he had collected over a million pounds.
Age treats humanity less mildly in the East, but U Khanti in his sixties
had still been walking up to the top of Mandalay Hill two or three
times every day.

They had had a passion for corrugated iron in Burma ever since it
first appeared, so I was not surprised to find the covered way up roofed
with it. The names of the donors were painted above the sets of steps
to which they subscribed. Two great cobras stood on either side of the
first flight. All the other representations signified something in the life

of the Buddha. A stag, a massive quail, an elephant and a lion commemorated some of his incarnations. There were two standing gilded
Buddhas, each thirty feet high. There was a green cage in which the
figure of Buddha was seen taking a farewell of his sleeping wife and
child. In the wife's leg there was now a fragment of shell. Then he was
beheld at peace, having achieved Nirvana. Doves were perched upon
his prostrate form, and at his feet stood the two figures, wonderfully
carved and painted, of Pain and Starvation, from which he was now
for ever free.

The various Buddhas all attracted their own particular devotees.
One was famous for granting people's prayers, and near it asters, blue
lotuses and small coloured candles were on sale as offerings. Another
courtyard showed the female Beeloo or ogress who used to live on the
hill and who was so much impressed by the shining face of Buddha that
she cut off one of her breasts and placed it at his feet. Four fearsome
male Beeloos were seated in each corner and everyone of them had
about a hundred tiny Beeloos behind him. The heads of many of those
were knocked off by the Japanese as souvenirs.

At the very summit of the 954-ft hill was a great arcade with pillars
of red brick and a plaster roof. The arches gave a wide view on every
side. Four red and golden Buddhas sat on the square pediment of the
central pagoda. A framed inscription at the entrance recorded that
Mandalay Hill was captured by the 4/4th Gurkhas on the night of
March 8th-9th 1945. This was put up by U Khanti, not by us. Dykes
gave me an account of this fight and of the combatants throwing
grenades at one another round the pillars. Then we sat in one of the
arcades, and he described most lucidly the whole operation by which
Mandalay was captured, the country below spread before us like a
huge map.

The capture of that arcade did not mean the capture of the whole
hill. The next position taken was an immense concrete roof, but unfortunately the Japs were underneath it and for some days they could not
be got out. We went down to where they had been and found a great
open hall, the roof being supported by iron girders used as posts. This
was the audience room of U Khanti, his throne being placed against a
background of glass mosaic. Below the audience room were tables where
refreshments were served to the pilgrims. We were given coffee and a
dozen raw eggs on a plate. Dykes pointed out the difficulties of getting
the Japs out without destroying the place. One could wish that the
Americans had always been as scrupulous in Italy. A bunch of twenty
Japs were burnt out of an arched tunnel that ran east and west behind
the audience chamber. The Japs were finally driven from there by two
companies of the Royal Berkshires and a memorial had been erected
to commemorate the fierce fighting in the clearance and final capture

of Mandalay Hill by the 2nd Royal Berkshire Regiment, March 10-12th 1945.

We descended by the 737 steps of the western covered way. The original approach from the south had 903 steps. A reproduction of the Buddha's footprint on Adam's Peak in Ceylon was impressive. So, too, was a forest of scorched infoliated columns beyond which was the printing press. This had been burnt out by the Chinese in 1942 to prevent its falling into the hands of the Japs. It is to be regretted that the Chinese did not fight as well as they looted and burnt; but they were badly led, and any chance of their being effectively used was destroyed by the bone-headed anti-British attitude of 'Vinegar Joe' Stilwell. On the whole, however, considering the fierceness of the fighting the damage had been slight; I could not help contrasting the lot of Mandalay Hill with that of Cassino.

As we walked down I noticed many *hpoongyis* in orange robes telling their beads beside the stairway. Merry family parties and bands of pilgrims were on their way up all the time. The whole place breathed happiness and peace. U Khanti himself lived beside the south entrance. He received us, supported by five young novices; now in his 81st year, he was frail and palsied. He shook hands with the men and offered a piece of his robe to Chrissie. He blessed us all in a quavering voice, and then sat back while we sipped coffee. I wrote my name in the venerable man's book, with the usual lame remarks about that astonishing place built by the faith and ardour of one man.

I went to a cheroot-maker's shop and ordered fifty cheroots for the next day. Four chips (six shillings) was the price asked by the bright-eyed woman who seemed to run the place with her daughters. A great bowl of ripened tobacco leaf stood in a corner, and from this my cheroots were rolled to the size I ordered.

At four o'clock we left for Maymyo which lay about 3,500 feet up in the hills 42 miles from Mandalay. It was a pleasant drive in the afternoon light. Shortly before six o'clock we arrived at the hostel run by the W.V.S. at which we stayed and where Chrissie dined at 7 o'clock, a remarkably early hour for that part of the world. I was to dine with Dykes at the Mess of the 1/6th Gurkhas.

The Gurkhas were in tents, but the anteroom of the Mess had a stone fireplace and chimney which allowed for a splendid log fire. We had some grand piping during dinner—The Road to the Isles, the Nutbrown Maid, and afterwards Over the Sea to Skye, Blue Bonnets, A Thousand Pipers, the Cock o' the North, and other Scots airs. I was taught a sentence in Gurkhali with which to thank Pipe-Major Shem S. Thappe and congratulate him on the programme.

Meiktila was our next destination. Major-General Crowther, commanding the 7th Indian Division, made us welcome, though I think he

was a little shaken by the prospect of putting up Chrissie. No woman
had ever stayed at that Mess. It faced the lake, and there was a beautiful sunset, the lake a luminous green, the sky orange turning to yellow
and blue-green.

I was up at 6.45 for the 360-mile flight to Myitkyina. The Dakota
was comfortable, having been adapted to carry six passengers in armchairs, but smoking was prohibited, much to Jim Thomson's relief. I
should have been glad of a cheroot as we flew over that green sea of
jungle; I was wondering what would happen if we came down in the
middle of it.

We heard with disappointment that we had to leave Myitkyina by
one o'clock. When we reached Myitkyina I found that the start of the
Ledo Road was fourteen miles away on a pretty bumpy road and that
we should not be able to leave before two o'clock at the earliest. Lt.-
Colonel Chappell of the 2nd Burma Regiment met us on the northern
air strip. He was depressed to hear we had so absurdly short a time.
He had gathered three or four officers who had been with 136 Force
to give me some stories and had expected we should stay the night.
We started at once for the Ledo Road, passing a group of wives
from the Kachin Regiment in attractive black and red dresses. We
drove over the southern and western of the two-thousand yards long
American air strips. On one was an abandoned Dakota. Beside another
stood a vast hanger. In a sandy bank charcoal burners were living in
dugouts.

At last we came to the head of the famous road built through the
jungle by 100,000 labourers, mostly Indians. It much resembled the
other end of it at Ledo nearly three hundred miles away. We drove
along about a mile and then had to turn round and go back to the
Mess. The immense expenditure of time, toil and money on that road
was a complete waste. It was finished in time for two or three convoys
to pass down it with supplies for China, and that was the end of its
utility. It would now revert to jungle, although a few lorries of the
Indian Transport Company were still able to make the journey to and
from Assam. Of the thousands of Americans who were once in Myitkyina all that remained were a 'Main Street' and 'Virginia Avenue',
some large tins of tomato juice, and by far the most luxurious thunder-
box I have seen. That was in the C.O's tent.

Brief though my stay was in Myitkyina, it was long enough to set me
wondering why the American and Chinese force, after seizing the air
strip in May 1944, failed for so many weeks to capture Myitkyina itself,
which lay as it were just across the road without any natural defences.
The contribution of the United States Airforce to the Indian Army's
final expulsion of the Japanese from Burma was of inestimable value;
indeed, without the help of the American flyers the Fourteenth Army

could not have been supplied. The contribution of General Joseph Stilwell's American and Chinese infantry was comparatively small. Yet owing to pusillanimity in London, where it was feared that the Japs were going to break through at Imphal, the vital importance of the long drawn out battle there was deliberately played down for fear of the effect on public morale if a disaster occurred. Simultaneously Myitkyina was played up to distract attention from Imphal. The B.B.C. announcers were even taught how to pronounce it (Mitchinah), and the public fancy was caught by a word which was pronounced so differently from the way in which it was spelt. The result was that to most people Myitkyina said more than Imphal or Kohima or Meiktila. A book was then published in America packed with Anglophobe lies and scurrility by the Public Relations Officer of that sour-faced, sour-mouthed, sour-brained fanatic, General Joseph Stilwell.

Next day Brigadier Miles Smeeton, then commanding 1st Burma Brigade, drove Jim Thomson and me round in a jeep to explain the battle of Meiktila. He was an exhilarating personality, six foot six inches tall, as thin as a lath, and with a nose on him like Julius Caesar. He was with Hodson's Horse in the Desert and commanded Probyn's Horse at the battle of Meiktila. Thomson asked him where our big hospital was. He pointed it out and said, "I remember the place well. I got a bullet clean through my nose and was inside for three days."

Smeeton told me the story of the Maharaja of Bundi's immediate M.C., and we saw where he had been separated from the rest of his troop and went charging on alone in his tank, shooting up the Japs all round him. He was wounded there.

The country round Meiktila would be rather like the Western Desert if it were just a little more bare. The low contours on the skyline were the same contours as there. The picture that the war correspondents had given of the Burma campaign as a kind of vast, dripping, green hell was one-sided. It was abominable the way the high ups at home played down those Burma battles. They could not believe that we should defeat the Japs and were afraid to tell the British public what the Fourteenth Army was doing.

The defeat of the Japanese was the first mortal blow to Nippon. Their naval defeats did not shake their morale because they always considered their navy of less importance than their army. The shock of that defeat may be judged by the fact that the last Japanese in Meiktila threw themselves into the lake, preferring to drown rather than surrender, and that the Japanese General in command committed hara-kiri. The daring and imaginative strategy by which F.M. Slim won that battle was incomparable.

For the next two days Miles Smeeton was coaching me about tank

warfare. There were two of Smeeton's Shermans which had been
knocked out in battle, and we went to look at their names—Captivation
and Allegro. They used to call their tanks after the stud horses of
Probyn's Horse.

"You really got as fond of them as horses", he told me.

Captivation was almost brought off the field, but had the bad luck
to run into a tree when he was turning, and he was still lying against
the stump of that tree. I wish I could reproduce Smeeton's own
description of the fighting.

"This is where we hooked round with Claudcol. It was the greatest
fun. Absolutely pirate show. Terrific sport. You see that haystack
there? I remember a Nip coming out of a haystack just there and running along down the road. He was hit with a Browning."

We came to the village of Yindaw which was surrounded by a wide
moat. That survival of medieval times defeated the tanks which could
not support the 6/7th Rajputs when they had crossed it and were trying
to get cover on the other side. The casualties were very heavy, and in
the end Yindaw had to be by-passed. 'Punch' Cowan[1] of the 17th
Indian Division must have been an inspiring commander in the field.

"He never let go of his objective", said Hulme who worshipped him.
"He stuck a big cigar in his mouth and went right ahead".

When 5th Indian Division was put in to give the Black Cats (17th
Division) a let up in the move south after Meiktila, the pace became
slower and the pursuit hung fire according to Smeeton and Hulme.
I noticed a tangle of iron beside the road and asked what it was.

"That's the remains of a bad show for 5th Division", and the two
Black Cats, looking at one another, shook their heads and shed a few
crocodile tears.

The competition between the Indian Divisions in that war was even
keener than regimental competition used to be once upon a time. They
accused one another of stealing the limelight like so many prima
donnas. Red Eagle (4th Division), Ball of Fire (5th Division), Golden
Arrow (7th Division), Clover Leaves (8th Division), St Andrew's Cross
(10th Division), Black Cat (17th Division), Dagger (19th Division),
Silver Sword (20th Division), Fighting Cock (23rd Division), Ace of
Spades (25th Division), Tiger Head (26th Division)—where should we
have been without them?

Before we went back to Meiktila we turned aside for a mile or two to
see Ye-we where Hulme and the 1/7th Gurkhas had a bad time. Ye-we
was unlike any village I had yet seen in Burma. Two of the pagodas
had snakes painted with red hearts coiling round them, the head of the
snake taking the place of the usual metal umbrella on the top. Outside

---

[1] Major-General D. T. Cowan, C.B., C.B.E., D.S.O., M.C.

one shattered shrine was a gilded Buddha of which only the feet and ankles remained. There was a domed temple carved with strange animals including *chinthis* with human faces, and a low arcade below in which Gurkhas and Nips chased each other round the columns— a smaller edition of the fight in the arcade on Mandalay Hill. On another pagoda, a bit of broken metal was swinging in the wind with the sound of a tinkling bell. Shells, dead and alive, were scattered all over the place. I nearly trod on a live grenade. The ground was covered with Jap bones. I saw a beautiful solanum with white flowers about the size of a tomato's and green bladders, inside which were seeds like small green peas.

Miles Smeeton had been anxious for me to see Pagán whence the 48th Brigade of the Black Cats with Probyn's Horse and the Royal Deccan Horse had made that advance on Meiktila in another February two years before. Major-General Crowther was good enough to arrange for that expedition, and on February 4th he with Michael Wauchope, his A.D.C., Smeeton, Thomson and myself set out in jeeps with the kit in a station wagon. We had an escort of Frontier Force Rifles as well as Smeeton's Karens and Chins.

We took the road to Kyaukpadaung where the Burmese Communists were strong and there had been trouble shortly before, but if anyone was looking for trouble that morning the sight of our jeeps bristling with tommy-guns must have made him look again. The road was very dusty and the country grew more arid all the time. The great triangle of Mount Popa was on our right for several miles, rising five thousand feet from the level lowland in isolated majesty. I was reminded of the way Samothrace rises from the Aegean.

In due course we reached the Chauk oilfields, which were the largest in Burma. It was a fantastic sight. Rust-red derricks everywhere, like dead trees among the withered herbage and low scant scrub. I had an impression of there being some hundreds of them. Every well had to be put out of action before the Japanese advance in 1942 and for the first time I fully grasped the magnitude of the task performed by the Burma Oil people.

I had had high hopes of Pagán, but the reality far exceeded anything that fancy had conjured up beforehand. Lots of people tire of pagodas but I never tired of their infinite variety, though I admit that their variety required a close view to be appreciated. Pagodas on distant slopes are apt to resemble one another; the most jaded traveller among pagodas would be wonderstruck by Pagán. It was once the capital of Burma, but it was abandoned after being sacked by Khubla Khan at the end of the thirteenth century. He could have found a thousand models there for the stately pleasure-dome he decreed. A little white pagoda on a hill the other side of the Irrawaddy marked the spot where

E

Buddha was said to have stopped and prophesied a future capital upon the site of Pagán.

The area of Pagán could hardly have been less than four square miles, and that was covered in every direction the eye looked with huge pagodas, small pagodas, whole pagodas, ruined pagodas, fragments of pagodas, and many temples as well. One dome at least was larger than St Paul's and the architectural influence of India was everywhere apparent. The greatest number were rose-red brick, the plaster (if they ever were plastered) having worn away in the course of over eight hundred years, but the dryness of the climate in that part of Burma had preserved the brick in the same way as I imagine Petra, the 'rose-red city half as old as time', has been preserved. It would be rash after such a brief glimpse as mine, to claim peculiar beauty for any single one of what was reputed to number 5,000 pagodas in some form or another, but the Nagayon Temple in which General Crowther had his head-quarters when he was commanding 89th Brigade of the 7th Indian Division was certainly one of the most beautiful. It was surrounded by a red brick wall eight feet high and then within the rectangle by another brick wall four feet high. Within its temple stood one giant Buddha facing north. It was an erect gilded figure, the right hand extended to receive what seemed the secret of the world. A huge cobra was coiled at his feet and wound up to show above the Buddha's head its own fearsome countenance with gilded hood. On either side in the alcove were twelve smaller cobras carved in a sort of wreath. At the end of a cloister beyond the central shrine, we scrambled up through a low door with a Gothic arch to where a steep flight of stone steps, none less than eighteen inches high, emerged on the shallow cupolas of the roof, whence by tiers of red brick one could have climbed to the base of the big central dome. Not all the pagodas were rose-red brick. Some were white as wedding cakes. One at least was covered with gold leaf. Others were plastered with stucco now a mellow grey. Those abandoned pagodas and the abandoned derricks of the Chauk oilfields provided a strange, indeed a startling contrast.

We reached the Dak bungalow at half-past one, where a police guard of honour saluted the General. This bungalow was built to accommodate the Prince of Wales and his Staff during his tour of Burma, but he did not manage to reach Pagán. On either side of the steps leading up to the verandah vendors of the attractive lacquer ornaments and utensils made locally were gathered with their wares spread out in front of them.

After lunch we set out to see the Ananda Temple. As it was still used for religious rites, we had to discalce. The covered way in, roofed as usual with corrugated iron, was built in 1920. A frieze of paintings illustrated Pleasure on the left, Pain on the right. Tortures of men and women by giant demons were the chief subjects of the latter. In one a demon was hitting women on the head with a mallet before they were thrown into a boiling cauldron. We hoped for a comparative frankness in the Pleasure series but were disappointed; most of them represented the insipid picnics of conventional oriental figures in a Christmas card landscape. The Ananda Temple itself was over 800 years old. Four gilded Buddhas, each at least thirty feet high, faced the four points of the compass from sombre Gothic-seeming alcoves, the gigantic doors of which were of carved and fretted teak, too heavy to close. Each Buddha was erect and made a different symbolic gesture with its hands. A cloister ran right round the six-foot deep windows with pointed arches and various images in recesses and niches. The pavement was peppered with desiccated bats' droppings which made walking in our socks an Agag promenade.

From the Ananda Temple we drove on to the Golden Pagoda, which was covered with fresh gold leaf and illuminated with electric lamps at night. We had to discalce again there because it was a contemporary centre of pilgrimage and prayer. The 'sexton' in attendance enumerated the nine wonders of the Pagoda. The first was a small hole in one of the praying flagstones which when filled with water held the reflection of the whole Pagoda. Another was that the shadow of the Pagoda never falls outside the sacred precincts. A third was that nobody could ever rise early enough to make the first offering of food in the great jars provided for this. Somebody had always put food there in advance. I cannot recall the other wonders. There were some rather tawdry architectural additions all round and the whole place resembled those Catholic churches designed to attract simple faith. The peace of the precincts was disturbed by the yelping of dogs belonging to the vendors of votive candles and flowers.

At about four o'clock we arrived in Nyaungu just beyond Pagán where the 7th Indian Division crossed the Irrawaddy and made it possible for a mobile column of the 17th Indian Division to pass through and reach Meiktila to the complete confusion of Japanese strategy. On the other side of the great river about a mile away stretched the long sandy beaches from which that vital crossing was made. Looking across the mighty river, pale blue in the light of the February afternoon, I heard my two companions evoke again those epic February days two years before.

Then we embarked on a patrol launch and crossed to the other side. The sun was setting behind a range of grey-blue zigzag hills when we embarked to return, and before we arrived dusk had fallen. The waters of the Irrawaddy were iridescent in the fading colours of the sunset. A great company of swifts was wheeling and swooping among the flies and midges on the river. Then as if to a word of command the swifts rose in a dark cloud and winged their way to roost, abandoning the dusk to a myriad bats. The *ti* or umbrella of the Golden Pagoda was lit up by electric lamps and round it other lamps were shining. The ivory moon, two days from her plenitude, had watched the sun go down, and was now robbing the stars of their silver as she climbed the sky. When we got back to the bungalow the vendors of lacquer were still sitting in the porch, their wares shimmering in the light of a Petrolux lamp.

I woke at half-past six and watched the dawn flush the high ceiling of my room. Outside a chorus of birds was twittering, cheeping, chattering and whistling in the trees round the bungalow, and the more distant air was filled with the crowing of innumerable cocks. If Pagán were made more comfortably accessible and a really good hotel built Luxor would take second place as a winter resort. The climate was absolutely perfect, the surroundings incomparably more impressive than Luxor, and the antiquities much more varied. Moreover, there were no Egyptians.

Miles Smeeton was in a mood of inspired reminiscence that morning as he drove his balloon-tyred jeep like a Pegasus over the sandy deep-rutted road to Meiktila. The air was champagne and washed down the dust in our throats. On our left as we came up the rise we saw the catacombs in the low hills which had been infested with Nips and gave 33rd Brigade so much trouble. In the end the Nips had to be sealed in. It is strange how one can write of burying human beings alive as if one was writing about the extermination of noxious insects. That part of the country was for tanks what the shires are for horses and hounds. Under the spell of Smeeton's vivid evocation I was able to visualize every hour of those marvellous seven days from the morning of February 21st until, at about six o'clock on the evening of February 27th, Probyn's Horse harboured on a ridge looking down over Meiktila, the capture of which decided Nippon's future in Burma.

The infantry of 48th Brigade were moving in motor transport along the road on which we were driving, while Probyn's Horse with the 6/7th Rajputs in their tanks kept pace with them over the open country to the right and the Royal Deccan Horse with the Bombay Grenadiers in their tanks ranged off to the left. The villages through which we passed had clustered round water and were like oases in the arid countryside. In all of them great tamarind trees spread their shade and they were surrounded by groves and colonnades of tall palms. One village was Oyin where the most bloody action of the advance was fought. Here the Nips attacked the tanks individually with boxes of picric acid. They held a deep cross road which ran through the village with high hedges, and the trees were full of snipers.

"They came falling down off that large dark tree over there like crows," Smeeton said.

We stopped for lunch where Probyn's Horse harboured on the night of February 24th. The slit trenches were still there and Smeeton showed us the perimeter inside which the tanks stood, the infantry bivouacked in front of them. He said the crews sometimes worked till 2 a.m. to keep their tanks in trim for next day's advance. For a month they were dependent on their own energy and ingenuity. Morale was at its peak.

"No one who took part in it will ever forget the excitement of that dash to Meiktila. The tanks moved along, deployed on each side of the road. They lifted their heads and flourished their tails, and took the little cactus hedges like a hunt across country, while the lorries of the infantry crowded down the road between them."

A mile or so before Taungtha we crossed a wide *chaung* along which the tanks saw a Jap company marching slowly.

"Extraordinary sight," said Smeeton. "They paid no attention to us, but trudged along, bent low over their heavy packs. Two tanks shot them to pieces, and not a Nip looked round or stopped marching."

Some of the bones which remained from this massacre were still scattered along the opposite bank of the *chaung*.

It was about six o'clock when we paused on the high ground by Milestone 6 to look down at Meiktila. The wide prospect was golden as a landscape by Claude. I could see that Smeeton was deeply moved by memories of two years before. It had been about six o'clock on the evening of February 27th 1945, that "Probyn's Horse and the Rajputs harboured on the high ground at Milestone 6 in sight of the Meiktila lake, on the identical piece of ground where they were later to kill many Japanese on March 9/10th, who however made full use of the slit trenches we dug that night. A Beaufighter circled round us in the dusk as if uncertain whether we could really have come so far, so fast."

I have failed to note where I found that quotation and apologize to the author for not giving the source.

Miles Smeeton left next day to join his Brigade H.Q. He would be leaving the Army in April and going to the island he owned in British Columbia. I was deeply in his debt for his contribution to the task ahead of me. As I look back to that day I spent with him twenty years ago I can say that in all my life I never enjoyed a day more.

Rangoon was our next stop where J. R. Bingley of the British Council put us up for the night. He was an old Magdalen man, some twenty years my junior. He asked me if I would sit on a Brains Trust—the first ever held in Burma.

Lots of young Burmans arrived and the proceedings opened with some rather half-hearted community singing. Then the Brains Trust started—a poet, a journalist, a civil servant, Daw Mya Sen, an extremely intelligent champion of women's rights, and a medical professor at the

University, Dr Burridge, who was formerly at Lucknow. The question
master was a young professor of biology. On the whole the questions
were good. I found myself in disagreement every time with Dr Burridge,
and in agreement every time with Daw Mya Sen. One question, which
I should like to hear put to a B.B.C. Brains Trust, was "what is love?".
I was amused to see the way the audience sat up and really did listen
to the answers to that. Another question was "Shall Burma join the
British Commonwealth?". I said there was a mistake in the phrasing
of the question. The wrong verb had been used. It should have been
'Can' not 'Shall'. This seemed to surprise everybody.

After the Brains Trust we went out in the moonlit garden to see a
film illustrating the British way of life. It was one of the most embarras-
sing half hours I ever spent. I sat with some beautiful young Burman
women in their bright *loongyis* and tight white bodices with high
coiffures decked with flowers. I can still see the bewildered expression
on their faces as they looked round at one another when the film started.
It was not poor Bingley's fault. He had not chosen the film which the
British Council at home had sent to illustrate the British way of life.
Even now with twenty years more experience of human stupidity I
can hardly believe that film was not a nightmare. Believe it or not, the
subject was a demonstration of physical training somewhere in England,
in which young women in a ghastly gym dress of bloomers and jerseys
went bounding about over a vaulting-horse, swinging along travelling-
rings, and doing hideous exercises. I thought of that exquisite dancing
I had seen at Kalewa and I was not surprised by the complete bewilderment of that audience before this display of occidental energy. I was
thankful when we went in again to listen to some Haydn quartets on
a new Deccola which had just been sent out by the British Council,
and that in spite of the fact that all the records were slightly warped by
their passage through the tropics.

What remains most vividly in my mind from the long drive of two
days to Moulmein is crossing the ferry of the Sittang river. There stood
the bridge with two of the spans gone and a third on the far side
sprawling into the river. This was where two battalions of the 17th
Indian Division had to be left behind when the agonizing decision
had to be made in February 1942 to blow the bridge in order to halt
the Japanese advance on Rangoon. Some hundreds were drowned in
trying to cross the river. That blown bridge was a haunted spot, the
paint on the metal work the colour of stale blood.

It was my friend 'Jacky' Smyth[1] who had to make that terrible
decision. As an epitaph I quoted in *Eastern Epic* the words of an officer
in the Burma Rifles:

[1] Brigadier Sir John Smyth, Bt., V.C., M.P.

"Controversy at the time was very bitter, but I'd like to meet the man who blew the bridge. He had a ghastly decision to make and I'd like to tell him that I think he was right, and that by his courage he probably saved us from being in a far worse plight . . . I was about the last man across, and so can't be accused of being an armchair critic, but I salute the man who made that courageous and ghastly decision."

In Moulmein Chrissie and I stayed with Leo Robertson, the Session Judge. He was one more of those whose hospitality I first enjoyed on this Odyssey who would become an intimate friend. Indeed, one day he would write a critical study of my work. He was a Chinese scholar, a philosopher, and a lover of literature. He had many tales of his life in Burma. My favourite was his tale of Ruth the leopardess. She came to him as a tiny cub, and for two years slept always at the foot of his bed. Then one evening a small girl came with a message and Robertson saw the menacing gleam of jealousy in Ruth's eyes. He knew that he no longer had the right to keep her at large in case of her attacking somebody. So he took her to the Rangoon Zoo where he used to visit her every day. She would purr and rub herself against the bars of her cage but as the days went by she became weaker and weaker and could no longer stand. She was starving herself for grief and died a fortnight later.

On our second day in Moulmein Lt.-Colonel Harmon of the Karen Rifles drove Jim Thomson, Chrissie and myself to see the graveyard at Thanbyuzayat where about 4,000 British, Australian and Dutch soldiers (of the latter about 200) were buried; the American bodies had been taken back to the States. These were the victims of the railway of death to Bangkok, every sleeper of which was estimated to have cost a human life. Many thousands of Indian coolies lost their lives on this railway as well as prisoners-of-war. The Pharaohs built the Pyramids with less human blood. Japanese prisoners-of-war, in order to preserve their morale, were now being allowed an afternoon a week to meditate on their contribution to the future of Japan. It might have been more seemly to allow them that afternoon every week to meditate on their own barbarism.

From the cemetery we drove on to Amherst. Jim Thomson, full of energy, scrambled down the cliff to explore the monastery on the spacious sandy beach; it looked rather like a pier pavilion. He found there among some gilded Buddhas in a heavily barred niche a silver pagoda. It was the missing Pagoda trophy of the Rangoon Lawn Tennis Club, which disappeared in 1942. Little did the annual winners whose names were inscribed upon it suppose that they would one day become an object of religious veneration.

After getting back from Amherst we drove up to the ridge and climbed sixty or seventy steep steps to see the old Moulmein Pagoda. The bells of the *ti* were being blown about harmoniously in the light breeze on the golden edge of dusk. The Buddhas there, whether seated, standing, or reclining, were all of glazed white earthenware, and looked modern. I cannot find any satisfactory explanation of Kipling's mistake about the aspect of the Moulmein Pagoda. The Burma girl who is looking eastward to the sea is a geographical impossibility. Presumably the road to Mandalay is the road of a troopship across the Bay of Bengal. I believe 'eastward' was a misprint for 'westward' and that having obtained currency Kipling decided not to correct it in a later edition.

On a sidewalk near the quay at Moulmein there was a statue of Queen Victoria sitting under a stone canopy illuminated by a solitary electric bulb. This was erected in 1897 to commemorate the Diamond Jubilee. The Queen had her back to the quay and surveyed, sceptre and orb in hand, the ruins of bombed Government offices on the other side of the road. There was not a chip to be seen in the statue, throne or canopy, and I would hazard a guess that the very bulb above her crown had survived the Japanese occupation. It was asking too much of the fancy not to attach to that statue a symbolic significance. In exactly fifty years the decline and fall of the British Empire had been consummated. Queen Victoria in Moulmein eyed the ruins.

Unwillingly I pass over the details of a militarily absorbing two days at Toungoo where Brigadier Jerrard who commanded 98th Brigade of the 19th Indian Division and whose nickname was 'Hindy' was a real Hindenburg of a tutor. My 'course' included a marvellously realistic Japanese night attack in the jungle staged by the 3rd Rajputana Rifles (Napier's). "The noise was terrific. Fragments kept falling on our roof. I suggested that we should probably find Toungoo evacuated when we got back under the impression that the war had begun all over again."

The 200-mile drive to Rangoon was mostly through monotonous paddy country but the time passed quickly thanks to Jerrard's lucid account of the break out to the Sittang in July 1945. Over 6,000 Japanese were killed for the loss of 93 Indian and British troops. They fell so thick in the sugar cane that bundles of dead bodies were roped together, dragged to the banks of the Sittang, and flung into the river, then in spate.

In Rangoon I was staying at Command House with Lt.-General Briggs[1] with whom I was to have some fascinating talks about Keren, Imphal, and of the break out of the 7th Indian Brigade from Benghazi, of which I should write in *Eastern Epic* as "a blend of audacity, coolness

---

[1] The late Lt.-General Sir Harold Briggs, K.C.B., K.C.I.E.

and skill deservedly blessed by fortune . . . under the inspiring leader-
ship of Brigadier Briggs, Lt.-Colonel Goulder and Lt.-Colonel Evans,
a military feat to which the annals of warfare offer few paragons."

I quote from my diary of February 15th:

"I had intended to write up the diary, but I found General Briggs's
quiet humour too attractive to deny myself a moment of it. What I have
enjoyed as much as anything during this tour has been the opportunity
of studying the diverse personalities of generals and brigadiers. In my
youth they were more stereotyped. I haven't attempted to present
snapshots of them in this diary, because it seems a breach of manners to
enjoy a man's hospitality and then rush into print about him. In fact
I find it difficult to write about anybody I have met until ten years later.
It's a form of shyness.

"The General gave a dinner party that night. Arthur Bottomley,
Parliamentary Secretary for the Dominions, was another guest. He is
dealing with the frontier tribes problem and had just come back from
the Shan States. I found him genial and, I should say, extremely competent. The more I see of these younger Labour Members the brighter
grows my hope of the future. Of course Conservative prejudice among
our people in the East is rampant, so rampant that Asians themselves
cannot yet believe in the decay and final disappearance of the Conservative Party familiar to them for the last sixty years. 'This awful
government' is blamed for throwing away the Empire, and people are
genuinely startled when I point out that the Conservatives, being
primarily responsible for the unimaginative incompetence which
directed our country's course between the two wars, are therefore
responsible for throwing away our position in the East, although the
muddle-headed advocacy of disarmament involves them (Labour) in a
share of the blame. Winston Churchill, since his return to the Tory fold
as a bell-wether, seems to have forgotten his political prime when as an
aggressive and wanton young tup he was always lowering his horns
and charging head on into the soggy earthworks of middle-class opinion.
And the irony of a surrender to party, as complete as Pitt ever made,
of 'what was meant for mankind' is that there is nobody out here who
any longer believes that his party is capable of producing an Imperial
policy which would counteract the policy of 'this awful government'."

Writing now twenty-one years later I have to admit sadly that those
bright hopes of the future are much less bright.

Back in November Commander J. Lawrence, the Chief of Staff to
Vice-Admiral Geoffrey Miles, had promised to do all he could to secure
a sloop in mid-February to take me round the Arakan creeks and on
by way of the Andaman and Nicobar Islands to Penang. Commander
John Dalison, with whom I had made great friends on the way out from
England, was Intelligence Officer to Naval H.Q. in Delhi. He urged

that a trip in the sloop would be a grand opportunity to fill in some gaps in Naval Intelligence. John Dalison was successful. We flew from Rangoon in a reaper-and-binder Dakota. It was much more comfortable than that fiendish reaper-and-binder in which we flew from Habbaniya, and they had fixed a deck chair for me in which I wrote up my diary during the three hours flight. I went forward two or three times to sit with the pilot and look down at the country. Arakan from the air resembled a faded jigsaw set scattered about a greenish-blue oilcloth. We made a good landing at Chittagong. It was grand to see John Dalison and Brigadier Roberts at the airport and we drove off to go on board the R.I.N. sloop *Narbada*, the flagship of the Indian Navy, Commander J. C. Mansell, R.I.N.

I must omit our exploration of the Arakan creeks and come to the most important objective—the reaching of the Admin. Box where General Messervy and his Divisional H.Q. were suddenly overrun by the Japs in February 1944.

The landscape became more attractive, bounded by the Mayu Range to the west and level as a billiard-table except for a small ridge prodigally clothed with trees on which there were more orchids than I had seen anywhere else. To my horror I discovered that my glasses were missing. I had put them in my trouser pocket and with the bumping of the jeep they had been ejected on to the road. Instructions were sent back for the children of Tatmingyaungwa to search for them, but I was pretty depressed about the prospect because even if they were found it was likely that one of the other jeeps would have driven over them in the thick dust. However, I put it up to St Anthony, and turned my attention to watching a water-buffalo enjoying a glorious wallow. At last we reached a dyke across the paddy and after driving over that we came to an end of any road negotiable even by the most optimistic jeep.

The villagers of Ngakyedauk had fenced in with bamboo a space beneath a spreading peepul tree, and there set out deck chairs and a table for our reception. Outside the fence they were gathered to the number of about two hundred—almost all Chittagonian Mussulmans— to gaze at the rare visitors. A deck chair slung on a bamboo pole had been arranged to carry me along the two rough miles from the Eastern gate to the Western gate of the Admin. Box. I was borne across three streams up and down a very rough path, and I felt sorry for the three villagers who took turns with the burden. The sun was blazing down and another villager walked beside the chair, holding an umbrella over me. From time to time we were refreshed by the shade of some really magnificent trees. It was fantastic to think that along this track only three years before hundreds of every kind of motor transport had passed.

Sinzweya, in which three years before there were thousands of vehicles and pile upon pile of stores, resembled an expanse of common land in a sylvan area at home and was surrounded by low wooded hills with one higher conical hill to the south-west which was completely blasted by our guns firing at point-blank range, but was now green again with the rapid growth of three monsoons since that February of 1944. Nothing now remained to recall that desperate struggle in the Admin. Box except a few tanks and the slit trenches gradually filling up. Cattle were grazing tranquilly. We sat beneath a tree and surveyed a scene of Arcadian peace. The local inhabitants had found a use for most of the debris which once covered the place. I was carried as far as a point from which one could see the road our Sappers had cut through the Ngakyedauk Pass, but it was rapidly falling to pieces so that even its trace would hardly be discernible after another couple of monsoons.

It was on February 19th 1944 that the Jap attack on Sinzweya began to weaken, and there three years later to the very day we were standing on the spot which marked the end of the beginning to destroy the military power of Japan. That green enclosure in its decisive influence upon the course of human history may stand beside the mound of the Athenian dead at Marathon. In the middle of the 'Common' we saw where Lord Louis Mountbatten stood on a soap-box and addressed the victors of the Admin. Box, having been flown there from his H.Q. at Kandy. I left that inspiring spot, conscious that very few Europeans were likely to see it again and immensely grateful to the energy and determination of Brigadier Michael Roberts which had made possible what everyone told me would be an impossible expedition to carry through.

When we reached the pavilion of the peepul tree where we were to eat our lunch we found the bamboo fence surrounded by a throng of villagers prepared to enjoy the spectacle. The officials began to hustle them away, but John Dalison and I intervened and they were allowed to come back and watch our demonstration of drinking gin, lemonade and beer, and the rapidity with which we could put away the hard-boiled eggs provided by the headman. Just as we were leaving, word came that a child had found my glasses and I asked for him to be gathered at Tatmingyaungywa for the reward.

Unit Craft of the Graves Concentration Unit arrived and offered to take us up the river next morning as far as Myan Chaung. Our basha was a rat-infested, primitive building, with a mud floor and sanitary arrangements at which even Adam and Eve might have raised their eyebrows. I was awake at four, watching the morning star winking through the roof of the basha, and through the 'walls' the kindling of a fire by the admirable Abdul, John Dalison's bearer, who might have

served as a model for Sinbad the Sailor. I had left the equally admirable
Gulaba Ram on board *Narbada*.

It was still dark when we left the basha and stumbled down the
bank to the water's edge. In the east, Lucifer was showing his incan-
descent lamp to guide the sun up, and the Great Bear's snout was below
the western horizon. The dawn was beginning to break in rose and
orange when we boarded the Unit Craft. Wisps of mist were rising
from the water like cold smoke, but the shades of the morning dusk
were warmer than at home and more like the dusk of evening there.
Flights of egrets broke into the pattern of a Chinese painting on rice-
paper as they winged their way to the feeding grounds. The trees on
either side of the stream were loud with bird-song.

A unit craft is not designed for comfort but to carry the remains of
those dead soldiers which were to be concentrated in certain cemeteries.
Those who fought in Arakan would rest in Akyab. The members of the
Graves Concentration Unit were all volunteers and the work they were
doing in those remote spots deserves a high tribute. After moving
upstream for about an hour we reached the mouth of the Myan
Chaung. At this point we transferred to a couple of sampans and made
our way up a *chaung* about the size of the Cherwell where it runs along
Addison's Walk in Oxford. A peasant carrying a large bunch of golden
pumpkin flowers beamed at us from the bank. The *chaung* grew nar-
rower and darker and shallower. The sampans which require only
eighteen inches of water seemed on the verge of going aground. The
left bank was fringed with abutilons in flower, their brick-red bells
swinging gently over the black slimy mud. We passed under a crazy
bridge consisting of one bamboo cane and a handrail across which a
party of cultivators were passing in single file. A couple of hundred
yards beyond this the sampans went firmly aground. Planks were taken
out of them and we scrambled up the steep bank without getting much
of the mud on our clothes. We walked across a stretch of paddy to a
small village.

After a while John Dalison and I were beginning to wonder whether
we should ever get back down the Myan Chaung by sampan and
walked over to find out the state of the tide. Both sampans were still
fast aground. So we walked back across the paddy fields, having left
word for the others to follow us when they returned. After a laborious
trudge of about half a mile we came to one of those formidable bamboo
fences, which, no easy job, we had to break through to reach the point
where the *chaung* enters the river. We hailed the Unit Craft, which was
backed in, and with the help of planks laid along the mud we managed
to get on board. The others arrived soon afterwards, Jim Thomson
caked with mud up to the knees. Brigadier Roberts left us to find his
way back with the transport to Shillong. I was sad to part with Michael

Roberts to whom I owed some of the best times of our tour. Just after
half-past five we were alongside *Narbada* in the war-shattered harbour
of Akyab.

We had two more days of exploring Arakan before we sailed in the
evening for Port Blair in the Andaman Islands two days later. It is
always Arakan, never *the* Arakan. Journalists were blamed for the
vulgar error, but probably the military were responsible. Certainly
they were responsible for the much more vulgar error of calling the
Near East the Middle East, which I was glad to find both Auchinleck
and Wavell agreed with me in considering prejudicial to the strategic
conceptions of 1942. We are such a nation of nominalists that it is
particularly dangerous for us to get a name wrong.

At sea in *Narbada* I was woken by Gulaba to say that a very big fish
was to be seen. Up on deck I found that our bow had hit and impaled
a young 35-ft Blue Whale which had crossed it during the night. Its
head was lolling to starboard and its body was streaming along close
to the ship on the port side. An attempt was made to get the carcass on
board, but when the ship slowed down for the difficult operation the
whale sank. It was probably killed by the first impact, for its neck was
half cut through. It was reckoned that our catch lost us twenty-eight
miles during the night.

We dropped anchor in Port Blair harbour early the following morning under a grey sky in warm and very sticky weather. The Deputy
Commissioner Michael Sullivan, the Cambridge and Olympic runner,
offered to drive Jim Thomson, Chrissie and myself across the island.
It was a glorious drive. The Andaman jungle seemed even richer than
the Burma jungle in variety of trees, for it had some of the characteristics
of the Malay jungle added. Besides the jungle there were many coconut
groves and wide valleys of paddy. We visited two Bhantu villages. The
Bhantus were transported there as one of the criminal tribes from the
United Provinces. Now they were to be sent back to Lucknow by their
own request. Only the older people could remember anything about
India and they had drawn a fanciful picture of life there for the younger
people. Probably the latter would be just as anxious to return to the
Andamans and plague the life out of officials in Lucknow as they had
plagued the life out of the Deputy Commissioner here. Sullivan had a
splendid way with them and I could see that every one of the extraordinary mixture of people respected him. And it *was* a mixture. There
were Moplah villages to which the rebellious Moplahs of Malabar
were transported. There were ex-convict villages which contained every
kind of Indian nationality. There were Burmese villages because before
the Burmese administration was separated from India Burmese convicts
were transported there. The Japs brought in a lot of Indonesians, so
there was one Indonesian village too. Then there were the 'local born'

Andamanese who were the descendants of convicts. There was a large
Anglo-Indian colony. Finally, there were the three kinds of Andamanese aboriginals—the Andamanese proper, now almost extinct, the
Jarawas and the Onges. Nobody knew much about the last two. They
were stone-age pygmy negritos, and the Jarawas shot at sight, but not
through a blow pipe as Conan Doyle thought in *The Sign of Four*. They
used the bow and poisoned arrow. The arrows used to be made of
wood, but they had learnt how to pick up and use old iron and their
lethal range was about seventy yards. So little was known about those
pygmy tribes that estimates of their numbers varied between five
hundred and five thousand. We had intended to cruise round North
Sentinel, a small island about fifty miles from Port Blair, in the hope
of catching a glimpse of those mysterious creatures, but everybody
assured us we should see nothing except an empty beach with dense
jungle round; as to land there might easily have meant getting shot by
an arrow, we decided to leave well alone.

After we had visited the Bhantu villages called Anna and Kate for
the daughters of a former Chief Commissioner, we found a place in
the jungle for a picnic tea and while we sat in the Dodge to enjoy it
an emerald dove pecked about in the road just beyond.

My mind was too full of the horrors of the Jap occupation which
Sullivan had told me about to settle down to diary writing when we
got back to the ship. Of 20,000 people they managed to exterminate
in one way or another over 7000. The kindest explanation for the
Japanese atrocities is to attribute them to panic. They were in a panic
throughout the occupation. When the British and Indian authorities
escaped in March 1942, the Indian Government asked for volunteers
to remain and look after the local population. Among those volunteers
was Major A. J. Bird, the Secretary of the Chief Commissioner, a man
in his mid-forties. A Benghali convict called Bagchi, who when manager
of a cinema (I think in Calcutta) murdered a man and received a life
sentence, had been employed by Bird and sacked for malingering.
So, to revenge himself, after the Japs had appointed him chief Naval
Intelligence officer, he forged a letter from Bird which purported to
give instructions about the establishment of an espionage service. This
letter he hid in a house, which he then urged the Japs to search. When
the Japs found it Bird was taken from the internment camp and tortured to make him confess. Finally he was paraded round the Bazaar
in Aberdeen and from time to time a huge Jap sergeant would fling
him over his shoulder after which the guards would kick him until he
rose on his feet again. Every brutality was watched with open glee by
Bagchi. At last Bird moaned for water whereupon the executioner, a Jap
naval officer, called for water which he poured on his own sword before
cutting off Bird's head by the edge of a trench dug to receive his body.

Bagchi was in jail in Port Blair, but the evidence considered legally necessary to hang him would probably not be forthcoming. The only hope of being able to make that vile creature pay any kind of penalty was to secure enough evidence to justify sentencing him to a term of imprisonment for forcibly procuring women to enter the Jap brothels. The method used was to drag before Bagchi some wretched woman— often enough a married woman—strip her naked and let a Jap doctor examine her with great brutality for venereal disease. One woman had testified that the doctor's hand was thrust up her so roughly as to draw blood. If after this she still refused to serve as a prostitute, she was beaten. If beating did not break her will, the guards would put lighted pieces of paper between her thighs. If in the end she still refused to give way she was violated by half a dozen soldiers. Women who suffered this kind of horror were still living in various parts of South Andaman.

Next day the Deputy Commissioner arranged for some of the victims of Japanese barbarism to come up and talk to me at his bungalow. I saw Mr McMullen, an Anglo-Indian, who had been Chief Jailer in the prison. He described the landing and the funk that the Japs were in. When Luty, the wireless man who had volunteered to stay behind and send out signals until the last moment, blew up the station the Japs all fell down on their faces and did not move for twenty minutes. Luty was killed by them later. When they got up they scampered around tying little Jap flags to the trees. A Swede called Cato who ran the match factory was allowed to go free at first, but they could not stand his contempt for them and took him away to Ross Island where he was murdered; nobody had been able to find out exactly where and how. In North Andaman there were four hundred and ninety Karens, mostly Baptists; the Jap general sent there was also a Baptist of the same American Mission. So until he was removed the people were decently treated. The three Indian National Army officers who arrived later in Port Blair all behaved well while they were there.

The Nips issued pompous proclamations about the mighty Nippon Empire after they landed, in which they promised to give the inhabitants an example of its beneficent rule. They then proceeded to cut down all the fruit trees and plant sweet potatoes and tapioca everywhere. There were four spy scares, and each one cost many lives. Men and women were tortured to make them confess. When they confessed to avoid further torture they were killed. Many others died in prison of beri-beri due to malnutrition. A group of seven or eight victims came into the Deputy Commissioner's office and the expression in their eyes as they told me what had happened I can never forget. The father of the young man who had fired at a Jap officer and wounded him in the cheek with two pellets of his shotgun (the only shot fired at the Japs) told me the story. They had been looting the bazaar and the young man

fired in a sudden burst of rage, after which he escaped. The Japs burnt
his father's house and threatened to burn down the whole bazaar if
Zulfiqar Ali did not give himself up. His father Akbar told how he had
given himself up for the sake of the rest of the community. His son was
put to death at the age of twenty after being tortured in public. I said
Zulfiqar Ali's was the only shot fired; I had forgotten that a Jarawa
on North Sentinel killed a Jap officer on the beach with an arrow.

Another little man, who was one of the Deputy Commissioner's
clerks, told how during one of the spy scares he and his family had been
dragged off to jail in the middle of the night. He had been tortured by
having red hot needles pushed half an inch under his nails. He described the water torture which, of course, was a favourite of the
Germans, and was much used by the English in the reign of King John
to extract money from the Jews. He was still unable to get up in the
morning without putting a hot-water bottle against his back—the
result of the beatings he had received. Another habit of the Japs was to
strip a man naked and tie him to a cane-seated chair with a candle
under his private parts. If he held out and would not confess to
espionage his wife was brought in and stripped. Then they were tied
together face to face and both were burnt in the same place. Several
of the island women were sterile as a result of the treatment they
received, the genital organs having been partially burnt away. Pouring
boiling water up the nose was used in the hill villages in Burma to
extract information about Force 136, but I did not hear of that being
used in the Andamans.

Perhaps what will show better than anything what those poor people
endured is the tale of an "old man (*sic*) of forty-five" whose heart the
Japs hoped to break by making him stand with his arms outstretched
and a green coconut in each palm. A green coconut weighs a great deal
more than the coconuts you see on a shy at a fair. When the 'old man'
let one of the coconuts fall he was beaten. At this story everyone turned
round to look at the 'old man' and laughed. Compared with the
sufferings of others what that "old man" of forty-five" had to endure
was a joke!

Some of the worst Jap criminals were hanged, but all too many may
have escaped retribution. I asked the people I was interviewing if they
could give me one example of Jap decency, and they spoke of a Doctor
Kamazo (?) who had been kind. He was very soon removed in consequence. They could not mention a single other instance of kindness.
The Imperial Nipponese Navy, Army, Police and Civil Service were
afraid of being bombed, and they all behaved like hysterical monkeys.
That inability to stand up to bombing was an interesting revelation of
Jap cowardice because the same barbarians in the field of battle were
often, indeed almost always, inspired with an insensate courage.

1a. On the way through Burma

1b. C.M. being carried in a dandhi on the way to Nepal

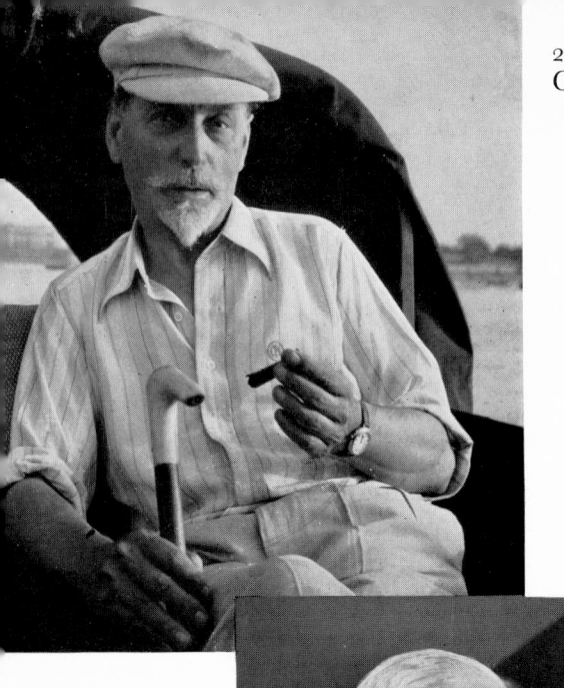

2a.
C.M. crossing the Ganges

2b.
Field-Marshal Wavell
and C.M.

2c.
C.M. with
Brigadier Condon at Simla

At noon the interviews finished, and we went up to see the jail, being received by Major M. Sendak, Indian Medical Service, who was simultaneously the Governor of the Jail and the Chief Medical Officer in the Andaman Islands. We sat in his office and heard about the convict settlement before the Japs arrived. Sendak himself was there then. All convicts on arrival spent three months in a cell. I looked at one of those cells on the ground floor. It measured fourteen feet by seven and did not seem as forbidding as the usual cell in one of our prisons at home. After the three months the convicts were to all intents free to work in different parts of the island. After seeing all over the prison we went into the courtyard to inspect the convicts who were awaiting trial in Port Blair itself. There were half a dozen Bhantu rioters, who no doubt would be sent to Lucknow with the others when the ship arrived for them. There was another dozen convicted of theft. Finally there were the Indian ex-jailers who had taken service under the Japs and had made a brave attempt to outdo their masters in brutality. Those fellows were all dull of eye, heavy of jowl, and low of forehead—the average human brute the world over.

Then I saw a small young man with the face of a weasel and the eyes of a viper. Sendak told me that he was Bagchi, whereupon a greasy propitiatory smile began to trickle over his face. When I stared at him without response he turned his eyes away. Appeals were being cabled from Bengal to the Chief Commissioner on behalf of Bagchi and I have never been able to find out whether misguided influence was brought to bear on his behalf. He deserved to be stamped out like a cockroach. Yet, what a narcotic time is! Sendak told me that when he first came back and was the creature responsible for the death of his best friend in Port Blair he could not look at him.

"And now I speak to him as I speak to the other prisoners," he added with a sigh.

I was much impressed by the personality of Major Sendak—a frail-looking man with sensitive eyes and mouth and sympathetic voice. He was of Czechoslovak extraction.

After lunch we reached a Burmese village and turned aside to visit a *hpoongyi's* school beside a small pagoda. The children were delightfully natural, and anxious to show their prowess in reading and writing the Burmese script on slates. The old priest himself in his faded orange robes had the gentlest face. He sat on the edge of a bamboo platform about eighteen inches above his scholars on the bamboo floor. A grandfather brought along his baby grandson who was wearing a gaily embroidered khaki cap and round his neck two fine cords, one with a golden sovereign older than the 1887 jubilee and the other with a silver half-rupee. Perhaps the former was a souvenir of some British soldier who loved a Burma maid before Kipling sang about the road to Manda-

F

lay. John Dalison knelt on the floor to photograph the infant who was held up on his feet by the grandfather, whereupon the infant behaved like some infant Cupid on a Renaissance fountain much to everybody's amusement. Even the old *hpoongyi* smiled.

That evening I met a Sikh Jemadar of Force 136 who had landed on one of the islands (not North Sentinel) where the Jarawas lived, and he gave me some information about them. He once saw a small boy shooting arrows at his mother's toes and laughing when she jumped in the air. He would pay no attention to her remonstrances, but at last his father came along in response to his wife's yells and gave the child a sound spanking. The Jarawas moved about from kitchen midden to kitchen midden in the way our Neolithic forebears did, and they had a communal sleeping hut, the sexes being divided by a spiked wooden paling. He had not seen a Jarawan widow going about wearing her husband's skull suspended by a necklace; this was a custom of the Andamanese aborigines. After the Japanese officer was killed the Japs bombed the Jarawa territory, and they retreated further into the interior. Since the Japs had left the Jarawas had been attacking the elephants of the Forestry Department, after an elephant had beaten up one of their villages. The bows they used required much strength, and they knelt to shoot like the long-bowmen of England.

Next day we went for a cruise in a steam tug among the Ritchie Archipelago twenty miles from Port Blair. Everybody except myself fished and had a great day's sport.

The greyish-white cliffs of Havelock Island had a menacing and macabre appearance under the grey sky and above the grey sea. The island was the scene of a Jap outrage only a fortnight before the surrender. Vice-Admiral Hara, the Japanese Commander at Port Blair, became apprehensive about the food situation and a round-up was made of six or seven hundred men, women and children, who were locked up in the cellular jail. About two hundred of them were released; but the rest, four to five hundred, were herded into boats and thrown into the sea off Havelock Island. Most of them were drowned or eaten by sharks; those who managed to get ashore perished of starvation. Rumours of survivors having been seen were always rife in Port Blair and the Deputy Commissioner had just sent another search party out; but if there were any survivors they did not know that the Japs had been defeated and would probably hide. As late as August 13th 1945, two days before the surrender, another batch of some three-hundred persons were taken overland to Tarmugli Island and there butchered. Thirty-seven Jap officers, seamen and soldiers were condemned to death after their trial in Singapore and those included Vice-Admiral Hara.

On the following afternoon we said goodbye to those who had made our stay at Port Blair so enjoyable. The atmosphere of the place was extraordinarily genial. Everybody liked the other fellow; I did not hear a word of criticism by one official of another. Co-operation was the rule. We steamed away from the orange sunset to turn south for Car Nicobar.

We dropped anchor off Malacca and Major J. d'Issa-Boomgardt, the Assistant Commissioner, came on board. He was in the 3rd Mahrattas and fought at Keren. We landed at the jetty built by the Japs of concrete walls filled up with sand. It was nearly a hundred yards long and it had always been declared impossible to build a jetty there before the Japs got busy and did it in three weeks. All the captains or headmen of the Car Nicobar villages were on the jetty to greet us, and we shook hands with at least thirty people. The island is 49 square miles in extent, almost completely flat and covered with coconut groves and rich jungle. The population was about nine thousand. The natives were passionately British. Every one of them had taken a British name besides his own Nicobarese name of which, like a small boy in a prep-school with his Christian name, he made a secret because to know a man's name gave you power over him. Rumpelstiltskin felt like this, and the same idea occurs somewhere in the *Odyssey*. They did not necessarily choose English proper names; one girl was called 'Yes please'.

We set out with Boomgardt in his jeep to make a tour of the island. The sandy roads were in good condition and ran in every direction through the coconut groves. The girls we met on the road were attractive. Half of them wore only a sarong, but the remainder covered their breasts with the thin white bodice of Burma. The men all greeted us with salutes. I could see that Boomgardt who had been there about a year was already much liked. He told me that it was impossible to get the Nicobarese to settle down to steady and regular work. They were capable of making a tremendous effort, but reaction always succeeded and the greater the effort the longer the fallow time. As an instance of what they could do in the way of exceptional tasks he told me that he had persuaded a number of them to carry for seven miles a Diesel engine and electrical equipment weighing several tons, which the Japs had buried. With his own knowledge as an amateur engineer he had got it working and was now able to provide electric light for many of the houses. That had been a joy to the Nicobarese and it had become the fashion to make up parties to sleep in one of those houses merely for the pleasure of gazing at the electric lamp. And beautiful houses they were, like large beehives thickly thatched with a kind of grass grown in carefully tended clearances in the jungle, which were tabu to other crops. The houses were built on piles with metal guards to keep out the rats, and one climbed up to the living-room by a narrow bamboo ladder. The cooking was done on the ground underneath. One third of the floor space in the middle was boarded. On either side the floor was of finely pleached cane which provided ventilation for there were no windows. Those floors were much better and stronger than the bamboo floor of the ordinary Burmese basha. The houses were built round about a village 'brown' of beaten earth on which I did not see so much as the husk of a coconut.

We drove on to visit the store of the only Indian traders now functioning. Before the Japs came the island had been exploited for years by Indian and Chinese traders, who had swindled the inhabitants ruthlessly over their coconuts. They had no system of measures or money, and they never received a fair amount of rice in return for their coconuts. Moreover, the Indian traders had managed to make them appear always in debt. They were much worried by the prospect of being handed over to India. For them it meant a return of trading tyranny. The existing store was well run and well stocked. I was impressed by the obvious decency and honesty of the Indian manager. Just inside the entrance one could read the following inscription in white lettering on a painted board:

> Always tell the truth.
> Give up your bad habits.
> Might is right.
> God Almighty.
> Don't spit here.
>   R. A. J. and Co.

From the store we drove to the church of the Reverend John Richardson,[1] a Nicobarese ordained by the Anglican Bishop of Rangoon. Mr Richardson was a man of fifty-three and as fine a specimen of good missionary as one could meet, with an attractive young wife. The church was beautifully neat, but the east window was smashed by the Japs and repairs were necessary. In the small side chapel stood a dry pomelo, which is a large fruit somewhere between a grape-fruit and an orange in flavour. I asked why the pomelo had been kept there and was told the following story.

A young Indian sailor came ashore from H.M.I.S. *Krishna*, when she anchored off Car Nicobar at the time of the Jap surrender, and cheated a Nicobarese by paying him for two pomelos the price of one. On returning to the ship he was seized with a kind of paralysis. His conscience tormenting him, he sent back the second pomelo with the request that it might be put in the church and prayers offered for his recovery. He was immediately cured, and the pomelo was preserved in the side-chapel as a perpetual reminder that honesty is the best policy.

Close to the church was the school presided over by Mr Ezekiel Joel,

---

[1] Bishop of Nicobar.

who was shortly to be ordained. He was much more High Church than Mr Richardson, but the two men were in complete accord. Among the brown pupils I noticed three little boys as black as coal, with glittering pop-eyes. They were Jarawas who with their sister had been captured during an affray with the police in which their parents had been killed. They wore light-blue cotton shorts and shirts and looked like the stock piccaninnies of the picture books. One of them was wearing a small electric-light bulb on a string round his neck. They were reported to be very naughty, but details of their naughtiness were withheld. Nobody was quite sure how old the eldest was. They suspected that his pygmy size was misleading people into supposing he was only about eleven.

Mr Richardson's flock was increasing all the time and he did not make the mistake of interfering too much with the old customs. The women of his congregation did not uncover their breasts, but I was told that this was not the missionary's order. It had come from the wife of the last Assistant-Commissioner; she had insisted that every woman and girl who came to see her should wear a bodice. I had noticed that occasionally when we passed girls with bare breasts on the road they had turned their backs and covered them with their hands. It was distressing to see those signs of self-consciousness.

We wound up a fascinating morning with lunch at the Assistant-Commissioner's house. It had been the H.Q. of the Imperial Nipponese Navy and still bore above its entrance the badge of the anchor and chrysanthemum. After lunch I went out on the veranda for a pow-wow with some of those who could tell me about the Japanese behaviour. At first the invaders behaved fairly well, but when we started bombing the airstrips they indulged in the same spy scares as on the Andamans. In all seventy-five Nicobarese were tortured to death. The most moving story was of the captain of Arong, a village in the remotest part of the island and completely animist. The captains of all the villages were ordered to surrender the Union Jacks which they had, and this was done by all except the captain of Arong. He buried his and would not reveal the place under torture. The flag was finally discovered by the Japs two years later, and after being tortured again the captain of Arong was put to death. "If the people of Great Britain are willing to disclaim responsibility for heroes like the captain of Arong the people of Great Britain deserve to sink into third-class insignificance."

The tortures used by the Japs on Car Nicobar were the same as in the Andamans with one exception. That was to make a man climb a coconut tree and remain all day balanced on a precarious branch. The Nicobarese have a keen sense of the ridiculous. They said the Japs were comic in their expression of hatred for Britain. If they found an English picture or an English book they would jump on it and chatter

like infuriated monkeys. After the surrender, while the Japs were still
on the island waiting for orders, the Nicobarese used to laugh at them
continuously. In the end the poor butts would not appear in public if
possible and were well on the way to a nervous breakdown before they
were evacuated. I was told there were fifteen thousand Japs in the
Nicobars but this was certainly an overestimate. Their habits were
filthy. No attempt at sanitation was made and the result was that a
plague of flies came to the islands with the accompanying dysentery.
From responsibility for the venereal disease which was sadly prevalent
the Japs could be absolved; it was introduced by the traders.

After the pow-wow about Jap atrocities we drove back to Mus,
where a representative island team were to play H.M.I.S. *Narbada* at
football. The sailors were inclined to think that the local yokels were not
quite the stuff for the champions of the Indian Navy to waste time over.
But what a game the local side put up! The result—two goals to none
in favour of *Narbada*—did not represent the run of the play; the game
should have ended in a draw. The Nicobarese played with bare feet
and kicked with great power; if they had been stronger in front of goal
they would have defeated the sailors. The pace was terrific. I was
excited and continually refreshed myself with delicious coconut milk.
When the match was over, the trunks of the coconut palms round the
field were stained with rose by the sunset.

From the match we drove to a dance in the village of Perka. Ninety-
six girls formed a great horseshoe round a bonfire of coconut husks on
the village 'brown', and between the chanting they stamped and
shuffled upon the ground. The sound of the shuffle was rather like the
sound of a calm sea running up a steep sandy beach and receding.
They moved round very slowly, and the pattern of the dance changed
from time to time. The girls were wearing white bodices, presumably
to save the modesty of the visitors. Round their heads they wore fillets
of cellophane. The half-moon was in the zenith. The grove around was
dark. The dancing forms caught the flickering of the bonfire. The
beehive houses were mounds of shadows.

Boomgardt had expressed a strong desire to visit the island of Chowra
next day. Rather unwillingly I agreed to go, for it meant giving up the
visit to Nankowrie and a meeting with the Queen of the Nicobars. She
was an old Indian trader who had acted as agent for the Government
and received a decoration in the First World War for frightening away
Captain Müller by hoisting the Union Jack when the *Emden* appeared
in the great harbour. He supposed that there must be a strong force on
the island. When the German raider had gone she sent a canoe to carry
the news to the nearest signal station, and the *Emden* was caught by
H.M.A.S. *Sydney* and destroyed in the Cocos Islands.

We left the anchorage at seven next morning and steamed south to

Chowra. We sighted a Japanese floating mine and after a lively bombardment lasting over half an hour the ship's guns managed to sink her. We reached Chowra four and a half hours later. It was a small island hardly more than two square miles in extent if as much. At one point from the sea it looked like the Dutchman's Cap—one of the Treshnish Islands off Argyll. At the south end was a square lump of rock, 343 feet high and perfectly level on top. The rest of the island was flat, hardly more than a mile across and two miles long, with a dazzling white beach above which, backed by jungle and coconuts, stood twenty large beehive houses.

The Assistant-Commissioner, John Dalison, Jim Thomson and I embarked in the motor-boat from which we transferred to a very narrow canoe with two outriggers. Each of us sat on a couple of bamboo thwarts no wider than his own behind and tried to keep his feet out of the water at the bottom of the canoe. Luckily the day was calm and blue, as perfect a day as one could hope for. We could never have landed at Chowra in our Andaman weather. A Union Jack flew from a pole above the beach. When we landed we found that the beehive houses there were guest houses and at that time empty. They were used by people who came to buy the Chowra pottery. Chowra was an island of magic. There were over five hundred inhabitants, and their chief occupation was making cooking pots for the other islands. The clay on Chowra was exhausted and it was obtained from the much larger island of Teressa about five miles away to the south. The people of Teressa dared not make their own pots for fear of coming under one of the potent Chowra spells. In the same way the Nancowry people fifty miles south had to pay a commission to Chowra on canoes they built for Car Nicobar a hundred miles away. If they did not, their canoes were bewitched by Chowra-conjured devils.

We found the villages of Chowra very different from those of Car Nicobar, and the people ugly. The men wore nothing except a red cache-sex with a long red string behind representing the tail inherited by the union between a woman and a dog after the flood from which the Nicobarese believed they sprang. In contrast, except for a few old hags the women covered their breasts with a grubby wrap. We asked the headman who had returned with us from Car Nicobar if this was done on our account, but it was apparently the rule. We saw unbaked pots as large as two feet across and more than two feet deep fashioned without a potter's wheel in perfect symmetry. We also saw them being baked on small bonfires and banded with black and red. The combination of black and red had a discouraging effect on devils; the devil-scarers in every house displayed it.

Chowra was much dirtier than Car Nicobar. The ground round the villages was littered with coconut shells and refuse, and flies were thick everywhere. There were many dogs and round the houses broody fowls in rectangular baskets were hung up out of reach of rats. The sun blazed down as we drank coconut milk, but even that did not taste nearly as good as the Car Nicobar product. We saw various devilish figures presumably intended to scare away other devils. The most depressing thing about the island was that practically the whole population was infected with venereal disease, not to mention elephantiasis, tuberculosis and malaria. The people had no medicine of any kind, and there was no room for them in the Car Nicobar hospital. The headman of Chowra brought men, women and children for Jim Thomson to look at. Even to be looked at by a doctor was something. Babies with syphilitic sores, small boys with gonorrhoea, women eaten away— all those horrors were to be found there in plenty.

After such evidence of neglect by the flag flown above the beach I was in no mood to investigate Jap atrocities there. However, there were none to investigate; I should suppose that the Jap company stationed there must have been too much depressed by those stricken people to commit atrocities. Anyway, they committed none and did not molest the women, which was hardly to be wondered at.

I wished we had not changed our itinerary by visiting Chowra instead of Nancowry, and yet perhaps it was better that we should not have left the Nicobars with only the lovely picture of Car Nicobar in our minds, when a place like Chowra existed. I have not tried to evoke the full horror of that small island where above that dazzling beach and azure sea the Union Jack flew, but the people who flew it with such pathetic pride and trust were phantoms of humanity. I wished that those who so willingly subscribed to missions for the cure of souls would subscribe to a mission there for the cure of bodies. A grave moral responsibility for allowing such a state of affairs was attached to the British Government. Few white men had visited Chowra. I was glad we did take the Assistant-Commissioner there; the Government would no longer be able to claim ignorance of the state of affairs.

That forever memorable fortnight was over and I was sad to say farewell to those shipmates when we landed at Penang. There we were disappointed to find that Brigadier A. F. Cumming had been held up in Rangoon because all the Dakotas were looking for a Dakota which had crashed. We were flown to Kota Bahru and I was able to see where the Japanese had first landed in the north of Malaya. I missed Cumming's guidance over the ground where he had won the only Victoria Cross awarded to a British or Indian soldier in that campaign. Unfortunately dysentery started for me at Kota Bahru and I could not fly over the various beaches of that Japanese landing. Cumming joined us when we reached Butterworth and while I was in bed at Ipoh he gave me an enthralling account of Kota Bahru and also of his time commanding 63rd Brigade at Tiddim in the autumn of 1943. I was the guest of A. V. Aston, the Resident Commissioner and his charming wife. I was extremely lucky to find myself in a house where my host and hostess managed to make it seem a pleasure for them to have a guest with dysentery. I was threatened with a week in hospital but, thanks to sulphaguanadine galore administered by Jim Thomson and my own determination to keep out of hospital, I was well enough to move on in two days to H.Q. Malaya Command at Kuala Lumpur. General Galloway[1] thoughtfully asked Mr Mohamed Youssif, the Chief Public Relations Officer, to accompany us to Malacca.

He was a grand cicerone. He came from one of the twelve clans who some three centuries before migrated to the Peninsula from Sumatra. Those clans were strictly exogamous and matriarchal. A husband who misbehaved could be thrown out of his wife's clan back into his own. All property passed through the females. Youssif spoke English perfectly, though he had never been outside Malaya. He hoped to come to London the following year to write a thesis on matriarchy. Malays are Muslims, but the stern religion had been much softened by the humid tropics. Fanaticism was non-existent. Even Ramadan was not scrupulously kept. Youssif's father had made the pilgrimage to Mecca and was a devout follower of the Prophet, but there was no attempt to force devotion on anybody else. Purdah had been unknown for centuries.

Malacca was high romance in one too brief afternoon. We saw the gateway which was all that remained of the fort built by Alfonzo d'Albuquerque in 1511, whose coat of arms stood above the gate. Once upon a time it was almost washed by the sea, which was now more than half a mile away. That relic of Imperial Portugal was overhung by two trees of Flame of the Forest, the petals of which stippled the grass around the gateway of the ancient fort and stained with vivid orange the red laterite of the gateway itself. The Portuguese were succeeded by the Dutch, and there were many Dutch houses of the seventeenth century in Malacca as solid as those built at home by the burghers of Holland. I thought of the elms in Amsterdam mirrored in the bottle-green canals where ducks and gulls swam side by side. We went up to look at the shell of the Portuguese cathedral of St Paul which the pious stalwarts of the Netherlands, who solved the problem of worshipping God and Mammon, turned into a fort. You could see their gun emplacements above the green glacis commanding the grey waters of the Straits. The body of St Francis Xavier lay there until it was translated to Goa in 1592. The empty tomb with the original grating of wrought iron above it stood in the middle of what was once the chancel of that roofless fane. Pious descendants of the old Portuguese conquerors still burned

[1] Lt.-General Sir Alexander Galloway, K.B.E., C.B., D.S.O.

votive candles to the saint, and the grating was knobbled with spilt grease. Ponderous Dutch tombstones of the seventeenth century, inscribed with epitaphs in Dutch and heavily carved with cherubs, skulls and other emblems of death and eternity were leaning against the walls all round. I noticed one to the wife of an Englishman, James Barber, who, arriving there pregnant, had been taken to the hospital in Batavia where she had died in childbirth. That tale was told in the sonorous Latin they knew how to write in 1702. The English finally obtained Malacca in exchange for land in Sumatra. They gave back Java to the Dutch after the Napoleonic wars, which was a mistake.

From the Cathedral we drove to Hereen Street in the old Dutch houses of which the Chinese millionaires had lived for a long time, so long that the houses had lost all their Dutch characteristics except solidity. The front doors were lacquered, and inside the rooms were decorated with exquisite tiles. In those houses the traditional life of a cycle of Cathay endured, but to appear a match for modernity several of the millionaires had built Riviera bungalows by the sea's edge outside Malacca. Youssif asked if we might enter one of those Hereen Street houses, and a grandmother, with very little of her still black hair left on her head, and three large tufted moles, made us welcome. There were daughters and granddaughters and grandsons everywhere. Delicious little girls in flowery pyjama dresses danced around, tinkling with laughter. On the walls of the first room were hanging ten large coloured engravings of Chinese landscapes and seascapes about a century old and between them four large framed mezzotints of Farquharson's sheep in Highland snowstorms. There never was a more absurd juxtaposition. Along one side of the next room, which was open to the sky, stood six porcelain keg-shaped stools perforated to allow the air to circulate and cool the sedentary behind. Beyond this kind of patio was the altar of the ancestors with joss sticks burning, and beyond this at least three more rooms opened out of one another, from the last of which a green-glowing doorway led to the garden.

From Hereen Street we drove out to the Chinese cemetery, which looked like a stretch of the Berkshire Downs. There for two hundred years and more the Chinese of Malacca had been buried. For over a mile the grass slopes of the hill were covered on both sides with large horseshoe-shaped embrasures of stone built into the hillside. At the opening of the horseshoe was a stone platform on which stood a slab of stone inscribed with the names of the dead. Children were flying white kites everywhere. I supposed that, white being the Chinese mourning, coloured kites were forbidden. We walked up to the summit of the steep grassy slope to look at the memorial to a Malay hero who fought the Portuguese. The Malays still came there bearing votive offerings and we could see the grease of burnt candles—the same kind of candles as St Francis Xavier was offered above his empty grave. Youssif told us that when the Japs let him out of prison the first thing his mother did, and she was a Muslim, was to come there and make her thanksgiving. Beside that tree-shadowed shrine was a pergola terrace with square columns much as one sees in Southern Italy. It was erected by the Chinese as a mark of respect to the Malay hero.

At last regretfully we had to shut our ears to the faint breeze whispering of rain and leave that tranquil green down. A grim cloud was darkening the sky and the children's kites were falling when we reached the car. As we drove through Malacca we passed a club at the corner of a street, opposite an old Portuguese church dedicated to the Holy Angels and still in use.

"Every night passing that club one heard shrieks of agony", said Youssif sombrely. "That was the headquarters of the Kempeitai."

The Kempeitai were the Japanese Secret Police.

We had to spend an extra two days in Singapore; objections were made to my going to Java and Sumatra because planes were being shot at in Indonesia. The real reason was probably official nervousness. There were complicated and fussy discussions about the journey on to Hong Kong, and the necessary information to be given about our passports. There was now a lot of red tape in Japan manufactured by the Americans who in spite of individualism turn out more of it than any other nation except Russia.

I had an agreeable tête-à-tête with Malcolm Macdonald who had recently arrived as Governor-General. Everybody was paying tributes to the skill with which he was carrying out his duties. I was glad to find that he had admiration and affection for De Valera; he agreed about the remarkable way in which he had steered Eire through the years of war, and that his neutrality had been consistently benevolent. He asked my opinion of Nehru; I said I thought he had the same kind of moral integrity as De Valera. The question was whether he could achieve for India what De Valera had achieved for Ireland, the vast difference in size and population making his task a thousand times more difficult. There was a disquieting parallel between the way certain elements in the Conservative Party were playing with the notion of exploiting the Indian Muslims as they had exploited the Irish Protestants.

My only disappointment in Singapore was Raffles Hotel. I had been hearing since youth stories about Raffles Hotel. It was quieter than the ineffable Shepheard's in Cairo, but it had lost the authentic stamp of a great hotel. There was too much chromium plate and too many squiggles in the decorations in an attempt to be modern. The result was hopelessly suburban.

We went one day to hear a bit of one of the war crime trials in the Victoria Hall. It was a queer scene. There was a concert platform, backed by an organ at the north end of the hall, with a battered-looking piano on it. At a table in front of the platform were seated the five members of the military court. Below them on the floor sat the interpreter, a Japanese with a foghorn American accent. To the left on a sort of village-inn settle with a high back sat the seven accused. They were all dressed in breeches, high leggings, and Kate Greenaway short brown tunics, the white collars worn outside adding to the Kate Greenaway effect. A number on a square of cardboard hung round each neck. At a raised table opposite the table of the court sat the defending Counsel—one of them a British officer, with an advisory brief for the Defence—and on the left was a female stenographer wearing very glassy glasses. Beyond them half the hall was filled with the public. We sat at right angles to the platform behind the witness box. The walls of the hall were hung with large portraits in oils of the civic and military fathers of Singapore, at least one Chinese among them. One of the former Governors in uniform was set against the background of a blue and white April sky at home. Fifteen fans whizzed round above and the big south doors were wide open.

As we came in Lt.-General Niashimura Takuma, the commander of the Imperial Guards Division, was answering his last question and on leaving the box was conducted back to the village-inn settle by two kilted Seaforths. The old Ross-shire Buffs provided the military guards for the proceedings. Takuma's place was taken by another Lt.-General whose name I did not catch. He saluted the Court and stood in the box at attention. The Japanese Counsel for the Defence read the questions from a sheet of paper, and these were translated into English by the interpreter. The seven men were accused of the massacre of at least twenty-five thousand Chinese after the surrender. It was the usual tale of Jap savagery, and I could not help thinking it was a mistake to allow a British officer to play any part in defending them. He was bound to plead that the massacre was perpetrated under military necessity, for that was the defence, and surely military necessity was not a plea that any British officer should make for an indiscriminate massacre. It allowed the Japs to suppose that some Britons considered their behaviour excusable. The Jap defending counsel congratulated the Chinese defending counsel on his presence as a sign of the fundamental understanding between the two Oriental races. I found it all a nauseating prostitution of fundamental morality to conventional justice.

The upset of the plan for going to Java and Sumatra gave Chrissie and me the chance of spending a rich weekend with Cunyngham-Brown, the Deputy Resident Commissioner, and his mother at Batu Pahat. Cunyngham-Brown was a Shetlander and a grandson of Clunies-Ross of Cocos-Keeling fame. From that rich week-end I must preserve a fragment from my diary:

"In one village we met a headman aged seventy-five, who was a very lively specimen of old age for the tropics. Yussif invited us into his house to drink a favourite mineral water called orange crush made extensively in Singapore. I should doubt if it contained as much as one orange to the ton. We took off our shoes which was the custom on entering a Malay house, although Yussif begged us to keep them on as in winter an Italian host in the south will beg a visitor to keep his hat on in the *salone*. Cunyngham-Brown said that compliance with the custom was always much appreciated. Inside, I was astonished to see a number of men, mostly elderly, with notebooks in front of them squatting all round a large room with their backs to the wall. In the middle was the teacher, seated in a wicker chair at a small circular table, for this was a sort of Sunday-school class for grown-ups from twenty-five to sixty. The exposition of the Koran was held up for a bit while Yussif, Cunyngham-Brown, the teacher and I drank orange crush."

On the other side of the road a Chinese school was having a music lesson to the accompaniment of a gramophone; and the contrast between the young voices and those elderly men taking notes on the Koran was piquant.

Cunyngham-Brown addressed the elderly scholars and told them I had written over sixty books, which evidently made a profound impression. After he had finished, our old host asked him where Cunyngham-Brown was nowadays, and on hearing that Cunyngham-Brown was himself almost embraced him. He pleaded his failing eyesight as an excuse for not having recognized him. Cunyngham-Brown had a splendid way with the Malays, young and old, and they obviously all loved him. He worked on the Sumatra railway, of which bad business few have heard. It was nothing like such a large undertaking as the railway from Siam to Burma, but the sufferings of those compelled to work on it were severe enough. Toward the end the Jap guards used to come in every morning and indicate by signs that the prisoners would be put to death that day. The latter expected to be massacred at any moment. That was when the invasion of Malaya was threatened, and there is no doubt that every prisoner would have been put to death when the invasion started. However, the atom bomb changed the whole situation, and any doubts I had about the rightness of dropping the bomb vanished after my visit to Malaya.

On March 26th we left Singapore for Bangkok where we should stay the night before going on to Hong Kong. We were to travel in a Sunderland flying-boat. General Cox, with whom we had been staying came down to the harbour to say farewell. The protracted stay at Singapore had been an irritating hold up of the programme and it was maddening that the people responsible for our not getting to Java and Bali could not have been frank from the start instead of not saying a word until a day before we were ready to go. 'Bouncer' Cox and his delightful wife never allowed us to suppose for a moment that we were outstaying our welcome, and their's was one more of the remarkable feats of hospitality we enjoyed.

Apart from the Sunderland's kicking about like a bronco in great billows of cumulus high above a blue sky it was an uneventful flight. I saw a phenomenon I had not seen before—a rainbow on the sea. Presumably this could only happen near the Equator. We came down in the grey-green river and had tea while we were waiting for the night luggage to come ashore. A ginger Siamese cat, not of the royal blood, miaowed in authentic Siamese and I gave her milk. A ginger female is rare in our country. Her light green eyes were set Siamese fashion, her ears were large and her tail was kinked at the end. After she was fed she crouched beside my chair in a typical Siamese attitude. I made friends at the hotel with a dark grey one.

The Ratanakosindr Hotel was ultra modern in design; but although the bedrooms were enormous, there were no bathrooms and only a minute basin and shower. Moreover, as there was no running water the shower was useless. A tub with a pannikin beside it provided the water. My bedroom was furnished with two immense beds and a quantity of extremely ugly furniture in the most degraded style. Mosquitoes were numerous.

Jim Thomson secured a jeep and we drove to the Temple of the Reclining Buddha. Door after door all round the high-walled enclosure was shut and we began to fear that we were too late when we found what must have been about the tenth wooden door open. We entered and found ourselves in wonderland. The numerous slim pagodas of graceful design were covered with porcelain mosaic and the colouring in pastel shades was exquisite. Great stone statues of men with fierce handlebar moustaches and what looked like top hats guarded each arched gateway within. Those gateways were encrusted with porcelain depicting various scenes in high relief—cocks fighting, dragons, warriors, grotesque birds, and posy upon posy of bright porcelain flowers. The shrines were all closed with black and gold lacquer.

The big Temple of the Reclining Buddha was shut. I have no skill in describing architecture, but the design of the exterior seemed austere in contrast with the colour all round. The walls were white with dark marble rectangles in relief like windows. The roof was steep, nine-tenths of it cinnabar-red tiles with the lowest line of black tiles. The roofs of other buildings had green and yellow and grey tiles in patterns of oblongs and squares, and at every gable point a kind of horn protruded. One could spend hours wandering about the courts of that enchanted enclosure in which rock gardens with small shrubs were peopled with the strangest human beings or occupied by dragons and mythical quadrupeds. Of one of those rock gardens a golden cock was the only occupant, he and a solitary baluster of green porcelain. The peace of the place was profound; although there were a lot of dogs all over it none of them barked. Now and then the sound of children's laughter rippled across the evening air, for there were schools as well as dormitories for the monks who in Siam wore robes of vivid chrome yellow not the more sober orange of the *hpoongyis* of Burma. There was a moment of supreme beauty when the setting sun lighted the gold and copper so that lamps seemed to be burning in the decorated gable tops and the gilded tiles on one of the porches of the shrines blazed.

Farther along, we found in the enclosing wall another door open in front of what looked like a small temple, with a placard outside to say that donations were welcome. I presented five Malay dollars to an ancient monk and expressed a desire to see inside the temple. When the door was opened a black and white cat sprang out with loud indignant Siamese miaows to demand a reason for her incarceration in what seemed to be a cross between a library and a large box-room presided over by a small gilded Buddha. I suppose she had been shut in to deal with the rats. Incidentally, I did not notice a single Buddha outside, which is the reverse of the arrangement of these holy places in Burma where Buddhas swarm in the open air.

Dusk was now deepening fast, and it would have been useless to take advantage of the monk's offer to unlock the Temple of the Reclining Buddha; the interior would have been dark. On signing the book we found that a donation of twenty-five ticals entitled the giver to a souvenir which proved to be a ring on which was engraved the Reclining Buddha. The monk blessed us in English before we said farewell, asking for us a happy life. The previous visitors in the book were six rubber-necks from Utah. How on earth or by air did six tourists from Salt Lake City reach Bangkok in those days?

The cicadas were loud in the trees outside the hotel when I woke. In the entrance lounge we were given coffee and tea, and when we left for the airport the dark sky was stained with the dull rose of dawn. People were hurrying along through the morning twilight. Mist was rising from the muddy canals. Birds were in full chorus, and the trams were crowded. At the airport we embarked for Hong Kong on the speedbird *Hamilton*, the sky now ablaze with rosy gold. I had my first view of the Pacific Ocean where it was rippling along the beaches of the large island of Hainan. Of course, it was technically the China Sea not the Pacific Ocean; I suppose one cannot call the Irish Sea the Atlantic. All the same, this glittering blue sea was the end of thousands of miles of that mighty ocean, and I saw no reason not to share the emotions of stout Cortez.

We landed from a launch in Hong Kong and drove to Government

House where we were to stay with Sir Mark[1] and Lady Young until we left for Japan. The G.O.C. Major-General Erskine[2] had gone to some trouble to ensure my getting full value out of my visit. He was married to a daughter of Sir Evelyn de la Rue who was a third-year man at Magdalen when I went up. To be the contemporary of a Major-General's father-in-law was a fresh reminder of age.

Those were days of concentrated listening of which I hope I made full use when I wrote the story of the Hong Kong tragedy in *Eastern Epic*. I owed a particular debt to Captain J. A. Phillimore of Public Relations, but I was indebted to so many people on this Odyssey that looking back at it twenty years later I am amazed at the kindness I was shown everywhere.

I went to see Dr Selwyn-Clarke[3] who was acting as Honorary Director of Medical Services. He was an outstanding personality. I have rarely been as deeply impressed by the moral force of an individual. He was a barrister as well as a doctor and was sentenced by the Japs to rigorous confinement for many months in prison after much torture and brutality. He was permanently lame from Jap kicking. His courage and humanity during the ordeal were continuous. Now he was repaying evil with good and trying all the time to help the Jap prisoners there. I was told that at Easter he would present each of them with a toothbrush at his own expense. He was inspired with a truly Christian faith in the power of good to overcome evil, and he practised what he preached. From Selwyn-Clarke's office we went on to visit Mr Ruttonjee, the owner of the Kowloon brewery, a wealthy and respected Parsee who survived the Jap occupation. His son Mr D. Ruttonjee was taken off one night, given the water torture, and badly beaten. He told me he could never forget the consolation of Selwyn-Clarke's voice, while he lay covered with blood on the floor of his cell, bidding him to take courage and to realize the ability of the human spirit to endure so much.

Next day was spent in making myself familiar with the topography of what was called the New Territories, some two hundred square miles beyond Kowloon on the mainland. The day was perfect—blue sky and a S.E. wind that turned the air to champagne. We drove through Kowloon until we reached the market gardens. What cultivation! Everything grown as well as it could be grown and looking as neat and exact as embroidery. I noticed one lovely square of carnations as rich as old velvet. Then we climbed rapidly up the road cut out of the hillside as far as Grasscutters' Pass where we had a magnificent view of the

---

[1] Sir Mark Young, G.C.M.G.
[2] The late General Sir George Erskine, G.C.B., K.B.F., D.S.O.
[3] Sir Selwyn Selwyn-Clarke, K.B.E.

3a. C.M. on the way to Bangkok

3b. Chrissie and C.M. in Patan street

4a. At Bahrein

4b. C.M. with U. Khanti at Mandalay

strait between Hong Kong and the mainland crowded with shipping. From there, too, there was a good view of the fifteen-mile stretch of defended hills known as the Gindrinkers Line between Gindrinkers Bay westward and the sea on the other side.

We got out of the car and walked up the grassy slope. There were white violets faintly tinged with palest blue and very sweet, a tiny Cambridge blue gentian, a deep lilac linaria, and a particularly spruce-looking small hawkweed. A grey-green fern, the young fronds red as they first uncrumpled, was in every cranny on the shady side. The soil was an ochreous decomposed granite. Northward the hills, nowhere higher than five thousand feet, rolled away in vast green billows of grass above the indented coast. Beyond the pale azure of the sea the hills of China were melting into the pale azure of the sky. I was loath to leave that spot, knowing that never again should I stand there and survey that vast serene view of land and sea, the March wind trumpeting in my ears and the air tasting of wine. *Hoc erat in votis*. This was how in the mind's prayers, which are dreams, I would have wished to gaze at China. And of Car Nicobar, too, I could have said *hoc erat in votis*. It was what I had prayed and dreamed a tropic isle might be.

On Palm Sunday Chrissie came with me to High Mass in the Cathedral. Between the Blessing of the Palms and the Reading of the Passion it was a long service and we were only just in time for a drive round the island which had been arranged.

In due course we came to the cemetery at Stanley. That cemetery must hold more various memorials of human misery in a small space than any similar plot of earth in the whole world. Stanley, which is a peninsula on the south-east of the island, housed the original garrison when Hong Kong was ceded after the China War of 1840. During the Second World War it was the internment camp of the civilian population and close by stood the prison, the wire fence round which was just below the cemetery. It lay on a slope overlooking blue waters and precipitous green coasts that reminded me of views along the Salernian Gulf and in various Aegean islands. The oldest graves had solid tombstones with large headstones. Those commemorated men of the 98th Regiment who were killed in an affray with pirates in 1844. There were some large gravestones from 1860 of the victims of the plague, and then from 1864 there were about a dozen high large tombs with rounded tops. Those covered the dust of children who died from the water of a well poisoned by the Chinese. The well could still be seen beside the road, sealed with a slab of stone. The largest of those large tombs was raised as "The Last Tribute of Affection" to an infant of ten months.

The little cemetery was thronged with the white crosses that marked the victims of the last war. There were graves of the internees, some in

G

their seventies who were too old or feeble to hold out against the Jap treatment. There was the grave of Captain Ansari of the Rajputs who endured fearful tortures rather than give away the names of the Chinese associated with his work. With him were buried twenty of those he tried to save by his own death. Captain Ansari was awarded the George Cross posthumously. Before he was taken prisoner he had been recommended for the Victoria Cross for valour in the field. There lay others tortured to death by the Japs.

There lay the remains of about a dozen unfortunate internees killed by an American air-raid in January 1945. There lay the remains of the nurses raped and murdered at St Stephen's Hospital on December 25th 1941 together with the remains of their murdered patients. I went afterwards to visit St Stephen's School—it was only a temporary hospital—and looked at the hall into which the Japs threw grenades among the sick and wounded before bursting in to bayonet them. On either side of the doorway into the hall, now full of desks again, was a huge thermometer advertising Stephen's Ink. Those thermometers were there on that Christmas Day of horror.

A short narrow rocky promontory like a horn of the hill above it was pointed out to me as the place used for the executions, from which the headless bodies were pitched forward into the sea. A soldier bathing from there a short time before had his leg nearly bitten off by a barracuda. Barracudas seldom attack bathers, and it was supposed that the barracudas round there had been accustomed to prey upon the bodies.

I left the cemetery at Stanley, chastened by the thought of what sorrow and suffering were enshrined on that slope above the sea, lightly shaded by blue-green casuarina trees and aglow with crimson hibiscus flowers. So far, I had seen sixteen war cemeteries in the course of my travels. Most of them were too far away for the graves to be tended with flowers from the hands of those that loved the dead within them. The hundreds of crosses white as bones looked desolate. At Stanley many of the graves were decked with flowers from the hands of those who suffered with the dead and were still living close to where they suffered so much.

Next morning John Phillimore drove me out again to the New Territories. This time we drove by the coast road to Fanling, The whole of the fifteen miles unfolded themselves in beauty. I recall the patches of seedling rice in the gleaming paddy fields as the most intense and lovely green the world can show. Beside it, emeralds and young apples, even young beech leaves, would lack verdancy. Presently those seedlings would be planted out and then sheets of that radiant green would cover the flats beside the sea. I was excited to see beside the road great bushes of white roses in prodigal bloom. I realized that it must be *Rosa Sinica*, of which the shell-pink garden variety, Anemone, flowers in May against a warm wall at home. I was back in Cornwall forty years ago, admiring its lustrous dark leaves and exquisite single blooms.

Lt.-Colonel D. Saunders commanding the 42nd Marine Commando met us at Fanling and drove us in his jeep to the village of Shan Tau Kok through the middle of which ran the frontier. Therefore one side of the street was in China and the other in the New Territories. We walked along the street, which was being patrolled by two commandos and a Chinese gendarme. The houses of Shan Tau Kok were all built of grey bricks and the street was full of dogs, children and flies. Gambling was forbidden in the New Territories. So the gamesters played on that side of the street and the money was paid to and from the Chinese side. The lawyers had been unable so far to get round this evasion of the law. We drove on by the stream which marked the frontier beyond Shan Tau Kok until we reached a narrow road winding up a fairly steep slope to about a thousand feet. A thin stone track for coolies went winding away into the heart of China and was lost to view round the shoulder of the farthest hill descending to the great plain behind. In 1917 I landed on the coast of Asia Minor to take off an agent and, waiting there on the beach, my ears sharpened for the tramp of a Turkish patrol, I thought with awe of the thousands of miles between me and China, no other beach between. When I saw that winding track it seemed to me that I had imagined thirty years before just such a track running right across Asia from where I had put my foot upon its soil for the first time.

Finally we reached Chick's Bridge, a Bailey bridge over the stream. Beside it was the bridge blown up to delay the Jap advance over the plain to invade the New Territories. We had a Commando post on our side of Chick's Bridge, the Chinese a post on theirs. Buses and wayfarers were searched at both. I saw a Chinese gendarme chasing some women across a field. The subaltern in command of the post told me those gendarmes were a brutal lot and thought nothing of beating up the women with their rifles when they caught them with smuggled rice. The road and railway continued across the plain to Canton a hundred miles away. There were many villages and the population teemed in every direction. *Hoc erat in votis.* Once again the view was what I had always pictured China would be.

Next morning I visited the University after which I went to the Gloucester Hotel, having promised to talk at the weekly Rotary lunch. I expect there are grand new hotels in Hong Kong twenty years later, but I remember the Gloucester Hotel being what Shepheard's and Raffles had ceased to be. Sir Mark Young, who had suffered considerably as a prisoner in Japanese hands, had come back to resume his Governorship but was on the verge of retiring. He was the guest of honour and made a brief farewell. I gave a dull talk, for I was feeling absurdly tired.

After lunch I had a talk with Mr F. P. Franklin, the editor of the *South China Morning Post*, who showed me a tome from America which claimed to give the history of Second World War. The whole of our Burma campaign occupied hardly a page of the eight hundred odd pages and the Hong Kong campaign was dismissed in half-a-dozen lines in which there were four misstatements of facts, one of which gave the handling of the guns to Americans. The author was Francis Trevelyan Miller, who once produced a book called "Photographic History of the Great War". Presumably this bowl of broth, in the making of which Mr Miller had been assisted by too many cooks, has been lapped up by myriads of Americans hungry for 'knowledge'. Franklin wrote a crushing review of the book in the *Hong Kong Telegraph* and received a letter from "Historian General Francis Trevelyan Miller (Litt.D., LL.D.)" addressed from "Historical Foundations, 15 West 68th Street, New York" in the course of which he wrote:

"Our chapter on China paid the highest tribute to China and the Chinese people for their heroic struggle. It seems to us that differences in time elements, exact dates, etc., while we desire to have them correct are minor matters in comparison to the principles we establish. The great thing is that the war is won!"

And he then went on to argue that all our greatest historians were in conflict over the facts. Mr Miller's letter was accompanied by a letter from Mr F. A. Barber, the "Executive Director of Historical Foundations", in which he pointed out that "Dr Miller's letter is typical of his courtesy and broad-mindedness."

Phillimore and I went to tea with Sir Robert Ho Tung at Idlewild. The 86-year-old patriarch was a superb figure. Benignity shone from his bright blue eyes. His complexion was rosy, his ample beard had not yet changed from grey to white. He spoke with enthusiasm of Bernard Shaw and H. G. Wells, both of whom he had met, and showed me photographs of himself with Ramsay Macdonald and Stanley Baldwin. The Japs pinched a photograph taken with Lloyd George. His charming daughter, Mrs Ho Cheng, was at tea, but the old gentleman wouldn't allow her to talk. I had to tell him all about the tour while his pretty young secretary stood by him and repeated in his ear anything I said which he had not followed. Tea was delicious, and afterwards we looked at wonderful ivories and brocades. The room was hung with greetings from friends on his 80th birthday (on October 2nd 1941) when he gave a reception to five thousand guests. He went to Macao to recuperate and while there the Japs invested Hong Kong. So he, luckier than most of his family, escaped the horrors of the invasion. I rejoice that I had the privilege of meeting that truly remarkable figure. Before we parted he presented me with a pair of gold cuff-links on which four Chinese ideographs had been cut—signifying, Happiness, Health, Wealth and Longevity.

When we got back to Government House there was a message to say that the weather in Japan was too bad for the plane and so to my relief, for I was extremely tired, our departure was put off for a day. I took advantage of the delay to spend much of it in writing up my diary. In the evening His Excellency took us to see *The Gold Rush* at the Lee Theatre. I enjoyed it in spite of beginning to feel more and more ill all the time. On the trailer I saw what were presumably intended to be *bonnes bouches* from the recent film of my book *Carnival*. They were worse than even I had ventured to fear, and I put my hands up to my face to avoid seeing any more.

"For goodness sake, don't do that," said Mark Young with a smile. "We are guests of the management and I shall lose face."

At midnight I went to bed with the prospect of getting up at four to catch the plane for Japan. I grew worse and worse, and after I was dressed I had to say I didn't think I could manage the journey. Jim Thomson was evidently relieved that I did not try to rise superior to my body. It was a typical demonstration of that accursed influenza with bronchitis in the offing. I undressed again and went back to bed. I felt too ill even to be disappointed about missing Japan. The struggle with influenza lasted for three days but I was free of fever by the evening of the third day when our Consul-General[1] in Saigon came up to my bedroom with his charming French wife. In spite of being in the midst of packing up for Mr Meiklereid to take on the Consulate-General in San Francisco they insisted that we should stay with them when we reached Saigon on April 8th.

On April 7th I woke at four o'clock in the morning with colic and had to lie up during the day, but somehow I had to persuade Jim Thomson that I was fit enough to travel next day. So I got up and dressed for dinner and we said goodbye to our wonderful host and hostess as we should be leaving Government House soon after six. The morning was chilly, and a Scots mist shrouded the harbour. When we reached the aerodrome at Kai Tak we were told that we should not take off before nine. This became ten, and finally eleven when we were told that a belt of bad cunim, that is cumulus-nimbus, two hundred miles wide, made any flight that day impossible. So back we went to Government House, feeling a dreadful nuisance. However, His Excellency and Lady Young managed to make us feel that they were really quite glad we had returned.

Next morning we were up at six again; the weather looked more

---

[1] Sir William Meiklereid, K.B.E., C.M.G.

promising and we were relieved to hear at the aerodrome that we actually should start this time. We were airborne after half an hour's tinkering with the port engine and recharging a battery. Taking off from the Kai Tak airstrip, which was surrounded by hills, was always a nervy business in those days. There had been some bad smashes. We were told not to unfasten the straps until we had been in the air ten minutes. One could sense the pilot's anxiety. We had to wear Mae Wests while we were over the sea, and I was glad of mine because it was cold and draughty in the plane. We came down at Saigon about two o'clock. The heat that blazed up at us from the airfield seemed an incredible change of climate to meet after less than six hours of flying. Mr Davies, the Vice-Consul, came to meet us and help with the wearisome form-filling. It really was ridiculous that we could not make a compulsory stop for one night without so much signing of documents; the 'free' world was already in chains.

Mrs Meiklereid was packing hard and therefore unable to come when the Consul-General drove Chrissie and myself round Saigon. The *place* was approached by tree-shaded boulevards. In the middle of it a well-designed Romanesque cathedral had all the room it wanted and left plenty of open space, round which ran a wide pavement in front of two or three cafés, a pharmacy, and lots of typical French shops. If it were not for the Annamites one might have supposed Saigon was somewhere a few miles from Grenoble. The dress of the women was the most attractive I had seen out there; white or black trousers with a kind of narrow tunicle of rich colour and design worn over them as far as the knee. We went to the Club where I enjoyed two of the nearest thing to Pernods. A Madame Jacquemar joined us. She had been caught by the Annamites in Hanoi and imprisoned for six weeks. A deep weal round each arm marked where she had been tied with rope. The French residents had a pretty bad time and about one hundred and fifty of them were still held *incommunicado*. An air of menace brooded over Saigon, which was garrisoned by battalions of the Foreign Legion there—mostly Germans. It was unsafe to venture away from the centre of the town, and to cross the river was fatal, the guerrillas being as fierce as they still are even twenty years later.

The Meiklereids had arranged a dinner party for the previous evening. Nobody at the Kai Tak aerodrome had thought it necessary to notify Saigon of the hold up of the plane, and the unfortunate Vice-Consul was kept hanging about all day. The casual behaviour of the R.A.F. ground staffs everywhere was a feature of their administration.

One of the guests at dinner had been the Crown Prince of Laos who had been disappointed to miss me but the Meiklereids asked him to come in after dinner next night. The throne to which he would ascend sounded as enviable a royal responsibility as the present could provide. Laos seemed to be one of the few Arcadias left. The Crown Prince was going to Washington for a few months and pressed me to go and stay with him when he returned. He was a distinguished, humorous and intelligent man, speaking beautiful French. He spoke with warm appreciation, as indeed did everybody, of the way Douglas Gracey had handled the situation in Indo-China when he went there in command of 20th Indian Division after the Jap collapse.

I have left that entry in my diary as I wrote it at the time because I did not want to suggest hindsight when I referred to that air of menace brooding over Saigon. As vividly as if it were yesterday I see that *place* and those lovely Vietnamese women in their trousers and gay tunicles walking gracefully along; we no longer talk about 'Annamites', I still hear the warning to keep away from the bridge over the river because of the guerrillas. I wish that I could have accepted the Crown Prince's invitation to visit his Arcadia before it was threatened by the world without.

If only Douglas Gracey could have been in Saigon to give some good advice to the Americans later on. He performed something like a miracle when after the Japanese surrender he and his 20th Division went to Saigon to handle the situation in Indo-China. He won gratitude from the French and Vietnamese alike. The former made him a Commander of the Legion of Honour and gave him the croix de guerre with palms; the latter made him an honorary *Citoyen de Saigon*. I have seen some of the wonderful gifts he received. I welcome this opportunity to pay a little tribute to the only officer in the Indian Army who raised a Division and commanded it until it was disbanded and who was for a while Commander-in-Chief of the Army of Pakistan. I still sadly miss a friendship that began when first we met in Bombay.

Early in the morning we left Saigon and about three o'clock in the afternoon landed at the Mingaladon airfield in blistering heat. There was something wild in having a bronchial cough in such weather but I was wheezing like an old gentleman with a winter cold in London. The rest-house for travellers in transit was worse than the worst Dak bungalow. Half a dozen people were crowded into each of the very small rooms; two lavatory basins and one privy was considered enough for more than twenty travellers. If the service had been free it would still have been a disgrace, but the R.A.F. charged as much as B.O.A.C. American travellers must have thought us mad to put up with such disregard of obligations. The 'food' in the reception place was served by the lowest class of grubby and nitwit Burman girls. A distorted radio blared away all the time. They hadn't even a room in which to lock up the luggage, and somebody pinched Chrissie's sponge-bag which was in the pocket of a hold-all.

We made no attempt to get into touch with people in Rangoon because some kind of political business was going on and transport for the twelve miles or so was unobtainable at the airport. So we sat on the verandah of the shoddy rest-house and read. I found an A.C.2 throwing stones at a house-lizard and asked him what he thought he was playing at. He said in an injured tone that he was trying to kill the brute because it was poisonous. I told him that the nearest poisonous lizard was in Arizona at which he gave an adenoidal gape and slouched off. The whole afternoon was intolerable because we had had to drive in a taxi in search of the office where air passages were granted and then in search of another office to get a warrant for Gulaba to travel by train to Delhi—a journey of twenty-five hours. Repeated misdirection, heat, dust, interminable form-filling, and the need to get the luggage to the station before dusk on account of the communal rioting, which was starting again, combined to make the whole business quite exhausting.

We were six hours late in reaching New Delhi where Chrissie and I were staying with the Commander-in-Chief, Lord Ismay.[1] Eric Mieville[2] and Martin Gilliat[3] were dining with the Chief next evening. I recall 'Pug' Ismay saying to me that 'Dicky' Mountbatten[4] had had no idea quite what a mouthful he had taken when he came out in March to be the last Viceroy of India. I said I would lay 2 to 1 on his bringing it off. Ismay said the right odds were 100 to 3 against. "Still", he added, "I believe he will bring it off." He was to be with the Viceroy until November as his Chief of Staff.

Chrissie and I were invited to lunch with Their Excellencies next day at Viceroy's House. The helpful and friendly A.D.C.s were the same but there was now much less formality. H.E. talked to me after lunch. He said that what gave him hope of success with the Indian problem was the memory of the state of affairs when he took over South-East Asia Command. There was lowest priority for everything there. It was impossible at first to persuade the people at home to be interested in the Burma Campaign. It was that lack of interest which had allowed the Americans to put out on the world the myth that *they* drove the Japs out of Burma. Stilwell's part in the whole business was a very minor one. The Chinese fought only one action of the faintest importance, which was at Toungoo during the retreat, and even that was without the least effect upon the situation. There was only one Ameri-

[1] The late General Lord Ismay of Wormington, K.G., G.C.B., C.H., D.S.O.

[2] Sir Eric Mieville, G.C.I.E., K.C.V.O., C.S.I., C.M.G.

[3] Lt.-Colonel Sir Martin Gilliat, K.C.V.O.

[4] Admiral of the Fleet Earl Mountbatten of Burma, K.G., G.C.B., G.C.S.I., G.C.I.E., G.C.V.O., D.S.O.

can brigade involved, and though they managed to capture the Myit-kyina air-strip they were held up for weeks by the Japs in the town itself. The only real help the Americans gave in Burma was in the air, and even that was always liable to be diverted to China. Yet everywhere I went people asked me if I got to Myitkyina as if that was the decisive battleground in Burma. The illusion of an American victory in Burma was helped by the Star on all the transport. Most of the Burmans supposed it to be an American star.

H.E. spoke highly of Nehru who he said had always behaved with complete sincerity and courage. Later I had a longish talk with Lady Mountbatten. She was certainly not sparing herself. The thermometer was already over 105° and she was visiting hospitals, etc., in the heat of the day without any let-up. She said she hoped I was going to devote some attention in my book to the great part played by the women of India in the war. I came away from lunch feeling that if any two people in the Commonwealth could win the affection and respect of the people of India those two could.

We had three or four days with Bill Condon and John Shaw getting all the arrangements in order for our visit first to the North-West Frontier and from there to Nepal. It grew hotter and hotter in Delhi and I began to wonder how any work was done there. I had to put quite a strain on my will power to bring my diary up to date.

Rawalpindi was the next place where we were to stay at Command House with General Messervy. We were disappointed to miss Lady Messervy and her delightful daughter Rosemary whose company we had enjoyed on the voyage out. They had left only a week before we got to Rawalpindi.

The jacaranda trees were even better than those in Delhi. Their flowers on the leafless boughs have the same quality of intensity in lilac-blue as the green of young rice in green. I see them vividly as I write these words.

I drove with Major Conroy (15th Punjabis) to Jhelum to see the regimental centre of the First Punjabis. This was the Auk's old regiment and was as well run as all the other regimental centres. I remember the drive back to Command House as the hottest I ever had. Conroy and I got out of the car like two eggs out of a frying pan.

After dinner we all tried our hands, or rather our mouths, on a six-foot long blowpipe used by the Sakai jungle-tribe in Malaya. Frank Messervy had a powerful blast. I was less successful, but at the second attempt I managed to send what looked like a miniature conductor's bâton against the wall at the far end of the passage.

Frank Messervy was in great form at breakfast, and extremely amusing about the orotund telegrams Winston Churchill used to send to the Auk in Cairo. He must have been a wonderful pick-me-up for his men. The fighting in Keren, Libya, Arakan and Burma all benefited from his presence.

We left Command House to drive the one hundred and six miles to Peshawar. The sun was obscured by haze and we could keep the windows of the car open without having our eyelids seared by what was more like blast than breeze. There was a kind of exhilarating austerity about this road, in which the only colour was in the fields of ripe wheat. The people themselves seldom added coloured stuffs to the prevailing white or faded lavender of their dress.

The crossing of the Indus by the Attock fort was as imaginatively nutritious as it could be. One had not a moment's doubt that it was one of the mighty rivers of history. The ghost of Alexander the Great haunted the place, and the great Attock fort round which the road swept down to the bridge with armed guards at either end seemed rather to have sprung out of those sunbaked rocks than to have been deliberately built. The Pathan War Memorial—a monolith in the shape of a gigantic cartridge—stood above the gorge of the Indus on the far side from Pindi.

Soon after Attock we reached Nowshera, the Regimental Centre of the Sikhs, and I went round to the quarters of the Boys' Company. Most of them were away, and the dozen left were off next day to visit the Commander-in-Chief in Delhi—much elated at the prospect. All those boys' companies were impressive; this and the Mahratta one at Belgaum were outstanding.

After Nowshera the road ran between innumerable orchards of pears which must have looked glorious when in blossom some weeks before. There were apricot orchards, too, and many oleanders, and arbours of pale pink roses. Cypresses were frequent. The landscapes of Arabia seemed to mingle there with those of India. In the haze the wheatfields were tarnished gold, and it was supposed that during the harvest the trouble along the Frontier might abate. We reached Flagstaff House to find that Major-General Ross McCay was expecting us in a plane from Ambala. However, as a buffet lunch for about a dozen people was going on, our unexpected arrival was not a nuisance.

The bazaars at Peshawar were more like the suks of Damascus than the usual Indian bazaar. We wandered up and down Arabian Nights streets, watching the coppersmiths, silversmiths and goldsmiths at work. There were myriads of flies, but the heat of the sun was tempered by the haze. A police wagon full of arrested demonstrators drove by, jovially chanting their Muslim slogans. There was an air of suppressed expectation of bloody events, and the small Hindu minority—only about ten thousand in a city of two hundred thousand—was feeling apprehensive.

For our tour of the North-West Frontier we were to have as our conductor Major Mohammed Yousuf[1] of the 18th Cavalry, to the command of which he would presently succeed. 'Joe' as he soon became, would remain a close friend. We always enjoyed his company when he was High Commissioner for Pakistan and the hospitality of him and his dear wife Zubeida in Avenue Road. Now in 1968 he is Pakistani Ambassador in Kabul.

The road from Peshawar ran for some miles across the wide plain between avenues of casuarina trees. We were in jeeps again because the Mullagori road was no road for staff-cars. The hills toward which we were travelling loomed in a haze of dust, and we had no chance of seeing the high snows beyond. We stopped at a police post and walked up on a parapet which ran round the square courtyard in which the charpoys of the men stood in the sun. In a corner a sentry was standing in the shade of what looked like a flying turret, gazing out toward that frontier whence for centuries the invaders of India had come. He did not expect Greeks nor even Russians then. The fierce tribesmen were the threat. Peshawar was well worth looting.

Not long after leaving the police post the road turned into the hills and we began to wind up through as arid and savage a landscape as one could see. A train of camels met us and seemed inclined to turn round and go back the way they had come. There was much shouting and tugging at ropes and at last they consented to pass the jeeps, with an expression of countenance even more supercilious and disagreeable than usual. We were driving through what was called tribal territory, which meant that one never went off the road. The road itself by a gentleman's agreement was exempt from the active side of a blood feud, and served as a sort of sanctuary for anybody whose enemy was sniping at him from behind a rock.

The policing was done by khussedars who were the equivalent of special constables provided by the tribesmen themselves. They wore a kind of uniform and were paid by us (one might say bribed) to keep quiet. After a mile or so of this savage road we were met by a khussedar with a big henna-dyed beard. The Prophet's beard was red, and it was the fashion for Muslims to dye their beards with henna when the first grey hairs showed and thus proclaim their potency. Punjabi Mussulman V.C.O.s dyed their moustaches instead. The khussedar with his rifle got into the jeep Chrissie was in, and on we drove. Few European women had travelled along that road.

A thousand feet below the road the dark green Kabul river was winding through a mighty gorge, and along one of its banks we could see tunnels. Those were relics of the metre-gauge railway planned by Kitchener and abandoned after a while under pressure from Russia

---

[1] Lt.-General Mohammed Yousuf.

as 'uneconomical'. We should have had a view of the great snow range
of the Hindu Kush and the lowlands of Afghanistan, but the haze
denied it to us, the limit of visibility being about five miles. In a way
the mysterious horizon and shadowy peaks were even more impressive.
There was a brisk wind, but the sun crackled in my ears as we took
hairpin bend after hairpin bend. We reached a fortified village with
adobe walls and watch-towers, where the dogs were large and fierce.
In the cemetery white flags were fluttering and here and there a red
one. White flags blew above the graves of men killed in action in some
tribal blood feud, while the red flag marked the grave of a holy man.
There were one or two blue flags, but Yousuf could not tell me what
those stood for.

About half way to Landikotal we came down to the Arcadian
village of Shilman. Along the banks of a stream flowing over round
grey stones were oleanders of every shade of rose from carmine to blush.
In the fields the wheat and barley glowed with ripeness, and a troop
of tawny dogs came charging at the car. The men of the village were
all carrying rifles. The strath stretched for several miles and at the
end of it we entered the main road leading up the Khyber Pass to
Landikotal. On either side were fortified villages, surrounded by high
adobe walls the colour of *café au lait*, each with a narrow entrance and
a watch-tower. Villages separated by hardly a hundred yards from
one another could be enemies.

It was strange to pass from this landscape of the centuries into the
tree-shaded Landikotal Lines and see 'Whitehall' on a signpost beside
the main entrance. Presently we turned in between iron gates to find
ourselves in what seemed like one of the smaller Oxford colleges. We
walked through into the 'quad', three sides of which were bounded by
the Mess and officers' quarters of the Khyber Rifles, the fourth by a
grey wall overhung by peaches, mulberries and other trees. There
were false-peppers, too, the heady scent of whose bunches of greenish
blossom brought back to me the boulevards of Athens. The lawn in
the middle was as green as an English lawn; the roses were as sweet.
The annual larkspurs were taller and brighter than I had seen them
in gardens at home; the flag-irises were already limp.

Poor Yousuf had to retire to bed after lunch with fever and a bad
throat, so Captain Dance and I drove down the rough winding road
to visit Charbagh Post. It was built beside a perpetual spring and from
time immemorial it was a key position in frontier fighting. The men
of one of Alexander the Great's columns must have watered there.
Outside the gate stood an immense *chinár* tree at least five hundred
years old beneath whose ample shade we sat gratefully beside the great
stone well filled with crystal water. Next to the *chinár* stood a large
white mulberry-tree, the ground strewn with its fruit like dusty pearls.

The figs and mulberries of that part of the world would not have served Adam and Eve, for their leaves are small oblongs and not the sycamore shape we know. The *chinár* is *platanus orientalis* of which our London plane, *platanus acerifolia* (the maple-leafed plane), is a sub-species. The leaves have sharper points than the London planes, and the trunks and branches do not peel so prodigally. In autumn the foliage turns wine-red. The spectacle of that grand tree defying the cruel landscape was magnificent; the grey trunk must have been twelve feet round. It was nothing like as large as the great plane-tree of Cos, but it had the same classic quality.

On the outskirts of Landikotal we passed a caravan, three hundred camels strong, preparing its camp for the night. It was there that Nehru was received with stones and objurgations by a wild mob of tribesmen and the windows of his car were smashed. Those caravans were sometimes over a thousand camels strong, not to mention three times as many small donkeys and numerous goats. Wandering tribes from Afghanistan came down into India every Autumn and returned in Spring.

When we got back to the Mess we found that poor Yousuf had been given an injection of ten grains of quinine for suspected malaria and ordered to stay in bed. So next morning Captain Dance drove us along the great sweep of road to Landikhana, at the head of the Khyber Pass, where we stood against the big notice-board which proclaimed the frontier between India and Afghanistan and were photographed like so many rubber-necked predecessors. Chrissie got too far over to the left and violated the frontier, which much excited the scruffy little Afghan sentry; I thought he was going to stick a bayonet into her. We did not condescend to mount a sentry. The lorries and buses from Kabul were stopped at the Customs house a hundred yards into India. We wandered up the parched slope following the line of the frontier. I asked about a largish building surrounded by trees and was told it was the headquarters of the American engineers who were re-metaling the road to Kabul. American commercial penetration was in evidence all over the East. Much of the American propaganda against British imperialism was the patter of cheapjacks attracting public attention to their own wares.

The parched slope had lots of interesting little rock-plants still in flower. I noticed a non-climbing convolvulus with silver-grey leaves and white flowers which much resembled *Convolvulus cneorum*, that star of the Capri flora. What excited me most was a miniature *arnebia*, which is known as the Prophet's Flower because the five yellow petals have five large chocolate-brown freckles declared by tradition to be the marks of the Prophet's fingers. Those freckles fade away gradually before the yellow flower itself fades. An old Pathan seeing me looking

at it, bent down and picked it and then told in Pushtu the story of how
the Prophet had one day made his ceremonial ablution and touched
the petal with the tips of his fingers and thumb afterwards.

From Landikhana we drove up a hair-raising road to see Big Ben
and Little Ben, which were fortified outposts during the war. The
trenches and the machine-gun bunkers were still there, but they
seemed as desolate as Hadrian's Wall. Below the two small plateaux,
where stunted poppies and thistles were twitching in the breeze among
the sparse herbage, the country surged away into a seeming infinity
of jagged peaks and deep remote glens. Immediately below the outpost
was a green abyss over which a pair of vultures were hovering and
planing—small light-covered vultures known as Pharaoh's Chickens.
A great deal of work was done on the frontier from the time war broke
out until Hitler broke into Russia, and even afterwards. This was the
only part of the world in which we did make a severe effort to prepare
for a possible enemy. If as much could have been done in Burma or
Malaya, what a different story!

I resist the temptation to write more about another wonderful day
which wound up with a *tikala* held by the Subedars and Jemedars, all
in mufti, in honour of Colonel Booth who had re-raised the Khyber
Rifles and was leaving next day to command a Brigade in Waziristan.
A long table was laid in the open and lighted with standard lamps from
the Mess. The British guests were given knives and forks; everybody
else ate with his fingers. When we arrived garlands of sweet white
banksia roses were hung round our necks. Although I ate more roast
mutton than I ever ate before at a single meal, I was reproached for
eating so little; I managed to redeem myself by eating two bowls of
sour curds.

Colonel Booth made his farewell speech and then we all adjourned
to the parade ground where we sat in a circle of at least two thousand
spectators to watch dancing by professionals from Peshawar. The
boys dressed as girls were hardly recognizable as boys.

To our great relief and pleasure Yousuf was well enough to come on
with us when we left the Mess of the Khyber Rifles where everybody
had put himself out to make our visit as fruitful as possible and another
bundle of memories had gone into the rich store amassed during that
wonderful tour.

On our way to Thal we stopped for a while at the entrance of the
Khyber Pass to look at the little room in the ancient Sikh fort of Jamtud.
Here the body of Hari Singh was kept pickled in oil for a week so
that he appeared to be sitting up in control of the situation and thus
the death of their mighty leader would not discourage his men from
resisting the onslaught of the tribesmen. The little room was now a
machine-gun post.

At Kohat the escort provided for the drive to Thal looked strong enough to deal with any martial emergency. We drove through fields of golden wheat and hedgerows of pink roses like miniature Dorothy Perkins ramblers. The orange trumpets of the tecoma trees and the orange-scarlet of pomegranate blooms took the place of the roses from time to time. Quail nets were frequent.

We reached the big fort in Thal after three hours' driving and were welcomed by Brigadier Roche and Major Stephen, his Brigade-Major. Yousuf and I were put up in the Mess, and Chrissie stayed with Major and Mrs Grice whose three brindled great Danes were enough to frighten even a marauding party of Pathans.

Yousuf and I went round the defences. The Valley of the Kurram was considered a likely way in for Russian tanks at first and for German tanks afterwards, so dragon's teeth had been sown all over the place. It was dark before we got back to the Mess and a cocktail party was already gathered on the lawn, where thousands of sparrows, perplexed by the illumination, were fluttering round the jacaranda trees like moths round a lamp. The Dogra pipe-band gave a splendid perform-ance of first-class piping, and when it was over I had the pleasure of drinking a dram with the drum-major (who was a juggling wizard with his staff) and the pipe-major.

During the night a band of Pathans broke through the wire of one of the small piquets round the fort, and before the Sikh sentry could pull out a grenade one of them shot him in the thigh, luckily missing the bone.

We started off soon after eight next morning for Parachinar, up the valley of the Kurram, a wide and fertile strath where the wheat was full golden at the beginning; the deeper we penetrated, the less golden it became, and before we reached Parachinar it was still green. About three-quarters of the way to Parachinar we turned off to the right along a dusty track to visit the Badama or Almond Post on the other side of the Kurbana or Apricot River. This lonely outpost stood at the entrance of the Kurram Pass which winds up into Tirah, a great tract of fertile country between it and the Khyber which was the home of perhaps as many as a hundred thousand Afridi tribesmen all armed with rifles. That small and remote fort was attacked about once a month by the tribesmen in much the same spirit as we might go shooting partridges. War there was essentially a sport.

The Subedar in command invited us to have a cup of tea, and then brought in a cold chicken and various other good things to eat. We protested that we could not tackle a chicken at 10.30 in the morning and then picked every bone clean with our fingers, besides eating a lot of eggs and nuts and slabs of bread baked on a large griddle. It was a pang to leave that little brown fort with the Union Jack fluttering above the rampart and to take a last look at the pass winding mysteriously into the heart of the brooding mountains. We walked to our cars across the sun-bleached yard in front, along which a double line of Persian lilac was in fragrant bloom. A Spitfire was humming high overhead when we turned back into the main road, and presently we saw the tribal plane tree—the *para chinár* which gave the place its name. Alas, the ancient tree looked like expiring of antiquity in spite of having been dosed with the bodies of twenty bullocks to revive its vigour.

How can I bring to the printed page Parachinar itself? The hexameters of Theocritus are demanded. The delightful house of Colonel Leeper, the Political Agent, was surrounded by lawns as green as any in Oxford. Bowers of honey-coloured banksia roses were everywhere. The wistaria racemes had not yet fallen on one side of the house and next it the single white rose known as the Rose of Mardan was in full perfection. The leaves of the daffodils were turning yellow, and the little tulips in the grass had set their seeds, but the irises were still in flower. We rested between a spreading *chinár* where on occasion Leeper dispensed justice at what resembled our land-courts in the Hebrides. Then we went on to lunch at the Mess of the Kurram Militia, the cosiest small Mess imaginable. There was an admirable library of at least a thousand volumes—rich in books of travel and history. We had a lunch to which I should like to apply an epithet of my youth and call 'spiffing'. They had so much asparagus that they even curry it. And spring onions as large and lustrous as Roman pearls in an enormous bowl!

After lunch we drove out to two or three Frontier posts. We stopped at Ali Mangat and gazed at the Safed Koh, the range of snowy mountains which presided over the plain round Parachinar as Taygetus, the line of which it resembled, presides over the plain of Sparta. On the way we passed groves of fruit-trees. They were planted long ago by Lord Roberts who intended to build a Residency there. It was Roberts who 'annexed' Parachinar. The residency was never built; its garden is a wilderness.

After seeing the Pathans I was certain the British Israelites were wasting time and money, and what was worse in those days, paper, in trying to prove that the lost tribes were to be found in Britain. The Pathans seemed like Jews unspoilt by urban life. Leeper said it was the custom to proclaim from the house-top the birth of a male child, and significantly to prolong the celebration of the Muslim Friday through Saturday with lighted candles. It is much more probable that the Jewish tribes were dispersed from Palestine by Nebuchadnezzar eastward, and the Afghan tradition of being descended from Saul may well have a Palestinian origin. There is also the Yusufzai tribe which definitely claims to be the children of Joseph. Their young men wore the side-curls, which are a characteristic of the Jews as far west as the ghettos of Poland.

We drove back to Parachinar and picked up our escort to return to Thal after a day of absorbing interest. When I looked out of the window of my room about half-past six I saw the Dogra drum-major rehearsing twirls with his staff on the lawn under the jacaranda trees. Evidently a real artist.

Yousuf and I started off early in a jeep driven by Major Stephen, the Brigade Major, to see Fort Lockhart. I hesitate to call the road up to Fort Lockhart—a six thousand feet climb—the most dizzy of all those we tackled, but there was one stretch of fifty yards where the road was built out on girders over an abyss about two thousand feet deep, and that was a bit of a tester for weak heads. Fort Lockhart stood on a ridge overlooking a vast stretch of mountains. I climbed to the top of a wooden platform by a rickety ladder and enjoyed a sublime view. Not far away was a memorial to nineteen men and two cookboys of the 36th Sikhs (later the 4/11th) who in 1897 defended a blockhouse against seven thousand Orakzais and died to a man before they could be relieved.

When we drove down again we transferred to a staff-car and went on to Kohat. Brigadier Parker had invited two Indian officers and their wives to lunch. The two wives, one a Hindu in a delicious sari and the other a Muslim in equally delicious trousers of white satin, were both lovely girls and moreover extremely good talkers, full of humour. I should have liked to stay talking to them for the rest of the afternoon, but as usual we had to hurry on.

That evening in Peshawar we were watching the Retreat of the 2/1st Gurkhas when a violent dust storm blew up and the electric light failed. I had promised to go to a Sergeants' Social in the Mess of the K.O.S.B.s. The oil lamps and motionless fans made it so hot that I thought I was going to pass out. Then the Colonel asked me to say a few words and I managed to pull myself together.

We left Peshawar on a blazing hot morning on the way to Malakand. Buses crowded with Muslims waving green flags and shouting slogans were coming into Peshawar from every direction in order to demonstrate to the Viceroy the solidity and fervour of Pakistan. Sixty thousand were expected to muster next day, but serious trouble was not expected. The demonstrators all looked extremely cheerful and the question at issue might just as easily have been the victory of a football team as the partition of a country. It was a relief to enter the Malakand Gate and start climbing out of the torrid lowland.

Malakand itself stood on a more or less conical hill with a superb view across a rich river-watered vale to the mountains of Chitral. This country was the scene of Winston Churchill's first book, *With the*

H

Malakand Field Force. Lt.-Colonel Evelyn Cobb, the Political Agent, with whom we were staying for the night, was keen on flowers and made my mouth water by describing a hillside of white eremurus in March. They would be *E. himalaicus*, I suppose. The asphodels are a wonderful lot, from the sweet golden bog-asphodel of the Highlands, hardly four inches high to those twelve-foot fellows defying Everest and Kanchenjunga. Our daffodils were originally 'affodils', which was a variant of 'asphodels'.

The drive to Yousuf's house in Risalpur was a griller, and there we enjoyed an altogether delightful lunch very much *en famille*. We met for the first time Begum Zubeida, his wife, who was to become a dear friend. We met, too, Yousuf's distinguished old father Shawbat Khan who had just come back from the Assembly. I was much amused by the ascetic air with which Yousuf declined a cocktail before lunch and presently made an excuse to go out of the room for a moment in order to gulp one down outside in the passage where his father could not see him. After lunch he kept going out to take quick puffs at a cigarette out of his father's sight. The house was full of children, Zubeida's and the twin sons of his sister-in-law, as handsome a young woman as I ever saw. She was the wife of Yousuf's brother the late Major Afridi, the malaria expert. I still have a souvenir of that happy gathering in a pre-revolution Russian plate which Zubeida gave to Chrissie.

On our way through Nowshera to Abbotabad we left Gulaba at the railway-station whence he had to go on to Delhi with our luggage. He had a fearful journey. The train was swarming with Muslim Leaguers. When asked if he was a Hindu he always vowed he was a Christian, and this possibly saved his life. Poor Gulaba, he had had a nervous experience on the Frontier.

We had a busy time in Abbotabad which was founded nearly a century ago and built to look like a village in the Home Counties with a Stoke Poges Church and all. Now it was a largish place and militantly Muslim.

On the second evening I dined with the 6th Gurkhas at their Regimental Centre of which Colonel Eustace was Commandant. The Mess was a grand room alive with history. After dinner we adjourned to the lines where we were joined by the ladies and saw some dancing. I was much amused to watch the faces of the Regiment's wives watching their men made up and dressed as women. They were splendid actors. It is strange that one of the most martial races in the world should be able to simulate femininity with such success. We sat at a long narrow table facing the arena, and the dancing was as good as the piping at dinner. Before I left, Colonel Eustace on behalf of the Centre presented me with a kukri with a decorative scabbard.

We left Abbotabad next morning at nine o'clock, making a circuit to avoid driving through a Muslim League meeting. In the paper I read of a bomb thrown and several shots fired at Flagstaff House, Peshawar, on the night after we left. I was a little disappointed we had missed that excitement. We were warned that there might be trouble in Haripur where a Muslim house had been burnt. It had obviously been accidental, but of course the Muslims were accusing the Hindus of having done it on the evidence of an empty petrol tin in the vicinity. Just before we reached Haripur the horn of our car after starting to hoot on its own without stopping, refused to hoot at all when checked, and we had to send the station-waggon in front to avoid an accident in the thronged streets. Fortunately the horn agreed to behave itself after we left Haripur. The drive on to Rawalpindi was a sizzler and we were glad to reach Command House.

We caught the plane for Delhi after a sad farewell with Joseph whose company we were going to miss. Ten years later when Major Yousuf was Lt.-General Yousuf and High Commissioner for Pakistan he introduced me to President Ayub Khan[1] who much impressed me. He, too, was a product of Sandhurst. He asked me why I did not suggest to the B.B.C. a series about the North-West Frontier.

"We'll give you transport and escort, and Joseph shall have leave to go with you."

I put this up to the B.B.C. but it was considered too expensive a proposition, to which a question was added.

"And are people interested in Kipling any longer?"

At Delhi we were met by John Shaw and Peter Goodwin who was to come with us to Nepal and take some of his splendid photographs. I had a longish talk with the Chief that night and it was nearly one o'clock when I went up to bed. I was half undressed when what I thought was a Sherman tank seemed to rumble past. It was an earthquake shock which lasted twenty seconds. The walls of the room vibrated but I did not feel any rocking. Captain Govind Singh, one of the Chief's A.D.C.s had just gone to bed after a party and saw his boots slowly walking along a shelf. He blinked, and then three pairs of polo boots on the shelf above began to walk about. This was too much for him and he went out of his room to seek advice. He was relieved to find that it was only an earthquake shock. Chrissie pointed out it was like the rumble of a V.2; she was right.

Next morning we had a comfortable flight to Bihta. The Area Commander was away, but we were met by Lt.-Colonel Miles Hoffmann and Colonel Chandler and after lunch drove on to Patna where we had our first sight of the Ganges. Patna was the sprawling seething

[1] General Mohammed Ayub Khan.

city where Mahatma Gandhi lived. Two Ducks were waiting to take us across the Ganges and as we went down the sandy bank I was reminded of old lifeboat launchings when the crews were practising during the summer holidays. The Ducks made a good deal of noise, but we sat in stately comfort in wicker armchairs. The mighty river stretched in a pale green expanse of water under the burning silver sunshine of the heat-hazed afternoon. Seven bloated vultures sat in a row on the farther bank while terns wheeled and darted and dived about us. They were the extremes of avian ugliness and grace. We saw the burning fires of cremation along the banks on the Patna side. After a while we overtook the ferry-steamer crowded with passengers, and in about half an hour reached the sandy slope below the railway station of Paleza Ghat. An unbroken stream of people from the train, many of them in vivid sulphur yellow, were toiling across the wide sandy slope to the ferry-steamer, and when we were almost at the top of this slope one of the Ducks jibbed. However, its companion came to the rescue with a kick in the rump and the summit was achieved.

A muddle had been made about our coach. We were supposed to have had the one that was meeting a mission returning from Nepal. The coach we were given was filthy and crawling with cockroaches. A great block of ice in the middle of the floor was making pools of dirty water. Colonel Hoffman argued in vain with the station-master that a mistake had been made and that the other coach was for us. Nothing could be done and, as it was fast growing dark by now, he had to leave us and get back to the Ducks.

The train crawled along to Muzzaffarpur where our coach was detached and shunted about to be attached to another train. The electric current was cut off, and we had to eat our dinner in darkness. At last we were hitched on to the next train; to our relief the light came on and one fan began to whizz round. We were all pretty tired and were glad to get into our berths, even if every time one lifted a pillow a couple of cockroaches ran out. Suddenly Chrissie gave a yell; she had been bitten on the finger by something, it turned out to be a yellow wasp that had got involved with the fan and had been flung on to her hand on which it took revenge. It was a nightmare journey. We hung about being shunted around at Segauli for over two hours. The metre-gauge train vibrated and jolted so much that sleep was out of the question, and when we arrived at Raxaul an hour and a half later we were exhausted.

We were met by the Overseer of the Legation Bungalow and walked along the railway line to it for about a mile. We lay down to sleep for the rest of that hot morning in the wired verandah. A great golden mohur in full bloom (*poinceana regia*) was a lovely sight but the heat was relentless until eight o'clock when it cooled off slightly.

Next morning we set out for the Nepalese railway station, which was next to the other one, and we found that we should have the state coach, a welcome contrast to the one in which we had travelled from Paleza Ghat. There were two comfortable armchairs and even a writing bureau, above which was inscribed "Long Live our Maharaja". The train was almost a miniature drawn by a small engine with a crimson cow-catcher built at Avonside, and it was crowded. The Nepal frontier was marked by a small stream just beyond the railway-station. We left Raxaul at half-past seven for the journey through the Terai to Amlekhganj, a journey of only thirty miles but it took three and a half hours to accomplish. There were many Gurkhas going home, most of whom had umbrellas, which they carried hitched from the back of their battle-blouses, and new hurricane lamps. They were the two gifts that the women at home demanded from their warriors. Money-changers with heaps of Nepalese silver coins in front of them were sitting on the platform. The Nepalese rupee was worth slightly more than the Indian rupee. The local band dressed in yellow-frogged tunics and hussar busbies with orange bags was playing *con brio*.

A storm was gathering in the north, and before we reached Parwanipur it was sweeping across the paddy fields in mingled rain and dust. Vivid mauve flashes of lightning at least five miles long rent the livid sky horizontally. Bullock-carts were galloping along the track beside the train rather faster than the train itself. After Parwanipur the storm showed signs of clearing. The hills appeared ahead of us under a pearly blue stretch of sky beneath a monotonous weight of grey cloud; by the time we reached the banyan-shaded station of Simra the sun was shining. We ate our lunch there, and presently the little train went jogging deep into the jungle of the Terai at about three miles an hour; from time to time branches touched the windows. That jungle was one of the most noted big-game haunts in all the East. Tigers abounded. The Terai and the Assam jungles were the last refuge of the great Indian rhinoceros. It was also one of the most fever-stricken stretches anywhere. The *awa*, a very vicious malaria, made it impossible for sport from the end of April to the end of October.

When I was in Rome in 1916 Sir Vivien Gabriel[1] who had been on special service in Nepal eight years earlier and was Secretary of the Coronation Durbar, told me that the Maharaja of Nepal had had a glade cut through the jungle which was lighted by torch-bearers on either side so that the Nepalese cavalcade returning from the Durbar could ride through at night to the foot of their mountains. It was that picture conjured up by Gabriel over a dinner-table in Rome thirty-one years before which fired me with a desire to see Nepal. The railway

[1] The late Colonel Sir Vivien Gabriel, G.C.S.I.

was only twenty years old. Before that everybody had to ride through the Terai to reach Nepal.

It was close on noon when we arrived at Amlekhganj. The mail bus was overflowing with passengers and luggage before our own luggage was out of the train. A Havildar of the R.I.A.S.C. who had a lorry for the returning Gurkhas offered us a lift. A Jemadar from the Airborne Division came along beaming to say he had shaken hands with me in Karachi.

The thirty-two mile drive to Bhimpedi was without doubt the bumpiest we had had during that tour and that's saying a lot. Chrissie and I sat beside the Havildar in front. Peter Goodwin and Gulaba stood holding on behind. The Havildar, who had been through the Burma campaign, kept pointing to the bare precipices towering above the lush vegetation and exclaiming 'Burma! Burma!' He was right about the comparison. The road climbed slowly all the way up from Amlekhganj and at Churia we came to a tunnel a quarter of a mile long through the rock. About fifty yards before the end it took a sharp turn and the weight of the rock was supported by twelve-inch rafters and posts. We were glad to reach the end of that wild drive and get out of the lorry at Bhimpedi, 3,650 ft. up, where we were followed by a crowd of children in any direction we went. There were no coolies or ponies or dandies, and while Peter Goodwin rushed around trying to find out where they were I meditated on the possibility of obtaining accommodation for the night in that swarming village.

Presently, the transport which had been waiting at the other end of the village, arrived. Chrissie entered a large black dandy with a hood and was hoisted on the shoulders of eight coolies. I entered a smaller dandy the shape of half a canoe and was hoisted on the shoulders of four coolies, with a relay of two. Peter Goodwin mounted a pony and off we went. We crossed the grey rocky bed of a river and ascended a precipitous mountainside in a series of loops four miles in all to the Maharaja's rest house at Sirsagarhi. We arrived at the rest house at half-past five and sat down to a high tea as soon as Gulaba could brew the tea.

The electric aerial ropeway from beyond Bhimpedi to Katmandu was a fascinating sight. One played with the notion of being strapped into what looked rather like chairs and making the journey which was made by so many packages. Yet to travel over abysses two thousand feet deep from ridge to ridge suspended from a couple of small wheels running along a wire might have been just a little too exciting.

In the early hours of next morning I woke to hear wind and heavy rain but by sunrise all was clear, and we set out on the last stage of our journey at seven o'clock with a cool breeze. The cloud effects were grand. All along the valley thousands of what one could call marbled black butterflies were dancing around the pomegranates and white roses and the candelabra cactus which were used down that warm valley for hedges.

We crossed the Markhu river and had a stiff climb up on the other side through the pass of Chisapani Garhi (over 6,000 feet) after which we proceeded through rolling downland for several miles, high above a rapid narrow river running through a wooded gorge. The steep slopes on the other side were terraced to the summit and beyond the grassy downland the cultivation was equally widespread. About one o'clock we stopped and ate lunch under a tree I could not name. Soon after we started again I recognized with pleasure some shrubs of *berberis nepalensis* which I used to grow in Cornwall. The leaves are of the mahonia type with yellow lily-of-the-valley-like clusters sweetly scented, and blossoming at home in early February. I noticed also what was probably *buddleia asiatica*. The white roses I had seen in the valley had proved to be *rosa moschata* with an exquisite scent. I saw, too, *rosa sericea*, which is a very small white rose whose beauty is in its fruit. A Chinese variety of this called *rosa sericea pteracantha* has large thorns like cornelians which if planted to catch the setting sun shining through them is one of the loveliest sights a garden can show. The grass beside the track was starred with what I was told was a miniature gentian, though the flowers were more like a *lithospermum*, and the shade was the same as that garden favourite 'Heavenly Blue'.

We reached the village of Chitlong at the foot of the Chandragiri Pass where we rested beside a small stream thick with watercress while the coolies got themselves tea. We could hardly believe that we could ascend the rampart of mountain in front of us which rose to seven thousand feet. The track up looked perpendicular. Over to the left a gash down the mountainside was pointed out as the elephant track. Our own track was strewn with small boulders and loose rocks. The strain on the coolies was painful; I felt ashamed of having to be carried.

The vegetation was beautiful. I noticed *rhododendron arboreum* and *rhododendron Thomsoni*, and I thought *rhododendron campylocarpum*. Alas, only a few scattered rubies still adorned the boughs, for their flowering season was over. We were too early for those lovely lilies, *Nepalensis* and *Wallichianum*. Cassias were in bloom, and another yellow-flowered tree I could not name. I saw also a tall scraggy hydrangea with rosy-buff flowers of the *paniculata* type which has a cluster of sterile incomplete flowers in the middle; I forget the technical botanical name for this arrangement. I looked through a list of Nepalese flora and found that three hydrangeas are indigenous—*anomala*, *aspera* and *vestiva*. I fancied the rosy-buff one must be *anomala*; I should learn that I was wrong. Many of the trees were draped with *clematis montana* at the peak of its blossoming—an exquisite sight. I saw a *viburnum* of sorts and what looked to me like *cornus capitata*. There were ferns in great variety and plenty of ilex.

From the top of Chandragiri we beheld the great valley of Katmandu, and Katmandu itself below us, but we were not granted the view of the Himalaya beyond. The equally precipitous descent of Chandragiri to Thankot, seventeen-hundred feet below, was of marvellous beauty. The vegetation was much more luxuriant on the northerly side, and the variety of greens seemed infinitive. The golden light of afternoon was falling slantwise, and the birdsong was continuous. Yet I actually saw only two birds—a tit and a large falcon hovering over the great punchbowl of greenery. Just before Thankot we passed a small stupa. That country, sacred to the memory of Gautama Buddha who was born in Nepal, was now predominantly Hindu in religion, but there were still many Buddhist temples and the two religions both took something from the other, nor did their worshippers quarrel.

At Thankot we got out of our dandies and into the Legation car which was waiting to drive us the nine miles from Thankot to Katmandu, along a road lined on either side with crimson bottlebrush trees and grevilleas in full faded-orange bloom. Somebody with a taste for Australian flora must have been influential in Katmandu once upon a time. Poor Gulaba's feet were much blistered by the seventeen-mile tramp. He attributed it to not wearing 'shocks'. I had tried to make him ride, but he always declined and it transpired later that he had twice been thrown off ponies in the past.

Lt.-Colonel George Falconer[1] the Minister welcomed us at the Legation, which had only recently been erected. It was not beautiful and like most modern houses did not look really lived in. After tea next day Peter Goodwin, Chrissie and I drove along to the Balajiri Garden. In a pond on a flagged terrace a large image of Narain— a manifestation of Vishnu—lay on its back in the water. It was put there for the King to visit because for some reason or other he was not allowed to visit the much larger Narain at a place near Katmandu. At this date the King was a figurehead and took no active part as a ruler, all power being in the hands of the Prime Minister who had the title of Highness and Maharaja. The Rana family were Rajputs not Gurkhas. His Highness was Sir Padma Sham Shere Jung Rana Bahadur.

Accompanied by an officer of the Nepalese army we went to explore Katmandu next morning. The first place we visited was the official residence of the Maharaja who did not actually live in it, preferring to remain in the house he had before he succeeded his cousin. It was

[1] Lt.-Colonel Sir George Falconer, K.B.E.

a large place with a profusion of tiles and marble, the latter quarried locally, a pinkish mauve in colour. The walls of the staircase leading up to the Durbar Hall were covered with paintings of a tiger hunt; the anteroom was lined with a dozen distorting mirrors, each of which transformed the spectator into a new grotesque shape. A crystal fountain played in the middle of the Hall at the end of which were two crimson thrones. Beyond it was a pink drawing-room of the late 'nineties with cosy corners and plush and silver photograph frames. The second Durbar Hall in another building was more impressive. A large gold and crimson carpet stretched in front of the thrones which were guarded by two metal leogryphs which at solemn functions were lighted internally and exhaled fiery breath. There were paintings all round of the Rana family, most of them Generals. The King's Durbar Hall, which we visited next was much smaller than either of the Maharajas, but it was surprisingly adorned by two large Winterhalter portraits of Queen Victoria and the Prince Consort—the Queen beside the throne, Prince Albert beside the door—separated by the usual portraits of Maharajas and Generals.

Having been shown those three examples of consciously magnificent modernity, we were free to explore the old Durbar Square, most of the buildings in which dated from the fifteenth to the seventeenth century. Many weeks would be needed to explore that phantasmagoria thoroughly enough to do even faint justice to it. A hurried walk round followed everywhere by a crowd of about two hundred people did not allow us to contemplate the details of the carved wood and ivory with which every house was covered.

There were temples everywhere. I recall most vividly the five-storeyed Temple of Talegu with its gilded Chinese-like roofs. It was opened only once a year when there was a procession of all the women of the ruling house to the shrine of Talegu, who as far as I could gather was another manifestation of the Goddess Kali. No men were permitted to enter this temple, and up on the balcony of the second storey we could see the female guardian of the place walking round. I recall the great bell in the middle of the square and near it two enormous kettle-drums, at least six feet across and six feet high, which once upon a time sounded the alarm. They now stood leaning against either side of a dim alcove. I recall the image of Hanuman, the crimson-faced monkey-god in a crimson robe who stood by an archway leading into the Court of Silence at the back of the old Royal Palace. The Court of Silence was surrounded by the apartments of distant relatives of the Royal Family with carved and fretted windows.

Back at the Legation I found a telegram written on paper made from the bark of a *daphne* or *edgworthia*. It was very thin and pale cinnamon in colour. The telegram was an enquiry from an American

publisher about the prospect of my being willing to write a life of
Winston Churchill.

Next day was devoted to exploring Patan, the second of the three
cities in the valley and practically joined to Katmandu. In some ways
the Durbar Square was even more impressive than that in Katmandu,
but the smells from the open drain running down the street were a
pretty tough proposition for the unfamiliar nose. There seemed to be
more children following us about than ever. They enjoyed standing
by the car and laughing at the reflection of themselves in the enamel.
I admired as much as anything the Machendranath, a temple standing
in a grass courtyard and overlooked by a row of ancient red brick
houses. It dated back to A.D. 1400. There was kept the image which
was carried in procession in the Machendra-jitra car to bring rain for
the harvest. No building in Patan was allowed to be higher than
that car. There are four stupas in Patan over two thousand years old:
but the amount to look at in a brief visit was so overwhelming that I
managed to record almost nothing.

On May 9th we drove to see Boddhnath which was a gigantic white
stupa over a thousand years old. It was at least four hundred yards
round and on each side of the *toran* or gilded tower which rose from
that mass of masonry were two enamelled blue eyes with a note of
interrogation to represent the nose; of course, it was not a note of
interrogation in any Eastern script. Those great eyes have gazed out
north, south, east and west for over a thousand years, although no
doubt the gilding and the blue enamel have been renewed from time
to time. That those eyes should have been gazing there since the time
of Alfred the Great is something for the imagination to ponder. The
stupa was surrounded by prayer-wheels, being a much venerated place
of pilgrimage for Tibetans who braved the snowy passes of the Himalaya
to reach that holy place. Notices in Tibetan hung outside the stairway
which led to the lustral path round the tower. The stupa was surrounded
by a road and a circle of houses curiously modern in appearance. One
of those was occupied by the Lamasery which we were allowed to enter.

From the stupa of Boddhnath we went on to Pashpatti. This was
one of the most celebrated Hindu places of pilgrimage. Steps led down
to the sacred river Bagmatti to which the dying were brought that the
stream might lave their feet in the last agony. Then the corpses were
burnt. One was being burnt when we arrived. Only Hindus were
allowed in the precincts of the temple, and a part of the steps down
the bank was reserved for moribund royalty. We crossed a stone bridge
and walked up among the trees of the opposite bank to a terrace
which gave a good view of the temple. I was disappointed to find that
so many of the roofs were of corrugated iron, but we were told that
that had been done as a protection against the sacred monkeys who

enjoyed throwing tiles at the pilgrims. The monkeys were all over the place, all of them with short tails.

We wound up the morning by visiting the museum. One room in the museum was devoted to the clothes of the predecessor of the current Maharaja. They included his uniforms, his helmets, the insignia of all his orders, and a pair of dress-shirts. The insignia included The Most Glorious Order of Rajunga, The Most Refulgent Order of the Star of Nepal, The Most Illustrious Order of the Tri-Shakti-Patti and The Most Puissant Order of Gurkha Right Hand. In a special case was the magnificent brocaded cloak of the Chinese Order of the Sacred Tripod. The succession was from brother to brother and then to the eldest son of the oldest brother. It was a bit complicated for a stranger to follow. Another snag was that various members of the Rana House arranged and spelt their names with a slight difference.

After lunch we went to call on General Sir Baber Shum Shere Jung Bahadur Rana who commanded the Nepalese contingent in the Victory March. He was a shrewd man with charming manners. His two sons were there, one of whom Mrigenda Shum Shere, was in charge of State Education, with obviously a fine brain. He said the idea that Gurkha soldiers would not serve under Indian officers was ridiculous. He also said that in Nepal they did not like calling the proposed Gurkha Division for the British Army Imperial troops. They would have preferred them to be called Commonwealth troops. I was interested to find anti-imperialism already strong with the younger generation in that feudal state.

Later we called upon the commander-in-chief of the Nepalese Army. He was next in succession as Maharaja. Finally we were received by H.H. the Maharaja himself. He was an impressive personality and was interested to find that he was only three weeks older than myself. He shook his head and said that in his country they were always ten years older for their age than we were. He asked me many questions about the likelihood of war in the near future, discussed the future of India and said that we had been too late in giving much to avoid giving all. Then he talked about the Government at home and was obviously amazed when I told him that unless there was an economic cataclysm not only would it last its full period but would probably be returned again in 1950. At that moment General Baber came into the room, and turning to him His Highness exclaimed,

"This is quite different from what we have been told."

However, he was clearly impressed by my conviction and said I must meet General Sir Kaiser Shumsher who was leaving to take up his diplomatic post in London soon.

The conversation with His Highness lasted for more than an hour and a quarter, and by the time it was over the room was full of people sitting round listening. If ever he was in difficulty with any of my replies he turned to his Personal Secretary, a son of General Mohun, who struck me as another acutely intelligent young man. I thanked His Highness for according me the privilege of visiting Nepal and expressed a wish to come back some day and study the flora. He assured me I should always be welcome and presented me with his photograph as Colonel-in-Chief of a Gurkha regiment and also a kukri in a silver-mounted scabbard. Before we parted I recall one remark he made was that we English had always been too 'superior' with the Indians, 'though never with us', he added quickly. Then he asked if it was true that somewhere in the Bible the last war had been prophesied in detail.

On our way back to the Legation we had the good fortune to be suddenly granted a view of the high snows of the Himalaya, which were hardly ever visible at this time of year. That view I beheld twenty-one years ago but it is as vivid as if I had seen it twenty-one minutes ago. We drove out to Swayambhanath, a Buddhist sanctuary on the top of a hill some miles from Katmandu. Here the eyes were grey-blue and black, with again that note of interrogation instead of a nose. A man in a red coat was taking round offerings on silver dishes to each shrine in turn, opening the trim lattice door and chanting some prayers. Pilgrims were walking round swinging the prayer-wheels, and it was evidently a resort for pious holiday-makers. All the little girls were in their best clothes. One little girl in vivid magenta was made up with lipstick and mascara. Babies had their eyes darkened with mascara, and even the cheeks of the little boys were rouged. Monkeys were climbing and running round everywhere, and as we left the hill-top we passed a house in which women were keening round the body of a man who had just died. We passed some elephant stables and went in to watch two of them having their evening meal. The large courtyard had about eight circular paved floors sloping gently down round a bulky tree-trunk post to which the elephant was tethered by a powerful cable from his front legs which were chained close together. Bundles of coarse grass were put down in front of the elephants which picked them up with their trunks and after thrashing them against their flanks to get rid of the seeds, masticated them ponderously, swaying slowly the while. The massive creatures were also given roots that looked like swedes, which they chewed up noisily with obvious relish.

When a wild elephant is trapped and proves difficult to tame, one of the syces tortures it for a week or two, brutally enough. Then another syce comes along, drives the elephant's tormentor away and treats it kindly. The elephant in gratitude to its rescuer allows itself to be trained for service by him. But let the syce who tortured it keep out of its way in future. Twenty years later that elephant will remember him, and woe betide him if he come within reach of that avenging trunk.

On the morning after, we visited the Zoo where a military function was in progress on the great green and absolutely level parade ground. Yet what I recall most vividly, although it was not entered in my diary, was a cage in which was a captive gibbon ape. There was absolutely nothing in the cage except a concrete floor and the unhappy animal was running round and round in what was obviously despair for the jungle from which it had been taken. I am still haunted by the expression in that gibbon's eyes.

In the afternoon we were driven to Bhatgaon, the third of the cities in the valley, seven or eight miles from Katmandu. Perhaps it was the most beautiful of the three. One temple was reached by a long flight of steps guarded at the bottom by Jaya Malla and Phatta, two local heroes with huge black walrus moustaches. Above them were two elephants ten times as strong as the heroes. Above the elephants two lions, ten times as strong again. Above the lions two dragons ten times as strong as the lions. Finally, above them were Baghini and Singhini, the tiger-goddess and lion-goddess, who were ten times as strong as all the others put together. The images were attractively painted. Indeed, the colouring of Bhatgaon was richer everywhere than either of its rivals, and the golden dome was unique. I shall not try to describe any more of those Arabian Nights places. They require months of close study because so much of their beauty lies in the pre-Raphaelite detailed decoration. Impressionistic writing does not convey the effect.

I am grateful to the good fortune which allowed me to wander round that forbidden city before it became as easy for tourists to visit as the Costa Brava. During the last fifty years only about two hundred Europeans and Americans had visited Nepal, and hardly a dozen British women. That same good fortune allowed me to travel in Spain and Morocco before the internal, or rather infernal combustion engine was invented.

On May 12th we left the Legation for Thankot on our way back to the present. We had the same dandies and several of the coolies who brought us to Thankot. The lucent various greens of the wooded heights of Chandragiri were even more lovely in the light of the morning than when we came down a week before. The birdsong too was equally rich. I could not enjoy the wonderful scene to the full because I was all the while too acutely aware of the strain upon the coolies of this long steep ascent. Some of the bends in the track were almost perpendicular. I saw a biggish white labiate which may have been *leonotis nepetifolia*. I had missed *piptanthus Nepalensis* on the way coming in, but I spotted two smallish trees of it on the return journey. It is a tree which finds its way into almost every nurseryman's catalogue. The flowers are yellow of the laburnum type and the foliage is a lustrous dark green. It strikes easily and stands up to our climate fairly well. Yet, in spite of its usually being obtainable, one seldom sees it in gardens.

We took our last view of the smiling vale of Katmandu from the top of Chandragiri, and the precipitous descent began. As we were going down a steep track to the valley of the Markhu we met a large herd of water-buffaloes coming up, and when we had nearly been tilted out of the dandies the coolies took another track across a very lively and narrow suspension bridge, which brought us through the valley on the other side and gave us some fine fresh views. There were several of those suspension bridges, each one more lively than the last, and they were built by John Henderson of Aberdeen. On the way up the last steep ascent we met women coming down with great bundles of foliage—a large shining oval leaf which I could not identify. They looked exactly like bushes walking along, for one could not see the bent woman underneath. Little girls equally invisible under smaller heaps were accompanying their mothers and elder sisters. It was a fascinating sight. Other women passed with white orchids in their hair.

At the top of the pass we got out of the dandies and walked what was supposed to be the last mile to Sirsagarhi, it was a longer and rougher mile than we expected. We met Gurkhas coming home, upward bound on the way to their resting place for the night. A Havildar of the 5th Royal Gurkhas stopped and spoke to us in excellent English. He was going home to be a schoolmaster.

"We must keep up the name of the 5th Royal Gurkhas," he said.

We reached the rest-house at seven o'clock. Gulaba, who was not quite so tired as on the way in, prepared our meal. Peter Goodwin had given him a pair of his own 'shocks' to wear. He had left Katmandu earlier than we did, and so had had more time to rest on the road. He had been much shaken by the food the coolies ate.

"Dirty food cooked a fortnight old, and dirty fingers, Miss Sahib, never can I see such a thing when I am travelling all this time with Master. I am never seeing such food in all my life."

And with an expression of disgust he shook his head.

Early of an exquisite morning we were away from Sirsagarhi, and the descent through the pines (*excelsa* and *longifolia*) was aromatic. I walked the first mile, but the track was not nearly so steep down to Bhimpedi, and the coolies had had a night's rest. So I could sit back in the dandy and enjoy the scene with a clear conscience. We passed several clumps of terrestrial orchids with small yellow flowers surrounded by pink bracts. At Bhimpedi we were met by one of the R.I.A.S.C. lorries. We put Gulaba in front and we sat on our bedding rolls, clinging to the side of the lorry. We nearly had a head-on crash with another lorry which came sweeping round a corner without hooting. I noticed many frangipani trees in flower along the road, and by far the largest *piptanthus Nepalensis* I had seen anywhere. It was not in flower, but the great head of lustrous green foliage was beautiful.

A quarter of a mile before we reached Amlekhganj we stopped at the R.I.A.S.C. camp. Our Havildar friend Karam Ellahi, a Punjabi Mussulman of Cambellpore, had put clean coverlets on the four charpoys in the tents and clean covers on the pillows worked by his sister in sampler style. He gave us glasses of what was called sherbet but tasted like sugar and water. Havildar Karam Ellahi had fever on him badly but the four R.I.A.S.C. chaps had no mepacrine or quinine, and the civilian doctor would do nothing for them. The Havildar who was only twenty-three was depressed because if he wanted to stay in the army he would have to lose his stripes and become a sepoy again. Round that part was as bad a malarious country as anywhere. The heat was intense and supplies were hard to come by. Nobody could have been more hospitable than the four Army Service Corps Indians in their arid, sun-stricken, dusty, malarious camp. They had adopted a Nepalese orphan boy who stared at the chip I gave him in recognition of his accomplished waiting at table as Aladdin may have stared at the treasure he discovered. Presently, a lorry bound for Bhimpedi stopped and Colonel Eustace who had given us such a grand evening with the 6th Gurkhas in Abbotabad came into the tent. He had had a foul journey with six changes, and sixteen people in the first-class compartment he entered at Lucknow. Travelling across India was no joke. However, he evidently thought a visit to Nepal was worth all the discomfort of getting there.

When he went jolting on to Bhimpedi we drove to the railway station. No Maharaja's coach, and the compartment without a fan was hellish hot. A man died of cholera on the platform while we were waiting. The journey through the jungle was blazing and we were thankful to reach Raxaul, where we were met by the Legation Overseer with the glad news that the General Manager of the railway had sent his own coach for us and that we could board it right away and dine there without going to the Legation bungalow. The coach was completely de luxe. Two bathrooms, armchairs, plenty of light and all the fans working. The only thing to worry about was whether we would reach Paleza Ghat in time to meet Lt.-General Francis Tuker[1] on the Bihta airstrip who was to pick us up there in his plane and take us on to Dehra Dun.

We were two hours late in reaching Muzuffapur and it began to

[1] The late Lt.-General Sir Francis Tuker, K.C.I.E., C.B., D.S.O.

look as if we should miss Dehra Dun. By the time the train started there were about twenty people on the roof of our coach and that of every other coach. No sooner had the train started than somebody pulled the communication cord, either because somebody had fallen off the roof or because a relation had not been able to clamber on to it. This happened twice, and then at last the train started on the last lap to Paleza Ghat where we arrived only a quarter of an hour before we were due to meet General Tuker at Bihta twenty miles away on the other side of the Ganges. However, Major-General H. Stable, who had kindly come to meet us, said he had arranged with the General not to reach Bihta until eleven o'clock and that we should just be able to make it. The Ducks behaved beautifully and waddled down the sandy bank into the Ganges without a quack.

Just before we reached Patna General Stable pointed out Mahatma Gandhi's little house beside the river, that little house from which such an influence upon the course of history had emanated. The Mahatma himself was not there at the time. We landed at Patna whence the car drove fast and we reached the airstrip at Bihta just as General Tuker's Dakota landed. Fifteen minutes later we were airborne and on the way to Lucknow. I had been led to suppose that 'Gertie' Tuker was a formidable figure, and no doubt he was a formidable figure to those whose lack of intelligence he deplored. He and I 'clicked' at once; I realized that he had confidence enough in my common sense to hand over various letters and records he had kept for me to read in the plane. He must have made up his mind about me during the quarter of an hour on that gridiron of an airstrip.

The letters that fascinated me most on that flight went back to the time when Tuker was commanding the 4th Indian Division in North Africa. I read his protest when General Montgomery left the Red Eagles behind to act as scavengers after the second Battle of Alamein. What was still more interesting was his letter suggesting that a night attack might be successful in breaking through the apparently impenetrable Mareth Line in Tunis. He suggested that this night attack might be started by his own beloved Second Gurhkas with their kukris. The reply was discouraging; it almost amounted to telling General Tuker not to make foolish suggestions. And then some days later was a letter from General Montgomery to say he had had an idea: could General Tuker's Gurkhas attempt a night attack with their kukris?

That night attack through the depths of the hills above Wadi Akarit was the decisive action of the Tunis campaign. Exactly a month hence I should see that maze of arid and ferocious hills which was the scene of one of the greatest military exploits of the war. There stands there now an austere monument to the men of the Fourth Indian Division. It is a monolith about eight feet high on the four sides of which are engraved the names of the fallen; it stands at the head of a steep flight of steps in as desolate a countryside as one could imagine looking across a waste of tumbled rocks and sand and withered herbage to the grim mountain called Fatnassa.

I was so much absorbed in reading those papers of Tuker's that the two hours' flight to Lucknow passed in a few minutes. Major-General Curtis[1] was on the airstrip to meet us. I had not seen him since we had cabins next to one another in the troopship on the way to Bombay. I was delighted to meet him again. He was in great form and drove Tuker and myself to lunch at Flagstaff House.

From Lucknow we flew to Saharanpur and from there we had a forty mile drive to Dehra Dun, where Chrissie and I were staying with Lt.-Colonel Wall (8th Gurkhas) and his wife. Chrissie remained to dine with her lovable hostess, and as soon as I was dressed our host drove me along to the 2nd Gurkha Mess. Here let me interpose to record one great difference between Bombay and Calcutta. In Bombay the men wore white jackets with black trousers; in Calcutta they wore black jackets with white trousers. I favoured the Bombay fashion.

After dinner 'Gertie' Tuker took me round the Mess and showed me a lot of interesting stuff. Much of the Mess silver had already been packed for dispatch to England. There was a discussion about the future resting-place of the trophies, relics and pictures of the ten Gurkha regiments. What was to be the place for their centre? General opinion favoured Winchester, the home of the Greenjackets. I suggested that it might be possible to find a suitable repository in Edinburgh Castle if there was not room for everything in Winchester, or failing that in Inverness. The historical friendships between Gurkha and Highland regiments would thus be preserved.

Next morning I was driven by Wall to the parade ground of the 2nd Gurkhas to see General Tuker give a couple of M.C.s to officers who had won them in the war and also the ceremony of swearing in the recruits. The famous truncheon of the 2nd Gurkhas presented to the Regiment by Queen Victoria was not at Dehra Dun at the time, and so allegiance was sworn upon the Union Jack. This truncheon had become a sacred emblem, and no 2nd Gurkha would tell a lie before it. In spite of the absence of the truncheon the ceremony of swearing allegiance was most moving. Indeed, that and the Retreat at Belgaum remain in my memory as the two most moving military ceremonies I saw during the tour.

After lunch we went to the bungalow of Colonel 'Fish' Armstrong who was Commandant of the 2nd Gurkhas Centre. There Francis Tuker and I had a very long talk, which was prolonged after tea

---

[1] Major-General P. C. Curtis, C.B., D.S.O.

I

when he walked back with me to the Walls' bungalow. He took me to several spots which had meant much to him in the past, and we walked across the polo ground, once considered the best in India. The warnings to keep off the grass were still in place, but the grass had gone sadly to seed. The General was in an elegiac mood. He was an artist as well as a soldier—a writer and a painter—and was admitted by all to have one of the finest strategic brains in either the Indian or the British army. My talk with him was of the utmost value and I have seldom spent as fruitful a day.

Alas, like too many of those remarkable men I met during my Odyssey Francis Tuker is no longer in this world. When he retired he went to live in Cornwall and became the victim of a merciless arthritis. He had to be wheeled about and was no longer able to paint. He bore his sufferings with the courage he had shown on the field of battle. I am proud to have been his friend and I salute his memory.

On our last night at Dehra Dun we had a quiet dinner with our host and hostess. Wall went to plant tea in Ceylon when he retired, and I have always regretted that I never succeeded in visiting Ceylon to enjoy their hospitality again. That bungalow in Dehra Dun set the seal on the marvellous hospitality we had enjoyed for months. Among the many good stories I carried away with me from Dehra Dun was that of the Gurkha Subedar who when asked what had most impressed him during his visit to England replied,

"The laundries and Queen Mary."

At Simla we were to stay at Snowdon, the house of the Commander-in-Chief. The original house was enlarged by Sir George White from a similar one lived in by Lord Roberts. Then Lord Kitchener obtained a grant to make the Commander-in-Chief's house really worthy of him, and he must have spent a lot of money on the synthetic Tudor and Jacobean interiors with their red corrugated iron roof. The ornate ceiling in the drawing-room was of papier-mâché from the military files accumulated in years. There was a large ballroom with a stage and a squash court right in the middle of the house. The view was magnificent—a fifty mile range of the Himalaya beyond a series of lower peaks. There was a signpost on the road TO TIBET. The garden was well planted and full of birds. The library of Lord Kitchener was an appropriate place in which to work at *Indian Epic*, among the ghosts and portraits and heraldic shields of bygone Commanders-in-Chief from Clive to Cassels. Only the arms of F. M. Lord Wavell and F. M. Sir Claude Auchinleck were missing. A swan song could not have a better setting.

We reached Simla in the afternoon, and found on our arrival that a muddle had been made and that we had been expected the day before.

Poor Mrs Kirkwood, who was looking after Snowdon for the Chief had sat up till midnight waiting for us. Even the police had been telephoned.

When we were being shown our rooms Chrissie looked critically at the wire-netting over the windows.

"That won't keep out mosquitoes", she exclaimed.

"But it isn't meant to keep out mosquitoes, dear," said Mrs Kirkwood, "It's meant to keep out the monkeys".

I still hear Chrissie's gasp of amazement.

There was an accumulation of letters which had mounted up during the last month. Among them were many about *The Vital Flame*, the expensive obituary I wrote for the gas industry on the verge of being nationalized. One from Harold Hartley[1], who will be ninety three months hence as I write these words, gave me great pleasure:

My dear Monty,

Over forty years ago I remember walking down New College Lane with you and talking about the possibility of our writing a book together. I have just read *The Vital Flame*, and if only I hadn't changed my job that possibility might have come true, as for twenty years I was in the thick of gas developments.

"It is far and away the best thing I have ever read about the industry. You really are a marvel at picking up all the star points. I broadcast about Murdoch in '39 and I was to have given the Memorial Lecture at the Royal Institution. He's a wonderful character and adequate justice has never been done to him. The book really is fascinating. What fun you must have had in your travels; how I wish I had been with you. I was in at the birth of both Fulham and Watson House—they were mainly staffed with my pupils.

"I was reading Faith's Autobiography again on Saturday night and wondering whether Polly (Christopher Stone) passed on to her one or two points I gave him for her Life of Cory.

Love from Gertrude to you.

Yours ever,
Harold Hartley

I went to Mass next morning and gave thanks for the safe end of our Odyssey. Yet the Odyssey was not over yet because it had now been decided that I should fly back to England at the beginning of June in order to see several people I had missed out here and if possible visit the battlefields of Italy and Tunis.

Four days after that Sunday a telegram came from Harris to say that Chrissie's father was critically ill and then another to say that he

[1] Brig.-General Sir Harold Hartley, G.C.V.O., C.H., F.R.S., M.C., D.C.L., LL.D.

had died on May 21st. I shared in her grief. Calum MacSween had meant such a great deal in my life as anybody who has read previous Octaves will realise. He was sixty-eight when he died and was buried two days later on the anniversary of the day his wife Barabuil had died in 1940.

Peter Goodwin had set his heart on coming with me to Italy and Tunis and had been successful in persuading the Historical Section at Simla of the historical importance of his photography in Italy and Tunis. On June 2nd he and I left Simla for New Delhi where I was to spend two nights. I quote from the entry in my diary on June 3rd:

"Delhi was an open furnace. Before dinner we listened to the Viceroy's broadcast. The Chief himself, Lt.-Colonel Sir Geoffrey Prior the Governor of Baluchistan, the Prime Minister of Kashmir and myself. Prior who was sitting next to me on the sofa suddenly whispered a quotation from *Extraordinary Women*, which he said he read once a year. Mountbatten broadcast well. Nehru's speech was deeply moving and a beautiful piece of sober rhetoric. Jinnah started off by talking about himself: 'I am glad to have been given an opportunity to speak at the microphone . . . . I hope I shall now have further opportunities, etc.' The rest was a good lawyer's speech, but suffered from following immediately after Nehru. I noticed that the Press next day cut out the bit at the beginning about himself. Baldev Singh spoke with evident sincerity. Claude Auchinleck in grey flannel shorts was pacing up and down most of the time. 'Pug' Ismay came in later. He has done a fine job behind the scenes. He hesitated to appear too confident about the immediate future but I felt that much of his anxiety was relieved."

The Viceroy had asked Nehru whether he would accept Partition if instead of waiting until June 1948 to abdicate from our Indian Empire we should abdicate in August of this very year. I have nowhere heard or read a warm enough appreciation of the courage Nehru needed to make that agonizing decision. The B.B.C. suppressed those opening words of Jinnah's broadcast. Last year I was recording a broadcast about the best year of my life and tried to find a record of that momentous occasion twenty years earlier. Apparently it no longer existed in their record library.

I do not think I fully realized at the time the historical magnitude of the occasion. Yet, as I watched the Auk pace up and down the room in those grey flannel shorts of his, which always looked as if they had started as a pair of grey flannel trousers, I do remember thinking that Claude Auchinleck himself must be seeing his life's work falling to pieces at that moment. The two last Commanders-in-Chief of the Indian Army were asked to perform impossible tasks, and when failure to perform them was blamed on them instead of on those who made the unreasonable demand upon them neither Wavell nor Auchinleck hit back.

On the day after that tremendous announcement was made Peter Goodwin and I reached the airport for our flight to Karachi at eleven but had to return to Delhi three hours later because a magneto in the York wouldn't behave itself. Finally, after a series of contradictory messages, we went back to the airport and were away soon after half-past seven, reaching Karachi four hours later. Douglas and Cecil Gracey were at the airport. They had arranged a dinner party but that confounded magneto messed everything up. However, they came and sat with me while I ate a very late dinner at the hostel and moreover stayed until we went off to deal with the formalities of departure just after one o'clock in the morning.

At Heliopolis the Egyptians were in their usual state of bloodiness with pompous customs and passport examinations. Bureaucracy is a world-wide malady due to human folly, but with them it resembles a venereal disease due to vice. The flight to Malta was most agreeable. The sea by Sidi Barrani and Sollum was a more amazing blue than ever. Dusk was rapidly deepening when we passed Tobruk, but I could still make out the masts of the sunken ships. A huge golden moon, slightly gibbous, had risen. We came down at Malta just an hour before midnight. The shrines put up for the Corpus Christi processions were still illuminated. We were airborne again at midnight.

We had been hearing a lot of bragging about a heat-wave but when we reached it England had given way to a 'tempestuous morn in early June' which by the time we reached Denchworth was a drench of rain. The next few days were spent in going up to town for talks with various generals. Lt.-Colonel W. Stewart of the 2nd Gurkhas who was to be my conductor in Tunis and Italy arrived, and another friendship began.

On June 15th we took off at Gatwick for Nice. We were twenty miles into France when Wing-Commander E. D. Crundall the Pilot said that the weather forecast was bad and we returned to Croydon. Just as well—another chartered Anson crashed in France that day. The flight to Nice next day was steady and the view of the Alps sublime. Mont Blanc behaved exactly as a classic mountain should behave and so seldom does. On the starboard side a bank of cumulus lighted by the westering sun tried to compete, and put up a very fine show. We went up to eleven thousand feet and came down on the Nice airport about six o'clock. The Azure Coast was in coloured-poster attire, and it was good to be back. We put up for the night at the Queen's Hotel. Swedes, Belgians and Swiss provided the bulk of the visitors, but there were quite a few English tourists all looking as if they were at Southend.

On the next lap of the journey we came down to refuel at the airport for Cagliari. I was moved to be standing on Italian soil after an absence of over twenty years and found myself talking the language fairly fluently. *Correntamente*, yes, but not alas, always *correttamente*. The airport had been terribly knocked about. We reached Tunis by half-past four and were met by Consul-General Gibbs,[1] Vice-Consul Manning, and M. Caunsu who was second in command to M. du Boisberranger, the Chef de Cabinet, all of whom were extraordinarily helpful. We had rooms at the Palace Hotel; as they were unable to serve anything but coffee and rolls we ate at the Majestic. M. Caunsu informed us that the Chef de Cabinet was putting a car at our disposal all the time we were in Tunis, and as soon as our lodging was fixed we went round to call on M. Boisberranger and thank him for the courtesy. He was sorry that the Resident was away and there would be no opportunity of giving me a formal dinner. Just before we left the Chef de Cabinet, M. Caunsu came in with a bit of red ribbon for me to put in my button-hole. I had happened to mention that in London I could only obtain the uniform ribbon of the Legion.

After leaving the Chef de Cabinet we went round to the Consulate-General. The building was modern, but our Consulate-General there was the oldest of all, well over three hundred years. Many negotiations must have been conducted in it to set free captives taken by Sallee rovers.

I had a good deal of rheumatism in the night, and the street noises in the early morning stopped any chance of dosing. Sharp at nine o'clock we were airborne on the way to the Mareth Line. We came down at Gabes and were met by Captain de la Rocque, who drove us to the house of General Dio, the Military Commander of Southern Tunis. The latter was a Breton with a chic Parisian wife. He was one of the first to throw in his lot with De Gaulle, and I noticed a large framed photograph of the great French patriot, inscribed "A mon Compagnon". A wall of the dining-room was covered with Hitler relics— swastikas and eagles and Nazi daggers. One looked at them as one would have looked at the spears, clubs and totem poles collected by an explorer from savages. The lunch was superlative. We went on eating and drinking for nearly two hours. The General expressed his intention of retiring to his native Brittany one day, but I noticed a glint in Madame Dio's eye which suggested that he was unlikely to get nearer to Brittany than the Parc Monceau. There are few things in life as agreeable as French hospitality at its best, and I should willingly have stayed on talking for the rest of the afternoon; but there was still a good deal to see and just before three o'clock we left the General's

---

[1] Sir Frank Gibbs, K.B.E., C.M.G.

house and drove with Captain de la Rocque to Wadi Akarit, thirty
kilometres away.

All that remained of the battle were two of the Italian guns that
were knocked out by Tuker's brilliant military operation and farther
along a German troop-carrier rusting away. When we got back to
Tunis we went round with Gibbs to the summer house of the Consulate-
General which was presented to the British Government by the Bey
of Tunis about a century ago. It was an attractive arabesque house with
a very large garden, and with that bewitching and subtle effluence of
the South of which Browning knew the secret in words.

Afterwards Gibbs drove us out to Sidi Bon Said where he was giving
us dinner in the restaurant which had a large terrace overhanging the
sea. However, the proprietor was firm and declared it was too damp
to dine outside. It was a good dinner of which the red mullet, my
favourite fish, was the best I ever ate. I recall saying to our host how
strange it was that the Germans who love the Mediterranean as
much as any nation had never been civilized or mentally cleansed by
those lustral waters. It was so difficult to avoid being civilized by the
Mediterranean. I fear that if I were dining in Tunis today I should
have to admit that the English tourists find it all too easy to avoid.

We left the hotel early for a long day's driving. Our first objective
was the glade a few miles from Ste. Marie du Zit where von Arnim
and his staff surrendered to General Tuker on May 11th 1943. It lies
some fifty miles south-east of Tunis at the base of the Cape Bon
peninsula from which the Germans had hoped to achieve another
Dunkirk. All the way along the roadside there was still plenty of
flowers and the dry water courses were full of oleanders in prodigal
rosy bloom. I have called the place of surrender a glade, but it was more
accurately a fold in the low rolling hillside covered with lentisk,
myrtle, cistus, juniper and rosemary. It was typical *maquis* or *macchia*
with few trees, and every step one took was aromatic. The year's
primal burst of bloom was past, but there were still flowers enough. I
noticed many plants of a small starry St John's wort, a Tyrian-purple
bugloss, a brilliant violet linaria, yellow thistles, a graceful yellow
umbelliferous plant, the most vivid blue eryngium I had ever seen, and
best of all an echinops with very large heads of pure sapphire.

Bill Stewart was with Colonel Showers of the 2nd Gurkhas when
they arrived, before General Tuker himself, to find about a thousand
Germans on parade dressed up in their best to surrender. It was poetic
justice that the Germans should surrender to three 2nd Gurkhas because
the night attack through the defiles of the hills above Wadi Akarit
when Subedar Lalbahadur Thapa of the 2nd Gurkhas won his V.C.
was the decisive action of the Tunis campaign. 4th Indian Division
began the fight for North Africa and it was 4th Indian Division which

ended it. The whole place stank of burning rubber when Showers and Stewart got there because the enemy had been destroying all his transport except two caravans and two staff-cars. The caravan in which von Arnim lived was now at Poona. One of the staff-cars lay as a derelict souvenir among the myrtle and the rosemary. Bill Stewart told me the Germans were still very cocky in 1943 and seemed to think that their surrender in Tunis was a mere incident.

From this memorable spot we drove along to the village of Enfida-ville, another forty miles south. We were unable to get up to the ridge, but from below it was easy to appreciate just what a formidable obstacle it was to our victorious advance. I looked with awe at the bald grey dome of Djebel Garci where the Rajputana Rifles, the 9th Gurkhas, and the Essex fought so gloriously. I saw the hill Takrouna on the eastern edge of the ridge, where a castellated village stood like a castle from a Doré picture. It was captured by the New Zealanders by an astonishing feat of arms. I saw, too, the wide stretch of open country across which the 4/16th Punjabis—the old Bo Peeps—advanced under very heavy shell fire as steadily as if across the dusty parade ground at home in Sialkot. The fathers of those men had saved the line at Neuve Chapelle, and fought a great bayonet fight at Festubert.

We drove on from Enfidaville to reach Medjez-el-Bab. The cross-country road depressed our driver because owing to the dust he could not go at more than forty miles an hour. His average speed on good roads was a steady sixty, and he often got up to eighty. We turned aside at Medjez-el-Bab to drive up to a much shelled farm from which we had a good view of the country across which the 4th Indian Division drove a way between the 1st and 4th British Divisions to reach the open plain and allow the 7th British Armoured Division to race through for the final kill. Yes, it was indeed a fine poetic justice which ruled that the two divisions which had arrived in Africa first should be the two to wind up so many months of African warfare.

Back in Tunis Gibbs took us round to see St George's Church where there was a monument to one hundred and fifty-two dead warriors of the 4th Indian Division. St George's Church itself was modern, but the ground on which it stood belonged to the British Government and it had been the site of a Church of some kind or another for over three centuries. At present it appeared to be run for the purpose of con-verting Jews and for the spiritual health of those already converted, the missionary having been appointed by the London Jews' Society. It was built in the middle of the native city and from the flat roof of the missionary's house one looked down on one side into Arab court-yards and on another into the Jewish quarter. On the flat roof across an alley a blindfold donkey was turning a water-wheel. This provided water for the public baths which were used by men and women on alternate days.

In the churchyard was a monument to John Howard Payne, the author of *Home Sweet Home*, who was born in 1791 and died in Tunis in 1852. In 1883 his remains were disinterred and taken across the Atlantic to Washington where they now rest. On a gloomy November afternoon in the year 1912 I was walking along that endless main street of Schenectady and feeling myself as gloomy as only that kind of street can make one feel in that kind of weather. I passed by a large stuccoed house set back from the road behind a grove of already leafless trees. A lot of small boys were playing some game with a ball and wearing away with their feet what little grass was left on the muddy expanse beneath the trees. I thought as I looked at this house in the November blight it was the most depressing house I had ever seen, and that if I ever wanted to choose a setting for some melancholy or sombre tale of thwarted hopes and frustrated lives I would choose as a perfect setting this gaunt stuccoed house with its dank leafless grove and muddy playground covered with green slime. Then on a pillar beside the gates, I saw an inscription which recorded that John Howard Payne, U.S.A. Consul in Tunis, had been born and brought up in this house. This house, in fact, *was* home, sweet home.

Gibbs and Manning were down at the aerodrome to see us off next day on our way to Naples. They had taken so much trouble to make our visit fruitful, and I was glad that Meiklereid would be succeeded in Saigon by a Consul-General as much in sympathy with the French as himself. It was a silvery scirocco day, damp and hot with hardly any wind. The summit of Etna was shrouded in cotton wool, and rain seemed imminent when we landed in the aerodrome at Catania. The officials there were much excited because apparently ours was the first strange plane which had landed since the Military Administration ceased. Half a dozen of them, all talking at once and contradicting one another about the procedure, dealt with the business of filling in the forms to be checked against our passports. Like all Mediterranean ink it was only just perceptibly coloured, and the pens were more like the quills of sea-urchins than pens. At last after interminable *chiaccieria*, the bureaucratic ritual was accomplished and we went off to eat motadella and drink beer in the refreshment room.

The coast was much obscured over the Tyrrhenian Sea. Cape Palinuro loomed out of the dense rain. On such a day might the steersman of Aeneas have been drowned, and the profoundest pessimism of Cyril Connolly about his own creative vitality (and everybody else's) been justified. We flew all round Capri where the air was clearer, and I was able to see how ruthlessly the trees of Ventrosa had been cut. I bought the whole front of Monte Solaro—the stomach of the mountain

—in the spring of 1914. Ventrosa was the only real bird sanctuary in Capri. Axel Munthe had a sanctuary below San Michele, but hardly any birds frequented its sparse Aleppo pines. In the ilex and arbutus groves and dense *macchia* of Ventrosa the birds flourished.

The rain was pouring down over the Bay and the airport at Naples seemed derelict. Great puddles stood everywhere on the runways; the seating accommodation in the reception office had been improvised out of packing-cases. There was a bureaucratic flap because neither Wing-Commander Crundall, the pilot, nor Bronson the wireless operator from County Kerry, had visas for Italy. Fortunately Crundall looked like a benign country parson, and even the most fanatical bureaucrat was softened by his amiable appearance, speech and manner. We pointed out to Naples that Catania had assured Crundall and Bronson that visas were unnecessary for the crew of a chartered plane. "That", said Naples scornfully, "is a *fesseria*." Jeaffreson, the representative of the Embassy's Public Relations Department who had come to meet us, was amiable. So was I. So of course was Peter Goodwin who was the very spirit of amiability. Jeaffreson and I agreed that without doubt it was a *fesseria*; but we amiably hoped that Naples would allow the crew to go on to Rome where they would be able to obtain a provisional *permesso de soggiorno* from the police. To this Naples, unable to resist our united amiability, finally agreed.

Jeaffreson had booked two rooms at the Continental and three rooms at the Vesuvio, the only two hotels that were functioning with reasonable comfort. Peter Goodwin and I went to the Continental, which had been really well done up. I stood on the balcony of my bedroom exactly opposite the Castello del Uovo and gazed once more at the port of Santa Lucia after so many years. The air was haunted by the faces and figures of the past. The rain had stopped and the bay was in a golden glow. In the old days we used to stay at the Santa Lucia Hotel and take the nine o'clock boat—the *Principessa Elena*—to Capri. Those topaz-bright November mornings after the chilly fogs of England and the long railway journey from Calais or Boulogne! The Santa Lucia Hotel had not yet opened again, but my balcony at the Continental looked out on the same heart-warming view. *O mihi praeteritos*!! Those two exclamation marks are sighs not shrieks.

The waiter, one of those venerable ecclesiastical figures into which only Italian waiters who remain in Italy can develop, came in with my coffee next morning to announce that the weather had recovered from its extraordinary behaviour of the previous day. It was almost as if he said, "the sun's apologies and he is shining again." Soon after ten we were away in a large Lancia. There was a lot of traffic on the road between Naples and Cassino, but we were in Cassino before noon. The town now looked like one of those boom towns which sprang up in America after the discovery of gold or oil. We drove up to the Castle Hill, but the condition of the road made it impossible for so large a car to get to the top of the hill on which the Monastery once stood, and I was disinclined to walk up and survey what I still consider was devastation caused by empirical tactics, the result of ill-considered and improvised strategy, and a link in the long chain of mistakes which marked the Italian campaign from the beginning. The soft underbelly of the Axis became in fact a mere rhetorical figment after the failure to turn the turtle over on its back when Mussolini fell.

Not without bitterness I contrasted what had been done at Cassino with the wonderful restraint of the fighting for Mandalay Hill. I remember having an argument with a Canadian officer soon after the destruction of the Abbey. His point was that the noblest edifice in the world was less important than the life of one man. My point was that either that dead man had an immortal soul or he had not. If his soul was immortal he would recognize in eternity that his earthly body was well worth sacrificing to something greater than that earthly body. If on the other hand that man did not possess an immortal soul, I was not prepared to accord his life any more importance than that of a monkey. Do we really believe that the lives of a few Venetians were more important than the Acropolis?

We lunched at the Risorgimento restaurant. Risorgimento was the key-note of Cassino. On the top of the Monastery hill the stones were being gathered and stacked in preparation for rebuilding. The town was alive with the spirit of rebirth. Every face was alight with energy. Indeed, throughout that Italian tour, I was impressed by the vitality and courage of the Italian people.

After lunch we drove on into the Abruzzi. The countryside was bright with flowers—poppies and broom, scabious and mullein. Everyone of the Abruzzesi girls we passed had a beautiful face, a perfect figure and faultless carriage. I have not seen anywhere so many good-looking women in the course of a few hours. Celibacy there was unimaginable. Yet, the Abruzzi produced a higher percentage of priests than anywhere in Italy.

By seven o'clock we reached Campobasso which was an industrial city, but clean and orderly with streets shaded by closely clipped and trimmed holm oaks. The Grand Hotel was not a luxurious hostelry, but it was reasonably clean, and we enjoyed a simple dinner of spaghetti and eggs. I saw the young moon from my open bedroom window in a calm green sky. I went to bed at nine for I had been in pain all day.

My leg was still giving me jip when we started early on what was to be a long and crowded day. The swifts were wheeling and screaming against the faded blue sky of the morning. The beauty of the countryside between Campobasso and Casacalenda was more powerful than the pain, and I drove for two hours in a rapture. It is limestone country, and the white road flung itself ahead of us for miles like a lasso. We travelled some of the way through the richly cultivated valleys of the foothills, some of the way round bald green hills. The cultivation displayed indomitable energy. The slopes on either side in the foreground were painted with the amber and gold of ripening corn in various shades; and in every sloping cornfield mighty trees such as you see in an English park provided contrasting shade, a luminous blue where it was aslant the sun. It was a landscape for Breughel, and he would have done justice to the human element—to the reapers in gaily coloured groups and to the horsemen who came riding along, each with a large long haired goat on a lead, itself the colour of ripe corn. Goats do not like motor-cars and when they saw ours approaching they would always leap aside off the road and drag the horsemen with them. In the grassy verges on either side there was as great a profusion of wild flowers as in any Alpine meadow—poppies, broom, a ladies' bedstraw twenty-four inches high and heavily scented, candytuft, love-in-a-mist, a brilliant crimson dianthus, larkspurs as blue as the finest ultramarine, corn-marigolds, a large crimson unscented pea, anchusa, a puce-coloured broom-rape, and any amount of *clematis flammula* which I used to grow over the ruined house of the old privateer in Jethou.

The road on from Casacalenda to Larino was a succession of avenues—avenues of limes, of stone-pines and Aleppo pines and acacia. There was one avenue of stone-pines at the entrance of the Piano di Larino, the ground between their dark umbrellas on either side of the road covered with mauve-pink thistles in full bloom, a most unusual floral effect, for the thistles looked as if they had been deliberately planted, so thick were they. The harvest in the lowland of the Piano was full ripe, and Sunday was no interruption to its being reaped. Presently we crossed the River Biferno, the first of those rivers all the way up Italy which cost so many lives in the crossing of them. We skirted Termoli and drove north along the coast road beside the pale blue Adriatic that was quiet as velvet on that summer's day.

Half an hour after midday we reached Vasto. There we looked at the Headquarters of the Eighth Army and remembered it was from that pompous municipal building that in November 1943 General Montgomery summoned spirits from the Vasto deep and proclaimed that the Eighth Army would be in Rome by Christmas. I wondered how much Livy he had read at the school of which we are both alumni.

When we reached Casalbordino we could not find a *trattoria* let alone an *albergo* or *ristorante*. Presently a signpost pointed to Torino, which much amused Vincenzo, our Neapolitan chauffeur. "Why leave out Rome?", he asked. By the time we reached the small village of Torino di Sangro it was half-past one and we enquired hopefully whether there was a chance of getting a bottle of wine. The population of Torino di Sangro felt that something had to be done about it. A reconnaisance party was sent out and finally it was reported that a willing host had been found. We turned down into a small side street and came to a cross between a stable and cellar. There was a lot of health drinking and a great deal of excited conversation. "*Brava gente,*" Vincenzo commented. Yes, fine people indeed. I still recall that sunny by-way and that cool cellar in which we drank the rough red wine of the country.

The great cemetery at Torino di Sangro where over three thousand five hundred dead warriors lie at peace occupied the most impressive site of the many cemeteries I had seen. It was reached by a private road running up at a steep angle from the main coastal road to Pescara and Bari. The expanse of white crosses took up the whole of a semi-circular bluff some two or three hundred feet above the Sangro River, and the effect was of a vast half-amphitheatre of graves. Below, the Sangro winds down a broad valley from the Apennine to the sea. Northward the land rolls in great billows to a skyline crenellated here and there by villages. Westward and north-westward the bastions of the Apennine, Maiella most prominent, towered indigo-dark against the sky. Eastward spreads the Adriatic, its waters on that morning a velvety Cambridge blue. Southward and level with the cemetery the countryside is intimate and fertile, a countryside of laden orchards and browsing cattle and lush grass. In due course the cemetery itself would become an extension of the little Arcadia it bounded; and I prayed that, when they whose dear ones lay there visited this spot in the kinder years for which we hoped, the beauty of the natural scene would shed upon their hearts a benison. I have felt nowhere a profounder sense of peace.

We drove on northwards through a battle-scarred countryside, and decided to reach Chieti by a third-class country road. We kept descending and ascending small deep valleys bosky with orchards and olives and bronzed with corn, and passing from time to time groups of bending reapers in bright attire, the rhythmic pattern of whose labour rejoiced the eye like the backgrounds of medieval art. In the bottoms of those valleys streams ran through lush reeds and grasses and white cows grazed beside them. On the third ridge we saw ahead of us the shattered town of Orsogna, the road to which was sometimes almost impassable on account of derelict German and New Zealand tanks. In a field behind one of those tanks men, women and children were reaping the corn and beside the merely obstructive monster was growing an unusually large clump of rest-harrow covered with spikes of rose and white flowers. That tough-rooted plant which baffled the iron teeth of the harrow had, as it seemed, arrested the progress of the tank. The whole scene was a fine subject for a symbolical picture. Presently we were driving through what used to be our front line. The more we saw of this country, the more clearly we realized that the whole of the Italian campaign was a vast improvisation. On the walls of the villages through which we passed there were fierce republican slogans painted in black, and then suddenly we came to a village with slogans for the Monarchy in blue paint. Among all those Vivas for the Republic or the King there was one Viva which perfectly expressed despair. On one wall somebody had painted '*Viva Niente*'—Long Live Nothing.

There remains vividly in my memory sitting for a few minutes in a small public garden at the edge of the sheer hill two thousand feet up on which Chieti stands. I still see that sublime panorama of the Apennine and the jagged peak of Gran Sasso d'Italia clawing at the majestic sunset. We spent an uncomfortable night. Bill Stewart felt he was being ill-repaid for marching in with his Gurkhas to liberate Chieti when the Germans abandoned the Gustav line and went surging back to the Gothic line.

We drove on next day through those lovely towns of the Alban Hills, all of them drenched with history. Perhaps the most beautifully situated of all is Arsoli with that magnificent grove of ancient cypresses on a green hill above the town. Arsoli, to judge by the slogans painted up, was strongly royalist. Some miles farther on we left the main road to visit Subiaco. I wanted to reassure myself about the damage done by Allied bombers. I found that a piece of the cloisters of the big monastery of Santa Scolastica had been smashed and a good deal of other damage done, but this building is, most of it, comparatively modern. The smaller monastery of the Sacro Speco had by the mercy of God escaped damage. The cave in which St Benedict spent three years in communion with the Divine Will is set in the hillside at the entrance of a deep ravine at least a mile away from Subiaco itself. The monastery which housed eight monks at this time, was built piece by piece round the cave through the centuries. Long before there was any threat of bombers there must have been a fear lest rocks from the hillside above should fall and crush the building which challenged by its position the malice of nature. The evidence of this fear was to be found in a life-sized statue of St Benedict in one of the small courtyards holding up his hand to avert the danger and inscribed in Latin: *Stay, O rock, do no harm to my sons.* His sons may have watched that arm held up to shield them when the bombs were falling all round the Sacro Speco. The attack was the mistake of a too enthusi-

astic American squadron which imagined it was bombing the re-
treating German Army instead of one of the most sacred fanes in
Christendom.

We were lucky enough to enquire the way up to the monastery from
a young monk who at once jumped on the running board of the car
and guided us through a courtyard to where one alighted for the
ascent of some two hundred steps through a grove of primeval holm-
oaks, not one of which could have been less than a thousand years
old. Dom Ignazio was the perfect guide. When I expressed my eager-
ness to see the portrait of St Francis of Assisi painted by one of the
monks when he visited the monastery in 1223, Dom Ignazio was not
prepared to accept so positive a statement. He would only allow that it
might have been painted by a monk. Anyway, the portrait itself completely fulfilled all my expectations. The fact that it showed the saint
without halo or stigamata was proof that it was a contemporary
portrait and the inscription 'Frater Franciscus' suggested that it was
painted by a monk. Even now, as I write about it twenty years later,
those two eyes are looking at me. Nor was Dom Ignazio prepared to
accept as more than a legend the grafting of roses by St Francis on
St Benedict's briars. The roses themselves were not in flower, and with
only the vivid light green leaves I could not say what kind of roses
they were, but I have seen nowhere any like them. The faithful have
cured their ills by drying those leaves and taking them as a powder.

The noise of Rome came as rather a shock to me. For so long the
Eternal City had seemed to my mind's ear the quietest capital of them
all. To find it more of a pandemonium than Naples was a blow. We
put up at the Grand Hotel, which had remained what the Grand Hotel
always was. I went to bed early. Too many ghosts from my golden
prime haunted the corridors and saloons of the Grand Hotel.

The hold-up by weather at the start of our tour had made it impossible for us to devote the two days we had intended to devote to the
campaign from Rome northward; there was no use pretending that flying
over the country was the same thing. It was tantalizing to peer down
at the terra-cotta huddle of Assisi, at the jade-green Tiber, at the olive-
green Arno, and at lordly Perugia upon its hill. The peace of Florence
after the din of Rome was quite exquisite. The very aerodrome itself
managed to look beautiful in that serene and classic landscape.
The sky was deep azure with snowy cumulus as artfully arranged as if
the brush of a great painter had designed its pattern. The encircling
hills were the perfection of chiaroscuro. Every cypress tree seemed to
have been planted by a master. I enjoyed a brief illusion that the world
had returned to sanity and civilization. The Grand Hotel in Rome
had been as full of *nouveaux riches* as it always was, but the guests in
the Grand Hotel, Florence, were as much a part of the scene as the

minor figures of a quattrocento picture. We had the luck to reach
Florence on the Feast of St John the Baptist, the chief patron of the
city. To be sure, it meant that all the galleries were shut, but it also
meant that the heavy traffic of business and industry was still.

It was in Florence that the emotional pleasure of revisiting Italy
after an absence of twenty-three years became so acute that a kind of
Pentecostal inspiration seized me and I found myself talking the
language with such fluency as to amaze myself and my listeners, who
could not believe that I had been so long away. By luck Yvonne's[1]
sister Babka[2] and her husband Zeno had just driven from England
and I dined with them that evening. Zeno Vinci kindly gave up his
seat, so that I could see the football match between combatants—they
really were combatants—in cinquecento costume. It was an unexpected
treat because it was the first time that the annual football match on
St John's Day had been held since the war. The game was played—or
fought—in the Piazza della Signoria between the Whites from this
side of the Arno and the Greens from the other side of the river. The
Piazza was turned into a true arena with sand. A round white ball
was used, but the game partook more of rugger than soccer. There
were twenty players on each side. Our seats faced the flying Campanile
which was as lovely in the floodlighting as one of the city's own lilies,
and the Michelangelo statues appeared to be divine visitors who had
descended from Olympus to gaze at mortal sport. There were thousands
of spectators in tiers round the Piazza and every window in the houses
was full. The audience resembled an immense bouquet of flowers,
and when at some crisis of the play they rose from their seats in excitement to shout "*Bianchi! Bianchi!*" or "*Verdi! Verdi!*" it was like a surge
of petals. The game was exciting, and it ended as it should have ended,
in a draw of one and a half goals each. We had missed the opening
procession round the arena, but we saw the same procession bring the
spectacle to a close with a ceremonious salute to the Communist
Sindaco of Florence sitting in the State Box. There was a bewildering
variety of medieval costumes and a cavalcade of young bloods of the
city clad in armour. I recall particularly twenty drummers in slashed
doublets and full breeches of blue and yellow. Such a procession at
home would have been marred by the self-consciousness of those taking
part in it, but here the illusion was complete because every single
performer in the pageant had gone back in spirit four centuries. Only
our own Yeomen of the Guard might not have disgraced themselves
at such a display. After the match was over we went round to Baglione's
and sat talking till half-past three in the morning when Zeno Vinci
added to my obligation by driving me back to the hotel. I cannot

---

[1] Mrs Hamish Hamilton.   [2] Contessa Vinci.

5a. Best Seller Quiz
lbert Frankau, Margaret Kennedy, Gilbert Harding, C.M., Ruby M. Ayres

5b. Nellie Boyte, C.M. and Chrissie

6a. C.M. crowning 'May' Queen at Denchworth

6b. Sant' Apollinare di Classe

remember a more perfect celebration of thus revisiting the glimpses of the moon than I enjoyed in Florence. Indeed, indeed, *hoc erat in votis*.

I was enchanted when we reached Rimini to see painted on the walls '*Vuotate per Malatesta*'. I found it highly romantic for the ghost of Francesca's husband or lover to be standing as a candidate for a post-war Italian Parliament. After booking rooms at the hotel we drove on to San Marino. We entered the territory of that age-long independent republic and presently went winding up that fantastic peak to its Gothic summit where the city of San Marino was waiting in a dream for tourists to return. I could fancy myself back in Capri before 1914 as all up the steep *viale* to the prison we passed chairs set out invitingly on little terraces for the tourist to refresh himself with Moscato wine.

From the battlements of the prison which dates back to the tenth century we had a view of at least fifty miles of country over which the 43rd Gurkhas Lorried Brigade performed prodigious feats of arms. San Marino itself was captured by the Camerons of the 4th Indian Division in a night attack.

Three or four miles before we reached Ravenna next morning we stopped to visit Sant' Apollinare di Classe, the oldest complete church in Christendom. It was built about A.D. 550. 'Classe' is a reminder of the days when the sea came as far as this, and half the Roman fleet (*classis*) was based there. The round tenth-century tower had been knocked about by shelling, but the marvellous Byzantine mosaics in the apse were undamaged except for a piece out of the corner by one window. The mosaics exceeded all my expectations. The texture resembled tapestry, and was not smooth-seeming like later mosaics. Apparently this effect was got by using tesserae of different shapes and heights. The design was beautiful, the most striking part of it being the twelve Apostles in the guise of lambs, a stem of madonna lilies between each one. I had a long talk with Giulia Goberti the Custode, who was a little frail old woman of ninety not much more than four feet tall. She told me about the bombardment when two hundred of the villagers, old and young, had sheltered in a side chapel for six weeks. One hundred and seventy-six shells had fallen all round the church. "*Cento settanta sei, signore mio*", she quavered to me. Her grand-daughter informed me that the old lady still insisted on digging in the garden for a couple of hours every morning. I wish I could reproduce the expression compounded of pride and humility on her face as she protested she could not do otherwise. I heard she was not able to get as much strengthening food as she required and I gave myself the gratification of handing her a 1000 lire note, which seemed to her a fortune but was now only the equivalent of ten shillings.

K

She was flabbergasted by this sum and promised to remember me in her prayers every day.

We had no time to visit more than a fraction of Ravenna's wonders but the Byzantine mosaics in San Vitale and the Roman mosaics in the tomb of Julia Placida were beyond any superlatives I can muster. By Divine mercy only one church in Ravenna was completely destroyed; the thought that San Vitale and Sant' Apollinaris de Classe might easily have perished sends a shiver through the mind.

From Ravenna we went on to see the Argenta Gap where the German forces in Italy received their death blow. Peter Goodwin had envisaged the famous Argenta Gap as a kind of Thermopylae. He would wake up from a doze in the car, burbling about the Argenta Gap, which he expected to be photographically the crown and glory of our rush through Italy. Actually it was a gap of dry land amid the wide floods and salt marshes all round, and as there were no floods at the time there was nothing for Peter to photograph, except another battered little town. We had no time left to explore what had been a hill of fighting and reached Bologna's almost deserted airport at four o'clock, much relieved to see the Anson waiting for us. We were warned that we should have trouble in Milan over the visas of Crundall and Bronson which had been causing trouble everywhere from Naples northwards. However, every official wanted nothing better than to help us. Milan was entirely under Italian direction and seemed to be functioning much more competently than Rome under American and a tiny bit of Italian and British direction. Milan hotels were full on account of the big fair; so at seven o'clock we flew on to Nice, all the officials speeding us on our way.

The flight along the Riviera di Levante in the roseate light of evening was miraculously beautiful. Genoa, Rapallo, Portofino, Mentone . . . what memories of the past were tumbling through my mind. An hour and a half after leaving Milan we came down on the Nice aerodrome. There was a bank strike in Nice and nobody seemed to know how we should be able to cash our travellers' cheques. By a grim coincidence as I write these words in another June twenty-one years later we are having the same trouble about travellers' cheques on account of the strike in France. Plus ça change . . . Next morning we were kept waiting for a couple of hours at the aerodrome, which was an ant-heap of officials. When at last we got away we encountered strong headwinds, and came down at Lyon to refuel. On the way to Croydon we dodged the bad weather successfully but for the first time in all those months I felt nervous in a plane and ever since my flight back to Delhi three weeks later I have never flown if a train was available. I said goodbye to Crundall our pilot and Bronson our wireless operator with real regret. Crundall had been the perfect pilot. He was imperturbably cautious and with his thirty years' experience of the air and his country parson kindliness he would reassure the most nervous traveller.

On the following afternoon Peter Goodwin and I left King's Cross at half-past three in what was intended to be a fast train to York with a first stop at Peterborough. Nevertheless, for two hours the wretched train wandered about in Hertfordshire, stopping just outside station after station. In the end we arrived in York two hours late. Our host and hostess, Lt.-General Sir Montagu Stopford, G.O.C.-in-C. Northern Command, and Lady Stopford were marvellously serene under the stress of guests arriving an hour late for dinner, and I soon forgot all about the sins of the L.N.E.R. in their delightful company.

Those talks with 'Monty' Stopford were as good as I had with any General, and we enjoyed much laughter. After a grand week-end Peter Goodwin and I left for Edinburgh where I had a good talk about 15th Corps with Lt.-General Sir Philip Christison, G.O.C-in-C Scottish Command.

Back in London I had talks with General after General, the longest and most absorbing of which was with General Sir William Slim[1] as he then was. He answered every question with complete frankness and never made any attempt to cover up what he said had been his mistakes. At this date he was head of the Imperial Defence College. He paid a warm tribute to General Sir George Giffard[2] as C-in-C 11th Army Group in S.E. Asia. When I went down to see Sir George at Winchester a day or two later I was much impressed by his frankness and he enlarged my knowledge of the almost impossible task the Indian Army had been called upon to perform. It was the more convincing because he himself was not an Indian Army man.

On July 12th I went along to Hyde Park Gardens to say goodbye to Sir Ian Hamilton. He was noticeably frailer than he was when he walked up those flights of stairs at St Mary's Hospital to tell me that I *must* round off my experience by seeing India. I thanked him now for that advice. I had been offered a cigar and was smoking it when Peter Goodwin was going to take a photograph of us both sitting on the terrace. Sir Ian demanded a cigar for himself and was rather indignant with dear Mary Shield when she offered to light it for him. That marvellous veteran born a year before the Crimean War had the most successful old age of anybody I have known. He was all but a day thirty years older than myself and I was privileged to enjoy his friendship for thirty years. That gallant young nonagenarian would not be there when I returned to England next year; he died in that October of 1947.

[1] Field-Marshal Viscount Slim, K.G., G.C.B., G.C.M.G., G.C.V.O., G.B.E., D.S.O.   [2] The late General Sir George Giffard, G.C.B., D.S.O.

Ralph Glyn[1], our North Berkshire Member, who had a good grasp of the position in India and strongly reprobated any attempt to make Pakistan another Ulster, kindly secured me a seat at the Bar of the House of Lords to hear the debate on the Government of India Bill— the last debate that would ever be held on Indian affairs. Lord Listowel read his speech, and I could not help regretting that there was no orator to introduce this momentous Bill. Lord Listowel was followed by Lord Templewood who spoke as neatly as the erstwhile Sammy Hoare always spoke. At the same time he managed to implant one or two spicules of doubt while protesting the Opposition's unequivocal support of the Bill. Lord Samuel came next with a brief, dignified and agreeably Ciceronian speech. It was Lord Halifax, however, who first made me feel that I was listening to the final words of a drama which had lasted nearly three centuries, and I should imagine that I was feeling what most of the noble Lords themselves were feeling. It was a moving speech, and it was difficult to believe that the man who made it was in his sixty-seventh year, so little really much older did he seem than Edward Wood speaking in the Oxford Union forty-five years earlier. Lord Halifax was followed by Lord Pethick-Lawrence, whose ten years' seniority to his predecessor seemed fifty. I had to leave the House after that speech by the man who made such a profound impression on Indian opinion by his essential goodness.

Next day I went to the Indian Office for a final long talk with General Scoones. He had been tremendously helpful over this rather hectic supplementary tour. I recall his saying to me that he hoped I had not been disappointed when my flight back to India in a York had been postponed for a day or two because my plane had been needed for an urgent priority. I was certainly not disappointed when the plane for which Peter Goodwin and I were originally booked crashed at Basra in a dust storm.

We left Heathrow for Karachi on the morning of July 18th. At six o'clock in the morning of July 20th we arrived. I had a glimpse of Douglas and Cecil Gracey who were in a state of domestic confusion because the Pakistan Government were taking on the military business of Karachi as the seat of the Dominion Government. He was wondering what his job was going to be in the new order. It ultimately turned out to be C.G.S. to Frank Messervy who was to be Commander-in-Chief of the Pakistan Army. Rob Lockhart was to command the Army of the Dominion of India, with Roy Bucher as his C.G.S. In due course Gracey and Bucher would become Commanders-in-Chief of the Armies of Pakistan and India.

We reached Delhi in time for lunch. The Chief, who was now to

[1] The late Lord Glyn of Farnborough.

become Supreme Commander and preside over the unwelding of an army it had taken ninety years to weld into its present shape, seemed in splendid form, but I could not help wondering how much his outward cheerfulness was covering up a profound sorrow for the end of that great Army he loved so deeply and had served so devotedly.

The abdication from our Indian Empire was fixed for August 15th and it was obvious that the original form planned for my book about the Indian effort during the war would have to be changed. I suggested a much larger work. It was furthermore obvious that I could not conceivably tackle such a large scale work during the two or three months when Snowdon would still be a live house. I suggested that if my publishers agreed I could put my diary in order, taking out of it pages and pages of military details. This would be published the next year by Chatto and Windus under the title *All Over The Place*. Claude Auchinleck approved of this idea. So did Bill Condon. I got to work on the diary as soon as I reached Simla. By now the terrific effort of will by which I had recorded the adventures of the last ten months had flagged and the rest of the year went unrecorded. So I have only my memory and a few letters to fall back on. I know that I shall have forgotten various interviews I had with people who played an important part in the war, but when I say that over twelve hundred people had signed their names in my birthday book since October of the previous year it will be realized that I was beginning to find that impressions of people were less sharp than they had been.

The morning of August 15th 1947 was an experience I find difficult to express in words. As I walked along the Mall at Simla the Indians, from the shopkeepers to the rickshaw coolies, looked at the British as if they had been mysteriously transfigured during the night. To be candid, I doubt if any of the British folk realized for a moment that they appeared transfigured; indeed, when I commented on the emotional effect they were having on the native population of Simla they obviously thought I was indulging my imagination. Alas, for what was to follow all too soon.

A fortnight later Lord and Lady Mountbatten and Sir Claude Auchinleck as Patron and Patroness and Vice-Patron of the A.D.C. who were in Simla for a day or two attended the performance of a play by Kenneth Horne called *Jane Steps Out*. This was the first time that the ex-Viceroy would see himself in a printed programme described as Supreme Commander Armed Forces India and Pakistan.

The Simla A.D.C. was the oldest Amateur Dramatic club in the world. Although most of the earliest records were destroyed by fire in 1889 there was still authentic evidence of numerous amateur productions as far back as 1838. Soon after the opening of the Gaiety Theatre in 1887 the A.D.C. was formally constituted and from 1888 until the present performance it had produced more than two hundred and fifty plays besides many other entertainments. At this date Bill Condon was President, Jim Thomson was Hon. Secretary and Alice Thomson was Mistress of the Robes, among various other honorary officials.

There were two or three more productions before the end of the year, but that performance on August 30th 1947 may be considered the fall of the curtain for the Simla A.D.C. It was also the fall of the curtain for any hopes that the complicated job of handing over the Civil Service and breaking up the Indian Army between India and Pakistan would be easily accomplished.

On September 9th I was writing to Faith:

I'm feverishly trying to get my diary ready as there's a faint chance of a serial which would help very much financially. After Auchinleck and Mountbatten went back to Delhi I had a tiresome five days in bed with pain. Mountbatten gave me a proof of his Report which will cause a bit of a kick-up. I doubt if Whitehall will allow him to publish the Report without cuts. I was to have gone through it with him but he had to get back to Delhi on account of the troubles, The situation is pretty tense. We had a chap killed just outside the gate yesterday morning, and in the afternoon one was brought in with his head severed. This morning there have been some more killings about two hundred yards away. The Sikh refugees from West Punjab who had been through hell with the Muslims are now massacring the Muslims in the East Punjab. The danger here is that the Muslims will fire Simla and that will mean a fearful holocaust. I think myself this is a fever which will burn itself out, and the Bishop of Lahore who has been spending the morning with me—such a delightful fellow—agrees with me, but it will be some time before it does burn itself out. All sorts of horrors have been perpetrated.

I hope your Italian trip will pass off well. I take it that only people going abroad after October 1st come under the financial restrictions. I also hope this letter reaches you. Posts have been completely haywire recently.

I wrote to Lord Mountbatten:

"It was a disappointment to miss the chance of talking to you about your Report. However, the Bishop of Lahore tells me that there is a possibility of your coming to Simla next month on the occasion of the centenary of the Lawrence School. In that case I hope that I may be given an opportunity to talk to you about the Report. I have read it through word for word and marked it. May I say that in its present form it is the most illuminating, indeed by far the most illuminating document I have read about the late war. I sincerely hope that you will fight any attempt to excise so much as a sentence."

I managed to get my diary into shape for print before Snowdon was closed down, and we took rooms at Clarke's Hotel. How that building managed to cling to the side of a sheer cliff without falling down was an architectural wonder.

On October 8th I was writing to Faith:

Posts here have been out of the question, but I got one letter before you were leaving for Italy. . . . There has been a lot of killing here and a good deal of mutilation. My present plan is to stay here till December and then go to Kenya to avoid the crush on Indian boats homeward bound. There are one or two generals I want to meet out there. This three months' notice that all British officers and officials, with a few exceptions, have come to the end of their jobs will strain the shipping to breaking point. Communication between here and Delhi is very difficult. The British people go by convoy. One with 50 wagons leaves tomorrow and somebody will post this in Delhi.

I do hope that you've been enjoying Italy and that your great-uncle William Cory is running along as smoothly and melodiously as his Eton Boating Song.

I think Mountbatten finds my completely disinterested approach to the administrative and emotional problems caused by this splitting of India into India and Pakistan rather a relief. He is coming up here for the weekend and writes "I am most flattered by what you wrote about the Report and shall be glad to have the chance of talking it over with you".

An extract from a letter of Chrissie's to Joyce Weiner recalls the atmosphere of Simla in this October.

"A lot of mail was lost during the frightful troubles in the Punjab. I wrote you a long letter in which I described all that had happened up here during those dreadful ten days of killing and terror. It did not affect us except that we could not get out as there was a 24 hour curfew for some days, but it was awful to feel that so many of the nice Indians whom we had got to know quite well were living in terror for their lives.

"One tailor who was making things for me just got away from Simla with his life, and the clothes he stood up in. . . . The bitterness between Hindus and Muslims is frightful, and there will be fearful misery and bloodshed if there is a war between them. Of course, it is the Sikhs who cause all the trouble up here as they want a Sikhistan with Simla for their capital. They have already cleared all the Muslims out of here, and now there is talk that they are going to do likewise to the Hindus. They swagger about with their great long kirpans (nearly three feet) while the others aren't allowed even a pocket knife or a walking stick with which to protect themselves."

When I said that Chrissie and I were going to drive the thirty or forty miles to Sanawar in order to be present on Founder's Day at the Centenary celebration of the Lawrence Royal Military School opinion in Simla decided that we should inevitably be murdered by Sikhs on

the way. I pointed out that the Governor-General was driving up
from Delhi and would be driving on to Simla to stay for a day or two
in the Governor-General's Lodge. I said I felt confident that Simla
had not seen the last either of Chrissie or of myself. Heads were shaken
gloomily but we set out for Sanawar. There was, perhaps not unnatur-
ally, the same kind of mood among the British still in Simla as there
was once upon a time during the Mutiny when the British residents
thought they were going to be massacred by what would become
Queen Victoria's Second Gurkhas; they all fled into the woods and
camped out under the deodars until they found that the Gurkhas
were their protectors not their enemies.

I was greatly impressed by the atmosphere of the Lawrence School
and admired the way in which Mr Hazell the Principal was running
it. The Governor-General as always made a good speech to the boys
and Lady Mountbatten was equally eloquent with the girls. I think
I had to make a speech. However, what remains most vividly in my
memory of that day was the Governor-General's suddenly spotting
a copy of *The Windsor Tapestry* in the School library.

"I was at sea when your book came out and missed reading it at
the time," he said. "I'll ask them to lend it to me."

On the way back to Simla, our car followed the Mountbattens' car.
I see now the Governor-General's head half-asleep on the shoulder
of his daughter Pamela and Lady Mountbatten knitting all the way.
It was dusk when we reached the end of the steep zigzag up to Simla.
The Moll was crowded thick with wildly enthusiastic Indians shouting
'Mountbatten ki jai' and many of them kissing even the wheels of
the car. I had a press photograph at the time of the Governor-General
standing up in the car to say a few words to the wildly enthusiastic
crowd, in his left hand *The Windsor Tapestry*.

I had two long talks with the Governor-General that week of which
I wish I had kept a record at the time. One of the things I asked him
was why he had encouraged that queer plot for the Eighth Army
Heads to come out to teach the Fourteenth Army how to fight in the
jungle. I had been told in Burma that the original plan had been for
F.M. Montgomery to come out as soon as he had polished off the
Germans in order to show the world how to deal with the Japanese.
Arnhem postponed any likelihood of F.M. Montgomery's reaching
South-East Asia and Sir Oliver Leese took over command of the
Allied Forces' proposed campaign in South-East Asia. The intention
was to land at Port Swettenham in September 1945 and the plan was
for this operation in Malaya to be carried out by a new Fifteenth
Army into which most of the Fourteenth Army would be incorporated;
General Slim was to be left behind in Burma with a brigade. This
was too much for 'Bill' Slim. He flew home and managed to get that

preposterous plan stopped. In the end the atom bomb in August made the landing at Port Swettenham unnecessary.

"Oh, as soon as I realized what was going on, I put my foot down," said the ex-Supremo.

It was in the middle of May 1945 that General Sir Oliver Leese sent for General Slim and informed him that he was being removed from the command of the Fourteenth Army. He gave as his reason what can only be called the eccentric opinion that Slim was not capable of planning or carrying out the forthcoming operations of the Army. He had then had what in a civilian might have been called the impudence to offer Slim the command of a Burma Army which would amount to no more than a garrison. This complete failure to grasp what the Fourteenth Army had achieved was too much for Slim.

I recall mentioning the great job that Douglas Gracey had done in Saigon and Mountbatten's telling me that he had wanted to send another Indian Division to Hanoi but that President Truman had objected because he thought it would upset Chiang Kai Shek, an objection which Attlee had had to heed. What a difference it might have made to the future of North and South Vietnam if Mountbatten's proposal had been accepted.

It was my privilege after one of those talks at the Governor-General's Lodge to meet the Rajkumari Amrit Kaur. To quote from *The Times* obituary when she died in 1964:

"She was one of the three great women thrown up by the nationalist movement, the late Mrs Sarojini Naidu and Mrs V. L. Pandit being the others."

The Rajkumari was a Christian and educated at Sherbourne School for Girls. She was a fine tennis player and won many women's tennis championships. She would be Nehru's Minister of Health for ten years. Edwina Mountbatten had realized at once what an outstanding woman the Rajkumari was and those two women behaved with heroic ardour and fortitude. They would fly together to cholera and typhus camps, rising sometimes at three in the morning to do so, and after an exhausting day Edwina Mountbatten would be hostess at great dinner-parties in the Governor-General's House, Delhi. The dauntlessness of those two women remains with me as one of the great moral examples I have been set in my long life.

I have a relic of those talks in the Lodge at Simla in a letter from Lady Mountbatten to me from which I quote:

May I say it is a breath of fresh air, knowing someone in a high position such as you hold has so clearly and fairly understood the real Indian picture. It has distressed me very greatly and saddened me beyond words, and we ourselves are

so particularly helpless at this present critical period. We do thank you for all
your kind sympathetic as well as practical support.

I suggested to Mountbatten that if he thought it would be useful
I would write to Aneurin Bevan and point out where instructions from
some of the Ministeries were muddling rather than helping things
out here.

"Nye is a great friend of mine and has imagination," I told him.

"But why write to Bevan? The only Minister who counts is Attlee.
Write to him."

"Well, you may remember that I was rather rude about him in
The Windsor Tapestry."

"That wouldn't influence him one way or the other if he thinks
your remarks worth while attending to."

So I spent two days writing and rewriting a letter to Attlee; unfortunately I have lost the copy of what I wrote.

I was surprised and gratified to receive a personal reply from Attlee:

> 10 Downing Street,
> Whitehall.
> 28th October 1947.

My dear Compton Mackenzie,

Thank you so much for your letter of 14th October. I will see that
the points which you raise are brought at once to the attention of the
Ministries concerned.

> *Yours sincerely,*
> *C. R. Attlee*

One more memory of those talks with the Governor-General in the
garden of the Lodge at Simla is of his letting me know what he had
suffered when at the age of fourteen as a naval cadet at Dartmouth the
outrageous campaign against his father, Prince Louis of Battenberg,
had been started by the Popular Press. It was argued that his German
connections made him an unsuitable First Sea Lord at such a time,
and Prince Louis resigned, to become a year or two later the first
Marquis of Milford Haven and change the family name from Battenberg to Mountbatten. The young Louis had vowed then that one day
he would himself be a First Sea Lord.

I realized that this ambition was still cherished by the ex-Viceroy
of India and present Governor-General, by the ex-Supreme Commander of Allied Forces in South-East Asia, and by a naval officer
whose active service had been outstanding in its brilliancy and daring.

In 1954 his appointment as First Sea Lord seemed imminent when
the Beaverbrook Press launched a campaign against that appointment, not of course on the grounds of his being pro-German this time

but on the grounds of his being too much involved with the Socialists.

At that time I was writing a weekly article for the *Spectator* and I denounced this campaign. I recall ending up my article by saying that Admiral Lord Mountbatten was about as red as the Admiral of the Red in the days of Nelson. He wrote to tell me that my article had done something to clear the air and his appointment as First Sea Lord was confirmed to the great advantage of the Royal Navy.

One day in 1942 Beaverbrook had said to him that he would now regard me as his enemy. He had never understood the reason for this vendetta. Gossip had all sorts of silly explanations for this vendetta, but the true explanation seemed to me obvious. Mountbatten had given expert advice to Noel Coward for his immensely successful film *In Which We Serve*. That film opened with a copy of the *Daily Express* floating across Portsmouth Harbour showing the actual headline on the front page on Saturday September 2nd THERE WILL BE NO WAR.

On October 27th I wrote to Faith:

I've had only one P.C. from you from Siena—in the last six weeks. The posts have got into a fearful jam. The English people here have panicked rather and the Press at home has been disgracefully partisan and alarmist. Some of the opposition are trying to make an Ulster of Pakistan, which will be fatal to any hope we have of keeping India in the Commonwealth and if we don't our economy will suffer badly. Of course the loss of life on both sides has been horrible but the figures estimated in the Press at home are ludicrously exaggerated.

My present plan is to leave Bombay at the end of December and go to the Seychelles, and thence on to Kenya to see two or three more Generals, getting home at the end of April. I'm working hard at reading some of the mass of material here. Pages and pages of blurred typescript which is trying to the eyes.

The expedition to Sikkim had to be given up because of the disturbed state of the country. This odyssey of mine has been pretty expensive, but I shall try to get a novel written, or at any rate a good deal of it written in the Seychelles.

That notion of mine to visit the Seychelles went back to boyhood when by some stroke of fortune I was able to brag of an almost complete set of Seychelles stamps. Thanks to Sir Selwyn Selwyn-Clarke's being now the Governor I was able to obtain a permit for Chrissie and myself to enter the Colony; Jim Thomson was equally successful in obtaining permits for himself and Alice with their two small daughters, Alice Mary and Marjorie.

On November 25th I wrote to Faith:

We hope to get away from here about December 28th, go down to Delhi for 3 or 4 days and then on to Bombay to catch the ship. Our stay in the Seychelles will depend on shipping. I'm sending home 4 of the trunks, all of them crated, from Bombay. The heaviest part are the papers. It is so lucky for us that the Thomsons with their two delicious little girls of 7 and 5 are coming with us.

I can't make out what game these damned income tax people are playing, but it's beginning to look as if it will be a hard struggle to earn the wherewithal to keep up Denchworth properly. However, I'm postponing that problem till I get home. . . .

Auchinleck has left, dodging Mountbatten's return. There was a bit of a tug-of-war.

I can't say how much I'm looking forward to the Seychelles and am wondering if I shall be disappointed. . . .

I was kept awake last night by a monkey battle on the corrugated iron roof of this hotel. At this moment a bulbul is singing at the top of one deodar tree and from the top of another an eagle is eyeing it balefully . . . .

The weather in England doesn't sound too good. Snow in November usually presages a cold winter.

That presage was to be fulfilled only too painfully for the people at home.

I had a farewell letter from Claude Auchinleck on November 12th. 'In the air en route to Peshawar.'

I am due to leave Karachi by air at the end of the month and hope to fly straight to Genoa via Malta. . . .

It is very good to hear that you are satisfied with your material and that you have such good hopes of the result. I am sure myself that it will be a great success —a resounding triumph!! I am sure I hope so. . . .

I realized what a bitter end to his Indian career was buried in those words '*I am due to leave Karachi by air at the end of the month*! His service to the Indian Army had been as great if not greater than any Commander-in-Chief's. It was tragic, but perhaps inevitable, that the Indians should get into their heads the belief that he was favouring the Pakistanis, and equally inevitable that the Pakistanis should feel convinced that Mountbatten was favouring the Indians. By the kindness of 'Reggie' Savory[1] who was Adjutant-General until the end of this November I am publishing in Appendix A some letters which I think have historical importance as faithful records of the feeling at this sad time about the end of the Indian Army. I have suppressed only the names of the officers and regiments concerned.

Those last days in Simla were full of hospitality both from the Indian residents and the British residents that were left. Among other events was the baptism of John Shaw's only son to whom Alice Thomson and I were godmother and godfather. There was a last production of

---

[1] Lt-General Sir Reginald Savory, K.C.I.E., C.B., D.S.O., M.C.

the A.D.C. when a good performance of Priestley's play *Johnson Over Jordan* was given. Finally there was a Boxing Day party for the children at which I played Santa Claus without managing to deceive the sharp eyes of Alice Mary and Marjorie Thomson.

By an agreeable coincidence a day or two later I received a letter which gave me exceptional pleasure:

Dear Sir,

May I suggest that your 'Santa Claus in Summer' should be republished? When I read the article on Children's Classics in the Times Literary Supplement I felt it fully deserved a place amongst them. It has always stood a good second to Alice in my children's estimation. Since they have been grown up it has been read and lent to innumerable children, who have clamoured to possess it, but I have never been able to get another copy.

I never can understand why it is not more widely known as one of the most delightful children's books ever written.

I am glad to think *Santa Claus in Summer* is still in print today, but I fancy it will seem old-fashioned to contemporary children, with welcome exceptions of course. After all, Alice herself is considered a suitable subject for these pestilent psychoanalysts to monkey about with and for Television to debauch.

I had not yet seen a copy of *Whisky Galore* which had been published in November, but I was encouraged to hear from somebody who had known Barra for many years:

I must thank you with all my heart for enshrining Barra again, in Whisky Galore. It is wonderful to hear my friends talking just as they do with that peculiar blend of cold common-sense and utter irresponsibility that makes poor Mr Waggett feel he is in a mad house.

A week or so before this I had heard from John Dalison who was leaving for an Admiralty job in Canada.

"I see there is an agitation to give the Auk a peerage. I must say he deserves one. . . . The short title for my job is BARCAN. What a triumph for the Admiralty joke section! It stands for British Admiralty Representative Canada and is the same job as that of a Naval Attaché in a foreign capital except that they make the fact that it is an excuse for not paying me a living wage. I have told all the pundits at the Admiralty that I would work for the Navy as many days a week as the pay enables me to and that I would take the remainder off in order to paint for my living."

Alas, while that fine sailor and artist was doing his job in Ottawa he was killed in a motor smash. I look back to those days with him in the *Narbada* as among the most memorable in my long life.

We had a formidably uncomfortable journey down from Simla.

I reached Delhi too late for me to meet Mahatma Gandhi as I had hoped. His weekly silence day had started when we arrived. Nor was I able to say farewell to the Mountbattens who were in Gwalior.

We were very tired when we reached Bombay where to our consternation we found that Cooks had made a muddle over booking rooms for us at the Taj Mahal Hotel. The Taj was full up, and so indeed was hotel after hotel to which we telephoned. As I remember, it was Peter Goodwin (he had come down with us from Simla) who just after dark found a cockroach-infested hotel on the sea front and called, believe it or not, the Sea Green Hotel. Here Alice Thomson, Chrissie and the two little girls were squeezed into one room. Jim and I slept in another with two Indian bookies for company. One of the bookies had had a bad time at the races and spent the whole night tramping up and down, muttering figures and odds, trying to work out his losses.

I was cheered up after that exasperating night by getting a postcard from Lord Samuel:

"I send you, for your collection, a 'literally' I have just received from a journalist friend in Lancashire taken from the 'Farmworker Journal'.

"He was born, literally, with printer's ink in his veins, and was an outstanding character in the field of local journalism."

The following night the Thomsons, Chrissie and I sat on the balcony of what we called the Pea Green Hotel to see in the New Year. It was going to be a bit of a job for 1948 to compete with 1947 as far as any of us were concerned. But the sirens hooting the New Year in down at the docks reminded us that the Seychelles would be a colourful opening for 1948.

WE fortunately did not have to depend on the Pea Green Hotel for our meals in Bombay after morning coffee. There was the usual abundant hospitality.

Archbishop Roberts asked me to lunch with him but had to leave immediately afterwards to go on board the ship in which he was sailing for England. He left me to the good offices of his Auxiliary, the Bishop of Tannis *in partibus*. I realised how anxious he was that his Auxiliary should be the next Archbishop of Bombay. Bishop Gracias (pronounced gracious) was a tall and handsome Goanese.

"You may not know," said Archbishop Roberts, "that when Bombay came to us with the dowry of Catherine of Braganza it was stipulated that the nomination for the Archbishop of Bombay should be made alternately by the British monarch and the Patriarch of Lisbon. When I give up the Archbishopric, as I hope to do as soon as possible, the next Archbishop must be an Indian."

The Patriarch of Lisbon agreed about this, and that is why Archbishop Roberts was succeeded by his Auxiliary, with whom I spent a couple of hours in stimulating talk. I was not surprised when Archbishop Gracias was made a Cardinal a few years later. Archbishop's House was, and I am sure still is, a source of light.

By special favour we were allowed to sleep on board the *S.S. Kampala* three days before she was to sail. The picture that remains in my mind on that afternoon of January 9th is of Gulaba Ram. He had given Chrissie and myself devoted service; we had been lucky indeed to have him as our bearer from the moment we arrived in Bombay to the moment we left it fifteen months later. He had given me as an expression of his sorrow at parting from us a green and white bed coverlet. I see him now as I write these words, standing forlornly on the quay, tears running down his cheeks, when the *Kampala* was taking away from him two people whom he was unlikely ever to see again. In the testimonial I wrote for him I tried to express my gratitude. He had, I gathered, a rather difficult domestic life, and I think that those months of moving round with us had been for him a happy escape.

Every cabin in the ship was occupied, and among the voyagers were several people we had met in one place or other in India and Burma. On the morning after we left Bombay, the *Kampala* stopped for a short while at Goa, but not long enough to go ashore and visit the old city some miles inland. I was struck by the air of perfect contentment with which the people of Goa were walking up and down the quay. It was inevitable that Nehru would have to give way to the agitation against what had been Portuguese rule for some four hundred years. That agitation was fomented outside Goa; the Goanese themselves had no desire to lose their Portuguese nationhood.

On southward with the weather getting warmer and stickier and the sky greyer; I remember saying that at any rate the horizon was not so dark as an idiotic film we saw called *Dark Horizon*. On the sixth day of the voyage we ran into as dense a downfall of rain as I ever experienced but although still grey it was not raining when we reached Victoria, the port of Mahé and the capital of the Seychelles.

Thanks to the kind offices of Dr Selwyn-Clarke, as he still was, his A.D.C. Major Burt, who was also Chief of Police, made our disembarkation ashore in a launch an easy matter. We were introduced to Maurice Michaud who would be our host at his guest house called Northolme at Glacis on the north-west corner of the island. He was a Seychellois belonging to one of the families of what were known as *les grands blancs*, that is to say one of the families of the original French settlers to whom the slaves had looked up as their lords and masters, and whom the emancipated Creoles still regard with much more respect than the British invaders.

I shall quote from a letter of Chrissie's to Faith:

The house is built of wood and is built on rocks almost overhanging two beaches on either side. The sound of the sea and the wind reminds me of the Hebrides and in fact conditions in this place are almost the same as staying at Coddie's except that the servants are black and coffee-coloured. The proprietor, Mr Michaud, is a delightful character and is French; his family have been here since the 18th century. He is married to an Englishwoman who used to travel all over the world with her mother who was a wealthy woman. She is quite young but is not very healthy—she has very high blood pressure and looks years older than her 41 years. She seems rather nice but knows nothing about running a guest house. In fact neither of them does. They bought this place and paid quite a lot for it but as they had no family it was much too big for them and they decided to turn it into a guest house. Actually that is better really because one can have what one likes and they are both very kind and sweet and want to do all they can to make us comfortable. C.M. has the best room in the place upstairs (the only room upstairs). It is a crazily built place but very attractive. His room has port-holes all the way round it with sea on all sides and it is really like being in a ship's saloon with the sound of the sea all around one. The port-holes slide open. The furniture consists of a bed, a very old and rickety wardrobe (not large), one small marble-topped table, one large table which covers the well of the staircase, two chairs and one card-table!! Fortunately plenty deep shelves here and there.

I bathe every morning with the Thomsons and their two children before

7a. C.M. with children at Katmandu   7b. C.M. on Chinese Frontier

8. Last photograph taken of General Sir Ian Hamilton with C.M.

breakfast which is at 8 and we bathe again before tea. But it is real surf bathing at the moment. They tell us it will be quite calm at the end of the month. We get masses of excellent fish, fresh eggs, fruit and very little meat. We have had roast sucking pig and chicken on two occasions. Supplies are difficult to get but I think Michaud tries to be self-supporting. They grow masses of egg-plants, papayas, mangoes, pineapples, bananas, pumpkins of various kinds (very dull). We have breadfruit instead of potatoes. Fortunately there are onions but other green vegetables seem to be difficult to grow here. What does grow seems to grow very easily—you just stick a plant anywhere and up it comes. Glorious amaryllis, bougainvillea, and what looks like a lovely red bignonia ramping all over a huge tree in front of C.M's room. And coconuts everywhere.

This island is quite high—3,000 feet at the highest point and there are huge rocks and boulders lying about, some of them fantastic shapes. I can well believe there is still a great deal of treasure hidden along the coast in many places. But it is very remote and far away and I feel that I would not care to live here for a very long time. I need hardly add that C.M. says he wouldn't mind how long he stayed here! I have to watch all our clothes in suitcases most carefully because there are flying cockroaches which eat things particularly woollen clothes and artificial silk.

I shall add to that description of my room that it was lined with pitch pine and that above the pitch pine ceiling was a roof of corrugated iron. I could look down over the winding path through the casuarina trees into our small bathing cove. I could look inland and watch the slow and dignified flight of the large fruit-eating bats as just before dusk they set out in pairs for their nocturnal feast. Westward I could watch the sublime sunsets behind the island of Silhouette. It certainly did have a magnificent silhouette, but it was called Silhouette after a French financial minister in the eighteenth century who was supposed to have taxed people so heavily that only their outlines were left and gave his name to a popular art-form which I wish could become fashionable again. They might be called . . . indeed the names of most Chancellors of the Exchequer from Lloyd George onwards would be equally appropriate.

Jim Thomson and I went on to Victoria to dine with the Governor on that first evening. I was depressed by a kind of a haunted atmosphere about Government House, as if it was a symbol of the decline and fall of the British Empire. However, Selwyn-Clarke was optimistic about bringing the house to life again after the inevitable neglect of it during the war. One amenity it did have, which had not been neglected, was a first-class croquet lawn.

The change from the frost and sun of Simla to the hot humidity of sea-level on the equator laid me out for that first week with a threat of dysentery and some lively rheumatism. I celebrated my sixty-fifth

L

birthday by taking forty sulfaguanidine tablets under Jim Thomson's orders; they successfully defeated the dysentery. The prospect of descending those steep stairs from my room day and night to the Northolme loo had not been bright. The Northolme loo was a fantasy. It was a kind of cave which must have been blasted out of the granite. Inside one mounted rocky steps to the throne, which had to be approached carefully to avoid cockroaches, scorpions and large centipedes.

In spite of the tiresome rheumatism I managed to write a long article for the *Literary Digest* and in a letter of January 23 I was saying:

Pain down now. I've decided to postpone writing 'Mrs Smith' and write 'Hunting the Fairies' instead.

Mrs Smith has not yet been written; if one day I decide to tackle it I shall have a Balzacian story of the *Cousin Bette* type.

I was well enough to go to a big dinner party at Government House next day, and on Sunday Maurice Michaud drove me to Mass at Glacis. The twelve parishes of Mahe were served by Swiss Capuchin friars, a remarkable body of men.

John Pape whom I had not seen for 45 years just after he won the Merton Grind came along that afternoon.

We had a good talk about old friends—most of them dead, I wrote . . . *Pape's last job had been running the Calcutta Sweep. When that was swept away he bought himself a house about a couple of miles from Northolme. He drove Chrissie and myself along to see it. The house was well built on the edge of a cliff and had a balcony like a quarter deck, with the best view I can remember, even better than the view from Casa Solitaria at Capri, and that is a big claim to make for a view.*

I am glad I was not able to tell Pape that when last I was at Merton in the fifties the Warden himself had never heard of the Merton Grind which in 1903 was considered the star point-to-point even by the Bullingdon bloods of the House. Pape himself was disappointed by his Seychelles experiment and offered to sell me his place for what he gave for it—£4,000. I was writing soon after this:

I like John Pape's place more and more. But the society here is pretty poor. Suburban of 30 years ago with the usual tug between the French and the English the former so far not being any more interesting than the latter. But I think it would be a good place of the hermitage style for a long job of work. I should like to write the earlier part of The Keyboard here.

Over a decade would elapse before I struck the first notes on *The Keyboard* which by then would be *My Life and Times: Octave I.*

I wrote the first page of *Hunting the Fairies* on January 26th and the next four pages on the following day. *These beginnings of books are a fearful grind,* I wrote. The effort to start a novel again after eighteen months was more of a grind than usual, though when I look back at it *Whisky Galore* had been just as tough. I was glad my first copy of it arrived soon after this because I wanted to check up on the names of my characters. My habit of forgetting everything I write as soon as it is published is a handicap when I am away from my old books.

I met at Government House the Acting Attorney-General A. G. Collet. The Governor recommended him to me as the most intelligent of the Seychellois. He was the son of a mason here with a good deal of colour who by guts and by brain had become first a doctor and then a barrister. This double profession naturally appealed to Selwyn-Clarke. Collet who was married to a French barrister, may have been pleased enough to get back on some of those white British or *grands blancs* who had snubbed him on the way up. At any rate he was causing a terrific upset by digging up fake income-tax returns made by various planters during the war, and initiating legal proceedings against them much to the embarrassment of the Lord Chief Justice who was a Cingalese.

On the day of King Charles the Martyr came the news of Mahatma Gandhi's assassination. I deeply regretted that I had failed to meet him. I felt that Earth was poorer for his leaving it and Heaven richer.

February came in blowing hard. There had been a cyclone at Réunion and we were getting the edge of it. The Seychelles themselves were too near the equator to have cyclones in full force. I found the weather good for work; *Hunting the Fairies* began to go ahead. I was starting to write early in the morning, which I had never done before in my life. I used to stop at dusk because the insects were a nuisance. The only insects that worried me in the daytime were the big carpenter bees so called because they excavate homes for themselves in wood. About half a dozen lived in the pitch pine lining of my room and like all bees and wasps and hornets they had an annoying habit of not making up their minds where they wanted to go. Not a carpenter bee ever found her own home until she had buzzed around the homes of other carpenter bees who would come buzzing out to ask her what she thought she was buzzing about. Once I was stung by a carpenter bee which had been investigating my rubber sponge. I banged it hard two or three times and flung it out on the sloping corrugated iron roof of the balconies on the ground floor. Like myself the ants thought it was dead and almost immediately it was surrounded by them and they were dragging it off to their headquarters. Half a dozen of these ants were running about on top of the corpse when suddenly the corpse came to life and flew off with the half dozen ants on its back. Carpenter bees have heads as hard as the wood on which they work.

Chrissie was writing to Faith on February 9th:

"I bathe every day, sometimes three times and have now learned to swim quite well. I study French every morning and find that my six years of French at school were more thorough than I thought as it comes back fairly easily. . . .

"You would love the warmth but you would not love the insects here. Last night I killed a flying cockroach of at least seven inches in length. It seemed to me like a whale! There is a huge spider (outdoors) which makes the loveliest web and she keeps two or three minute husbands in her web, and eats them when she has finished with them! —like the praying mantis. At first we thought the small spiders in the web were her babies—so small are they in comparison with herself. She has very long black and orange legs and a black body about the size of a large bee—perhaps bigger. I haven't yet met one of the enormous centipedes but Alice Thomson nearly sat on one in the loo the other evening. Jim Thomson is kept hard at it D.D.T.-ing."

I was writing home on February 14:

It is getting hotter and hotter but I am determined to prove that it is possible to work in the tropics. I am writing 7 or 8 hours a day in order to maintain my schedule of seven pages a day. On Ash Wednesday I saw the young moon on her back, holding the old moon in her arms under a rim of silver and dipping down with the old moon toward the ocean horizon.

I get a marvellous swim every afternoon to reward me for my diligence, and believe me I really do overcome temptation by refusing to bathe till the seventh page is written.

I met a fellow who writes school stories for the Amalgamated Press—an aggressive fossil of 66. He said severely that the Seychelles were no place for adultery. I was not surprised wandering bachelors came here to live with Creole girls. The British married women were almost all unspeakably dull. 'No Place for Adultery' would make a good title for a novel.

Lent was lightened for the people of Port Victoria by the arrival of Archbishop David Mathew, the Apostolic Delegate in Africa, which meant an unusual open-air procession for the season. Father Gervase Mathew, his Dominican brother, was with the Archbishop. David Mathew was a rich personality with a remarkable career behind him. He had started at Osborne and Dartmouth and was a midshipman when the Great War ended. When he left the Navy he had a scholarly period at Balliol. He had been Bishop Auxiliary at Westminster to Cardinal Hinsley, and had written some good books. I was lucky enough to have given in the *Daily Mail* his first book *The Celtic Peoples and the Renaissance in Europe* its first good notice. One always remembers kindly the man who gave one's first book its first good notice and David Mathew has always remembered me kindly.

The Archbishop's job in the Seychelles was to reach an agreement about the future of Education. The Catholic Bishop whose name I have forgotten was making things difficult for the Educational plans of the Colonial Office. I recall being shown a new school which had been built in Port Victoria and being shown with pride the pictures which had been contributed by the British Council. Those were engravings of works by the English painters of the eighteenth century. I hardly thought that Reynolds and Constable would have a great appeal to the young Creoles of Port Victoria. Nor did a large framed photograph of Stoke Poges Churchyard strike me as absolutely appropriate.

The Governor had asked me to come and play our Thursday game of croquet and stay on to an informal dinner to meet the Archbishop and his brother. The Governor and I had a dour game which lasted for nearly two hours and was finally won by Selwyn-Clarke, three hoops ahead. It was '*a really good evening of civilised talk*' as I wrote home. What I recall from that talk was the Archbishop's suddenly saying to the obvious surprise of the Governor, "You know I always feel rather sorry for the Devil", on which I commented "Like Marie Corelli".

The Governor had invited the Northolme party to go to Praslin in the Governor's launch when he went over there for three days. I was now halfway through *Hunting the Fairies* and felt I was entitled to a short holiday. I am glad I did; that expedition to Praslin was worth much more than 28 pages of my book.

We were up at 6.30 and on the pier by eight o'clock to embark on the *Jeannette*, a very lively craft. Those three hours were a long three hours for the Northolme party. Jim Thomson still maintains that he was not seasick; the rest of the Northolme party were all seasick. I seem to remember cracking a joke about Sick Transit Glorious Monday and being reminded rather peevishly by one of the victims that it was Tuesday not Monday. To my mind the major compensation of senescence is that by the time a man reaches the mid-sixties he is immune to sea-sickness. The more the *Jeannette* bucked about the more I enjoyed that crossing. However, that sick transit was forgotten when we found ourselves in a bungalow by the water's edge kindly lent to us by its owner.

A few yards from the Lanier bungalow lived a retired Gunner Colonel whose name I have forgotten. He was a strict teetotaller with one eye and a rupture, but he was dressed impeccably and his bungalow was as spruce as himself. The Colonel had plenty of intelligence and I was impressed by the way all the local Creoles obviously liked and respected him.

I did not enjoy my bathe; the water in the lagoon was really too warm; I did not stay in long but came out and sat in a deck-chair tackling *Times* crossword puzzles in a few copies of the journal the Governor had lent me. The *Times* crossword puzzle was presently put down to watch a sunset more lovely than any I had seen yet, and the Seychelles sunsets remain the best I have seen anywhere. There were stretches of green sky southward, as green as grass, and above them stretches of blue with plum-dark clouds over the small neighbouring islands. As the sun went down it vanished in rose and copper with fire behind. At dawn I woke to an equally superb sunrise of rose and gold with a lemon-yellow full moon setting behind the palm groves along the shore.

Before eight o'clock we were off on our long walk to the only valley in the world where the *coco de mer* grows wild. This tree is a survival from an earlier world. The nut itself is a huge oblong and has an exact resemblance to the female genital organ, pubic hair and all, while the fertilizing stem attached to the palm resembles the male organ. Sometime in the 'eighties General Gordon was sent to report whether the Seychelles would be suitable for a naval and military base in the Indian Ocean. He was not impressed by their suitability for that. What he was impressed by was that in visiting the Seychelles he had obviously visited the site of the Garden of Eden, and he wrote a report to that effect, which is now in Mauritius. By a piece of good luck a week or two after I had written the account of our expedition to Praslin I found the copy of a letter from General Gordon to Kew. This is printed in Appendix B and many of those who read it will agree with me that General Gordon made out a strong case for his theory.

During the middle ages and indeed as late as the eighteenth century those mysterious nuts which sometimes floated ashore in Ceylon were regarded as a powerful and infallible aphrodisiac. One of the Austrian Emperors paid the equivalent of several thousands of pounds for a specimen.

It was a tough climb up to the valley in the heat. I started off in the only rickshaw on the island, which the Creoles call a push-push, but I felt so sorry for my 'pusher' that I walked for most of the four miles to the valley. It was an awe-inspiring experience and as we walked through that antedeluvian world our voices were almost hushed. Most of the palms were over three or four hundred years old and there was one, the tallest of the lot, which was believed to be over eight hundred years old. On our way to the valley we had passed clove, coffee, cinnamon and allspice along the road but the valley itself had nothing except primeval vegetation of which the giant pandanus was the most impressively gloomy. As we walked along through what was almost a twilight we hoped to see one of the black parrots that only here in all the world may be seen. We had been warned that it would be very unlikely to see one, the sight of which was said to give seven years of good fortune, but no parrot did we see. At last we reached the hut above the valley where we rested and prepared to eat lunch. I recall watching with fascination a canary-yellow hunting wasp at work building her marvellous nest of mud against the wall of the hut.

Then suddenly to our joy four black parrots flew along to alight in a casuarina tree and chatter away at one another. Twenty-eight years of good fortune! They were near enough for Jim Thomson to get a shot of them in his cine-camera and I can see those parrots on the screen today. When we told people we had seen four black parrots they would not believe us but there they are in Jim Thomson's film. I was thankful to hear the birds were being protected now, but I hoped they would be more effectively protected than the telephone wires which the people of Praslin kept cutting to make strings for their guitars and violins.

We were given some vanilla pods by the owner of the bungalow when we got back from our excursion, absolutely whacked. The plants creeping round the trunks of the trees would not have their white lily-like flowers until July. It is an illustration of our willingness to abandon our imperial responsibilities that when we reached England with those vanilla pods we were charged duty for them. Presumably this duty was imposed to protect those dreary bottles of synthetic vanilla which provide all but a happy few with the illusion that they know what vanilla tastes like.

My memories of the following day when Jim Thomson and I went for a cruise right round the coastline of Praslin are confused. What remains clear in my mind is the sight of the Creole lepers coming down to the beach of a small island and waving to us as we sailed by. After that we landed on another small island where we talked to a lonely planter, the son of a thrice-married Englishman whom he described to us as a drunkard and a *gaspilleur*. His wife was in hospital and he seemed quite unable to manage his eight children. But the most memorable experience for me that day was my first taste of *coco de mer* which I thought absolutely delicious with the texture of a muscatel grape.

I had just written that rather hazy account of our cruise round Praslin in which I had omitted to mention an island called Cousin because I did not feel sure of the name, when the post arrived with a bundle of letters held up by the strike in France. One of those letters was from Mrs Bushill-Matthews inviting me to a 'Seychelles Safari' with the Birmingham Branch of the World Wild Life Fund which was raising money for the purchase of the Island of Cousin as a wild life sanctuary.

We embarked on the *Jeannette* next day about noon. The Governor came armed with some anti-seasick medicine, remembering that sick transit of three days ago. However, the sea was calm and everybody was lively. Alice Mary caught a bonito to her pride and delight. I told her I should call her Mrs Jack Horner. It was soon my turn to be teased because I let my malacca cane fall overboard. The *Jeannette* put about and at last we sighted it floating gallantly. One of the matelots hooked it back on board.

I was writing on February 28th:

I had a tough job getting down to work again after those colourful three days in Praslin. The temperature was 87°, and very sticky. My knees were badly sunburnt and very sore, and on top of that there were three punctures in my air-cushion to mend. After three hours of writing I had only done two pages of Chapter 12. However, after lunch I worked for 5½ hours without stopping and in the end produced 9 pages for the day which shows that it is possible to write in the tropics if you have the necessary determination.

Chrissie was writing to Faith:

"C.M. loves being here and has been able to work very well. But I don't know how he does it as some days are *so* hot. He just lies in a large bath-towel with nothing on but short pants whilst writing."

The S.E. Monsoon was early, and as I struggled on with *Hunting the Fairies* the weather grew hotter and hotter with violent squalls. Prickly heat started to be tiresome and the sciatic nerve competed with it. I recall from that struggle to finish *Hunting the Fairies* one night when two of the ports in my room blew in and when I woke in the morning finding myself covered in leaves like a babe in the wood. I finished the revised manuscript on March 12 and celebrated the occasion by drinking the book's health in some Mauritius rum flavoured with vanilla and prunes. I was writing on Good Friday:

Finished last 20 pages of typescript which means Hunting the Fairies was written in exactly two months to a day.

I went to Mass on Palm Sunday, carrying my palm with me to be blessed. It was a long business but nearer to the original Palm Sunday than ours at home with those little faded crosses handed out to one already blessed. The 'palms' or sallow buds must have been taken to church like that in the Middle Ages. The High Altar and Sacred Heart Altar were completely covered with palms. Our Lady, St John the Baptist and St Francis were covered with bougainvillea.

I don't know when there will be another mail. The last lot we sent off with H.M.S. Loch Quoich, and they were to be posted in Trincomalee. I thought the arrival of that ship with a loch from the Western Highlands a good omen for the Fairies. I had a welcome cable yesterday from Chattos congratulating me on finishing the book.

While I was doing my revision I've been reading Evelyn Waugh's 'Handful of Dust' which is very good indeed. I like it best of his books. I was also reading Willie Maugham's Round Dozen. Of course, his minor adulteries under the palms are technically excellent but for me the technique is too apparent, and somehow the result is artificial. He makes odd mistakes like 'illusive' when he means 'elusive', but in the story about a world-famous herpetologist whose wife goes off in the usual Maugham way with a young man he makes a real howler because the herpetologist talks of being stung by a snake. From that moment I could not believe there ever was such a herpetologist and in a novel I must be able to believe that the people really did exist. I thought 'Of Human Bondage' splendid when I read it 30 years ago and I shan't read it again because I hate being disillusioned in maturity by a book I enjoyed in youth. Much of the success he had with the young men of the 'twenties was his provision of a kind of ready-made cynicism which they mistook for worldly wisdom.

I was feeling the reaction of finishing the book and cried off a grand party the Governor was giving for the officers of *H.M.S. Loch Quoich* to which the Thomsons went. I went to bed early and enjoyed an unusual experience for me; at 1.15 a.m. I was woken from deep sleep by a smell. I got up and looked round the room with my torch for a dead rat. I could find nothing. The smell was more violent. I wondered if it was fermenting palm toddy. Then I wondered if I had contracted some odd disease of the nose since I went to bed, and hoped if I had that Jim Thomson would be able to diagnose and prescribe the right cure. I went back to bed and somehow in spite of the smell I managed to sleep again.

In the morning the mystery was solved. Some time ago I had happened to tell the Governor that there were two fruits in Malaya out of season when we were there which I longed to taste. One was the mangosteen of which I had read in the Vailima letters when R.L.S. planted it in Samoa without much hope of its succeeding. This I had managed to taste thanks to somebody's garden in Mahé, and most delicious it was. The other fruit was the durian which the Malays themselves esteemed their noblest fruit wondering why we liked the pineapples which they despised. There was a durian tree in the garden of Government House and the Governor had sent one back for me with the Thomsons. They had put the large oval fruit with its thick knotted green skin on a table at the bottom of the stairs leading up to my room. Even the Northolme dogs who barked at everything and everybody were silenced by it and slunk off with their tails between their legs. A fellow guest of ours at Northolme, an elderly Australian, who was waiting for a passage to Durban on his way home was woken by the smell and thought the main drain must have burst and considered waking up Milhaud.

With a certain lack of foresight the durian was put into the frigidaire with the result that for a week or two the butter smelt too. We decided to eat the durian before dinner. The moment it was cut open the smell vanished but only Chrissie and I were bold enough to take the first spoonful. It was delicious, the most delicious fruit I had so far eaten in the tropics. To me it tasted like a mixture of Irish stew and apricots. Chrissie liked the flavour of onions, but Alice Mary who was braver than her parents did not like onions and she thought the durian delicious. I should add to apricots and Irish stew, a taste of strawberries and cream with the faintest hint of paraffin.

Harry Savi, the owner of Frigate Island, had invited Jim Thomson, myself and Thomas, a jolly Welsh tobacco grower from Rhodesia on holiday, to spend a week-end with him. The confounded S.E. Monsoon blew and blew and we had given up hope of the expedition before we sailed to Mombasa when the weather became kinder, and on Friday, April 2nd after lunching at the club we sailed for Frigate in Harry Savi's speedboat. There was still a heavy swell but it was growing less all the time. Of the voyage what I remember is the sight of two turtles copulating. Savi slowed down for Jim Thomson to take a photograph but what may be called the two turtle-doves were more embarrassed than the young *avant garde* of today in films and plays and books; they submerged.

Frigate turned out to be a classic island, and the memory of it has consoled me for my failure to reach the South Seas. Some years ago I put up to the B.B.C. a proposal for a T.V. series in which I would start in Edinburgh and follow R.L.S. through the places of his career to Samoa, winding up by his tomb above Vailima. The B.B.C. thought it would be too expensive for them and doubted whether there was nowadays enough interest in R.L.S. to make the expense worthwhile.

It was about five o'clock when we reached Frigate, the surf by now not being too heavy to land on the beach. We sat on the verandah of Savi's bungalow. I remember the two great banyan trees covered I thought for a moment with big white blossoms, which in fact were roosting terns. I still hear the sound of the banyan seeds falling on the roof of the verandah. I still see Venus very bright in the west and the Great Bear nosing down into the north-east. I still see Arcturus rising, Saturn just above Mars, and Sirius bright as Venus. As I see that equatorial sky I hear the chattering of the terns in the banyan trees. Two shades of pink remain in my memory, the pink of a zephyranthes flower and the pink of the coral. And a last memory of that dusk as we drank our whiskies or Dubonnets the sight of a puppy industriously chewing up a packet of Thomas's cigarettes.

Next morning the others went off fishing early. I walked around with Savi's manager. The black soil was very fertile; the palms produced

60,000 coconuts a month. I saw the copra and the tobacco drying. I saw the yellow flowers of the musk from which scent was made. I walked through a grove of wild oranges and saw a large black butterfly with circular white spots, giving a domino effect. There were a lot of baby turtles in a tub which would be emptied when they would have a chance of getting safely down to the sea. Too many of them were the prey of various enemies immediately after hatching. Finally I was shown a pen of giant tortoises, not one of which I was assured was less than 300 years old. I was also told that when the Seychelles were first discovered in the middle of the eighteenth century there were crocodiles up to 40 feet in length, but I was never shown any remains to justify that assertion. What I did see, however, when I went to the privy out in the garden that night were three black scorpions, each of them at least eight inches long, and defying me with open claws and curling tails to do my business until they had retired. These black scorpions were peculiar to Frigate; so too was a magpie-robin I saw.

On Sunday morning the others all set out to go stalking; I could not learn how there came to be red deer on the island, but red deer there were, though Frigate was only a square mile in area. The stalking was a failure because in spite of the size of Frigate they did not see a stag or a hind. I said I believed the red deer on Frigate were unicorns.

That afternoon we sailed back to Port Victoria in an exquisite apricot sunset as we came along the quay. It had been a truly superlative week-end.

The last week was full of farewell calls of which I remember going to tea with the Laniers who had been so kind to us on Praslin. Suddenly Madame Lanier jumped up and put covers over her mirrors. This was because a cardinal bird had arrived on the verandah which used to attack the reflection of itself. These brilliant carmine birds were immigrants from Madagascar and had by now made themselves the cock-sparrows of the Seychelles by getting rid of nearly all other small birds. I gave a talk in the Carnegie Hall with the Governor in the Chair. I forget what the talk was about. We left Northolme with regret on April 10th. Neither Maurice Michaud nor his wife is still alive but I record my gratitude to them. Chrissie and I stayed at Government House that last night, and after a dinner-party I sat up with the Governor till half-past one talking about the various problems of the Seychelles. The most immediate was the Income Tax war between the Deputy Attorney General and various planters. I was much disappointed to miss the arrival of Dr Selwyn-Clarke's wife and daughter. I have not mentioned that the Governor had a delightful summer bungalow high up above Port Victoria. The Seychelles had been a place for exiles. The French began it by banishing two or three dozen terrorists. We wound up by inexplicably banishing Archbishop

Makarios there a century and a half later. He was housed in that
summer bungalow. The Archbishop and I had a talk about the Seychelles in Athens. He has a sense of humour and had been much
amused by the idea that his banishment would help to solve the
Cyprus problem.

The morning after our night in Government House we went aboard
the *S.S. Tairea* bound for Mombasa. Captain Macdonald was an
Australian whose mother was a Mackenzie of Applecross. He was as
warm-hearted a skipper as I ever sailed with. We had three days of
deep blue water sailing in perfect weather on the way to Mombasa
where Archbishop Mathew and Father Gervase were on the quay to
meet the *Tairea*—I hope I have her name correctly. David Mathew
had asked me to stay with him, and Chrissie was the guest of C. C.
Ricketts and his wife. He was the headmaster of the Arab school, and
they were a charming pair. I see now Father Gervase in his white
Dominican habit hurrying along the quayside like a large newspaper
blown by the wind.

I think that by this time my brain must have felt that it had been
asked to record too much during the last eighteen months. For what
would be the last month I cannot hope to be sure of my accuracy
whether about time or place or people. The first problem was to decide
about our return to England. News that the first ship would not be
sailing until June 10 at the earliest decided me, much as I disliked
the notion, that we should have to fly home. Accordingly we were
booked to fly from Nairobi on May 16th.

On Sunday I went to Mass in the African church which was
completely packed. There must have been at least 800 in the congregation. Men predominated because they used to leave their wives at
home to keep the land going while they came down to Mombasa. I
was impressed by the devotion of the worshippers and also by the
enthusiasm of the three Irish missionary priests with whom I break-
fasted after Mass.

That afternoon Chrissie and I set out for Nyeri where we were going
to stay with Tom Corbett[1] and his wife. It was a long and for much of
the way a tedious journey. The man-eating lions which used to raid
the sleeping-cars had long been disposed of.

We reached Nairobi next morning and the journey from there on
to Nyeri took hours because the railway wound about along the
hundred miles like a river. At one station we saw some Kikuyu women
with their heads covered by red mud, one of them with a green and a
red plastic comb stuck on either side. They were all in pink dresses
and carrying tattered umbrellas, all laughing happily and shaking the

---

[1] Lt.-General T. W. Corbett, C.B.

fantastically large lobes of their ears. The festival in prospect for them to which they were obviously looking forward was their circumcision!

Tom Corbett whom I was very glad to meet again and with whom I was looking forward to more rewarding talks about military events in North Africa met us at Nyeri. They had had some much needed rain and the road to his house was so slithery that he had to use chains round the wheels of his car. I do not think I am exaggerating when I say that the only good road in Kenya at this date was one which had been made by Italian prisoners-of-war on their diet of zebra meat.

The Corbetts' house at Mweiga was on a wide plateau with a superb view of Mount Kenya rising for 17,000 feet to a snowy sharp and ragged peak that reminded me of Etna.

Tom's first wife Flora made us warmly welcome. During our stay in Kenya she impressed me with her wisdom. She was a little older than her husband and died three years later.

Tom Corbett was full of his plans for the future. I recall his showing me a bamboo and wattle house being built for his herdsmen, but I must not start telling what the people in Kenya were hoping to do. Among those whose dreams of the future were dispelled were Billy and Ruby Beyts. He had been one of the Dagger Division's Brigadiers who had taken part in that famous crossing of the Irrawaddy. We spent many enjoyable hours with Billy and Ruby and their entertaining children. A letter from Chrissie to Faith written on April 26th brings back to me that Kenya of twenty years ago:

"One loses all sense of time here—it is really very remote and now that the rains are on it feels like being on an island rather. Still, we have been able to get about a bit. It is quite chilly now, although far from cold. We have met quite a few of the people who live nearby. All of them have lovely houses and even more lovely gardens with enormous lawns most beautifully kept and hand weeded, all of them, by the Kikuyu women and not one weed to be seen in any of the beds. They grow quite a lot of our English flowers and of course also lots of tropical plants. We have been out to lunch but one doesn't go out much at nights because the roads are so bad—just mud in which you stick very badly. . . . The other afternoon we saw a flock or herd or whatever you call it of ostriches. When they saw us coming they moved away very fast; they looked enormous. Lots of smaller birds including the widdah bird which dances in the most extraordinary way (the cock bird of course) while the hen birds sit around and look on. It was fascinating to watch them and as they have long floppy tails they looked most attractive. . . .

"The famous Tree Tops Hotel is quite near here but I don't think we are going. It is rather expensive and I must say the thought of walking a mile to it with the possibility of meeting a rhino face to face is not my cup of tea at all. There are rope ladders here and there for people to get up into the trees in the case of danger."

The Outspan in Nyeri was by far the most attractive hotel to look at that I had seen in my Odyssey but I enjoyed more the clubbable atmosphere of the White Rhino. The Outspan had a series of three-roomed cottages for guests in one of which Tom's uncle, Jim Corbett was staying with his sister. I found the most renowned slayer of man-eating tigers a most attractive personality. I look back to his talk as I sat beside him in the little garden of that cottage and watch the sunbirds with quivering wings bathing in the jet of the fountain.

The days went on with visits to one enchanting house and garden after another. I have to confess that I remember more vividly the flowers than our various hosts. I think the importance of remembering the personalities of so many soldiers had undermined my memory for civilians. I could write a bit about flowers that would run to half a page but I shall mention only the thrill of picking rose and white amaryllis in a meadow as I might have picked buttercups at home. Another sight that is still vivid is of two hornbills playing cup and ball with wild olives.

Next day we were packed up to go to Nairobi to which we were to drive by car. We were sad to leave Tom and Flora Corbett. He had clarified my views on the Malayan campaign. We stayed at the Norfolk Hotel in Nairobi which was said to be the best; it was certainly the most pretentious.

Next day General Heath[1] drove in from Limoru to take us back to stay with him for a couple of nights.

"We've never met," he said, "but we have corresponded. When I was commanding the 1/11 Sikhs you sent us the original despatch you wrote about the battle of the fourth of June at Gallipoli."

I told him how much my own morale had been stimulated by that wonderful letter[2] of his eighteen years ago, and what a privilege it was for me to meet the commander of the 5th Indian Division at Keren and of the 3rd Corps in Malaya.

The chief occupation of 'Piggy' Heath's retirement was the management of a large flock of turkeys. Lady Heath, a New Zealander, whom he had married after the Eritrea campaign had been a Queen Alexandra nurse. Both had suffered from Japanese captivity. She had had a still-born child. Now they had a jolly baby boy called Christopher not quite yet two. Heath's sight and hearing had been affected by Japanese brutality. He had been wounded in Mesopotamia in the First World

---

[1] The late Lt.-General Sir Lewis Heath, K.B.E., C.B., C.I.E., D.S.O.
[2] The letter may be read in Octave 6.

War and his left arm was permanently stiff. When the Japanese commander thought he was not being saluted with sufficient respect he ordered his men to punch Heath. When I read about students all over the world squealing about the brutality of exasperated policemen I wonder with what courage most of them could have faced real brutality.

I learned a lot about Eritrea and Malaya from long talks with Heath. Next day he drove me to the escarpment road made by the Italian prisoners-of-war. They somehow persuaded the Public Works Department that they knew more about road making than the P.W.D., and as I have mentioned made the only good stretch of road in the whole of Kenya. They built for themselves a little church at the head of the drift with a glorious view. I made a note of the motto over the door. Stet crux dum volvitur orbis. Pax vobis. Deo gratias. I was sad to hear that no Masses were still being said in that little church.

I dined that evening with the Governor, Sir Philip Mitchell.[1]

"We first met nearly sixty years ago," I told him.

My greatest friend at Colet Court had been his elder brother Alan Mitchell, who was in the Indian Civil Service but was now dead. Philip Mitchell had been a rather noisy year-old baby who disturbed our Saturday afternoon tea-parties in Kensington.

I recall one remark by Philip Mitchell. "My job here as Governor is an easy one. I do not have to consider what is the right way to tackle the problem in Kenya. The problem is insoluble."

Yet he loved Kenya and when he retired as Governor not long after this he remained on his property in Kenya.

A packet of letters which had been chasing me round caught me up at Nairobi. One was from Watson to say that after long argument Sir Michael Balcon had agreed to pay £500 for the film-rights of *Whisky Galore* with a further £1,000 if it covered more than its expenses. I was not impressed by the terms but I was grateful even for £500 because two years passing without a book from me was going to make it financially heavy going.

Our drive through the national park was a splendid wind up for our wanderings. I wrote:

"It was a wonderful experience . . . Hippos, wildbeestes, jackals, hyenas, impala, eland, Thomson's gazelle, Grant's gazelle, giraffes, the nose of a crocodile, secretary birds roosting in small trees (an absurd sight), bustards, but alas, we missed the pride of lions, though we drove where they had been that morning. Notice boards warned people "Stay in your car. Beware of Lions".

As I copy out that letter the most vivid memory of that drive is

---

[1] The late Major-General Sir Philip Mitchell, K.C.M.G.

of a solitary giraffe standing motionless on a small hill against the skyline and of giraffes loping along at what looked like a slow canter but what was in fact a very fast gallop. I have always been much attracted by giraffes since one of them leaned over its fence at the zoo and started to chew the flowers in our governess's hat.

On the last day I had a few minutes with 'Mo' Mayne.[1] He had been the first general I talked to about my Indian tour in June 1946 and it was only fitting that he should be the last when the Odyssey was over. After that call we went to have our luggage weighed. It was twenty pounds overweight and we had to leave one suitcase for the Thomsons to bring back when they sailed in the *Matiana* next month.

On my last evening I gave a talk for the British Council to which Bingley had been moved from Rangoon. The room was packed out.

At the airport where we had been told to arrive by six o'clock there was a long argument about which plane was to leave first. Then one of the planes had engine trouble and we were driven back to the hotel. Finally we were airborne at eleven. Chrissie had secured that large ham; the arrival of that ham in England was her only concern. She carried it along over her back. I recall landing at Khartoum to refuel and what seemed a blow in the face as we left the plane but what was simply the heat. She was writing to Faith about that sacred ham a fortnight before:

"C.M. says I cannot take a ham back with me, but if I am willing to be weighed with it on my back I don't see how it can be included as part of our luggage. They charge twelve shillings a pound for every extra pound overweight but I should love to be able to manage it as my personal weight. I wish I could bring back some sausages—the kind one used to eat pre-war and of which we had forgotten the taste. I would like to put some in his dispatch case and not tell him anything about it."

On the way to Cairo we heard that Egyptian troops had seized Gaza on the way into Palestine. We were the last plane to land in Cairo and had to stay the night. The customs were as intolerable as usual. One unfortunate Englishwoman who had been very sick on the plane was without a transit visa and was made to sleep in the waiting room all night under an armed guard. It may have been Chrissie's ham that persuaded the Egyptian officials that we were not Zionists. At any rate, we were allowed to leave with the ham for the Heliopolis Palace.

Next morning which was Whit Sunday we left the hotel at five o'clock, but we had a two hours wait at the airport, and reached

[1] The late General Sir Mosley Mayne, G.C.B., C.B.E., D.S.O.

Castelbenito in Tripoli about one. It was a relief to find Italian officials
after those wretched Egyptians. We bought five bottles of olive oil,
one of which I dropped and broke in pieces on the way from the plane
at Heathrow.

The flight across Tunis, the Mediterranean and France was very
rocky almost all the way on account of thunderstorms. It was not
reassuring to hear of two plane crashes in France; I felt it would be a
pity if we crashed on this last flight. I decided that I had had enough
of long-distance flying. The weather was perfect when we landed at
Heathrow that evening. The customs officers were pleasant and helpful
unlike the customs officers at Tilbury when our heavy luggage arrived.
I was even charged duty on the vanilla pods we brought back.

I spent two or three quiet days at Denchworth walking round the
garden with Faith in lovely weather and going through a pile of correspondence which had accumulated during my absence. One letter
from P. G. Wodehouse was a great treat:

                                        2 East 86 Street,
                                           New York.
                                      March 7th 1948.

Dear Monty,

I have been a long time answering your letter, which reached me
after a lot of wandering, as I wasn't sure where to write, you being
on the move so much. I finally decided that the best plan was to write
to Denchworth Manor, so that you would find my letter on your return.

"What an exciting time you must have had, and what a fine book
you will make of it. Talking of books, I have just re-read 'Buttercups
and Daisies' (called 'To Let' over here) and enjoyed it just as much
as the other six or seven times I've read it. I have also caught up with
'the Winds of Love', so I am feeling fine.

"I have been concentrating on theatre work over here, as the magazines are a hopeless proposition. My adaptation of Molnar's 'The
Play's The Thing' goes into rehearsal tomorrow and the revival of
'Sally' for which I have done the lyrics, on Friday, so things are
beginning to move. I have done four other adaptations, two of them
Molnar's, and I should think these ought to be put on eventually.
Everything in the theatre here depends on whether you can get the
production money. (I suppose it always did, but nowadays the
established manager with solid backing seems to have died out). You
need at least 180,000 dollars to put on a big musical, and apparently
the only way to get it is to give a series of 'auditions' to the angels.
It's a pretty loathsome process.

"By the end of April I shall have had a year in New York and shall
have to get out of the country, my visitor's visa having already been

M

extended once. I think I shall go to Canada or somewhere and try to get back on the quota, as America from a writer's point of view is very much the centre of things. In order to get theatrical work, one simply has to be on the spot. What I would like would be a small house about an hour's train journey from New York.

"We have had the most poisonous winter, the worst but one on record. Everyone is fed up and longing for the Spring. I wish you would come over here for a visit. Some of the plays on now are great. The American novel, on the other hand, is a mess. I can't find a thing to read, so in another week or so shall probably start in on 'Buttercups and Daisies' again!

Yours ever,

Plum."

After the brief rest I went up to London to get my complicated commitments in order. I had undertaken to write a history of McAlpine. I had to arrange with Chatto's about the timing for *Indian Epic*. I had to discuss various proposals for the future with the B.B.C., and I had to meet the film people at Ealing about *Whisky Galore*. I was kept for a day or two in Denchworth by a ridiculous interruption of my various jobs in London in the shape of two nests made by jiggers (or chigoes) in my two big toes. I had been warned about walking about on bare feet and I had heeded the warning scrupulously. I had severely admonished Chrissie for sometimes forgetting to put on her slippers. Yet here was she jiggerless and myself at the mercy of that infernal flea which lays its eggs in people's big toes.

By the greatest of luck a younger doctor with Squires called Lenward had had practical experience of extracting the nests of jiggers at which he was as skilful as the natives of Kenya. It was not a comfortable business but Lenward performed the extraction with aplomb, and my toes were soon free of those exasperating tenants.

The Savile was for me what once upon a time it had been for Robert Louis Stevenson. I recall my gratification when I found that the 20 years crusade some of us had waged to get the bridge players out of the room they had collared for themselves when the Club moved from 107 Piccadilly to 69 Brook Street had been successful. The card-room boys had been routed and driven upstairs; the bar was in the right place at last. What hours of talk I had with dear friends like John Moore, Humphrey Hare, Peter Rodd, Norman Edwards, Walter Greenwood, Richard Church and others. As I write these names I think with a pang that I shall never again sit up till three in the morning with John Moore or Humphrey Hare. One evening we were talking about another much loved member of the club, Boulenger or 'Bully', who had left us two years before. Bully and I had been dining with Thelma and Vivyan Holland (he too gone), and the next day Bully was taken ill at the club. Walter Greenwood had got him back to Polperro where two or three days later he died. Walter told me that on the way to Cornwall he had hardly spoken until suddenly he said, "Extraordinary bugger, Monty, I don't believe there's any subject of which he doesn't know something." Alas, today there are all too many subjects of which I know nothing.

I dined with Ralph Glyn who was our Member and whom I had known since Gallipoli days. The Lord Chancellor[1] and Lady Jowitt were the other guests. I held forth for a bit about India. I asked why the Government had been foolish enough to hand over the Andaman and Nicobar Islands to India. I argued that they were vital for the defence of Malaya.

"India's only claim on them is that we used Port Blair as an Indian and Burmese penal settlement. Do you know the finest potential naval harbour in the whole of the Indian Ocean is in one of the Nicobar Islands?"

"The Indians made a great point of having the Islands," said Bill Jowitt.

"But they're fifteen hundred miles away either from Calcutta or Madras."

"Are they as much as that?" Jowitt asked vaguely.

I could see he was not interested, and presently he went on to wonder why Mountbatten had been sent as Viceroy. I said it had been entirely Attlee's idea which seemed to surprise him. I went on to say that it would be a good idea to send him as Ambassador to Greece. I believed he might effect a great job of reconciliation. Jowitt said Mountbatten was determined to go back to the Navy. Then I suggested that Mountbatten should go with a warship and hand back to Hellas the Elgin Marbles. Jowitt achieved an inch or two of levitation, and I still hear the echo of his voice as he thundered "NO!"

"Well, I hope you'll keep the British Museum authorities in order. They nearly ruined the Marbles by their bad cleaning and had to keep them out of the public view until they recovered from the mess made of them."

Jowitt changed the subject by telling a story of his time at New College, when one night he was back in College just five seconds after midnight. Next morning when sent for by the Warden he had explained it was because Rosemary Spooner had dropped the key of the Warden's Lodgings and he had helped her to look for it.

"The Warden of New College is no relation to that young lady," said Spooner, and fined Bill Jowitt a pound.

[1] The late Earl Jowitt, D.C.L., LL.D.

The Lord Chancellor told another story about a contest in hymnology with Asquith.

"Quote the third verse of the hymn 'Brief life is here our portion', Asquith challenged.

"I had to mumble the first two verses to myself before I got the third. Then I challenged Asquith to quote the fourth verse of 'Onward Christian Soldiers'; he rolled it out correctly without a moment's hesitation."

Another story I recall his telling that evening was of meeting Haw-Haw's wife in Germany and as it was he who had secured the death penalty for Haw-Haw he felt a rational embarrassment.

"So I asked Mrs Joyce if I could do anything for her. 'Yes', she replied. 'Get me a bedroom to myself.' She was in a dormitory with a dozen other women."

Lady Jowitt reminded me of that evening at the Savoy in November 1937 when she and Albrecht von Bernstoff were beckoned over to the table where Winston Churchill was dining with Bob Boothby and myself.

"Yes," I said. "I can hear Winston now asking who that pretty woman was with Albrecht—and when we said he must have met Lesley Jowitt Winston saying he never had and waved you over.

Albrecht von Bernstoff who with unbroken courage had worked against Hitler throughout the war was hanged with others like Canaris in that last April. The victims were stripped naked and slowly strangled. A film was made over which that 'bloodthirsty guttersnipe' as Winston called him gloated.

Lady Jowitt told me that Albrecht had gone back into Germany from Switzerland and that he had been denounced to the Nazis by a sister-in-law who coveted the estate.

It was just after that dinner with Ralph Glyn that the Silver Jubilee of *The Gramophone* was celebrated at which I saw many old friends. We are now forty-five years old and I shall have to make ninety if I am to attend a cocktail party for the Golden Jubilee.

On June 15th Monya Danischewsky, the producer of the *Whisky Galore* film, was writing:

"Dear Mr Mackenzie,

When we met I told you that I am most anxious to retain in the film 'Whisky Galore' the atmosphere and flavour of the book, and indeed of the island which the book captured so well.

"Film writing, as you know, is not primarily a literary process. It is really notes of guidance for the director to enable him to tell the story in visual terms. I have had first class technicians converting your book into a film, and I think that they have made a very good job

of what was a difficult task. In the process, however, a great deal
of Compton Mackenzie has gone out of the film, and now is the time
to put a great deal of Compton Mackenzie back into the film, if you
will please help us to do it.

"May I please see you for a few minutes at the earliest opportunity
to discuss whether it will be possible for you to help us on the script?
I do hope that you will be able to, because I believe that if we can at
this stage infuse your dialogue and characterisation into the script,
then we shall have something really worthwhile.

"Do please telephone me as soon as you can. Even if you cannot find
time to work for two or three weeks on the script, a consultation with
you would be invaluable. But I do hope that you will find the time
to work with us, and that the very slender budget alloted to me will
be elastic enough for us to meet your terms!

Yours sincerely,

M. Danischewsky."

I felt it was important to know what was going to happen, and ten
days later I dined at the Ivy with Danischewsky and Sandy
Mackendrick, the director. My leg was being troublesome, and that
script of the proposed film was no sedative.

"Another of my books gone west," I muttered. "Well, perhaps
the trouble with this script is that it has *not* gone west. It has gone
south. It must be entirely reconstructed and be given authentic dialogue."

"But that's what I wrote to you about," poor Danny, as he soon
became, protested. "Micky Balcon is coming back from South Africa
in a fortnight and I promised him we should be ready to go on location
when he gets back."

"It will want at least one scene from *Keep the Homeguard Turning*."

Danny looked apprehensive.

"But this is my first experience as producer, and it was my idea to
make the film on Barra. The trouble is that £60,000 is the most that
Ealing will allow. We couldn't possibly buy the rights in another of
your Highland books."

"You can give me a box of cigars for the scene I should want from
Keep the Homeguard Turning. The best thing will be for you and Sandy
to come down to Denchworth from time to time while I am writing
the script and you can then put in the technical directions."

"But Micky is coming back in a fortnight," Danny pressed.

"So what? It won't take a fortnight to write a script."

During the next fortnight I worked hard on *Whisky Galore*. Angus
McPhail who had done the original script was cooperative and did
not seem to resent my criticisms. The film was to start going into

production as early as possible in July. I felt that Micky Balcon when he got back from South Africa was treating Danny like an indulgent uncle. It was clear to me that he was feeling very doubtful indeed about its being a successful film.

While work on *Whisky Galore* was taking up most of my time I had other contracts and duties to claim my attention.

Dr Selwyn-Clarke had asked the Colonial Office people to see me and learn my impressions of the situation in the Seychelles. I cannot remember what I said to Sir Charles Jeffries, the Permanent Under-Secretary. What I do remember is that on my way to his room I was following my guide down a long corridor lined with books and that I saw an old gentleman with a long white beard searching for some volume. As I passed him he took it from the shelf with obvious satisfaction. I saw on the outside ANTIGUA 1821. I banished the mischievous thought that came into my mind. I tried to feel sure that the Colonial Office in 1948 were not looking for guidance from what happened in Antigua in 1821.

I find in Faith's Diary on Sunday June 27th:

Three film men arrived for lunch. They were very nice and easy. Chrissie and I waited at table.

After they left Monty and I went to a party at Rosamond Lehmann's Manor at Little Wittenham between Didcot and Abingdon. Dadie Rylands of King's, Rupert Hart-Davis, David Cecil, Maurice Bowra, the Warden of Wadham, Barbara Rothschild, Enid Starkie, etc., Cecil Day-Lewis singing Irish songs was unforgettable. I've not read any of his poetry but Monty says he is the only real poet of the group. Rosamond was looking lovely and the house is charming.

Ella Coltman who had been Cory's pupil in Greek died in her eighties. Faith had been helped with some reminiscences. She cut out a tribute to her in *The Times* with a tale of Queen Victoria that deserves to be in a book.

"Granddaughter of Sir John Ross, the Waterloo Field-Marshal, even as a child of three she proved herself resolute, observant and enquiring. One wintry afternoon at Windsor, Queen Victoria, still in deep mourning for Albert, had come to tea with her aunt. Observing the intent and studious little girl on her footstool by the fire she summoned her to her knee and asked to see the book. It was 'Alice in Wonderland', and the page exposed showed Alice swimming in her own tears. The child surveyed the austere but kindly face and inquired gently, 'Do you think *you* could cry as much as that?' "

The day after that party in Rosamond's Manor where Beatrix Lehmann, as I remember, had an attractive home in a barn, I had to go to Cardiff and Port Talbot to look at various contracts carried through by McAlpine's for the account I was to write of that great firm.

I evidently over-tired myself, for I succumbed to the worst 'go' of pain I had had for eighteen months. It lasted for over a week and at the end of it I was summoned to Ealing to read the final script. Three days later Chrissie and I were on the way to Barra. We went by the night train from Euston and from Glasgow flew on to Benbecula, where we had a little time with Dr George Mackinnon and his wife Morag. My godson Angus was now ten years old and grown into a really delightful boy. There was a great reunion when we reached Barra where we stayed in the Coddie's house, the bungalow of once upon a time.

I was moved to find beside my bed a copy of *Treasure Island* which I had given to the Coddie's second son Neil in 1933. He had entered up his various addresses on his way through the Airforce. Then came an entry 'eat, drink, and be merry, for tomorrow we die'. That was the last entry. He was lost in a Beaufighter off the west coast of France.

I made one last attempt to restore the scene where the islanders are waiting until midnight before they could break the Sabbath by setting out for the whisky in the wreck. In the book the agony of the Protestants on Great Todday was intensified by the thought that the Catholics of Little Todday were getting at the whisky before themselves. In the film it was merely nervous agitation about getting to the ship before she sank. However, it was no use. Everybody was firm about taking no risk of offending religious prejudices. When *Rockets Galore* was made into a film some years later, Little Todday was allowed to be Catholic.

I told Danny that the ship they had in the film would break up in the first sou'wester. This happened in due course and a wrecked ship was rigged up at Pinewood where at the end of October I said my three lines as Captain Buncher, the scene keeping me up all night till it satisfied the director.

That fortnight we spent on Barra when the film was being made had moments as funny as the film itself. I have not returned to Barra during the twenty years that have gone by since. Those who have read the previous Octave will know what Barra was to me and what Barra did for me. I cannot bring myself to go back there and look round in vain for so many much loved friends.

I must pay a tribute to Monya Danischewsky for the way he preserved the humour of *Whisky Galore* by becoming *persona grata* with the people of Barra as the 'fillum' who understood them best. They were all known as 'fillums'. I hear somebody saying when I asked where Chrissie was that she was away at Faire na h'Abh with one of the 'fillums'; that particular 'fillum' was Catherine Lacey.

Basil Radford's memorable performance as Captain Waggett was partly due to his inability to understand why people thought that Waggett was a comic figure. In his view Waggett's attitude to the behaviour of the islanders over the whisky was exactly what it should have been. He really believed that his condemnation of the islanders' lawlessness was in complete accord with that of any Home Guard commander who appreciated his responsibility.

Sandy Mackendrick was a little worried because not enough was being made of the love affair between Bruce Seton as Sergeant Odd and Joan Greenwood as Peggy Macroon. In the scene from *Keep the Home Guard Turning* that I contributed for a box of cigars Chrissie gave Joan Greenwood the Gaelic accent which Joan Greenwood achieved to perfection, and Bruce Seton accepted my coaching for his part. When the scene was shot it was perfect but Sandy Mackendrick thought that it was not sufficiently 'sexy,' and it was done again but the magic of the first shot was not recaptured.

The next problem that arose was the title. I gathered that Arthur Rank was worried about *Whisky Galore*, and the American reaction was firmly against using it. As I remember, *Golden Treasure* and *Liquid Treasure* were suggested as possible titles. I wrote to Micky Balcon that it was not an author's vanity which was being wounded by abandoning *Whisky Galore* but that it was my long inherited knowledge of the theatre which recognized a great box-office title. At this date whisky was still in short supply everywhere and the mere sight of *Whisky Galore* outside a cinema theatre would fetch in a thirsty audience.

Micky Balcon was writing on July 23: "Mr Rank at the meeting this morning handed me your letter of the 20th July, only because it is a matter with which I should deal in the ordinary way, and in any case I had a note to discuss the matter with him this morning.

"Please don't get into your mind that a change of title was forced on us by Mr Rank or any member of his organisation. In the first place it was suggested by us that the title might have to be changed for reasons which I will mention to you when we next meet. Also, as you know, the Code authorities in America refused to pass the title. In any case we have now decided to revert to WHISKY GALORE as our standard title, making such changes in other territories as Code authorities and others might insist upon.

"Mr Rank particularly asked me to give you his kindest personal regards."

The Code authorities in America remained impenetrably virtuous. I suggested *Tight Little Island,* and that was accepted as not too offensive to the feelings of the prohibitionists. Unfortunately what would have been the perfect title had not yet been invented: that would have been *Scotch on the Rocks.*

On August 16th Danny was writing to me:

"It is awfully difficult to schedule Captain Buncher ahead firmly, owing to the alternative schedules depending upon weather. On the other hand, we do want to have you with us again as soon as possible so, if you are agreeable, may I suggest that you come here for the first or second week of September, whichever suits you best, and we will try then to fit in the Captain Buncher scene with your visit.

"The film is going well but a little slowly. We hope, however, to pick up tempo. We are getting more and more accustomed to coping with conditions that were at first strange to us. All the scenes in Waggett's Den are finished and today Catherine Lacey has gone back to London, her part completed. James Justice is here now and we have today finished the scene inside Hector Macrurie's bedroom. Altogether, we have between twenty and twenty-five minutes of the film completed. The reactions from Mick have been good all along the line, so far as the direction and playing of the scenes is concerned. We have come up against one or two technical snags—photography, for instance—but these have not been serious. Mick's only comment so far has been to express his doubt as to the pay-off for Mrs Waggett, but he is reserving his judgment until the whole sequence is assembled. I can understand his bewilderment, because we did rather spring the hysteria scene on him. Incidentally, Catherine Lacey played it superbly I thought.

"As the King used to say, in his Opening of Parliament speech, our relations with foreign powers continue to be friendly. As for myself, I find myself more and more enchanted by the island and the people here.

"I look forward to seeing you very soon and I know that all the Unit will wish to be remembered kindly to you."

Back at Denchworth I had as good a laugh as any in *Whisky Galore* from a 'literally' sent me by Lord Samuel.

"From *News Chronicle* 31.7.48 on the Olympic Games:

Biggest thrill of yesterday, however, was reserved for the closing race, in which Zatopek (Czechoslovakia) literally pulverized the ace distance runners of the world."

After Barra I was up in Edinburgh discussing with the Lord Provost a Scottish Year Book which Foges had wanted to do. He also wanted to do a souvenir of the Glasgow Industries Exhibition in 1949. Andrew Murray did not want the proposed Year Book till 1950 and was against the idea of my editing a souvenir of the Glasgow Exhibition. He said that personally he should have no objection but that Edinburgh certainly would.

I had a curious experience in the train from Paddington to Challow when I was going back to Denchworth. There were three other men in the compartment. One of them sitting opposite asked me the name of the tobacco I was smoking. I told him it was Warlock but that it was too strong for most pipe-smokers south of Newcastle. Then a man in the corner on the other side leaned across and said that the last time he had seen me was in a tent at Imbros, whereupon the man in the farther corner said that the last time he had seen me was in '32 at a debate in Trinity College, Dublin.

"More people know Tom Fool than Tom Fool knows", I observed.

My next memory is of a perfect weekend with Barbara Rothschild at Tackley Manor beyond Woodstock. Her three children were there and we played a variant of croquet which was as indecorous as rounders. Mary Hutchinson and Rex Warner were other guests. On Sunday we drove over to Burford and lunched at the *Bay Tree*. My Burford of over forty years ago was not actually obliterated but for me it was like a beautiful woman with erysipelas. The rash of cars had completely destroyed what Burford had been once upon a time. Maurice Bowra and Rosamond Lehmann arrived for dinner that night and we had an enchanting evening of good talk and good wine.

I had one painful moment, and that was when Maurice Bowra said that he could not understand the silly fuss made about Jane Austen. He found her unreadable. I rose and said I should be compelled to leave the dinner-table unless the Warden of Wadham withdrew his observation. I forget exactly how the argument finished but I did not feel called upon to leave the dinner-table at the end of it.

My history of the McAlpines took me up to the Midlands where I spent two or three days in the good companionship of Tom McAlpine. That visit provided a unique experience. For the first time in my life and for the only time I watched a professional soccer match, Birmingham against Chelsea. I have not seen even West Bromwich Albion, my mascot team since 1894, in action. I was disappointed by the ragged play; I had expected a much more attractive performance by professionals. It was a sunny day and thousands of Birmingham fans watching their team defeat Chelsea by a goal to nil looked like a washed up mass of pebbles.

My visit to the Midlands was cut short by an infernal attack. McAlpine's sent me home in a car, and I had a painful drive. After three days of pain I think I overcame it by hearing of the death of Benes and being rung up by the B.B.C. to ask if I could do a ten minute tribute to him on the radio five days later. I had been moved by the death of that little man and set to work at once on the broadcast. I had been able, when engaged in writing his life, to appreciate his true love of humanity and his deep anxiety for everybody in this world to be given his chance. His enemies the Czechoslovak Communists were a nasty lot. Yet only now twenty years after the death of Benes do the people of Czechoslovakia seem to be waking up to what they have lost under that tyranny.

I had asked if at a certain cue the Dumky or lament from a Dvořák quartet could be played softly.

"Rather theatrical, don't you think?", had been the reply.

"There are moments when a scene requires incidental music."

The B.B.C. was indulgent; I was allowed my theatrical accompaniment, and I am glad to say it was declared successful.

Faith had gone to Italy at the beginning of the month and we had hopes of selling Ventrosa to relieve the financial situation. We were not successful in doing this but she had a rich two months in her beloved Italy.

I look back at that last quarter of my sixty-sixth year and give up any hope of recapturing it in sequence. McAlpine's, the Book Society, lectures, broadcasts, television, brains trusts, dining out, writing *Gramophone* editorials, answering at least fifty letters a week. . . . I give up and shall record one or two occasions which have remained in my memory but whose date I have forgotten.

The dinner of the 19th Indian Division at the Connaught Rooms was a great evening. 'Pete' Rees failed to arrive because on his way back from South Africa in a Dutch ship he was carried on to Antwerp. 'Monty' Stopford's plane failed to make it. So Frank Messervy and I had to carry the brunt of the speech-making. After dinner when we adjourned for good-bye drinks and a final quack a Colonel invited me to have a glass of brandy with him. When we had exchanged healths, he said,

"You know we were all a little disappointed this evening."

"I am sorry to hear that."

"Yes, we had all hoped that you and General Messervy would say something to us about the Dagger Division's crossing of the Irrawaddy and capture of Mandalay."

"But General Messervy and I each talked for at least twenty minutes about the exploits of the Dagger Division."

The Colonel looked completely bewildered.

"Did you?", he said in what was a tone intended to show hospitable politeness to a guest but at the same time obviously unable to believe what he was saying. "Did you?", he repeated. "I never noticed it."

What a wonderful way of surviving the speeches! The loyal toast. 'Gentlemen, you may smoke.' A cigarette which he finishes during the opening remarks by the Brigadier in the Chair. Then an exquisite oblivion as he falls asleep and does not wake up until the company is adjoining for a final drink.

Another good evening was the 5th Indian Division dinner at the Mayfair Hotel. Bob Mansergh[1] was in the Chair supported by a glow

---

[1] General Sir Robert Mansergh, G.C.B., C.B.E.

of generals including the Auk and 'Bill' Slim. I sat between Denys Reid[1] and Frank Messervy who nobly stood champagne.

There was an enormous dinner of the Printers' Pension Association at the Connaught Rooms on November 11th. Earlier I had lunched with Francis Queensberry[2] who had shown me the letters between Oscar Wilde and Alfred Douglas.

Colonel Hazell of the great printing firm was in the Chair, and among the speakers were Prince Philip, Lord Reading, Beverley Baxter and myself. I was sitting next to 'Boy' Browning,[3] Daphne du Maurier's husband, who was Controller of the Household of Princess Elizabeth and Prince Philip. I remember saying to him that I wondered if when my turn came to speak I should have to begin 'Your Royal Highnesses'. I am sure that the Duke of Edinburgh that night was wishing he were anywhere but at a large public dinner. In the event Prince Charles was not born till three days later sharing a birthday with Pandit Nehru and Aneurin Bevan.

But what I remember most vividly of that evening was Browning's telling me I ought to have been at the War House that morning when the outgoing C.I.G.S. heard that his successor was to be Bill Slim.

"Montgomery was almost hysterical. He was dancing about and protesting that the British Army would never stand for a C.I.G.S. from the Indian Army."

I have heard various explanations for F.M. Montgomery's prejudice against the Indian Army, but without confirmation of them I abstain from passing what may be false currency.

I told in Octave Seven of my first experience of television at its very beginning. This autumn I gave three talks. At this date Alexandra Palace was having a bit of a struggle with Broadcasting House which was inclined to treat T.V. as an unwelcome upstart. I recall that when Val Gielgud was appointed head of T.V. drama he regarded it as a come down and was not happy till he was back at sound drama of whose success he had been the chief architect. Norman Collins told me of his struggle to get the B.B.C. T.V. to realise what the future of television was bound to be. It had certainly made a great advance from the days when we had a lamp nearly burning the back of one's neck but it was still in its early days. One's face was still being painted yellow before one appeared.

The talk I remember best was about Elgar. In those days a television programme would run on for three or four minutes over the time announced for it but when I reached Alexandra Palace for the Elgar

---

[1] Major-General Denys Reid, C.B., C.B.E., D.S.O.
[2] The late 11th Marquess of Queensberry.
[3] The late Lt.-General Sir Frederick Browning, G.C.V.O., K.B.E., C.B., D.S.O.

talk at 8.45 p.m. the announcer asked me if I could possibly time it exactly to ten seconds before nine o'clock.

"We are showing the boxing at Harringay this evening and our viewers will be annoyed if they are kept waiting."

"Well, if I am going to stop ten seconds before nine o'clock I must have a clock."

This was a problem for Alexandra Palace and the big central studio had to be ransacked before an electric clock was found and plugged in for my guidance.

I started off on what was a tricky bit of narrative with the march to the scaffold from Berlioz's Symphony Fantastique to come in at the right moment from a gramophone record. I had been talking for about seven minutes when I put an eye to the clock on the floor off right. To my surprise it showed that I had been talking for only three minutes. I knew I had been talking for at least seven, and I looked again. The clock still showed three minutes. Evidently somebody had stepped on the wire lead leading to it and disconnected it. I hoped for the best and when the talk was over the announcer came along, beaming.

"Marvellous," he said. "Fourteen minutes fifty seconds. I *am* so glad our clock was so helpful."

"Helpful," I exclaimed. "Your bloody clock nearly wrecked the show. Look at it."

The time was still twelve minutes to nine.

"However, the boys playing the Berlioz record up there were a great deal more helpful than your clock. They were not a second too soon or a second too late and had the needle down on exactly the bit I wanted to illustrate my Elgar story."

Faith had come back from her two months in Italy where she had dug out a lot of interesting material for the book she was proposing to write about the English colony in Lucca but which she never managed to write. We were happy to get a long letter from Francis Brett Young from Leighton Road, St James, Cape Province, South Africa. 20.10.48: "My dear Monty,

We have been thinking and talking about you and Faith quite a lot recently and feeling that we have rather 'lost touch' with you. Probably you and I are to blame, but in any case it is a great pity that survivors of the deluge, who still have memories of Paradise, should be thus isolated in a post-diluvian (or mid-diluvian) world whose inhabitants don't even know what we're talking about when we speak the language of civilisation. So let me bring our friendship up to date —it has never languished—by telling you what's happened in the etw een .

"We last saw you, I think, either in that house at Petersham or in an ambrosial night at my lost, beloved Craycombe, nearly seven years ago, since when we have both become elderly gentlemen. As I think you know, we gave Craycombe to the British Red Cross for the duration of the war, and never had as much as thank you from them. Then, in 1944, the combined strains of farming, defence work, and four years of writing *The Island* culminated in a heart breakdown (legacy also of 1914-18) which forced me to part with Craycombe, the material possession I loved best in the world and in all my life; and as soon as the war was over I managed to persuade our lords and masters to let me go to South Africa, where I fully intended to write the third book of the City of Gold trilogy. It hasn't been written, because my health was still too rocky and the inclination to work was lacking. We found and bought a sufficiently pleasant cottage on the shores of the Indian Ocean, 17 miles from Cape Town. But, for all its amenities, the suburban life has never suited us; we are country people at heart, and now we are on the point of migrating once more to the outskirts of a village called Montagu in the lesser Karroo, about 120 miles North East of the city. It lies in a shallow valley, at an elevation of 800 feet, surrounded by mountains rising to 5,000 feet and washed by a pellucidly clear Alpine air, whose dryness (rainfall about 8 inches) we find deliciously stimulating after the moisture of the Indian Ocean: the best climate, indeed, I have yet discovered in the world. We have $2\frac{1}{2}$ acres of garden, with plenty of water. We can grow oranges, lemons, grapefruit, guavas and even paw-paws; but in winter the lawn is often white with hoar-frost. Most of our garden, however, is of wild Karroo veld, unbelievably flowered with gazanias, moreas, gerberas, and innumerable mesembyanthema of every hue. I wish you could see it; for, as you know, the S. African flora is of a startling richness.

"The village which lies below us, grows deciduous oaks, and its vineyards are irrigated, so that there is no lack of greenness. It grows the best peaches and aprocots I have ever tasted: an oasis in the midst of an almost lunar landscape of rugged mountains from which issue a number of radio-active hot springs, which, by the way, completely cured me of fibrositis when I visited the place ten years ago. Twenty miles away in a fold of the foothills at about 4,000 ft, there is a region of apple and pear-orchards. So, you see, we have a great variety of climate, within a small space. The inhabitants of the village are mostly wine and fruit farmers, Dutch Afrikaners, and we have found them most courteous and helpful when once we got to know them. We are living, in fact in a society which has not changed since the days before the first war. Yet we are within three hours drive of Cape Town, which is a gracious little city still, in spite of the inevitable process of Americanisation with good shops and excellent libraries, and an orchestra, small in size but extremely proficient, under the conductorship of a Basque,

Enrique Jorda, who previously had the Liverpool Philharmonic. Albert
Coates has settled in Cape Town, and our musical scene has lately
been enlivened by a visit from Tommy Beecham, rather the worse for
wear, I am afraid.

"Mainly as the consequence of my long illness, Jessica also developed
a patch of bad health, but now, thank God, she is very much better and
has completely recovered her old sense of humour, which, as you know,
was a thing without price. Indeed, we are both well and happy in
Montagu, and have almost ceased to think of our dear Anacapri, whose
life had something of the same placidity as this.

"Do you ever talk to a man named C. P. Snow at the Savile? He is
in treaty to buy Fraita, and has paid a deposit on it. He has not visited
the island himself, being overwhelmed with the claims of novel writing,
a Civil Service Commissionership, and a Directorship of English
Electric, an enormous concern which has recently absorbed Marconis.
Before this he was Tutor of Christ's at Cambridge, and in direct
succession for the Mastership. But he wanted some quiet place in
which to write, and Fraita seemed to fill the bill. Unfortunately the
emissaries he sent to Anacapri to survey the repairs to Fraita appear
to have fallen foul of Edwin Cerio, and he is convinced that with
Edwin as an 'enemy', who evidently led them to believe that the island
was his private preserve, he is convinced that life in Capri would be
intolerable. If you do meet him, you might explain to him that Edwin
isn't as all-powerful as that, and that his vagaries should be treated as
the delightful joke which they are. From all I can hear, Capri seems to
have been completely corrupted by the American occupation as
well as by hordes of Neapolitans, full of money and denied egress from
their country. The contadine, according to Marietta, are all lipsticked
and wildly promiscuous. Edwin himself has become in old age his
father all over again; is always *braccia sotto braccia* with signorine, and
has acquired as a secretary, the young and beautiful daughter of—.
Serena is looking after our affairs, and Costanzo Desiderio has our
power of attorney as far as the reconditioning of Fraita is concerned.
—recently died in his little house, stone-deaf and unhappy: the greater
part of his establishment occupied by his monstrous and slatternly
servant, her husband and a diseased family. Nannina still lives, but is
very ill and poor. The incredible—s are returning to their house below
the Migliara. Borselli, after leaving Frances *plantée*, went off with the
red-haired maid to Sicily, and has died there. Not a cheerful picture
of our Arcadia. But we did live there in happier days, didn't we?

"Is Christopher still running the Gramophone? If he is, I wish you
would ask him to post to me regularly and send me the bill. I still
have Davey's latest electric E.M.G. and records are fairly easy to get
in Cape Town, as is everything else. Did you have the aged Strauss's

exquisite Oboe Concerto? We have been playing a great deal of Mahler lately, and get a good deal of pleasure out of him.

"Remember, we want to know all about Faith and yourself, for we still hold you in the greatest affection. I hear that Rupert Hart-Davis is publishing Hugh's diaries—the most interesting part of which must surely be unpublishable. You know, my dear Monty, apart from Frank Swinnerton, you and I are the only samples of that admirable vintage left. So don't let us remain so shockingly disconnected. An air-mail letter only takes three days at the best; and you can fly to Cape Town, the only accessible Mediterranean climate (sterling area) in even less time.

"We both send you our love.

Yours always,
Francis"

I should see Francis again for the last time, a year or two later when dining with Charles Snow and I should have the pleasure of advocating Charles's remarkable novel *The Masters* as Book of the Month for the Book Society.

I do not remember who it was that bought Fraita in the end, nor do I remember who ultimately bought Ventrosa which Faith had had great hopes of selling when she was in Capri that autumn. That letter from Francis stirred up many memories of the past, and Faith became less and less interested in the future of Denchworth. For me the past is always the present and I can write of it without the slightest nostalgia because it is still as much alive as the present. My only quarrel with old age is the tiresome way in which it muddles one's last years and destroys the sequence of events, thus thwarting my passion for accuracy. People much younger than myself assure me that forgetting names and dates happens to everybody as they grow older, but I am not consoled. However, when I am slightly disturbed by the news of old friends leaving this world mentally and remaining in it physically, I think of Plum Wodehouse and Frank Swinnerton, one a year older, the other a year younger than myself, both of them still writing better novels than most younger people. I think of my old publisher, Martin Secker, whose opinion of a work is as much worth while hearing as it ever was.

It was soon after that Printers' Pensions dinner that Frank Owen and I had a great evening at Camberley with the Staff College. At this date Frank was editing the *Daily Mail* but managed to leave it long enough to come down to Denchworth and drive with me to Camberley and take part in the debate to which we had been invited. I have forgotten what the subject of the debate was. What I do remember is that it did not get really going till midnight because the debaters had to brace themselves for the ordeal by drinking whiskies after dinner to conquer their self-consciousness. Frank and I much enjoyed ourselves and when we got back to Denchworth sat up talking till six o'clock. Somehow he managed to catch a train next morning and get back to editing the *Daily Mail*.

From a crowd of dinners and lunches at the end of November I recall lunching with the Birkenheads in Chester Street and meeting for the first time David Margesson[1] by whom I was much attracted. As Chief Whip during what I thought were the two disastrous 'National' Governments and as Minister for War when war came I had expected to find ourselves completely out of sympathy. The Birkenheads had to go off to some affair at Church House soon after lunch, but Margesson and I stayed talking until half-past four. I wish I had made some notes of that talk but alas, what he told me about the Abdication, about Baldwin, and indeed about so much in that fatal decade of the thin-faced 'thirties was not recorded by me at the time and I do not think it is fair to commit somebody no longer alive to statements the accuracy of which are at the mercy of an old man's memory. What I do know is that it was one of the most absorbing conversations I have ever enjoyed.

My next memory is of a November day of thick fog. I had been sitting for a portrait by Michael Ayreton in the morning and had momentarily fallen asleep to be woken by his reminding me that he was not making a death mask. I had promised Alexander Korda, who had taken an option for a film of *The Monarch of the Glen*, to go and see his Prince Charlie film, but to my relief the fog was too thick to get to the cinema. Later I managed to reach a restaurant where I was to dine with Arnold Haskell and meet Karsavina.

In my second Octave I was able to boast of finding a letter from Taglioni to my mother congratulating her on my birth. I could now congratulate myself on meeting the greatest prima ballerina of a later generation. At this date Tannia Karsavina was sixty-three years old; I had not seen her since those evenings at Covent Garden in 1911 when I was writing *Carnival*. I wrote in my fourth Octave:

"It is idle to attempt to convey a dancer on the printed page. I must just thank heaven that I have seen Karsavina and Nijinsky dance to the air of Weber's Invitation to the Waltz, *Le Spectre de la Rose*."

As I looked across the dinner table at Karsavina on that foggy November night I was back thirty-seven years to the blazing summer of 1911 and to that evening at Covent Garden when I saw Nijinsky come bounding through the window to the enchanted Karsavina. (I still see that exquisite moment in colour fifty-seven years later.) I

---

[1] The late 1st Viscount Margesson of Rugby.

forget what we talked about at dinner that November but I remember
that when Arnold Haskell and I had escorted her to her home by
Primrose Hill I said to him as we walked away in the fog that Karsavina's mind was still as agile as once upon a time had been her body.

At the end of the month Chrissie and I were away for a packed
fortnight in Scotland. I started off in Glasgow and went on to Edinburgh, giving at least half-a-dozen lectures to one society or another.
What I remember much more vividly than the talking is meeting
Dunstaffnage just outside the Caledonian Hotel in Edinburgh.

"Hallo, Angus, I've just passed the final proofs of that novel I
wrote in the Seychelles. It's called *Hunting the Fairies* and I've got a
marvellous portrait of Miss Donaldson and that younger woman who
used to live with her."

"Well, you'd better be careful", said Angus.

"Why?"

"Miss Donaldson is a great hand at threatening people with libel
actions."

"But she's dead."

"She certainly isn't."

Miss Donaldson had written two or three excellent books about the
Highlands. She was a passionate Episcopalian and the bitterest enemy
of all Campbells whom I have met. I have told in an earlier Octave
of the house beyond Ardnamurchan. In *Hunting the Fairies* I had called
her Miss Lamont and it might have been possible to maintain that I
had suggested a lesbian attachment and certainly that I had brought
her into ridicule. I went back to the Caledonian and rang up Constables
who were printing it.

"I know you're ready to go to press with *Hunting the Fairies* but I
have some corrections to make. Send me round two sets as soon as
you can."

As soon as the proofs arrived I set to work to change Miss Lamont
into Aeneas Lamont and Miss Lamont's dearly loved friend into his
sister. I never spent such hours of concentration in my life. Of course,
I had to make Aeneas Lamont an obvious pussycat, for otherwise the
original Miss Lamont's way of speaking would not have suited a too
masculine man. Unfortunately I lost the set of proofs with the change
of sex. If ever they turn up they will be a literary curiosity.

We went on north to stay with Eric and Marjorie Linklater at
Pitcalzean to which they had moved from Orkney. Central heating
had not yet been installed and in spite of roaring fires it was unmistakably mid-winter. However, I was never cold inside because the company of kind hosts is always heart-warming. I went to tea with Lady
Cromartie at Tarbet House among the crowded portraits of bygone
Mackenzies. She had always given me great encouragement over my

Highland stories. I told her about the hairbreadth escape I had had over *Hunting the Fairies*.

"It must have been the fairies themselves who came to your rescue," she declared.

Eric Linklater took me to see Admiral Sir Patrick Macnamara[1] at Ardgay to get his opinion about the Singapore defences but what I recall was his boy at New College home for the vac telling me that Magdalen was now the reddest college of Oxford.

I crossed over to Cromarty by the Nigg ferry to see Willie Mackay Mackenzie and tell him that Chattos were going to do an eight-volume edition of *The Four Winds of Love*. Cromarty seemed rather sad. Personally I thought its situation at a dead end in the Black Isle was a welcome relief from the ever growing stream of cars through other little towns and villages. I went to look at Sandilands, the home of my forefathers and found that the old tiles had been stripped from the roof and corrugated iron substituted.

Eric Linklater drove us to Inverness on our way back south; I recall stopping on the way to drink a bottle of port with Hector and Christobel Munro-Ferguson. Eric's car began to behave erratically but we reached Inverness in time to catch the train. To my pleasure Alastair Fraser[2] joined the train and we had a good gossip as far as Perth. His youngest boy Simon was now at Magdalen and confirmed the redness of the college at this date. Alastair and I as Magdalen men of earlier days when the only red about the college was the colour of the cox's blazer in Eight's Week were not enthusiastic. Yet as President of the Greek League of Democracy I was being painted red at this time by the Athenian Press of the Right.

There were no porters at Euston owing to the strike. The birth of British Railways in this year had certainly been premature; indeed, they might have called it a miscarriage. The Government could not have chosen a worse moment to nationalise the four railway companies, and if one searches for the primary cause of the economic position in which the country would be twenty years later many might claim it was that ill-advised take over at the wrong moment.

To quote the Annual Register:

"Equipment was being exported while the shortages at home, the disrepair of the permanent way, congestion and overcrowding were accompanied by mounting costs from wages and the high price of coal, the poor quality of which hampered efficiency. . . . The appointment of General Sir William Slim to take charge of public relations for the railways was amply justified."

[1] Rear-Admiral Sir Patrick Macnamara, K.B.E.
[2] The late Hon. Alastair Fraser.

Unfortunately for British Railways but fortunately for the Imperial General Staff General Slim had only nine months in charge of public relations, and it was significant that a week or two after he became C.I.G.S. there was that strike of porters. If the Government had made railway travel free except for those able to afford travelling de luxe and if freights had been levelled all over Great Britain, being charged by bulk and not by distance, I believe that not one line would have had to be closed and that the stream of lorries would have been dammed. The fatuity of paying large sums to business tycoons without any experience of railways to make them pay is among the major follies of our time.

There was another crowded week of lunches and dinners in London with late night sitting up in the Savile or Pratt's. I shall leave them unrecorded because they are difficult to sort out and I shall wind up this year with what is today a very poignant memory.

I told in my last Octave of a brief stay at Ipsden with Rosamond Lehmann, and of Sally Philipps, her enchanting small daughter whose face I still see as she listens to my fairy tales. Sally was now fifteen. Her mother and Beatrice Lehmann had brought her over to Denchworth during her summer holidays. I had been having two or three days of pain but that visit of which I have a precious souvenir in a note from Rosamond, had been a perfect sedative.

Oh—I do hope you are none the worse. I worried last night about the possibility of a bad reaction from too much expenditure of yourself for our sakes. . . I don't think I need tell you what a glorious treat you gave us: it must have been plain in our almost fatuously beaming faces. Sally said: "I could listen to him forever!" We came home in a state of wild affection, exhilaration and chuckling.!

On December 11th Rosamond wrote from Little Wittenham Manor:

Sally is to be christened here on Dec. 28th—as one of her godmothers, my cousin Nina Drury, will be staying with us then. Do you think you could possibly come over to lunch and attend the ceremony afterwards? It will be the ceremony "for those of riper years" . . . and those present are called witnesses and not godparents . . . I thought you would let me know if it was against your principles to officiate at an Anglican ceremony. You were Sally's choice and I left it at that! I myself hold no dogmas on theological doctrines of any sort—indeed I am an agnostic, believing only that Love might mean God, or God might mean Love—and that there is a mystery about the universe which science does not explain. Sally seems disposed, at the moment, to have a grain of faith—but of course that is common at her age and may not last.

She is embarrassed about this junction but is determined on it, as confirmation follows at school next year! I only want to make it all seem simple, loving and real for her—would hate her to go through it feeling self-conscious and awkward.

Anyway, darling, do come if you can, and also Faith if she will pardon the peculiar circumstances.

I thought your introductory talk to the 3rd Programme Light Music series quite admirable—but oh dear, was bored by the music itself, I fear. In any case the 3rd Prog. is now so interfered with by a background of what appears to be a French monkey and parrot house that I mostly have to give up the effort to listen. I'm so furious about this. Are you in the same plight? Everyone is complaining all over England.

A week before the christening I was laid out with influenza but with a Christmas dinner in bed of marrons glacés and cheese I was well enough to see that beloved child baptized and sign the register.

All too soon after her marriage to Patrick Kavanagh, Sally left this world. She was in Bali and was struck down by a violent poliomyelitis. Requiescat in pace. Her mother has written an exquisite book of reminiscence called *The Swan in the Evening*, which was published in 1967. This more than any book I have read evokes the magic of once upon a time, and from the past that beloved daughter lives again.

AT one of Edwin McAlpine's great annual lunches at the Dorchester in December I had said a few words about India and I was much encouraged by a letter from James Maxwell, the General Manager of Cook's:

"I would like, if I may, to congratulate you on the most inspiring remarks you made today at Edwin McAlpine's luncheon. I had not for a long time listened to so much sound commonsense on a subject which, I fear, is all-too-little known and understood by many people in this country whose power and influence count so much in the immediate shaping of the world in the East, the result of which will so largely determine the course of international developments in the next few years.

"It is good to feel that your forthright views, based on recent first-hand experience, were so well received by an audience composed of such responsible people as was at the Dorchester today. You will be doing a great service if you continue to preach the gospel loud and wide.

"I came back from India a few days ago . . . and it gives me the greatest pleasure to support the views expressed by you that the standing of Great Britain and the opportunities for young Britishers of the right type surpass anything yet known in the East. . . . But the next few years are vital in our handling of this great and delicate question. We have a heaven-sent opportunity based on the respect and confidence so manifest towards us at the present time by the leaders, political and commercial, of India and Pakistan, to bring about an understanding such as we could never have dreamed of pre-Partition. I hope we will be worthy heirs to this fine inheritance.

"Mountbatten has done one of the greatest jobs of all times . . . ."

There was still a great of deal of ignorant comment on India being paddled in the duckpond of conventional opinion. What was more serious was to find people who should have known better quacking with the flock. At some meeting of the British Empire Society in Northumberland Avenue Sir James Grigg,[1] a Minister for war in the 'National' Government, was addressing a gathering of patriots and condemning the precipitate way in which we abdicated from our Imperial responsibilities. This had led to what were estimated at five million casualties, though he feared those casualties were

---

[1] Rt. Hon. Sir James Grigg, K.C.B., K.C.S.I.

hardly less than ten million. I nearly choked to hear an ex-Minister splashing about figures like an exuberant kid in his bath. After his speech I asked him if he was serious when he talked about ten million casualties.

"At least", he said firmly.

"Do you know what is the population of the Punjab?"

"Not exactly, offhand," he admitted.

"I'll tell you. The last census of the Punjab put its population at thirty-one millions four hundred thousand. Are you asking me to believe that while I was in the Punjab one third of the total population was being exterminated without my noticing it? Not only is your ten million casualties a ridiculous figure, what you called the estimated casualties of five millions is equally ridiculous. If I allowed you half a million, which God knows was bad enough, I should be much too generous."

"Oh, well, you're entitled to your opinion but I maintain that my figures are nearer the truth."

I regard the inability of the average human being to grasp quantity as a menace. This has nothing to do with mathematics; it is due entirely to loose and self-indulgent exaggeration. How often will you hear somebody talk of the hundreds of letters he has had when you know that probably ten was the most he received. I do not pretend to any more exact grasp of quantity than other people. If I were left a million pounds I would not have the least idea what spending power it gave me as for instance what sum I could afford to bid for something at Sotheby's. This inability to understand quantity is responsible for the mad extravagance of the Welfare State. Not one member of any government of late years is capable of grasping that an economy of £250,000 does not compensate for an extravagance of £25,000,000.

On January 15th Rosamond Lehmann wrote to me of my god-daughter:

Our sweet Sal went sorrowfully but philosophically back to school yesterday— her fifteenth birthday! I persuaded her not to take the crucifix which has been beside her bed since you presented it, and shown with triumphuant awe and pride to all the boy and girl friends. She agrees it better remain in my care, and I have put it in the drawing-room. It is so perfect in materials, design and workmanship that it jumps to the eye wherever it is placed.

I gave a dance last Tuesday for about 40 teenagers. I wish you could have been there to see the Budding Grove, and especially your goddaughter, in flowing silvery-white net off-the-shoulders frock, looking quite bewitchingly charming and gentle and peach-faced. She is going to be such a beauty in another two years.

I feel as I read that letter of all but twenty years ago a reinforcement of my belief in the eternity of the present. As I write these words on the edge of my 88th year I am becoming so much more and more aware of the sacredness of life that the obliteration of it by death becomes continuously more incredible. Those who believe in a future for that sacred life enjoy one supreme advantage over the unbelievers. If they are right they will have the laugh and if they are wrong they will remain ignorant of their mistake for evermore.

I had signed up with the B.B.C. that January for three months on the panel of the Brains Trust. I find many letters from listeners agreeing with my opinions on various topics but inasmuch as I have completely forgotten those arguments of twenty years ago I do not feel justified in trying to squeeze them out of old letters. Eric Hooper,[1] Professor Bronowski and Cicely Hamilton were three others on the panel, and it would seem that I was usually disagreeing with the last two. The only vivid memory I have is of that great Canadian Leonard Brockington as a guest. When we were moving to our perches after the preliminary dinner at Broadcasting House he offered me a cigar which I gratefully accepted.

"Tell me," he said, "why is it that in this country only rich men are supposed to enjoy cigars?"

That is a question that might well be repeated in 1969. If the Government, Tory or Socialist, really believes that cigarettes are a menace to the nation's health why is not the duty on pipe tobacco and cigars halved? The humbug of prohibiting advertisements of cigarettes on television is a contemptible pretence of morality. We often read allusions to Victorian humbug among young writers who are apparently completely unaware that they are just as much at the mercy of humbug to-day.

Another memory of the Brains Trust is my success in persuading the B.B.C. caterers to believe that a glass of gin and the synthetic vermouth offered to guests as an apéritif was not a glass of gin and IT but a glass of gin and NOT-IT. I asked for a vodka, and after they had recovered from the shock the B.B.C. restaurateurs produced vodka before the next sitting of the Brains Trust.

This gives me an excuse to tell a story of vodka of some years later. I was lunching at the Athenaeum with Sir Selwyn Selwyn-Clarke and Lord Nathan.[2] The latter was an Old Pauline half-a-dozen years junior to myself, who had lived a life devoted to welfare. He once gave me the largest cigar I ever smoked; it lasted for two hours and a half.

Before lunch Sir Selwyn who was the host asked us what we should like as an apéritif. When I said I should like a vodka the effect was

---

[1] The late Sir Frederic Hooper, Bt.
[2] The late 1st Baron Nathan of Churt.

rather like a picture by Bateman 'The Man who asked for Vodka at the Athenaeum." One could see the aprons of bishops flapping in a wind from the East. The people near our table who heard seemed to be looking apprehensively at the fireplace as if they expected to see the ghost of Stalin coming down the chimney. The elderly waitress who was waiting for the order said with icy dignity, "We do not have vodka."

If the contemporary Athenaeum has lifted its ban upon vodka I apologize for telling this story about a forgotten piece of conservatism.

The endless argument with the Inland Revenue whether the sale of my first twenty copyrights recorded in Octave 8 was capital or income went drearily on through this year. I find a letter to *The Times* at the end of this January:

"Sir,

Mr Milne's whimsies do not help the argument. He challenges Mr Charles Morgan to define 'exceptional' or 'non-recurrent' earnings. I should call the outright sale of a series of books which had already been taxed for income a capital transaction, and I should expect that the sum received, however invested, would find the income it brought in taxed as unearned income. To this no author would object. His complaint is that it is assumed by Inspectors of Taxes that he cannot capitalise his exceptional and non-recurrent earnings, and that the capital transaction must be taxed as part of his regular income. This assumption should be challenged by the Society of Authors and an unequivocal decision sought from the judicature.

"Mr Milne's sentimental epilogue about young writers has even less to do with the case than 'the flowers that bloom in the Spring.'
Your obedient servant"

A recent business in which I was involved was an attempt to get Stafford Cripps to remove the purchase tax on gramophone records. I wrote a long appeal which I sent to various people. It may be read in Appendix C but I give here the letters from those to whom I appealed.

From Somerset Sir Arthur Bliss wrote:

Dear Monty,

By all means include me in your petition to the Chancellor of the Exchequer. Would it not be a stronger argument if we restricted ourselves to the finer type of record (e.g. Gold and Red label). It seems to lose strength if we include the many thousands that are really the equivalent of 'No Orchids for Miss B' in the book world—but perhaps you intended this.
Yours ever,
Arthur Bliss.

From the B.B.C. Sir Adrian Boult wrote:

"*Dear Mackenzie,*
So many thanks for your letter and the enclosures which I return.

It seems to me quite excellent, but, alas, being a public servant the B.B.C. does not like the idea of my signing it.

I am so very sorry, but, as I am staying on here, I suppose I must be a good boy. I do wish you every kind of success, and I am sure everyone else will too.

Yours very sincerely,

Adrian Boult."

From the Royal College of Music Sir George Dyson wrote:

"Dear Mr Compton Mackenzie,
I will gladly sign your proposed letter to the Chancellor asking for relief of tax on gramophone records. The question of accompanying a deputation I must leave until a date is suggested.

Yours sincerely,

G. Dyson"

At this date I had never met T. S. Eliot who wrote from Faber and Faber, the publishers, of which he was a director:

"Dear Mr Mackenzie,
I must apologise for some delay in answering your letter of 1st of March. I am not very well informed on these matters and therefore I do not think I could have any useful criticisms to make on your very interesting draft letter to the Chancellor of the Exchequer.

"I was at first somewhat doubtful of my suitability as a signee of this letter considering that my only qualification is as a representative of those few poets whose work has been recorded whether by themselves or by some other interpreter. If this were a letter for publication in the Press I should still feel hesitant since I think that a public letter should only be signed with names, the appropriateness of which is obvious. But for the purpose of a private address to the Chancellor of the Exchequer I see no reason why I should decline as your suggestion seems to me eminently reasonable.

Yours sincerely,

T. S. Eliot"

John Masefield wrote from Burcote Brook:

Dear Mackenzie,
Thank you for your letter, and for the admirable appeal to the Chancellor of the Exchequer. This I return to you signed, with every wish for its success.

I am not very sure of being able to go on a deputation, having been warned off such jaunts.

Hoping that the politicians may for once show wisdom.

            Yours sincerely,

                        John Masefield.

Boyd Neel wrote from Hogarth Place:

"Dear Compton Mackenzie,
    I will be delighted to sign the petition to join the deputation, because it is something that I have very much at heart. I congratulate you on your action. I will await further news from you.

            I am
                Yrs sincerely

                        Boyd Neel."

Vaughan Williams wrote from Dorking:

"Dear Mr Mackenzie,
    I send your letter back with my signature.
    "My only stipulation is that if by any chance the other proposed signatories, or most of them, do not sign, I should not be left alone at the end of the letter. But of course, without a large number of signatories you would not want to send it.

            Yours sincerely

                    R. Vaughan Williams"
                    (R. Vaughan Williams)

Ernest Newman, the leading music critic, wrote from Tadworth:

Dear Mr Mackenzie,
    I must apologize for the delay in replying to your letter. I have had trouble with my eyes lately, and both work and correspondence have been intensely difficult for some weeks.
    I shall be very glad to sign the proposed letter to the Chancellor. I don't see that anything can be added to it; it's a perfect statement of the facts and the conclusions that follow from them.
    Putting in an appearance with the deputation, is I am afraid, beyond me. I don't go up to town but once in a blue moon, nor do I want to be hanged for homicide. The sight of the Chancellor, within easy clubbing distance might be more temptation than I could resist.
            Yours sincerely

                        Ernest Newman

It was all a waste of time and trouble. Chancellors of the Exchequer do not consider the Muses respectable females. I can think of only one Chancellor in my lifetime who tried to help the Arts; that was the present Master of Trinity, Rab Butler. Kingsley Wood tried hard to put a purchase tax on books and was only deterred by his fear of what the Methodist Conference would say if he taxed the Bible.

As I look through the letters that have survived from the first two months of this year I find myself being asked to write an article for a publication by the Shipwrecked Fishermen and Mariners' Benevolent Society, for the R.H.S. Daffodil and Tulip Year-book, for the Iris Society Year-Book, for the centenary celebration of David Copperfield in *The Dickensian*, for *The Debater* at my old school, and half-a-dozen more. Would I go to Paris and address the Comité Française d'Aide à la Grèce Démocratique, and half-a-dozen more requests for 'talking' not to mention being given the honour of opening the new Central Library in Swindon.

On February 14th I gave a talk on Valentines in Woman's Hour of the B.B.C. and had some nostalgic letters from listeners and three exquisite valentines of the past, the most beautiful of all well over a century old. On that Valentine Day a valentine reached me from Francis Brett Young and it recalls for me so much of a time past it seems an essential leaf for *My Life and Times*. It was written to Faith and myself:

"How good it was to have your two letters . . . Denchworth sounds delightful. I have hunted you down on the ordnance map, and can find nothing against it except when I remember one or two wintry days when I drove over the Berkshire Downs in an open car to Appleton and reached my friend's house in a state of rigid congelation (if there is such a word). It is, of course, the cold which has always scared me since my malarial days of the last war—particularly at the time when I was liable to be prostrated with a devastating migraine. That is why I stop my ears to Monty's appeal, charm he never so wisely. I never want to see the *nives diffugere* again. Even Anacapri was sometimes too cold for me. . . . My wretched heart condemns me to a more or less static life, however bitterly I resent it. As for 'dropping out': I feel I have run my race; and honestly I have no wish to compete with our juniors, who, in any case seem to me a short-winded lot. Most of what I had to say, such as it was, went into *The Island*; and though my laurels are of an unfashionable kind, I prefer to rest on them and to resist the lures of ambitions, which I have so happily surrendered, no less than the admonitions of yourself, whom I still regard as the truest of friends.

"I envy you your long orientation. It is nearly half a century since

I went out East as a ship's surgeon, and visited Korea during the
Japanese occupation. Not that the East ever enchanted me of itself.
I was never charmed by its tormented arts—not even in China;
and I must confess that I regard its reanimation with horror. No,
apart from Europe, which now seems to me perilous and unfriendly,
Africa is—and always has been—the only continent for me. I don't
expect you liked Kenya. Lovely as the Highlands are, their European
inhabitants were never to my taste. But I do wish I had been lucky
enough to see the Seychelles, though I distrust General Gordon's
identification of them with the Garden of Eden. Perhaps we may see
them after all; anyway we shall soon be traversing those seas, as we
have booked passages to Italy and leave Durban on March 16th.
C. P. Snow, with whose work Desmond Macarthy is enraptured, has an
option on Fraita, which currency restrictions prevented him from
taking up, and we may possible sell it to a young man in the American
Embassy. In that case, we shall be, like Faith, temporary (or even
'acting') millionaires; though that aspect of the matter does not
embarrass us, since S.A. Nationals can get exchange outside the sterling
area up to £5 a day. Fraita suffered rather badly from the Italian
military occupation, and must be rewired and re-decorated (alias
biancheggiato); but Edwin Cerio has offered to lend us a cottage just
below the Tragara, so we shall not be homeless. The ship is the
Gerusalemme of the Lloyd Triestino, and we hear from the new First
Secretary of the Legation, who has just come out in her, that conditions
are quite tolerable. In six weeks time we shall therefore be at sea,
consuming maccheroni and drinking Chianti, which will be very
much to our liking. We look forward to seeing old friends, who by now
may be distressingly older (like ourselves) and though I can't climb
Solaro, I may be able to struggle up to the piazza. Yesterday we
lunched at the House of Assembly with an ex-Speaker who had just
spent a fortnight in a house near the Piccola Marina. He says that the
last traces of the American debauchment have now gone, and that
living is fairly cheap and food abundant. This, from a South African,
means quite a lot. How marvellous it would be if we could all four meet
on the scene of those early ardours and endurances which the company
of Lawrence made so amusing! I still think of those days as the happiest
of my life—the long walks through the olives with Douglas, the high
comedy of Munthe, our Sunday lunches at Solitaria. *Tempi passata.* . . .
We sail from Venezia a few months later, returning to Montagu for
the Karroo Spring. Perhaps, like Faith, we may sample Bagni idi
Lucca and see Percy Lubbock at Lerici.

"I see that one of your neighbouring villages is called Goosey and
another Balking. These suggest the shivers which I know only too well
and the frustrations of the Berkshire climate and the chillness of the

'stripling Thames'. Altogether Denchworth suggests something rather like Kelmscot, though I gather the style is later. Is it of Cotswold stone like my beloved lost Craycombe, with Grinling Gibbons fireplaces in place of my Adam?

Oddly enough, when I recall your long series of houses, which reads like an agent's catalogue—Solitaria, Herm, Jethou, Hampstead, Burford, Eilean Aigas, Barra (which I never saw) Ham Common and the rest—I look back with particular affection to that cold little eyrie looking down on Wells, which I suppose, was really Faith's. That must be because of the Mendip blood in me from those Rowberrow grouviers whose unbroken descent and permanence in the daffodil valley below the batch I can trace just as far back as the records of Churchill go. The earlier ones, alas, were burnt somewhere about 1700; but I've no doubt that those rugged ancestors of mine 'poured to war' at Sedgemoor for that pretty boy Monmouth, and I'm quite certain they were as unresponsive as the rest to the persuasions of Hannah More. That is a stubborn country, and I'm sure we were a stubborn race: a Celtic island persisting in the middle of the Saxon floodwater which drowned the flats. Did I ever tell you that my grandfather was a celebrated dowser, whose name is mentioned in all the textbooks of that mysterious art?

"We both send you affectionate greetings and hope you will both write again—and soon.

As always

Francis"

That letter from Francis Brett Young makes me ask myself whether in continuing to write I am competing with my juniors, and I can reply with sincerity that I have never been aware of competing with anybody throughout my life. I suppose that I must have reproached Francis for 'dropping out'. But I should not have been thinking of a race; I should have been talking of life itself.

What always reassures me is to find evidence of the continuity of my beliefs. For instance I was glad to find in one of the many Brains Trust letters that I expressed an opinion I still hold today:

It was good to hear you insisting upon the fact that the French Nation is the most civilized in the whole world. I don't think there can be any doubt of it, for the simple reason that they enjoy life and do daily what the Brains Trust does for about an hour once a week for a short period each year.

Another letter which arrived just before the publication of *All Over The Place* gave me much pleasure because it seemed a good omen.

"I was much amused at the time at being in one of your books of memoirs. I am, or rather was, so many years ago now the 'rosy-cheeked young woman' in the General Staff Office in Malta whom you most wrongly accused of losing a file. You cannot imagine the excitement your arrival caused among us in Malta. I tried to meet you and as a preliminary made up my mind (I was fairly young then) as I could not get an introduction in any other way and as you were staying at the same hotel in which I was billetted, that, tennis-racket and all I would fall downstairs outside your door. I did the fall but it was the wrong door and was opened by an infuriated Naval Officer!"

The publication of *All Over The Place* brought me many letters, one from an uninfuriated Admiral:

> Flag Officer Commanding,
> First Cruiser Squadron,
> c/o G.P.O. London.
> 21st February, 1949.

My dear Compton Mackenzie,

"How very nice of you to send Edwina and me a copy of your Diary out in India and South East Asia. I have already glanced at 'All Over The Place' and shall look forward to reading it during some of the cruises.

"I am looking forward very much to the publication of 'Indian Epic'. You say it will be the swan song of the old Indian Army and, you hope, a bugle call to the new armies of India and Pakistan. I think it will achieve much more than this. I think and hope it will achieve a continuity of thought, tradition and service which will make the armies of India and Pakistan feel that they really are the continuing entities of the old original Indian Army.

"I have now practically completed a close study of the despatches written by all my Commanders-in-Chief and I have also read most of the books written by British and Americans about the campaign in South East Asia. I have been through the 48 foolscap pages of remarks put in by the British Chiefs of Staff and next month I am starting work on the comments put in by the American Chiefs of Staff. The report itself I hope will be published some time this summer. I am therefore pretty well up-to-date in all aspects of my campaign and if there are any questions you wish me to answer please do not hesitate to write and ask me. . . .

"Wishing you the best of luck in your great work.

> *Yours very sincerely,*
>
> *Mountbatten of Burma*"

I was surprised and much gratified to get a letter from that paladin, Lord Birdwood,[1] now in his eighty-fifth year:

Ford House,
Drewsteignton,
Devon.
3 Feb

Dear Compton Mackenzie,

Having just had the great pleasure of reading and absorbing "All over the Place" I feel I must drop you a line of thanks and gratitude for it. As you may know I served 47 years in India—where I followed a father and grandfather and was followed by son and g.son. You will realize what my feelings of affection for the country people are, for I speak comfortably 4 of their languages. . . .

I wonder if you have come across my Khaki and Gown, (was 47 years soldiering and 7 years Master of Peterhouse) of which the late King George wrote "Every soldier and all interested in India should read it". I'd love to go out there again but at 84 one reaches by Hindu astrology "the age of beatitude" (7 planets × 12 signs of the zodiac) and I can no longer face such a journey—indeed I am a poor creature at present.

I specially liked what you wrote about Kohat and the frontier. . . . I much enjoyed too your Nepal. . . .

Please excuse writing but suffering from heart attacks I have written at intervals and as the Babu said "My pen has become constipated". All good wishes and hoping to see you later on.

Yours sincerely

Birdwood.

The Field-Marshal added a long postscript in pencil.

I much liked to realize you share with me and my family a love for gardens and trees.

He went on to write about gardens made by his father and uncle in India but time has made that postscript almost illegible.

As I read that long letter of which I have only printed extracts I was back on the beach at Anzac thirty-four years earlier and hearing somebody say 'Birdie's coming'. I see him still as he was then. Peterhouse made a wise choice when they elected him as Master in succession to Lord Chalmers of whom I wrote in earlier Octaves.

An author who has just received a letter like that may be forgiven for feeling exasperated when *All Over The Place* was placed in the 'also rans' of the *Times Literary Supplement* and dismissed as a dull chronicle of lunches and dinners in a few lines. The T.L.S. had been

[1] The late Field-Marshal Lord Birdwood of Anzac and Totnes, G.C.B. G.C.S.I., G.C.M.G., G.C.V.O.

so just and kind to my books since my first novel was published in
1911 that I felt the injustice of this review more than I should have
felt it in another paper. But what really angered me was the reflection
it cast not only upon myself but upon those who had directed my
course. I was not prepared to write a letter for publication because I
have never written a letter to any paper protesting against a review.
However, I sent the editor a stinger for himself and here it is:

"I invite your attention to a notice of my last book *All Over the Place*
in the current issue of the *Literary Supplement*.

"Your reviewer is either lazy and dishonest or merely dishonest,
and if you will give yourself the trouble of turning over the pages of
my book your editorial conscience may be pricked. I know that I
should sack any of my reviewers in *The Gramophone* who misrepresented
a book in such a way.

"Hostile criticism is one thing: the deliberate publication of a lie is
another."

I shall charitably not quote the Editor's evasive reply in the style of
an ancient sophist.

Letters from Monty Stopford and Douglas Gracey smoothed the
feathers ruffled by the T.L.S.

From the letter of the former:

..... *The whole story has been a joy to me ... bringing back many memories
of my earliest days of soldiering in 1911 ... I was particularly interested in
what you wrote about the Andamans and Nicobars as at one moment towards
the end of 1943 I was on the point of being entrusted with their capture from
the Japs, and I had the uncanny feeling that the result might be the same as
that which befell another of my name at Suvla Bay.*

*I'm glad that you liked Douglas Gracey, Frank Messervy and Miles Smeaton
as they are all friends of mine who played a tremendous part in the antics of
33rd Indian Corps ....*

Two or three days later came a long letter from Douglas Gracey.
It was impressively headed by a large dark green circle in which were
the Crescent and Star above two crossed scimitars with 'Commander-
in-Chief Pakistan Army'. The C-in-C's House was in Rawalpindi:

*How very nice to send us your enchanting book... What a marvellous journey
you had! .. I must say my reading was tinged with great envy. I would dearly
have loved to have gone with you on all your travels, and fought some of my
battles over again with you. ...*

*Pakistan is most peaceful and friendly, for all the rumours and reports abroad
to the contrary. The country side is very pro-British, and we are on the whole
welcome boon to the 'intelligentsia' who have realised what a funny chameleon*

O

the British officer (an official) is, and how much we are doing and will go on doing to help them put their houses in order. . . .

Sometime early in that Spring I wrote an article on the remarkable achievement of Lord Louis Mountbatten in South-East Asia. This appeared in the *Daily Mail* but I have failed to keep a copy of it.

Lady Mountbatten wrote to me from Malta:

> Villa Guardamangia
> Pieta
> Malta

Dear Mr Mackenzie,
Your very generous and completely unexpected article in the 'Daily Mail' touched us very much and I felt I would like to send you this little line of appreciation. I was so particularly glad for Dickie as I do think he did a magnificent job and had got a good many kicks for it ! !

As for me I would have liked to have done so much more and am only too conscious of the very small contribution I made.

But India gave me and my daughter a quite overwhelming welcome when we returned as their guests a few weeks ago, and we felt so grateful and rather humble! They have made such brave and amazing progress too in spite of so many appalling problems and obstacles and it was a joy to see.

I hope we may meet once again before too long has elapsed; I so often think back on our interesting meetings and talks in India. You are a very good friend of theirs, and of ours—thank you!

> *With warm wishes*
> *Yours sincerely,*
> *Edwina Mountbatten of Burma*

Walter Greenwood asked me if I would play a small part in a film that was being made by Pilgrim Pictures called *Chance of a Lifetime*. Bernard Miles was playing the chief part; Walter had written the script.

"The part is a bank director on the Montagu Norman level and in this scene he refuses an overdraft," he told me.

"I ought to be able to play that, Walter. I have had a lot of experience in being refused overdrafts."

The scene in which I was to appear was to be in the banker's Mayfair house and we did actually play it in some house in Grosvenor Street. I recall a brief preliminary scene with my mother before Bernard Miles came in to ask for the overdraft. My mother was played by an actress of the old school and I recall her saying to me after I had opened the door for her to leave my room.

"Thank goodness for somebody who knows how to shut a door behind one without a bump."

What staggered me was the amount of shots the camera-man took for one scene.

"Why can't the players rehearse a whole scene until they have it right before being shot? No wonder it costs such a lot to make a film. It all seems to me so infernally amateurish."

However, Bernard Miles himself was a competent enough professional and I was pleased to get a note from him on March 9:

"Dear Monty,
Just a note to say your performance is splendid—just what I wanted, and we look forward to continuing next weekend.
Yours ever
Bernard Miles"

The Duke of Windsor was in town that April and Walter Monckton invited me to a cocktail party that was being given for him at a house in Upper Brook Street. There were not more than about thirty people if as many, but by the freakish behaviour of memory the only guest I remember being present was William Jowitt. Perhaps it was because I was surprised to see him at this gathering that his presence stuck in my mind.

There was nothing wrong with the Duke of Windsor's memory. While we were talking he suddenly said.

"I see you're still wearing those excellent brogues."

The allusion was to the brogues I had been wearing when I was presented to him at Beaufort Castle fifteen years ago.

I was going up to town regularly for Book Society meetings. The choice of books to be recommended was decided by Veronica Wedgewood, Sylvia Lynd, V. S. Pritchett, Daniel George and myself. I remember being much excited by the Kon Tiki story and holding out for its authenticity. One or two of my colleagues were inclined to think it had been made up. Jack Priestley had given up working for the Book Society by now. I say 'working'; it was really hard work. Besides attending the meetings in Grosvenor Place one had to read a certain number of books and write two or three reviews of the choices and recommendations. Inevitably one asked oneself if it was worthwhile. However, the grateful author was a compensation.

Pamela Frankau was writing that April from California:

Dearest Monty,
I've just received the Bookman with your heavenly review of 'The Willow Cabin' and I send this hurrying across 6,000 miles to kiss your hands. . . .
I am so glad you like it, and I could not ask for a better review, and this novel was written with all my guts and in a time of dark unhappiness and I minded

more about its reception than about the reception of anything else that I have written. So you see why I am incoherent and ungrammatical. . . .

I feel that a letter to one whom I really love like yourself—after so long a gap in time—should contain autobiographical and geographical detail, but the hell with that. What I want to know is whether you would like me to bring you anything from here; food-parcel, clothes?—and do take this offer seriously, please.

In letter after letter from abroad at this date kind friends were offering to do what they could to relieve the 'misery' caused by the severe restrictions of Chancellor Cripps. The pity was that the Labour Government had lacked the courage to refuse the American loan. However, they funked the effect on the working classes of a famine of cigarettes.

I was talking about you for a long time on the drive up from the desert to Los Angeles yesterday with John van Druten and if you got a wave of it it must have been a nice wave to get.

Please give my love to Faith and hug yourself in triplicate.

Pamela

Mrs Marshall Dale Junior on the surface, but much the same below the skin.

You told me once about seeing the complete conception of a work of art all in one flash; that happened to me with The W.C. (unfortunate abbreviation!) You have two devoted fans of The Winds of Love here.

I am glad to have found that letter and know that I had been able to give a moment of pleasure to that warm-hearted and utterly unaffected woman. A few years before this she had been received into the Catholic Church, and that step brought her the mental happiness for which she had been searching ever since Humbert Wolfe died early in 1940, a loss alike to literature and the Civil Service. Pamela herself left this world only a month or two before I wrote these few words about her. She put among her recreations in *Who's Who* roulette, and gambling was her delight. I see again the contents of her handbag scattered in the entrance of the Ivy restaurant and Jack Priestley stooping to pick them up. I see again Jack Priestley holding up a ticket for the Irish Sweep and hear him rebuking her for idle extravagance. I hear again her deep voice asking him if *he* would not like to win £30,000.

It was in the Spring of this year that the first long-playing records made in America were issued in Britain by Decca. I had the tiresome job of having to do what I had had to do when electric recording started: that is to warn the readers of *The Gramophone* that the long-playing record was in its youth and that they must not be in too great a hurry to turn away their ears from the 78's. The dealers would have been upset if I had gone into raptures about the new long-players before they had unloaded their 78's. Reproachful letters from enthusiasts for the new recording accused me of being an enemy of progress.

I gave a half-hour talk about Cockney on the Third Programme which brought me a lot of letters to answer. In the course of it I gave an imitation of my father reading the trial scene from *Pickwick* who himself had imitated Charles Dickens's reading of the scene. I condemned Bernard Shaw's phonetic and 'phoney' Cockney, and involved myself in answering letters of agreement and disagreement.

The situation in Greece was another preoccupation. The ex-Foreign Minister Sofianopoulos cabled to me in March:

"Profoundly grateful your and League's efforts arouse Greek people stop appeal to you do utmost prevent unfree elections thirty-first March."

What was distressing me most was the condemnation to death of Manoli Glezos, that young hero who during the German occupation of Athens had dared to pull down the Swastika that was defiling the Acropolis and hoist the blue and white standard of Hellas. Not even that heroic gesture had secured him against the anti-communist bitterness in Athens. With Broniewski, Joliet-Curie, and Stig Viebel I signed the following telegram:

"Nous faisons part nombreuses protestations indignes condamnation a mort Glezos heros resistance nationale et ses compagnons. Au nom peuples democratiques demandons annolation immediate."

At the same time I sent a personal telegram to the King of Greece, begging him to reprieve Manoli Glezos.

In May I received a letter from John Jobson, the Editor of *Greek Outlook* (Monthly Progressive Review):

"Below is the copy of a letter which it is proposed to print in the May 'Outlook'. I send this to you in order that you may comment on it, if you wish.

"I delighted in your tribute to the Mountbattens."

This letter came from Pat Sloane of the Communist-inspired Greek News Agency:

"Mr Compton Mackenzie writes that "General Markos sought mediation and "Markos has been eliminated" and draws the conclusion that "the Kremlin" is against mediation in Greece. I am afraid I cannot follow Mr Mackenzie's reasoning, but I can state, with the fullest knowledge, that the Provisional Democratic Government, both under Markos and under Partsalidos, continued to strive for a peaceful settlement if this is humanly possible."

I was anxious to demonstrate that Liberal opinion was not necessarily Communist opinion. I had retained my presidency of the Greek League for Democracy in spite of many Communist members because

I felt that men of Liberal ideas should have the courage to express them without being afraid of being smeared with red paint by unintelligent political fossils.

The *Greek Outlook* printed my comment under the letter from Pat Sloane:

"My reasoning is crystal clear. What I want to know is whether the Provisional Democratic Government of Free Greece proposes to be both Democratic and free, or whether it proposes to follow in the wake of Poland, Bulgaria, Rumania, Hungary and Czechoslovakia. An unequivocal answer to this question is required. It is essential for those of us who are not Communists and yet deplore the present state of affairs in Athens to know where we stand and to what we are committed."

As much may be observed about our attitude to the Greek Colonels as I write these words, I find Communist cashing in on Liberalism as tiresome as harvest bugs.

On November 12th I was pleased and relieved to hear from the Chief of H.M. The King's Civil Cabinet:

"In reply to your cable of the 21st March, 1949 to H.M. the King, I have the pleasure to inform you that on the 9th November His Majesty graciously reprieved the death penalty of Manoli Glezos, following his petition duly submitted to the competent Authorities."

In the middle of that argument which seemed to have been going on for thirty years and is still going on, alas, it cheered me up to get a letter from a little Indian girl in Simla, to whom I had sent my childrens' story *The Naughtymobile:*

My dear Mr Mackenzie,
Thank you so much for your lovely book. Baby Austin was very naughty. Daddy gave me a Hornby train. I collect stamps now.
I hope you are very well.
                    With love and
                        kisses
                      your loving
                         friend
                          Vijah

And underneath was a little girl's picture of the Naughtymobile.

Another letter came at this time from Lady Londonderry to whom I had written after the death of her husband:

My dear Compton,
So very many thanks for the very charming letter you have sent me—which I appreciate so much.

We were only talking of my Charley and Father John (from whom I had such a nice telegram, dear old boy, the other day)—that afternoon when they sang songs and brandished the whisky bottles ! ! What fun those days were—I am very glad for his sake that his trials here are over. I only hope he has been able to appreciate all the countless nice things that his friends like yourself have said about him.

All my thanks again
from
Circe

I had been thinking of those days in Barra of which I have written and wishing that the film of *Whisky Galore* had been allowed to include the portrait of Father John MacMillan which I had painted. Then came a long letter from the Coddie who would appear in *Whisky Galore*. The feeble Prince Charlie film had been shown at Fort William, and Lochiel had been persuaded to introduce it.

Lochiel made a very true remark that every Highlander was a Jacobite at heart. My father could not read or write. I got hold of a Gaelic history book and began to read to him the history of the Prince, but when I came to the defeat at Culloden he told me to stop reading it at once. He never would allow me to read to him anything out of that book again. When I grew up in life I always thought what a real Jacobite he was at heart.

We all join to send you all our sincerest and dearest wishes. Do charaid dileas
Coddie

The joint committee of the Order of St John of Jerusalem and the British Red Cross Society had a Hospital Library Department of which Arthur Bryant was Chairman. This year he was ill and unable to attend the annual conference. Mrs Harold Raymond the Vice-Chairman asked me if I could go to York in May and make a speech.

"H.R.H. the Princess Royal will open the Conference, and the other speaker will be Professor Turnbridge of Leeds University who is dealing with the 'Problem and Value of Reading as a Therapeutic Aid', so do please be entirely literary and beg the librarians in the audience to keep the flag of good literature flying. If you would do 20 minutes we should get you comfortably to your train."

I recall an extraordinarily stimulating audience who laughed away because the Princess encouraged them to laugh by laughing herself. When I was presented to her I remember saying what a tonic her elder son[1] had been with the letters he used to write from Eton to *The Gramophone*. His knowledge of music, particularly of opera, was truly remarkable for a boy of fourteen. I can see now the smile and shake of

[1] The Earl of Harewood.

the head as she answered "Don't I know!" For all the speeches I have made I never had a more sympathetic chairman.

Vera Raymond wrote to me on May 13th:

"I don't think I have ever seen an example of 'good measure pressed down, running over', such as you gave us at York. It was the most lovely speech and there was something in it for everybody in that audience, and it put them in such a good humour—including H.R.H. who literally never stopped smiling until she went away at 5.0."

The next excitement for me was the trade show of *Whisky Galore* before it opened at the Gaumont Theatre in the Haymarket. A fortnight earlier Ealing had decided that the film was too long and an expert was brought in to cut twenty minutes out of it. This made it a second feature film, and those cuts must have been regretted when after the trade show the critics were so unanimously enthusiastic, though I do not suppose any critic or anybody connected with the film world would have dreamed that after that first performance in the blazing June of 1949 it would still be running in 1969.

An anonymous postcard from Glasgow sent to me at Barra was heartwarming:

As a Gaelic speaking islander, University graduate, and schoolmaster I write to thank you for 'Whisky Galore' which I had the privilege of seeing in the "Gaumont" this afternoon . . . I laughed till the tears dimmed my glasses. The characters were so natural that I quite forgot they were acting a part. Their actions and reactions were so true to nature, and so like life in the Hebrides that I loved them all even the Englishman!

I am not giving my name but just want to tell you that I have not enjoyed a picture like 'Whisky Galore' for 25 years. Strength to your arm!

The Coddie wrote:

I am exceedingly pleased to hear and see by all the papers that Whisky Galore is a great success. I am thoroughly pleased, and confident that my prayers got a hearing. During my career in the Studio I always went to the Craigston Church where I used to pray in my innocent days. The intentions this time were all for the success of the film and the tremendous venture you risked. Now I am thankful to God for your success.

People suppose that the film of *Whisky Galore* made me rich. In fact, the whole amount I made was £2,275 which includes what I was paid for re-writing the script. This may not seem much but the value to me has been not for my purse but for my name. Nothing brought this home to me more than when last year the *Depêche de Toulouse* headed an interview with *Compton Mackenzie, Le Père de Whisky à Gogo*.

The B.B.C. proposed an interview on television in which I was to ask questions of Claude Auchinleck and Rob Lockhart. The Auk felt disinclined to run the risk of a topic's arising in which he did not want to take part. So instead of him Frank Messervy was to accompany Rob Lockhart.

I was writing to the latter:

"What we want to avoid is the stock B.B.C. interview, but if you and I and Frank Messervy talk it out at lunch we can have a complete rehearsal at Alexandra Palace in the afternoon and it ought to be all right. . . . We'll hold Messervy as much as possible to his personal adventures like that Eritrean cavalry charge when he was caught bending. The main problem of television is timing, but fortunately they always have room for a runover: in broadcasting one has to finish to the second, but I shall insist on going through the whole business with the lights on because a first experience of them is apt to dry people up completely."

It amuses me to recall the early days of television at Alexandra Palace. The two Generals and I were in the cramped baronial hall of the stock T.V. set. There was a sofa at right angles to a fireplace above which was hanging a large map of India. One General was to sit on the seat of it, the other General on the arm. In the middle was a cocktail stool.

"What's this for?" I asked.

"That's for you to sit on."

"Look, I don't ever sit on a cocktail stool in a cocktail bar. If you think I'm going to slide off and on that damned stool as I walk over to point a finger on some place in that map of India you'd better think again."

"I'm afraid it's absolutely necessary for you to use the cocktail stool, Mr Mackenzie."

"Why?"

"Because we have to get the light across you on the Generals and have to think of the angle."

So, an obedient pro, of course I gave way and agreed to slide on and off that confounded cocktail stool during the interview. The Generals were in a state of nervous apprehension. Frank Messervy who had been through some desperate moments in the war and borne a charmed life under fire was more nervous than Rob Lockhart. He was sitting on the arm of the sofa and mopping his dewy forehead during the rehearsal. However, all went well on the night.

I had a kind note from Rob Lockhart:

I must say that quite contrary to my expectations I greatly enjoyed our day (and evening and night) when we televised. You made it all so delightfully easy and happy.

I came back from that television to find Faith gravely ill with inflammation of the lungs and we had an anxious time at Denchworth. She was having repeated spasms of high blood pressure and Dr Squires felt he should have a heart specialist over from Oxford. When he arrived her blood pressure was normal and he was amazed at being called in unnecessarily. His fee of fifty guineas may have helped to soothe the irritation.

In the end it was decided to get Faith into a hospital in London, and I was luckily able to find a room for her in the Hospital of St John and St Elizabeth in Grove End Road. I realized that the true cause of her illness was nostalgia for Italy and by the beginning of October she was able to go there.

After Faith went to the hospital I had a bad ten days of pain due to the strain of writing what was still called *Indian Epic*, the anxiety over Faith, and the interminable argument with the Inland Revenue. However, I was well enough to keep a date I had made with Christina Foyle to speak at a Foyle's Literary Luncheon during the Malvern Festival. The other speaker was Beverley Nichols; Lord Beauchamp was to be in the chair. I had not seen him since Capri in the early 'twenties. He like his uncle Henry Lygon before him had been at Magdalen. I have written of Henry Lygon in earlier Octaves.

Christopher Stone drove me to Malvern from Denchworth, and as we did not have to pass through any traffic heavier than that in Oxford, which Christopher could have managed blindfold, my thoughts of Malvern when I had last seen it in July 1885 were not disturbed as they sometimes had been when being driven by my brother-in-law.

The Malvern Festival had been founded by Roy Limbert, the producer of many plays in London. He was a great Shavian, and had made Bernard Shaw the totem of the Festival. Until recently Shaw himself had always attended the festivals to enjoy the veneration of his devotees.

During my speech I indulged in reminiscences of the Malvern of sixty-four years ago. I think most of the people supposed I was romancing but they were nice and polite. They were not at all polite to Beverley Nichols because he took an opportunity in his speech to criticize the reverence for Shaw which he argued was being exaggerated by Malvern. I privately agreed with Beverley Nichols but I did not think this was a tactful occasion for him to proclaim the emperor's lack of clothes.

The Lunch was being held appropriately in the Winter Garden across which a chill wind blew. Dear John Moore spoke up for Shaw as if he were an Old Malvernian like himself, but Shaw's fiery champion was Frances Day who dealt with Beverley Nichols as Boadicea might have dealt with a Roman centurion. I can see now Jimmy Drawbell's mischievous grin, for although Beverley was one of his most successful

feats of journalism his sense of humour was always too much for
him.

Hunting the Fairies was published sometime in this summer and was
given a kindly reception from the reviewers, who managed to read
it more carefully than the surveyor responsible for the *Annual Register's*
summary of the year's literary output; he described it as a Jacobite
romance.

Just after the Malvern Festival I received a long letter from which
I give an extract or two:

*I am writing to you on the advice of Beverley Nichols, as he tells me you
sympathise with our efforts to safeguard from Silkinism the lovely hill of Dulcote
which overlooks Wells. . . .*

*Believe it or not, but Silkin has sentenced to death the amenities of a city,
to which the whole world pays lip-service, without once visiting it in person. . . .*

*Do help us somehow. B.N. is writing us up in the 'Sunday Chronicle'. He
is trying to get the Kemsley papers to support us, but so far they are cold. . . .*

*Our most vigorous supporter in Parliament is Christopher Hollis . . . and the
best man in Wells is Councillor Duncan.*

The Rt. Hon. Lewis Silkin[1] was Minister of Town and Country
Planning.

On September 15th I wrote to *The Times:*

Sir,

*Is it yet too late for sane, decent and civilised public opinion to shame Mr Silkin
into withdrawing the permission he has accorded a private company to quarry
along the whole length of Dulcote Hill and thereby ruin the natural frame of
the lovely city of Wells? He consoled his critics by telling them he had made it
a condition that, when the company had quarried away 140 feet of the sky line,
they were to plant a wood to cover up the damage. 'Progress must come before
sentiment', the Minister of Town and Country planning warned them.*

*But why stop at the frame? Why not sell the stones of Wells Cathedral and
indeed the stones of every old edifice in England which has survived the Reforma-
tion and the German blitz?*

*The impossibility of making a silk purse out of a sow's ear has been observed;
but the possibility of making a sow's ear out of a silken purse has unfortunately
been overlooked.*

Your obedient servant."

Dear Bill Casey,[2] one of the most lovable men I ever met, after being
Deputy Editor of *The Times* from 1941 to 1948 was now Editor. He was
a graduate of Trinity College, Dublin and had been called to the Irish
Bar. He always printed my letters, and indeed under his editorship

---

[1] The late Lord Silkin of Dulwich.
[2] The late William Francis Casey, LL.D.

the correspondence column was much better reading than it has been under any editor since. Bill Casey printed my letter but cut out the last paragraph.

"There are limits you know to my ability to indulge you", he told me at the Savile.

By an amusing coincidence I was able to show him a letter without address signed "T.C.II".

As a temporary clerk in the Ministry of which Mr Silkin is the nominal head, may I refer to your letter in today's "Times" and respectfully remind you that you cannot make a Silkin purse out of a sow's ear!

Macdonalds published a new edition of *Sinister Street* in one volume on the anniversary of the original publication of the first volume in September 1913. The obstinate life of this third novel of mine has always been an agreeable surprise to me. Even today in 1968, when it is fifty-five years old I get at least a dozen letters a year from young people who have read it for the first time, and significantly today from more young women than men. For the first thirty years I did not have one letter from a young woman. Now they write and tell that the youth of Michael Fane is their own youth. Besides the young people who write to me I get letters from the septuagenarians who read it when it first came out and find in it now a kind of elixir of youth. A French translation came out this year called *L'Impasse*, which had a perceptive introduction by André Maurois and was well received by the French reviewers.

Macdonalds were pleased by the way *Sinister Street* had been received, particularly by the *Times Literary Supplement* which may have been an *amende honorable* for that absurd notice of *All Over the Place*. They were now preparing to publish next year the two parts of *Sylvia Scarlett* in a single volume. Since writing those words in 1968 about *Sinister Street* Macdonalds and Penguins have reissued the book and B.B.C.2 have announced that they will be doing six episodes, beginning in May 1969.

I paid a tribute to Dr Beneš for a large gathering at London University. The Czech translation of my book about him had become a crime to possess in Communist Czechoslovakia; even copies in English were confiscated. I received a letter from Brno in October which was an echo of that ban:

I happened to borrow your English book about Dr Beneš which gave me a real thrill and very great pleasure, especially the way you wrote about politics and the then contemporary events in Europe. It is my ardent wish to own this book in English, a dream which cannot be fulfilled today.

A Czech exiled in England wrote:

May I add one personal line of appreciation of your illuminating and expressive tribute to President Beneš at London University which recalled so vividly that vital, sincere and penetrating personality.

It is a tragedy that once more our democratic freedom loving people should be under the yoke of a tyranny as uncompromissary as any we have previously suffered.

Since I wrote those words we have had that panic invasion of Czechoslovakia by the U.S.S.R. The invasion of Hungary at the time of Suez was similar panic. The chief threat to the world's peace is this unfortunate liability of Russians to panic. God knows they suffered in the last war and one can sympathize with their fear of a Germany armed with nuclear weapons but there is no more likelihood of an attack from the West than of an astronautical invasion of Mars. I pray that one of those panics will not lead to a greater crime against humanity than even Hitler committed.

Mick Balcon wrote me an encouraging letter on September 22:

"To say that Whisky Galore is going well in Scotland is a slight understatement. I happened to be there and saw it playing with an audience and it really was exhilarating . . . I was at a public dinner at which the Duke of Edinburgh was in the Chair. The film had been seen at Balmoral, and he spoke about the appreciative audience of ghillies, etc., There is no doubt about it in Scotland or anywhere else . . . It was tried out in New York the night before last and I have a most enthusiastic cable from Michael Truman whom I sent over to make any slight amendment necessary for the American market."

One amendment was calling it *Tight Little Island*. In London *Whisky Galore* had run for a fortnight in that blazing June at the Gaumont in the Haymarket and a small cinema theatre near Marble Arch. After that every cinema theatre in London was booked. Paris would make up for that next year.

Thanks to the generosity of the Maharaja of Mysore the Philharmonia Concert Society was able to announce for the season of 1949-50 8 orchestral concerts, 4 Lieder concerts, 4 piano recitals, 4 chamber music concerts and 4 concerts of 20th century music.

My brief meeting with the Maharaja two years ago had been a lively grain of mustard seed, but it was Walter Legge who created the Philharmonia Society after going out to Mysore.

I find a note from him dated October 8:

"H.H. The Maharaja of Mysore has asked me to express to you his personal gratitude for your kindness in consenting to act as a member of the Music Advisory Committee of the Philharmonia Concert Society."

I fear I was never any use as an adviser but I am still a trustee of the Society.

On October 17th I received a note from an officer in the Historical Section of India and Pakistan in Westminster. The Army Council had asked him to check the figures in a footnote to Lord Mountbatten's Report of his Command in South-East Asia which the Chief of Staff were busy passing before it was published. *Can you help me?*

"Of the three and a half million men in the Indian Army the overwhelming majority remained loyal to the Allied cause. Of those in the notorious prisoner-of-war camps, fewer than a third were persuaded to join the 'Indian National Army' raised by Subhas Chandra Bose to fight alongside the Japanese. This 'Army' which totalled some 60,000 men, proved to be of very inferior fighting quality; and this was soon realised by the Japanese."

The letter from the Army Council went on:

"It may be considered that it would be more suitable to express the number of Indian nationals as a percentage of prisoners in enemy hands rather than of the number in Japanese hands only, for the Council is aware of attempts to suborn prisoners held by the Italians and Germans also."

I replied on October 20th:

"My information is that there were 2,250,000 men in the Indian Army. 3,500,000 is a wild over estimate.

"As you know I have been trying to extract from Simla details about the I.N.A. after Mohan Singh was out, but so far without success. The figures for the first I.N.A. are enclosed.

"If you can work out a percentage on that for the whole of the war in the Far East you'll be a better mathematician than I am. On the whole the I.N.A. didn't do much good, but they did knock sparks out of either a West African or East African Division in Kalapanza in Arakan.

"I am sorry I can't give more help but Simla is unwilling to give any figures about the I.N.A. All I have are what was written about the Malay campaign before the Historical Section in Simla was handed over in August 1947."

No wonder I was writing to Faith in that October: *Life becomes a railway station after sixty.* She had been well enough to travel to Italy for which she was longing to stay with Mrs Waterfield at Poggio Gherardo Settignano outside Florence. Mrs Waterfield had been Lina Duff Gordon before she married and was a niece of the famous Janet Ross whose house she had inherited.

On October 19th Faith was writing:

Saw Francis Toye at a British Institute Concert, at which Mrs Waterfield said 'everything delightful but the music'. Indeed except for folk songs by Keith

Faulkner it was pretty awful. Worst of Debussy and Delius, and delle Pirecole
12—tone nonsense which reminded me (on violoncello) of our pig at Denchworth.

On October 25th I was writing:

I'm staggering along with the book, but it's becoming clear that I shall need
two volumes. I had an agreeable evening as guest of the 4th Indian Division at
Simpson's last week. Slim was in Hong Kong. So Wavell took the Chair.
Pamela Frankau and G. B. Stern came over from Blewbury on Saturday, the
latter just able to squeeze through the front door. Pamela sent you many messages.
I'm rather tired, in fact very tired, but I dealt with the Siamese Cat Club
Show and was glad Mrs Hindly got the second. I always remember her kindness
to our beloved Sylvia.

On All Souls' Day I was writing:

I'm so glad that you are feeling so much better and that as always you have
been refreshed by Italy. . . . I'm doing a broadcast for the overseas people about
my library.
I've been asked to write a National Trust Book and another for the bicen-
tenary of 'Coalport China'. I shall try to squeeze them in next year.

I was getting fed up with the Income Tax argument going on and
on; after a date had been made for the first hearing in December I
was now told this had been postponed to March. I heard of what
sounded like a perfect house in Tipperary and feeling I must escape to
a land that was not being slowly smothered by bureaucratic pillows
I made a hurried visit to this house, in the garden of which was a
superb collection of rhododendrons and lilies. I was sorely tempted,
but the eighth in my puritan ancestry asserted itself and I surrendered
to common sense.

I was writing to Faith on November 12th:

The notion of migrating to Ireland has not been well received by either The
Gramophone or Chatto's. Don't worry. I've abandoned it . . . I've just had an
exhausting 3 days in London. I presented the MS. of the 4 Winds of Love to
my old school and addressed the first 100. I recorded a talk for overseas service
and finally spoke at the Sunday Times Book Exhibition. Ralph Richardson and
I drew the two biggest audiences. The Third Programme want me to repeat the
Henry James talk with an extra 5 minutes.
I have a quiet fortnight (I hope) ahead as I've refused all talkings.

Faith was writing on November 23rd:

At tea with Bernard Berenson were Ronald Storrs (who says you promised
him another copy of Extraordinary Women or Vestal Fire which were burnt in
his Cypriot holocaust) Bob Gathorne Hardy, with his Logan Pearsall Smith
book just out, and Alan Morehead who has Baudelaire's diary to review and

thinks it rubbish. "Why not say so?" asked Bernard Berenson, who turned to me and said that your broadcast of Henry James was quite perfect, the impersonation lifelike and would I tell you so.

On November 23rd I was writing:

I am getting very tired, but I ought to be able to finish Vol. I (600 pp) by January's end. Florence sounds amusing but I remain romano di Roma. I always feel that Rome is Oxford and Florence Cambridge. . . . I understand the Italian Press is being very anti-British at the moment over the colonies. Getting out of Egypt has made us unwilling to relinquish Tripoli and Libya. That was to be foreseen. I suspect we shall hand over both to the Arabs. That will be a disaster for the future of mare nostrum. Moreover, it will encourage Tunis, Algeria and Morocco to revolt against the French. This passion of British politicians for Turks and Arabs is to me incomprehensible. We have steadily let down the Greeks since 1920 and I should not be surprised if we let down the Jews presently.

Charles Morgan had a great vogue in France. There was a society 'les amis de Charles Morgan' and he was an honorary Docteur of Caen and of Toulouse Universities. I was glad to see a picture of him in the *Illustrated London News* being prodded about by a tailor as he tried on his uniform as a Membre de l'Institut de France. I wrote to congratulate Charles; on November 15th he wrote from Campden Hill Square:

Dear Monty,

I returned from France this morning, not too cheerfully and it was a great joy and encouragement to find your letter. Yes, there are other English "Immortals", Winston for example, but no other novelist except Kipling. I think I am at any rate unique in having bought the uniform! What male could resist the opportunity to have an embroidered habit vert designed by David and executed by Lanvin!

Thank you for writing. The English are a silent race, and there are no congratulations I value more than yours. I am glad that the French put a Thistle, as well as a Rose and Fleur-de-Lys on the hilt of my épée.

Yours ever
Charles Morgan.

I was touched by that letter because it was obvious that I had been almost the only person to write and congratulate him, and there was a tendency now to laugh at him behind his back. I am always being called a 'romantic' by the critics for some reason I have never been able to ascertain. Charles Morgan really was a Romantic, and I welcomed the honour from France he had so well deserved because I knew what romantic pleasure that honour was giving him.

On November 30th, our wedding anniversary, I was writing to Faith:

A scrawl of augury for this date. I tried to telegraph this morning but the 'phone chose to go off the air. I've been up to town opening a circus exhibition for Anthony Hippisley-Cox at Simpson's in Piccadilly and have to go up again tomorrow for chores of various kinds. I'm getting more and more involved in doing things, but say 'no' six times for one 'yes'. I'm glad Bernard Berenson approved of the Henry James broadcast.

Faith was writing on December 4th:

Lina Waterfield makes me go to the lectures at the British Institute. She thinks a lot of Francis Toye and of his lectures. His Chairmanship at other people's lectures is not so good. He sat on the platform while Storrs lectured looking pale with boredom and making hideous faces. For Alan Morehead he introduced him and then retired to the back of the room. Morehead was left at the end not knowing what to do, so drank some water and Toye didn't do anything. He may have thought too little of the lecture but it was not very good manners for the President or whatever he is.

On December 17th I was writing:

I've been having a hectic time and am feeling a bit tired. I was the guest of the Savage Club at their annual dinner. Alan Herbert was in the Chair at the top of his form. I was Question Master at a Brains' Trust of 5 M.P.'s. Lunch with Francis Queensberry to celebrate the publication of his book about Wilde and his grandfather. A tough Snooker tie at the Savile in which I was beaten by Gyp Wells. The annual McAlpine lunch. Big business pullulating. I should think the gathering represented about £50,000,000.

Waxwings have been seen which means a hard January. I think you should stay in Italy till February and aim to get back by Valentine's Day.

Ian Parsons had managed to put in a night at Denchworth and wrote me a most encouraging letter from the King's Head Hotel, Aylesbury, where I had stayed when I was seeing Beneš about my life of him.

I did so much enjoy my evening chez vous and by no means least the chance of hearing parts of 'Indian Epic'. All that you read me filled me with admiration, and I now feel no doubts whatever that you were right to insist upon two volumes . . . and I continue to be amazed that you have managed to cover so much ground in such detail in the time at your disposal. If Vol. II. is as moving as Vol. I., and I'm sure it will be, there is nothing to fear—and everything to gain—for a 2 volume edition. . . .

You'll be glad to hear that we have now sold 33,500 copies of 'Whisky Galore' and a fourth impression of 5,000 is on the way. Not bad, eh? And 'Hunting the Fairies'—well past 20,000—is going great guns. Well done, Monty!

P

Claude Auchinleck came down to Denchworth for the weekend. Chrissie excelled herself at the kitchen range and I still had a bottle of the '33 brandy.

I was very anxious to extract the Field-Marshal's views on the way the abrupt change in command of the Eighth Army had been made. I had just received a remarkable album of gramophone records called *Sounds of Time*. There were speeches by the King and Queen down to J. B. Priestley, a remarkable tribute to the impression his braodcasts during the war had made. Among the speeches was one made by General Montgomery to the Eighth Army, which I put on after that good dinner. In this the General told the Eighth Army that he had given back to them their soul. It might not be actually true to say that another Field-Marshal listening to him in my study achieved levitation but I did have the impression that he rose at least two inches from his comfortable armchair. After that speech he talked more freely than I had ever heard him talk, not of course for publication. One comment I cannot resist quoting. Of one General he said, 'I made a mistake. I should have known better. He was a bad fagmaster at Wellington.'

I have a souvenir of that evening in the note Claude Auchinleck wrote to me:

> *5 St James's Street,*
> *London. S.W.1.*
> *19th December 49*

My dear Monty,
Thank you a thousand times for a most delightful and stimulating weekend. I enjoyed it all tremendously and was supremely comfortable and happy—though I was too well-fed and wined!
I hope that you are well and that you will have a very good Christmas and a good beginning for 1950. I am most enthusiastic about the book after hearing about it from you, and I feel it will be a triumph.
You may be sure that I will do all I can to help.
With best wishes to you all at Denchworth.

> *Yours ever*
> *Claude*

On December 20th I was writing to Faith:

Claude Auchinleck talked more freely than he has ever talked yet, but I expended more vitality in 48 hours than in the whole of the tour! He has really been very badly treated but he never gave any sign that he thought so himself. Only once, obviously moved for a moment, when I played a record of Montgomery addressing the Eighth Army as if he were Moses, Abraham and Aaron in one, did he show a sign of emotion.

I'm changing the title from 'Indian Epic' to 'Soldiers of the East' to avoid hurting Pakistan susceptibilities.

On December 28th I was writing:

A Happy New Year! I've had to sweat at this broadcast 'A year I remember 1900.' It has been a sweat too because it will last for an hour.

I went to midnight Mass in Wantage on Christmas Eve. The little church was chock-a-block but they have heating, so my rheumatic ribs did not get any worse. . . . Leo Robertson has got his proposed book about my work all mapped out.

Next day I had an agreeable Christmas present from the *Daily Express*.

The Editor wrote:

"You will have seen the announcement in the *Daily Express* that the script of 'Whisky Galore' has been voted the Script of the Year by the Daily Express Film Tribunal. May I as Chairman of the Tribunal extend to you our sincere congratulations."

He went on to say that the Treasury would not allow them to offer cash prizes this year.

"However, we would very much like you and Mr Angus McPhail to have mementoes of your award, and I suggest that you let me know what sort of gift up to the value of £50 you would like. This could be suitably inscribed if it were in metal.

"With renewed congratulations on the brilliance of your achievement.

Yours sincerely,
A. *Christiansen*"

I went to the Goldsmith and Silversmiths in Regent Street. I was wearing the wrist watch given to me by Harry Pélissier in 1910, and indeed I am still wearing it as I write these words. What puzzles me is that in old age it gains time instead of losing it. And certainly it is true that, at any rate for me, time is galloping along faster than ever.

I was much taken by the thinnest watch I had ever seen. It was of platinum with tiny rubies round it. The assistant at the Goldsmiths told me it was second-hand and a great bargain. The price was £100 so I joined with the *Daily Express* and awarded myself £50. I had it inscribed inside the lid.

I was amused to get a letter from C. T. Onions (of Dictionary fame), the Librarian of Magdalen College:

I have just acquired for the College library a second-hand copy of your First Athenian Memories which we did not before possess. In fact, I find that your works are very poorly represented, viz. only Sinister Street, Pericles and The Oxford Point of View. I should be grateful if you could inform me which of your books you consider the College ought to have in order that your works in general may be suitable represented.

I think I sent Dr Onions copies of any books of mine still in print and am under the impression I sent the library a manuscript.

On the last day of 1949 Christopher Stone wrote:

I have sent back the proofs of Faith's book about our great-uncle William Cory. I think she has done a really good job. This morning in a cheerful mood I told Pollard to send this cable to Mysore: "Greetings to your Highness from Compton Mackenzie, Christopher Stone and Cecil Pollard stop may the building on your musical foundations in 1950 be blessed with beauty and security." I hoped it wasn't too florid. Walter Legge is out there.

Too many people the world and I would miss died in 1949, but that happens more and more frequently with every year I live.

Axel Munthe died, and this was a further obliteration of the Capri that was. That great woman Sarojini Naidu died. Evan Tredegar died, and with all his absurdities I missed him sadly. Two Hellenes of outstanding merit died. Themistocles Sophoulis who was the only man in Greece able to carry on the spirit of Venizelos; his death at the age of 88 when he was trying to unite the people of Greece after the miserable civil war was a tragedy. Demetrius Caclamanos died; with him I had been in close touch during the glorious fight of Hellas against the Italians and the Germans. Douglas Hyde, the President of Eire. Sir Henry McMahon, a former High Commissioner in Egypt and much loved member of the Savile died; I had known him since Gallipoli days. Another who brought back memories of my youth died; that was Dame Irene Vanburgh.

As I look back on my account of 1949 I feel more than ever that life after sixty is like a railway station.

I FIND a birthday card from Leo Robertson who had been chosen as the Liberal candidate to contest Chelsea at the General Election with as much chance of getting into Parliament as of reaching the planet Jupiter in a balloon. The card was a picture of the Peter Pan statue in Kensington Gardens. The suggestion in a verse of his own was that I enjoyed perennial youth. In fact on that birthday I was feeling as old as my old school which would be 441 years old this year. I find a letter from the Librarian, Anthony Richards written on January 18th:

The M.S. of the West Wind arrived safely this morning, and now that The Four Winds of Love are here together I want to thank you once again for your magnificent gift, not only for its certain value to us as a treasure, but also, I hope, for the encouragement it may prove to persuade other Pauline authors to follow your lead.

Yours very gratefully

By an encouraging coincidence I had just come across that letter when I received a letter from Tom Howarth, the High Master, to say that the move from the Fourth School to the Fifth School in Barnes was to be celebrated in March 1969 by a dramatic sequence performed by the boys called Res Paulinae. In this sequence would be an interview between myself at fifteen and that awe-inspiring High Master, Dr F. W. Walker whose portrait I painted in *Sinister Street*.

The reason for my feeling so much unlike Peter Pan on this 67th birthday was the exhaustion of my work on what was presently to be called 'Eastern Epic'. I had written to the Historical Section at the beginning of January:

"It has now been decided to bring out *Indian Epic* in two volumes. As each will be 200,000 words you will realise the impossibility of bringing it out in one. From the beginning of February onward I shall be sending you a copy of the revised typescript which please return as urgently as possible. . . . I do not know what the position is with regard to Pakistan, but I understand that the Pakistan representatives have withdrawn from Simla. If this is true it will presumably be necessary, or certainly courteous, to send the typescript to whatever Pakistan authorities occupy themselves with this sort of thing.

"The first volume will tell the history as far as the end of the Second Battle of Alamein in October 1942 . . ."

My absence in the East for nearly two years had compelled the

Income Tax people to keep quiet, but by now they were yapping like a pack of dogs in their anxiety to prove that the sale of my first twenty copyrights to Macdonalds in 1943 was income not capital and claim that my income in that year was £13,000 odd. In the next three years the argument would go on. The Incomes Tax Commissioners would give it against me. Mr Justice Danckwerts would give it against me and finally the Lord Justices of Appeal would give it against me. I have included in Appendix E the statement of my case. I do not propose to say anything more about it until I recall the proceedings in the Court of Appeal.

As soon as I had finished the first volume of *Eastern Epic* I found myself involved in keeping rash promises. I realise the feebleness which makes me say 'yes' when I should be saying 'no', and I almost feel that I am bragging when I mention that somehow I managed, most unwillingly, to refuse to take on a history of Glyndebourne and the astonishing operatic achievement of John Christie. However, I was already committed to a history of the House of Coalport to celebrate its bicentenary. Like my book *The Vital Flame* about the gas industry it must now be regarded as an obituary. Coalport was not nationalized like gas but that beautiful china is no longer made.

It was Edward Liveing, of whom I have written when he was running the North West Region of the B.B.C. with headquarters in Manchester, who secured the Coalport job, and did all the donkey work. He and I set out to explore a part of Shropshire which was once a centre of industry. We too often have to lament the destruction of rural peace and beauty by the 'proggress' which is purely material progress. Today the signs of industry have almost vanished; rural peace and beauty have returned.

In 1862 a connoisseur of china was writing in *The Art Journal*:

"Brosely, whose clay pipe manufactories were as famed as they are now . . . Jackfield famed for its earthenware. . . . Iron-Bridge with its famous one arch bridge spanning the Severn. . . . Madeley with its extensive iron furnaces. . . . Coalbrookdale whose iron works are known throughout the world . . . and a score of other busy hives of industry are gathered together in the district, close around the Coalport China works."

When Ted Liveing and I stood on that iron bridge and looked down at the Severn in spate we prayed that talk about pulling down that astonishing bridge would come to nothing. In 1950 it was closed to everything except pedestrians who paid a toll. We thought that Much Wenlock, the civic centre of that district rivalled even Chipping Camden and Burford in the beauty and interest of its buildings. It was a local squire, the Bailiff of Much Wenlock who in 1750 decided to add to his agricultural revenue by embarking upon a traditional industry of the neighbourhood with clay and coal to hand upon his own estate of Caughley Hall. Squire Brown's 'workhouses, shops, and appurtenances thereto' were taken down and moved brick by brick to Coalport in 1814-15 and all that remained was what was now a gamekeeper's cottage of red brick mellowed by the years. The tiny hamlet of Caughley a few hundred yards away was invisible. The view was of undulating fields and woodland down to the hidden river a mile away. The only sound audible was the lowing of a distant cow and the first birdsong of earliest Spring. We could hardly believe that this really was the relic of that busy past, and then suddenly we saw that the garden of this cottage was still strewn with innumerable fragments of china, mostly blue, the blue of the Willow Pattern which Coalport was the first china made in England to use. The contrast between that cottage and the works of the Coalport china in Stoke-upon-Trent was much sharper than the contrast between the two rivers and that was sharp enough.

I went to Chester that February to give the Miln Memorial Lecture of the Chester Natural Science Society. I have always enjoyed visits to Chester since in 1886 Judge Hughes gave me a signed copy of *Tom Brown's Schooldays*. My father was at one time part lessee of the Royalty Theatre. I take from the report of a local paper:

"The theory that the decline of compulsory Latin and Greek in education 'may have lost us the British Empire' was put forward by Mr Compton Mackenzie. . . .

"He said the giving up of compulsory Greek at the Universities of Oxford and Cambridge was one of the great education disasters of the age, and went on 'Most statesmen and soldiers today do not have a thorough knowledge of the classical languages and so they have lost a certain wisdom, a sense of the past and of the repetition of human experience'. . . . . . .

"Mr Mackenzie's talk was entitled 'Landmarks in my Reading', but its theme was a possible decline in the enjoyment of literature. He said he wondered how much reading would be done in fifty years time when besides radio, television and rapid travel there would be many other enemies of reading, and went on 'you cannot be educated by radio and it will be worse when television will come to the fore. There is so much competing entertainment already that I doubt if many boys can become absorbed in a book as I could once upon a time.' "

As early as 1903 when compulsory Greek for Responsies was retained by only a couple of dozen votes I had realised that compulsory Greek would very soon be voted out, and in *The Oxford Point of View* I prophesied that its abolition would mean the end of the British Empire. I made that prophecy as a piece of undergraduate humour, not really believing it of course. Less than fifty years later I was to realize that many a true word *is* said in jest. Now seventy years later I feel more sure than ever that contemporary education is encouraging human nature to achieve the Insect State. At the risk of writing something that might be quoted as an example of the old-fashioned human beings who were blind to the splendour of glorious technology I doubt if a century hence much imaginative literature will be written or read. The fact that more books are published than ever before does not mean that people are reading more; it means that publishers are manufacturing more books to keep up with the growing lust for quantity instead of quality. But I must dismount from my hobby-horse. . . .

I did about half-a-dozen broadcast talks besides various talks in England and Scotland. I was also tired after finishing *Eastern Epic* and there was still a great deal of checking to do and meetings with British, Indian and Pakistani officers to verify various facts. I recall particularly a couple of talks with Brigadier J. G. Smyth[1] who had just been elected M.P. for Norwood. He won a V.C. in World War One and was set as hard a task as any Commander in World War Two. Those first talks I had with 'Jackie' Smyth led to a friendship I value. We share a love for Siamese cats about whom he has written two or three perfect cat books.

Halfway through April I had an enjoyable four days with the Yorkshire Bookmen talking in Dewsbury, Huddersfield, Cleckheaton and Leeds. A Yorkshire audience is one of the best that any actor can play to or any speaker address. Yorkshire was a great influence during my childhood and boyhood as my first two Octaves recall, and the following letter made me pleased and proud:

"It is not everyone who is accepted in a Yorkshire that prides itself on its own qualities . . . Lord Elton made the mistake of underestimating Yorkshire intelligence, but you made no mistake, and brought a friendly sincerity to which we respond, and I hope you found a cup of tea and the sandwiches refreshing after the tiring ordeal of travelling and meeting new friends."

I had been invited by the Senate of Bristol University to give the two Lewis Fry Memorial Lectures of this Session. I suggested as a subject 'The Indian Army from its beginning until its division between India and Pakistan in 1947'. It was evident from the reply to that suggestion of a topic that something literary would be more acceptable. So in May I gave two talks on 'Reading and Writing for 50 years' and was bucked when the audience on the second day was twice as big as the first day.

I spent a memorable evening of good conversation and good wine with the Senior Common Room, and I look back to a completely

---

[1] The Rt. Hon. Sir John Smyth, V.C., M.P.

civilized evening in which the ultra modern furniture seemed out of place. I was staying at the Royal Hotel and when it was time to be going down the hill from the University to Redcliffe Square Charles Malcolm MacInnes,[1] the Professor of Imperial History, offered to escort me to the hotel because it was easy for a stranger to the city to lose his way. This may not seem an unusual courtesy but what made it an outstanding courtesy was the fact that Professor MacInnes was blind. He had defeated his blindness more successfully than any man I have known. At the Savile he immediately recognized a fellow member by his footsteps. I salute that Canadian Scot for his courage and his scholarship, and for his continuous kindness to young and old. The friendship begun that night when he was piloting me back to my hotel was for me a tonic.

I paid a visit to Bristol Grammar School with John Garrett, the Headmaster, and was much impressed by the intelligence of the boys. I seem to remember hearing that the Grammar School was being converted into a Comprehensive School and what a dreary affair it will be compared with the Bristol Grammar School of twenty years ago.

From Bristol I went on to Salisbury where the British Red Cross Society was holding its annual Conference. Arthur Bryant was still kept by ill-health from attending as Chairman of the Hospital Library Department and as at York last year I was asked to talk at the meeting of the delegates. H.R.H. the Duchess of Kent was to preside this year.

I recall arriving at the hotel where I was to be collected by Mrs Harold Raymond, the Vice-Chairman. The room was packed with Colonelesses, Majoresses and Captainesses of the Red Cross. By the window was seated a solitary male and I made my way through a regiment of female uniforms to keep him company.

"Thank God to have another man to talk to," he said, "I'm Somerset."

It was the late Duke of Somerset. I recall from our talk his saying,

"During the war when they were having that drive for paper I did something I've regretted. I let them have all our family papers."

The thought of those Seymour papers being turned into bumph for bureaucrats made me speechless for a moment. My face must have expressed my horror, for the Duke added,

"Yes, I expect as a writer you feel shocked by what I did and I do realise now what a mistake I made in a moment of patriotic hysteria."

The meeting of the Library delegates was a success. Indeed, no meeting presided over by Princess Marina could have been anything else. I had not seen that beautiful Princess since she and her sister

---

[1] Professor Emeritus C. M. MacInnes, C.B.E., LL.D.

Princess Olga as small girls with her English governess came into the room of her mother the Grand Duchess to announce that they had met a cow on their walk among the pines of Kephissia. That was in September 1915. Alas, that fairy tale Princess has left us.

Before I set off to Bristol and Salisbury I had sent the last chapters of *Eastern Epic* to Chattos. Norah Smallwood cheered me greatly by writing:

"I think yours is the most remarkable assimilation that I have ever come across. The book flows on as though it were all in your head and you hadn't recourse to notes at all. . . . Now for an exciting bit of news, which I hope will cheer you up after all your hard labours. The Reprint Society want to do *Whisky Galore* as a World Book Choice for 1951 or early 1952. They think that they will be requiring something above 150,000 copies. . . ."

I read that remark about assimilation with a twinge of envy. The difficulty of assimilating the material for these later Octaves with readability is all too often too much for me twenty years on.

In that May F.M. Lord Wavell died a week or two after his birthday. I had seen him last at a dinner of the 4th Indian Division. There was a press photograph of Wavell and myself which I no longer have because I gave it to his only son Archie John when he came to spend a day with me at Denchworth later that summer. Archie John who had already lost a hand in the war insisted on active service again with his regiment, the Black Watch, to fight against the Mau Mau in Kenya where he was killed in action. Our country was the poorer for the loss of a father and a son.

In June I was writing to Simla apologizing for the delay in sending the completion of the revised typescript. Some quotes from that letter will show the amount of tact that I had to use in my correspondence:

"I shall consider very carefully all your suggested amendments and omissions. I shall write you at length when I have your comments on the complete script. I agree about leaving out all Mutiny references and thought I had done so. The only one that offers a difficulty about leaving out is the 2nd Gurkhas, but I will try and get this in without stirring up old memories. So far as the Japanese atrocities are concerned, with the exception of the Hong Kong hospital, my information is entirely derived from Historical Section documents. I went into the Hong Kong business in Hong Kong very carefully and the evidence is unanswerable. I took evidence on the spot in the Andaman and Nicobar Islands, and though this will not come into the book it satisfied me of what the Japanese were capable, and I think it would be a mistake to ignore entirely terrorist methods used with deliberate intention. I cannot agree with you that so long as Russia denies the help that was given to her my comments are unfair. What can any historian do more than hope that our effort in the way of getting supplies to Russia was worth it?"

I was proposing to spend my time while waiting for what was going to be the formidable task of correcting the proofs of the first volume of *Eastern Epic* by writing a Highland farce called *The Rival Monster*. However the opportunity to produce an enjoyable pot-boiler presented itself and *The Rival Monster* was postponed.

My old friend George Rainbird had left Adprint by now and was the moving spirit of the Naldrett Press which had been commissioned to produce a book for the National Trust. I was invited to write the text, and those journeys I made in July and September all over England and Wales were a kind of sedative for the worries of this year —mostly financial but added to by Christopher Stone's having a slight stroke which put him out of action for a couple of months and by having to make up my mind about the future of *The Gramophone*. I am grateful twenty years later for my ability to make a decision which proved vital for the future of the paper. I recognized the potential of young Anthony Pollard, though I cannot pretend I thought he and his late father Cecil Pollard would raise the circulation to the figure of which it can boast today. That decision I made in 1950 has enabled me to write *My Life and Times* without financial worries.

The book I wrote for the National Trust was called *I Took a Journey*, and it was a journey of 3,500 miles through 38 of the counties of England and Wales.

The first expedition was in July to the Lakes. It was raining in buckets when I caught the 'Lakes Express' at Euston, and it rained without stopping until at a junction somewhere in the extreme north of Lancashire the clouds had vanished and people were gossiping under a sky of delicate turquoise. Many of us have left London in the sunshine to find it raining in the Lakes. Very few of us have left London in a drench to find the prime of summer in the Lakes.

I intend to indulge myself for a few pages in recalling some of the moments that have remained most vividly in my memory. One is of lunching in a medieval inn at Hawkshead with Sir Robert Ewbank, the Chairman of the Lake District Committee. I thought Hawkshead as fascinating a little town as any place in England, full of houses jostled together at all angles with arched entrances and small court-yards. In the Grammar School I saw the desk on which Wordsworth had carved his name as a boy, but I fear I was more moved when I heard that Sir Robert had been the immediate successor of Pirie-Gordon and myself at 43 High Street, Oxford, forty-six years earlier. Miss Prince and Miss Allen, our two landladies, had given him a highly colourful account of my behaviour. What Miss Allen had recalled most vividly was my sitting up all night doing my Schools drinking champagne and black coffee, and eating quails in aspic from Cooper's great station warehouse opposite. I remembered the coffee and the quails but I had forgotten the champagne.

The other link with my past on that tour of the Lakes was a visit to Keswick which I had not seen since I was seven months old. I had a faint, a very faint hope that I might see again those black rabbits and white rabbits running about in a field on the outskirts of Keswick. Of course, I was disappointed. Yet even as I write these words I still see with my mind's eye those rabbits of eighty-six years ago.

The next journey was through Wales in the agreeable company of Humphrey ap Evans, the Regional Representative of the Trust. Humphrey's uncle G. P. Evans had been a contemporary of mine at Magdalen, where under the handicap of being partially crippled by polio in childhood he was one of the best loved undergraduates in the College. I enjoyed every instant of that survey of Wales.

One delightful experience was the time we spent with the three Misses Keating at Plas-yn-Rhiw overlooking Cardigan Bay. They had already given fifty acres round their seventeenth-century manor house to the Trust and bequeathed to it the rest of their property. The view of sea and mountains refused to behave itself by retiring into a haze and the Misses Keating were naturally distressed because it drained the view of all its colour. Nevertheless, that visit remains full of colour in my memory because I still see with the mind's eye a great mauve *Iris Kaempferi* beside a grey wall, the loveliest iris I ever saw.

That single iris was the herald of an enchanted visit to Bodnant. The late Lord Aberconway had just presented the finest garden in Great Britain to the Trust, and I enjoyed the privilege and the pleasure of being taken from terrace to terrace by Lord Aberconway himself. That was all but twenty years ago but every flower, shrub and tree at which I marvelled is still a visible memory. By the time we returned to the house I had travelled with Forrest and Wilson in remote provinces of China and camped with Kingdon Ward in the floral wonderland of farthest Upper Burma, and as from the darkest recesses of memory I dragged to light botanical names I had not uttered for many years I could almost have felt florally at ease in the presence of Sir Joseph Banks and Sir William Hooker. Lord Aberconway showed me a Monterey pine, *Pinus insignis*, he had planted on his twenty-first birthday in 1901 when it was a twelve-inch seedling; it was now nearly 100 feet high! I expect this noble pine is still growing. To me it is the symbol of a great gardener and his achievement.

I had a curious experience in Barmouth when I went into a barber's shop to get a shave, to be told there was a ban on shaving imposed by every barber in Barnmouth. I could not persuade the barber to tell me why. I wonder if that ban is still imposed.

I am grateful that I have seen the beauty of Wales before its beauty has been robbed from it by the Forestry Commission people, the electricity people and the reservoir people. As I wrote in *I took a Journey!*
"Why do we constantly allow such lazy utilitarianism to ruin our landscapes? I use the adjective 'lazy' deliberately because these crimes against nature are almost always due to the laziness which infects officialdom and makes it seek the easy way."

Humphrey ap Evans who had been such an indefatigable guide all through Wales handed me over to James Lees-Milne, the Secretary of the Historic Buildings Committee, at Coughton Court by Alcester in Warwickshire. No more romantic house exists in England. It was built by the Throckmortons early in the fifteenth century, and they still live there on a long lease from the National Trust. The contents of the house are not the property of the Trust, but they are shown on the days when the public is admitted.

"And what enthralling contents," I wrote. "There is the chemise in which Mary Queen of Scots was beheaded at Fotheringay, stained with drops of her blood. There is a purple velvet cape embroidered in gold by Katherine of Aragon. There is a chair made from the wood of the bed in which Richard III slept on the night before Bosworth Field destroyed Merrie England and brought in the black Tudors. . . . There is a pair of gloves of James III and VIII and a garter ribbon of Prince Charles Edward; there are locks of their hair and of the hair of His Royal Eminence the Cardinal Duke of York. In contrast to those relics of a tragic past may be seen the Throckmorton coat hanging in the front hall. Sir John Throckmorton in 1811 wagered that the wool on the back of one of his sheep at sunrise on a summer day would be a blue cutaway coat on his own back by sunset. And he won his wager."

It was in the lovely gatehouse on the night of November 5th 1605, that Lady Digby and other ladies waited for news of the Gunpowder Plot, only to hear from Catesby's servant that Guy Fawkes had been captured. During the great Rebellion the Roundheads sacked Coughton and set it on fire, but after the Glorious Restoration it too was restored. Then in 1688 an Orange mob destroyed the Catholic chapel, and with it the whole of the east wing, leaving it as it stands today three sides of a quadrangle.

If a motorist finds himself on the road from Alcester to Birmingham he should turn aside and drive up that wide avenue of elms to enter a little world as richly coloured as the margin of an illuminated missal.

After an absorbing tour of the Midlands James Lees-Milne drove me to Long Crichel House in Dorset where he handed me over to Eardley Knollys, the Regional Representative for the South-West. Eardley Knollys lived with Raymond Mortimer, Eddy Sackville-West and Desmond Shawe-Taylor in what was an extinct rectory a few miles from Wimborne. Raymond Mortimer was away on the two nights spent in Long Crichel House, Desmond Shawe-Taylor and I sitting up late listening to records on their remarkable Enock gramophone. Alas, Eddy Sackville-West is no longer with us; his musical criticism was one of the pillars of *The Gramophone*, and I am thankful to say that Desmond Shawe-Taylor, another pillar of criticism, is still supporting it.

There was one incident I recall with a smile; Eardley and I had just got back from a day of Trust sightseeing to have tea with Eddy and Desmond when it was announced that a Mrs X—was waiting for the answer to some local charitable appeal. The other two insisted that Eddy must go and explain to Mrs X— that what she wanted, perhaps the arrangement of a concert, was not possible. As I remember there were two large square rooms on the ground-floor into one of which Mrs X—was shown to be joined by Eddy. Presently after a very short interview Eddy was showing her out again and we heard,

"Yes, Mrs X—, but you must realize that we are all rather elderly people here."

Perhaps indignation would be too strong a word for the expression on the faces of Eardley and Desmond but neither laughed.

I feel so humbly grateful for that chance I had when drawing near to seventy of touring through the West country; it was a prolonged delight. Perhaps Stourhead was the peak; it enshrines an era of English history more completely than any house and gardens of which I have knowledge. Situated seven miles from the nearest railway-station it is not the easiest place in Wiltshire to visit, but I can imagine no better way to spend a summer's day than wandering through the rhododendrons beside those bespelled lakes, exploring the Grotto and the Temple of the Sun, dreaming in the spreading shade of those great beeches, and stepping from room to room among the Chippendale furniture of Stourhead House where Gibbon as a boy of fourteen received his call to write *The Decline and Fall of the Roman Empire*.

On we went into Somerset which to my belief exceeds any other English shire in the variety of its scenery and architecture. Think of the city of Bath, the city of Wells, the fat vale of Taunton, the past-haunted Mendip Hills, the vale of Avalon with its apple-orchards and rhines and green knolls, Sedgemoor and Athelney with their great bogs, Minehead with the sea—not the sea in its glory but still the sea —the Cheddar Gorge, Wookey Hole, and almost all of Exmoor. Dunkery Beacon nearly 2,000 feet high crowns the variety of Somerset. Add to all this Glastonbury, whose Tor with the most sacred view in England belongs to the Trust, and the noble towers of so many churches, Somerset can confidently challenge any county to produce its peer;

it even has some coal-mines to add to the variety. A year or two after this I made this claim in an article in *The Spectator* and not a correspondent from other counties accepted the challenge. I was glad to see the great honey-coloured house of Montacute; my grandmother was a Somerset Montague and I could suppose that remote forebears of mine had once lived in that ancient village.

From Somerset we drove on through the deep lanes of Devon to visit various Trust properties, and finally two or three days later I crossed the Tamar by the great bridge and once again stood upon the soil of Cornwall after thirty-seven years. I seldom indulge in sentiment but it was impossible to dismiss too abruptly the thought that Cornwall had been the making of me as a writer. Here I had written my first two novels and a large part of my third. Yet I was glad that we were not going to penetrate beyond the extreme east of the Duchy. I wanted to keep West Cornwall in my mind as it was when I lived there for six years.

The only Trust property I visited was Cotehele House. This medieval house was built when the last white petals of the rose of York were fast withering, by a partisan of the tight-lipped Henry Tudor, probably in the year when Richard Plantagenet fell on Bosworth Field. The two victories I most deplore and the victory in which I most rejoice all begin with B— Bosworth, the Boyne and Bannockburn.

Next day a train dawdled through Devon into Exeter. I was sad to see the way the red Devon cattle were being displaced by the black and white Frisians standing about in the fields like bloated dominoes.

The next tour was of Kent, Surrey and Sussex which began at Tunbridge Wells where I was met by Ivan Hills, the Area Agent. I had not visited Tunbridge Wells since the sopping June and July of 1888, and my guide was rather shaken when I pointed to a turning and asked if it did not lead to the Pantiles; it was quite easy really because I remembered the steps up to the pavement. A nearer past came back to me when we visited Ellen Terry's little timbered house at Smallhythe where she lived from 1900 until her death in 1928. There was a Lyceum room with relics of herself and Henry Irving including many of the stage dresses in most of which I had seen her act. In her own tranquil bedroom the spirit of that beloved actress seemed still to abide. Another memory of my youth came back when we drove on from Smallhythe to Henry James's house in Rye.

Ivan Hills' house in Frant where I was spending the night looked across to Eridge Park; I described the farmhouse in which I had stayed in the summer of 1888 and the lane leading from the farm to the high road which I had once seen covered by a rain of frogs. My host immediately recognized the farmhouse from my description and drove me there next morning. My photographic memory had not failed me.

The farmhouse and its surroundings were exactly as I remembered them from another July 62 years ago.

There was an ornithological event in Frant in the shape of a pair of choughs which had arrived there late in the previous Spring. To protect themselves against the jackdaws they roosted nightly beneath the eaves of a convent, where I caught a glimpse of one of them in the dusk but not clearly enough to distinguish the red legs and beak. I recall telling James Fisher in the Savile about those choughs and James spluttering with contemptuous incredulity, even when I reminded him that Gilbert White wrote of their nesting on Beachy Head. I believe that James did investigate those choughs and discovered that they had escaped from a private aviary.

At this date Charles Sackville[1] was a week or two away from his eightieth birthday. I rang him up at what I thought was the tactful hour of 9.15 a.m. to say we were visiting Knole for this National Trust book and hoped he would be in. The answer came back that his Lordship was on the golf-links.

I do not believe I exaggerate when I say that Knole is probably the most wonderful house in the world. It once upon a time belonged to the See of Canterbury, but Henry VIII thought he would like it for himself. Much against his will Cranmer signed it away as he had signed away his Royal master's marriage to Queen Katherine. I once slept in Cranmer's own room in the Green Court. It is on the ground floor and the Archbishop's signature is scratched upon a pane with a diamond. I hardly slept, for I kept waking all night to fancy that ghostly visitants were in the room. This is the only time in my life that I have felt a room was haunted.

As I went round the treasures of Knole again with as much enjoyment as ever, I envied the man who visits Knole for the first time.

Nevertheless, only a month ago at Long Crichel House, I had asked Eddy Sackville-West if he intended to live at Knole when his father died.

"Oh no, my dear Monty," he replied in a shiver of pained astonishment at being asked such a silly question, "it's much too suburban."

The tour of Kent, Surrey and Sussex finished at Polesden Lacey which Mrs Ronald Greville had left to the Trust and which will provide posterity with a picture of the background of a famous Edwardian hostess. At the Burford Bridge Hotel I was handed over to the guidance of Carew Wallace, the Area Agent for London and the Northern Home Counties.

I was glad to revisit Ham House and eyed Sudbrooke Lodge with some regret; by now Denchworth Manor was beginning to seem an impossible financial task with which to contend.

---

[1] The late 4th Lord Sackville.

We wound up one of the days in the Buckinghamshire countryside at Stoke Poges where the Trust owns a field just beyond the Church-yard which had been turned into a garden of remembrance. The rude forefathers of the hamlet were now sleeping under a patchwork quilt of flowers and the turf, far from heaving, was like a suburban lawn. Few places can be less suitable for the contemplation of mortality than this country churchyard today. A stream of visitors was flowing in and out; motor-horns were honking, making a good deal more noise than the beetle's droning flight; bicycle bells were much shriller than the drowsy tinkling in distant folds; the churchyard in fact was uncomfortably near to the madding crowd's ignoble strife. Yet when I had last seen Stoke Poges thirty years earlier it was not greatly different from what it was when Gray wrote his Elegy. Mercifully Gray's Field with its dignified monument to the poet belongs to the Trust and preserved enough tranquillity to make it not quite necessary yet to call it *Elegy Written in a Suburban Churchyard*.

The biggest surprise I had on this survey of England and Wales was the Ashbridge Estate of 3,500 acres, a wonderful stretch of country of infinite variety without a suggestion of Metroland. In Frithsden Beeches I could have fancied myself a boy back in some Hampshire wildwood when it was Oberon's horn I could hear upon the distant air before it was drowned by the hoot of automobiles.

At the *King's Head* in Aylesbury I was thinking of those days I spent with Dr Beneš in 1944 at Aston Abbots where that indomitable little man was dreaming of and working for a sane Europe after the war. When I think of Beneš I can sympathize even with the most acute American hysteria about Communism, for no man was so monstrously betrayed by his own toleration and charity to the forces of evil. I wonder how much those Czechoslovakian Communists who licked the boots of Stalin enjoy licking the boots of lesser men today.

It was September before I could make my last journey for the National Trust through East Anglia. For this I had the stimulating company of Joshua Rowley[1] who was Deputy Secretary of the National Trust. Our first call was Flatford Mill where John Constable worked for a year and immortalized in the *Hay Wain*. I had what for me was the thrill of seeing for the first and only time in my life a Large Tortoise-shell butterfly. There were half a dozen of them honeying their way up and down a herbaceous border in the garden of the Mill House.

The next visit was to the Horsey Estate, nearly 2,000 acres of marsh and marram and farm land which had been acquired from Major Anthony Buxton and of which living in Horsey Hall he was now the

----

[1] Sir Joshua Rowley, Bt.

lessee. He was married to one of my beloved Maxwells galore to whom
Octave Seven was dedicated. Anthony Buxton was the ideal man to
preside over this naturalist's paradise. I found him nearer to my
notion of Gilbert White than any contemporary writer about birds . . .
and what birds he could write about! Those like the marsh-harrier
and the bittern which bred here, and the migrants that could be
observed from the wooded garden of Horsey Hall, the only sheltered
spot for miles. There could be seen or heard golden orioles. Anthony
Buxton supposed that they did not stay to build their exquisite
nests in Norfolk for lack of the large green grasshoppers on which they
feed their young.

While we were walking in that immense landscape always in peril
of being flooded by the sea, Buxton told me that his headkeeper carried
a glass not a gun, and that his policy was to leave the wild creatures on
the estate, game and vermin and the rest, to fight their own battles.
Would that every English landowner would give his keepers glasses
instead of guns.

It was close on dusk when at last we tore ourselves away from the
fascination of Horsey. We were to spend the night with Sir Edmund
and Lady Bacon at Raveningham. The eccentric signposting in
Norfolk combined with a deluge of rain and a night of ebony blackness
made us feel at one point hopelessly lost. However, we did manage
to reach our destination. We had a great evening, and next morning
Joanna, the eldest daughter, did the honours of the garden. One of
the pleasures of life is walking round gardens with schoolgirls between
the ages of eight and fourteen; the conversation is always racy and the
gossip good. I was sorry when we had to move on.

By the time that survey of mine was finished I had seen every
cathedral in England and Wales except Canterbury. Among those I
entered for the first time was Ely. Evensong was in progress; I stood
at the west end of the great Norman fane, staggered by its sublime
beauty. It was built in three blocks in three different centuries in three
different styles, but by a miracle consummated in stone the whole is
as perfectly one as the music of Palestrina's inspired polyphony.

I was charmed by the Cambridgeshire country side and what is
left of fenland. Cambridge rightly boasts of her poets and Oxford has
to admit that her list of great poets is completely overshadowed by
the younger University. Why have those Cambridge poets all failed
to celebrate the countryside in which they first communed with their
muses. We have come to accept the Cambridgeshire scene as dull;
nothing could be less true. If Matthew Arnold and William Morris
had been at Cambridge they would have allowed to the Cam as much
beauty as they sang of for the stripling Thames. The failure of Tennyson
is notably inexplicable and even more so of Gray. I do not recall a line

about Cambridge by Wordsworth. Of the older University he wrote:

> Yet, O ye spires of Oxford!
> domes and towers!
> Gardens and groves! your presence
> overpowers
> The soberness of reason.

In spite of her great poets I ask myself whether Cambridge may not be fundamentally anti-poetic.

The last property of the National Trust we visited was Hatfield Forest, some three miles from Bishop's Stortford.

I wrote in *I Took a Journey:*

"The morning and early afternoon had been beautiful with a sky like turquoise matrix beneath which the wide level countryside looked its best. There was, however, an immense leaden cloud in the offing. The weather continued perfect all the way south to Royston, but as we approached Bishop's Stortford that livid cloud drew rapidly nearer so that the grass in the foreground in the apprehensive sunlight took on that shade of metallic green in which Millais' Blind Girl sits. We had hardly cleared the picturesque streets of Bishop's Stortford, crowded for market day, than the cloud caught up with us and emptied a torrent accompanied by loud thunder and spectacular lightning. Turning right by *The Green Man* we reached the car entrance to the Forest."

There we were met by Theresa Buxton, a sister of Anthony Buxton, whose father had managed to save what was left of Hatfield Forest after a timber merchant had got hold of it by buying it and presenting it to the National Trust. Miss Buxton took me into her car and followed by Joshua Rowley drove with great skill through chase after chase. In my mind's eye is still a grove of hornbeams which had made me want to alight from the car to stand in the downpour and venerate them. The rain stopped when the time came for us to leave the Forest Lodge by the lake, and to my joy I saw the largest and most resplendent of all our dragon-flies—*Anax Imperator*—that great flying sapphire.

I have recalled some of the highlights of those 3,500 miles of driving about all over England and Wales because they were an invaluable sedative from the struggle with the Inland Revenue, the many meetings with Indian and Pakistan generals and brigadiers, the final checking of the typescript of *Eastern Epic*, the growing realization that Denchworth Manor was financially an impossible burden, not to mention a good deal of physical pain. I think that almost the greatest blessing humanity has been granted is the way one is able to forget pain and indeed hardly to believe that there is such a thing as pain the moment it leaves the victim. I find in letters from the people I was with on that

National Trust expedition kind enquiries about my leg. Yet without those letters I should have completely forgotten that I had as much as five minutes of pain during that July and September.

On St Bartholomew's Eve I was in Edinburgh as a guest of International P.E.N. at the dinner which wound up the conference. Eric Linklater was in the Chair, and the dinner had just begun when he asked me to carry on as chairman because he had to go off to see the first performance of a play of his at the Gateway Theatre. I protested that a guest at a dinner could not suddenly turn himself into a chairman. It was no use. He was as deaf as a Viking to my protest. I am under the impression that he hurriedly introduced me to a female Turkish novelist before running out of the George Watson's Assembly Hall to see his play, but that female Turkish novelist may be a figment of what was to me a nightmare.

At the very end of September I went over to Paris for the first night of the French film of *Whisky Galore*, which was called *Whisky à Gogo*. Simultaneously the French translation of my book was published, also called *Whisky à Gogo*. Ealing had sent over to Paris large supplies of whisky which the critics drank with enthusiam, and the Marignon cinema theatre in the Champs Elysées that night was the nearest thing to a Bacchic revel imaginable in this twentieth century. When Joyce Weiner reminded me of sitting in a box that night I could not and still cannot recall it. Presumably I too was a reveller. What I do vividly recall was a party given for me by French P.E.N. Various French writers were present, all of whom were generously appreciative both of the film and of the book. The only thing that worried them was that *l'esprit* was *gaulois*, not the kind of wit they associated with the other side of *la manche*. Their perplexity was lightened when I told them that I had *une arrière-grandmère française*.

"*Alors, ça s'explique*," I hear one writer exclaim with relief.

So *Whisky Galore* was written not by me but by my half-French great-grandmother.

Joyce Weiner stayed on in Paris after my three days there, and wrote a week later.

"I visited les Editions de Flore and met the translator, a most charming middle-aged man speaking perfect English . . . M. Belmont Perrier asked me to tell you it was 'pure joy' to translate Whisky Galore. . . . I was told André Gide was one of the first to see the film and came out with a broad smile on his face. . . ."

In November I was bucked to hear from Philip Gee:

"My friends of the Scottish Whisky Association join with me in inviting you to dinner at the Savoy Restaurant (Pinafore Room) on November 28th. We want to congratulate you on the wonderful success of 'Whisky Galore'."

I still have the menu card of that dinner at which both Monya Danischewsky and Sandy Mackendrick were present. On it is printed:

DINNER

to celebrate a great conception

"WHISKY GALORE"

And now twenty years later you may see *Whisky à Gogo* as the accepted sign over bars all over the Riviera and even as far as Naples.

A few days before that dinner I received a cheque from Ealing Studios for £1,000. When I accepted £500 for the film rights I had stipulated that if the production was covered by the takings I should receive an extra £1,000; that had now happened.

In the previous June I had received from J. F. Kilfredder, the Auditor of the Historical Society of Trinity College, Dublin, an invitation to repeat the visit I had enjoyed so much in the autumn of 1932.

Here is the letter which gives a clear picture of the occasion:
"Dear Sir,

May I, as Auditor of this Society for next session, extend to you a cordial invitation to address the Inaugural Meeting to be held here in Trinity College, Dublin, on Wednesday 1st November 1950.

"As you may remember the meeting is by no means confined to an undergraduate audience, and leading figures in Diplomatic, Government, Academic and Professional circles in Ireland will be present in the audience of five hundred which is the capacity of our largest hall.

"The form the meeting takes has remained unchanged since it was founded by Edmund Burke. The Auditor, the equivalent in status of the President of Oxford or Cambridge Union, reads a short paper normally touching upon some live issue of the day. I hope to make International Affairs my subject with special reference to Ireland and the problem of Partition. This is but the overture to the main part of the evening when four distinguished guest speakers, under the thinly veiled pretence of proposing a vote of thanks, deliver themselves of their opinions on or off the subject as they please."

Terence de Vere White's paper in 1932 had been 'Communism', with Maurice Dobb and H. N. Brailsford on one side and Desmond Fitzgerald and myself on the other. This year Kingsley Martin was to be my partner, both ready to attack Partition whose cause was represented by two extremely agreeable Ulstermen. I have no record of the occasion and have regrettably forgotten their names.

Dear Kingsley whom we lost so short a time ago as I write these words was a most lovable man and his own peculiar tactlessness always seemed to me like the tactlessness of a paradisal innocence. I feel now the chill that fell upon that audience when Kingsley said 'from life to death or as I should prefer to say, from the sperm to the worm'; I could have fancied that the decorations worn by various senior members of that audience tinkled like icicles.

When the speeches were over Kingsley Martin asked me if he had said anything that seemed to upset the audience.

"No, no, Kingsley, nothing except that all those old boys will probably wake up with bad colds tomorrow from the drop in the temperature after that remark of yours."

"Well, at any rate you made one stupid mistake," said Kingsley. "Do you realise you made yourself out to be 67."

"Well, I am 67, Kingsley."

"What? Do you mean to say you're fourteen years older than me?"

"Yes, in actual years reckoned by the sperm, but a century older in the ways of the world."

Next day Kingsley Martin and I were guests of the Irish P.E.N. and having a splendid time at Jury's Hotel. At least, I was but Kingsley was wandering round looking worried.

"Astonishing people, these Irish," he observed to me. "I'm perfectly willing to talk for twenty minutes about Shaw and not one of these Pen people has asked me to do so."

"But, Kingsley, at the dinner yesterday we all stood up for a silent two minutes as a tribute to a great Irish writer, and for a roomful of Irishmen to remain silent for two minutes was a tribute indeed."

During that visit to Dublin I spent a memorable two hours with Eamonn de Valera, talking with him about the state of the world as the first half of the twentieth century was drawing to its close. He was at this date the Leader of the Opposition in the Dáil. I had not seen him for eighteen years. Remembering the impression he had made on me in 1932 of a kind of embarrassed self-importance on finding himself Taoiseach, I was astonished by the mellow wisdom of the man just three months older than myself. I regard him as one of the few really great men I have met, and believing as I do that the Christian creed offers the only rational guide to an otherwise incomprehensible universe I am always refreshed when I have the privilege of meeting him nowadays. I no longer hear stupid people making stupid remarks about President de Valera. They reserve them nowadays for President de Gaulle. At one time I had to put up with stupid people making stupid remarks about Archbishop Makarios. It is useful to remind oneself from time to time how stupid people can be. So I have kept a few examples of epistolary stupidity. One of these I received in that week of November.

A quarto sheet of writing-paper was headed by the author's name in large capitals under which in middle capitals was 'Author'. One quarter of the sheet of paper was filled with a catalogue of novels this author had written, of newspapers to which he had contributed, and finally the announcement of three broadcasts for the B.B.C. and the script of a religious film for "J. Arthur Rank, Esq".

Here is the letter:

"Dear Mackenzie,

I have written 75 novels with only one short visit to France during the First World War. Why do you find it necessary to visit the Seychelles to write a book? Is it supposed to be a sign of intelligence?

Faithfully,
X— Y—"

Dr Tom Walsh whom I had never met wrote to ask me if I would talk to the circle he had managed to form in Wexford to hear and enjoy operatic records. So before leaving Ireland I went to Wexford for a night and gave a 'lecture' to that circle in the old gaol, which is no longer used for such occasions nowadays. At the end of my talk I asked why the people of Wexford were bothering to listen to me babbling about operatic gramophone records. Here with the old theatre still standing and with the memory of Balfe who had spent his early years in Wexford, why did not Wexford bring opera back to life instead of listening to it on records?

I little imagined what an inspiring answer that question would receive. A few months later Tom Walsh would be writing to tell me that the Wexford Festival had come to life and that a year after I had asked that question in the old gaol of Wexford Balfe's opera *The Rose of Castile* would be performed in that old theatre. I was touched to hear that I had been elected President of the Festival, and as I write these words in 1969 I am still President. I have included in Appendix G the first three letters I had from Tom Walsh because I like to preserve the seeds of what became the most intimate Festival imaginable, unique in its spontaneity and remarkable for its music.

That autumn the B.B.C. decided to celebrate the end of the first half of the twentieth century by a broadcast for each decade. I was picked for the first decade—in fact mine was a decade and a half from 1901 to the start of the Great War for Civilisation. I managed to persuade George Robey to illustrate my music hall memories. I asked him to sing a song I had heard him sing at the Canterbury in 1905.

> "Say no more about it,
> Not another word.
> You've earned your shilling,
> You've done your work
> Say no more about it."

"I never sang a song with those words", the Prime Minister of Mirth declared.

However, at last, I managed to persuade him that he had sung those words to the driver of a hansom-cab who had received no tip for a fare after driving the full two miles for a shilling. The long-forgotten song was found and as I listened to George Robey I was back in 1905, sitting beside Faith in the Canterbury a week or two before we were married.

For the end of that hour's broadcast I had planned a musical accompaniment to my recollection of the journey home from Italy in July 1914. I asked Francis Collinson who was composing the music for the broadcast whether it would be possible to start with a popular song which by the time the railway journey, of which I wrote in an earlier Octave, was over it would have turned into Wagner at his most sombre and menacing. Frank Collinson carried out my suggestion perfectly. It was the finest piece of incidental music I had ever heard. The broadcast went out on the evening of New Year's day and was well received by listeners and radio critics.

In that autumn Scotland was indulging in a mood of Home Rule which usually recurs when Scotland is getting sick of the government in power. John MacCormick was elected Rector of Glasgow University by a majority of 25 over Lord Inverchapel who had a majority of 4 over Maxwell-Fyffe; it was a close call. As I record that result of 1950, Scotland is again in a mood of Home Rule; I hope it is not just a mood of irritation with the Labour Government.

I was writing in the Nationalist Rectorial Magazine:

"John MacCormick has carried on the struggle to rouse Scotland from despondency ever since he was himself a student with a grim tenacity of purpose for which the triumphant result of the Covenant has at last rewarded him.

"Nevertheless, it is still maintained by party politicians that there is no real demand for a Scottish Parliament and the defeat of John MacCormick in the Rectorial will put a deadly weapon in the hands of Whitehall, for, make no mistake, it is Whitehall which turns even whiter at the thought of a Scotland independent of its bureaucracy. I am not going to take up space with arguments about a Scottish Parliament, or the economic potentialities of the country. John MacCormick himself has been arguing long enough, and the support the country gave to the Covenant suggests that those arguments of his have at long last convinced Scotland that the hour is at hand. It is incredible that the students of Glasgow University who lead the van of a forlorn hope twenty-two years ago, will choose, at the culmination of five centuries of their great and ancient University's existence, to line up with the camp followers of English party politics."

I had realized by now that the expense of Denchworth would be impossible however hard I worked. I was worried about Christopher Stone. He had recovered from his stroke but his mind was entirely preoccupied with the broadcasting of popular music for Luxembourg and I knew that his London editorship of *The Gramophone* would soon become a merely nominal affair. When it was suggested that the shares held by Christopher and myself should be put in Trust for young Tony Pollard and in their stead that life annuities should be paid to Faith, Christopher and myself I did not hesitate to agree. I decided to hold on at Denchworth until I had finished the second volume of *Eastern Epic* and meanwhile to look out for a flat in Edinburgh.

I was up in Scotland to attend the lunch given in commemoration of the centenary of R. L. Stevenson. James Robertson Justice and I were trying to get a Scottish film company going. This was to be run as Albyn Films.

When the news came of the successful rescue of the Stone of Destiny from Westminster Abbey my superstitious tendency made me fancy that the successful feat was a sort of assurance of the wisdom of my decision to abandon Berkshire for Midlothian.

In *The North Wind of Love* I had written of an attempt to rescue the Stone of Destiny which failed. Whether it was that or whether it was an article I wrote defending the action of the rescuers, I do not know, but sleuths, presumably from M.I.5 came sniffing about in Wantage and the neighbourhood, to see if they could find any evidence of my having buried the Stone in the garden of Denchworth Manor. It was appropriate that on Boxing Day I should do a broadcast about the Drury Lane pantomimes of over sixty years ago. I find a tribute to that great comedian Harry Nicholls. I was pleased to get a letter from his daughter to say my broadcast had "brought back many happy memories of those lovely days." And she added a little story:

In the nursery I was always 'Sir Augustus Harris' and my sister was 'God'. One day father heard a terrible commotion, dashed in and found that 'Sir Augustus' had eaten 'God's' sweets!

An article in *The News of the World* about the Stone of Destiny brought me some long letters from British Israelites and one or two Jews. My failure to take seriously the tradition that the Stone was the stone on which Jacob's head had rested when he had the vision of the heavenly ladder was severely rebuked. The persistency of the belief that the lost tribes of Israel landed in the north of Scotland is remarkable and even more remarkable is the belief that somehow or other those lost tribes permeated England. I was sad to receive a heart-broken letter from Alan Donn, the Dean of Westminster, reproaching me for expressing sympathy with the robbers of the Stone.

In the end the robbers notified the police that the Stone would be left in the Abbey of Arbroath where it was collected by police from Scotland Yard and driven back to Westminster in a Black Maria, a typical display of bureaucratic bumbledom.

WHEN I came to 1912 in that New Year's broadcast I naturally talked for a minute or two about 6 North Street, Westminster, of which I have written in Octave 4. Among the letters I received was one from a Mrs Partridge which I preserve as a footnote:

I was extremely interested in your broadcast. No 10 North Street is the first home I remember. I lived there from about 1891-1912. Sir Herbert Tree moved into No 12 and owned the first motor-car I saw. It was a large white one. The tenants of No 8 made pills in the basement and on wet days we children helped to sugar them. A butcher lived at No 6. Phyllis and Zena Dare frequently stayed at a house in Smith Square; it had a door in North Street so we often saw them.

As you spoke of No 6 I could see the old fig tree and the three cottages. Unfortunately I never went inside them. There was a fourth cottage where we took the washing to be put through an old box mangle at 1/- per dozen. The mangle completely filled one room.

At home we always cooked the Sunday joint on a roasting jack, a high thing with a screen round it and a dish, which separated the fat from the gravy, under it.

There was a rumour that a passage ran from the wash-house at the bottom of the garden and the Houses of Parliament but we never found it.

I shall never forget the old house but should not like the problem of running it nowadays.

It was welcome news to hear that Mrs Partridge, who was fortunate enough to have tasted real roast beef in her childhood, found the tinned foods and baked beef and delights of today a problem compared with the domestic cooking and washing of once upon a time.

The vandals of the London County Council pulled down number 6 North Street and destroyed a superlative plaster ceiling; the police bagged the brass dolphin to be a knocker for some police nursing-home. I was fascinated to hear of that rumoured secret passage. That was obviously a survival of the gossip when Lord North used to spend the night with his lady love after a long sitting of Parliament. I hope the G.L.C. will commit fewer crimes against London's past than the L.C.C. but it is only a faint hope. The L.C.C. managed to think they had made their peace with history by calling North Street Lord North Street.

The Festival of Britain with which the government decided to celebrate the dawn of the second half of the twentieth century was an attempt to make the British public forget the rigours of the immediate post-war years and believe that England was 'merrie' again, even if Scotland and Wales were still gloomy.

I found myself on a panel with Peter Fleming and Osbert Lancaster to decide upon the choice of authors for the exhibition of books by the National Book League at the Victoria and Albert Museum. The two sections we had to choose were of 'Venturers' and 'Uncommon People'. John Hadfield was the organizer of this exhibition. Gerald Barry[1] had been appointed director of the Festival of Britain, and he like myself suffered the loss of a dearly valued friend when Philip Jordan,[2] not yet fifty years old, died that June.

I looked back over twenty years to the time when Philip Jordan and I were wrestling with the problems of the weekly I started for radio criticism. *Vox* unsupported by the wireless trade lived only six months in sad contrast to the monthly *Gramophone*. Philip Jordan's last job had been the Prime Minister's liaison with the Press, and he had served Attlee well.

In words spoken by Gerald Barry at the Memorial Service for Philip Jordan at St Dunstan-in-the-west:

"It can't, in the nature of things, always be easy going to please both a Prime Minister and the Press. Yet those who know best assure me he did both with a poise, a devotion and resourcefulness that won him new friends and admirers."

At the same time as I was helping to pick authors for the exhibition of books the International Music Council of Unesco asked me to be a member of the working Commission for the Unesco Anthology of Contemporary Recorded Music; the other members were Maurice Dallez (France), Gilbert Chase (U.S.A.) and Ernest Ansermet (Switzerland).

Later on Lord Esher, the President wrote:

"At the Inaugural meeting of the British Institute of Recorded Sound on June 13th the Council, by a unanimous resolution, decided to ask you to become a Vice-President. . . .

"The Council which is composed of representatives nominated by the British Museum, the B.B.C., the Public Record Office, the Universities of Cambridge, Edinburgh and St Andrews . . . will feel deeply honoured if you are able to accept their invitation. A similar invitation is being sent to the Earl of Harewood."

I felt this was a good omen for the Silver Jubilee of *The Gramophone*; as I write these words its Golden Jubilee is only four years away.

I was now asked to take part in 'Spotlight on the Best Seller', a film to be made for the Sales Expansion Committee of the Publishers' Association by Rayant Pictures at their Wembley Studios. My companions were to be Margaret Kennedy, Gilbert Frankau and Ruby M. Ayres. I think it is worth printing in Appendix H the 'Final

[1] The late Sir Gerald Barry.
[2] The late Philip Furneaux Jordan, C.B.E.

Treatment' as a record of film work before that kind of work for films was made obsolete by television.

After an exhausting day at Wembley I was glad to hear from the Managing Director:

"We are all quite delighted here with the rushes. . . . I felt very guilty making you do so much yesterday as you were feeling a little under the weather. . . . I hope that you did not find the proceedings too long winded."

I was laid out by influenza and pleurisy just after this but I managed to finish a Highland farce called *The Rival Monster*, correct the proofs of *I Took a Journey*, and record a reading of *Carnival* for the Light Programme of the B.B.C.

It was just before Easter that a crippling go of pain made me do something I had never done before and have never done since.

Angus Wilson gave a talk on the Third Programme about the four younger novelists whose prospects Henry James had considered in the *Times Literary Supplement*—Hugh Walpole, Gilbert Cannan, D. H. Lawrence and myself. In the middle of agonising pain I listened to the radio and presently heard 'who now remembers *Carnival*?' Above the Third Programme in *The Radio Times* that week was a photograph of myself then reading the forgotten book in the Light Programme.

If I had not been in such pain I should probably have laughed at what would have seemed an addled egg-head talking. As it was I sent a telegram to the B.B.C. threatening a libel action.

I was amused to hear later that the Third Programme *côterie* had all been fetched up to London from their Easter break, but two days afterwards I had forgotten all about my threats of libel and forgotten my momentary irritation. I fancy that what upset the Third Programme *côterie* more than the interruption of their Easter break was the suggestion that they ought to have known anything at all about the Light Programme.

In justice to Angus Wilson whom I met a year or two later he condemned his own broadcast and accounted for it by having been at Westminster after his elder brothers were at St Paul's. He had been annoyed by the way they talked about it and for that reason refused to read *Sinister Street*.

That reading of *Carnival* brought me the pleasure of being invited by the London Cornish Association to be their guest at a dinner; I felt that my attempt to evoke the Duchy in my second novel had been approved by Cornishmen which, after all, was much more important for me than the approval of the Third Programme.

As usual I had been finding pain an incentive for a comic novel and by the end of March I had sent off *The Rival Monster* in time for publication in the autumn.

I had much enjoyed and greatly admired C. P. Snow's[1] novel
The Masters. I told him so at the Savile. Charles Snow was naturally
pleased because *The Masters* was to be his first book with Macmillans.
At the same time, I told him I thought he had made a mistake in
having a forsythia in bloom against the wall of a Cambridge court in
February, and suggested that it must have been a winter-flowering
jasmine.

I did have an argument with another member of the Book Society
Committee who disagreed with my choice. However, Daniel George
supported me. In a letter of March 20 Charles had written:

*Do take care of yourself. Don't worry about the Book Society or similar
activities. Your one duty is to live to an enormous age and go on delighting the
public and your friends. It is, incidentally, about time you worked less hard.*

Charles had known then that I liked *The Masters* but I do not think
he had the least idea I was intending to back it for a Choice when I
came to town next.

On April 3rd Charles wrote:

*I have just heard that The Masters is the fiction choice . . . for July. I know
that this is your doing, and I shall never forget it. Even more because you were
too ill to have any business to be busying yourself at other people's books.*

*I was also (as Pamela will tell you) completely delighted by your letter. To
be praised by you for the natural scene! on character I know, without false
modesty, that I can hold my own—but I was just overwhelmed by that particular
praise. I shall correct the forsythia if I can retrieve the proofs. . . .*

The Brett Youngs were in London at the end of that April and I
was glad to see Francis and Jessica when I dined with the Snows at
1 Hyde Park Crescent. Yet what I recall most vividly from that dinner
party is Pamela Snow's mother, a personality of great simplicity and
warmth. Now in my eighty-seventh year my sharpest pleasure is to
meet somebody whose simplicity and warmth is immediately apparent.

I felt that Charles Snow's advice about not trying to do too much,
good as it was, would be impossible until I was out of reach of London,
but set as I was on retiring to Edinburgh I was not prepared to migrate
from Berkshire until I had found the right flat for the future. I was much
tempted by one in Ramsay Gardens with the best view almost any
city in the world could provide but there was no lift and 72 stairs were
not the stairs for my legs.

One day in May I was in the Savile when Richard Church came into
the Sandpit.

"Well, I've done it", he exclaimed, evidently under the influence
of high mental excitement.

---

[1] Baron Snow, C.B.E.

"Done what, Richard?"

"Given up Dents with whom I've been working for twenty-one years. I hope everything will be all right. The problem is how I'm to make by writing the £1,000 a year I had from Dents."

"You'll find no difficulty, Richard, and you're going to enjoy a masculine change of life at around 58 much more than you've enjoyed all those years as a publisher's handyman.

"Anyway I've done it at last," said Richard, half to himself.

I hope I offered Richard a drink to celebrate his release from Dents because just after Richard had made his announcement I administered a severe shock to my old friend.

"Well, Richard, I've just been down in Bath for this west country writers gathering. After that I went to Gloucester. I wanted to see the cathedral because it was almost the only cathedral in England and Wales that I had never seen. Indeed, there is now only one cathedral I have never seen."

"Oh, which is that?" Richard asked with as much interest as he could withdraw from that problem of his financial future as a poet, novelist and critic.

"Canterbury," I told him.

"You've seen every cathedral in the country except Canterbury?" Richard gasped.

"Yes, I think that is rather amusing."

"Amusing," Richard repeated severely. "The sooner that ceases to be amusing the better. You must be the guest of the Canterbury Luncheon Club at the end of the month."

I have a relic of a delightful two days I spent with Richard and his remarkable wife Katerina in a letter from the Oast House, Curtisden Green:

To remind you that you are to speak at the Canterbury Luncheon Club on May 17th and to come down to us the previous day. . . .

. . . I'm still feeling slightly bewildered about severing my connection with Dents. . . .

For the first time in my life I have no regular income! So far I've not begun to worry.

The Friends of Canterbury Cathedral were gathered to show me round the Cathedral before lunch. I fear I failed to assure them that I had found Canterbury more interesting and more beautiful than Durham, Ely, Lincoln or St David's, my favourite cathedrals. Nevertheless, they were tolerant of my failure.

An enjoyable memory of that visit to Kent was going with Richard Church to meet H. E. Bates for the first time. I had long admired his writing and I looked forward to a talk about Burma where he

had been in the last war and about which he had written at least
two good novels. Within a few minutes I felt as if I had known him
all my life. By an agreeable coincidence I had just written those words
when I read almost the only article of common sense about the position
of authors today written by Bates.

At the end of May I received a letter from Father John MacMillan
in Barra to thank me for some thing or other. After a couple of lines
it stopped and it continued with a letter from Matilda MacPhee, his
devoted housekeeper, to tell me Maighstir Iain had not been able to
go on and that he was very ill. A few days later he died. Those who
have read in earlier Octaves about my life in Barra will know what
sorrow I was feeling for the loss of a friend who had played a truly
inspiring part in my life. I was grieved I could not get away from a job
I was doing in London to attend the funeral and hear the five pipers
play the lament.

Canon Ewen MacInnes wrote from Castlebay on June 6th:

*Last Sunday we had a solemn Requiem Mass for him on an altar erected
outside the Craigston Church as no church in Barra could accomodate the vast
crowd. . . . Afterwards the funeral procession went down the 'machair' to
St Brendan's Cemetery where he was laid to rest beside his "spiritual father",
the Rev. William Mackenzie. 1,200 were counted at the 'Aird' gate and many
more waited in the graveyard . . . Neil Angus led the five pipers.*

I was grieved I could not be at Father John's funeral, and yet in a
way I was glad because I should have found the reminder of my happy
life in Barra too poignant. I sent an inscription to be translated into
Gaelic for the gravestone:

"Here rest all that is mortal of John MacMillan who for many years
was the parish priest of Craigston. He loved alike the language of his
forefathers and the conversation of his fellowmen. Out of the abundance
of his vitality he gave so much to life. Priest, poet, and humanist, of all
the sons of Barra none was better loved. He was born on May 11th 1880
and died on June 1st 1951. He lies at last where he wishes to lie
beside the ocean, and may Almighty God grant him eternal peace."

The job I was doing in London was writing a history of the Savoy—
the manor, the theatre, the hotel. I stayed for some time in the hotel
and talked with numbers of those who were responsible for the running
of the greatest hotel in the world. It was a fascinating experience.
I quote a brief extract:

"Amanda of the Restaurant and Luigi of the Grill are personalities
as different from one another as the Restaurant and the Grill, but they
have in common that distinction only Italy in all the world can give,
a distinction which so many pictures have immortalized. In *quattrocento*
Florence or in *cinquencento* Perugia, in the retinue of a Medici or a

Sforza or for that matter in the retinue of Peter of Savoy himself, either would be as completely characteristic as they are where they are in this twentieth century of ours."

Twenty years later Luigi's personality may still be recognized at Claridge's.

I stayed in different rooms about the hotel. In one the floor-waiter was Roy Heath who had written an excellent book about rare Alpine plants. I quote:

"I must say I find it exhilarating to be discussing with a floor-waiter the comparative beauty of rare bulbous irises and the difficulty each one offers to the enthusiast.

" 'Why don't you give up waiting and devote yourself entirely to the rock-garden?', I asked him.

" 'I prefer to remain an amateur, and I like being in the Savoy,' Roy Heath replied."

"In another room the floor-waiter who brought in my breakfast commented,

" 'Still faithful to your coffee and grapefruit after thirty years.'

" 'How did you know my tastes?'

" 'I used to bring you your coffee and grapefruit when you were staying at the Royal Hotel, Guernsey in 1921—just after you leased Herm and Jethou.'

"How much we owe to waiters, and I take this opportunity of recording my thanks to them for all that waiters have done to make the fugitive hour well spent."

In that August John Richardson who was now Bishop of the Nicobar Islands came to England for a conference of missionary societies. I was privileged to give a broadcast about that saintly man. I received many generous letters including one from the Press Officer of the Society for the Propagation of the Gospel:

"May I say how very warmly I appreciated your broadcast and also express my sincere thanks. In doing so I am speaking not merely personally but also on behalf of this Society and all Christian people. . . .

"I wonder if I might ask a favour. This Society has a very complete set of archives going back over the last 250 years. The script of your talk will have a very definite place in these. I wonder if you could possibly let me have a copy."

A letter which arrived from Wales about the same time was a joy:

I felt I had to write to tell you of an amusing incident that happened. Your picture was in the 'Radio Times'. My seven year old daughter looked at your picture for quite some time, then she said, "what is this man's name, mum?" I told her and she said, "Do you think he's married?" So I said, "Oh, I expect he is", and she replied, "Pity, I'd ask him to wait if he didn't have a wife.

He's just the sort of man I'd like to live with in my house in the woods, when I'm grown up."

One or two critics have sniffed at my habit of telling about letters from children in these Octaves of mine. I am impenitent and sometimes wonder if sour grapes come into it.

Bishop Richardson spent a night with us at Denchworth. Chrissie decided to give him a dish of rice such as we had enjoyed with him four years ago in Car Nicobar. The Bishop's face lit up when he saw that dish. We fancied he must be very tired by now of cold mutton after preaching on Sunday in one church after another. When he had polished off that great dish of curried rice we felt it would sustain him until he got back to those enchanted islands in the Indian Ocean.

There was a correspondence in *The Sunday Times* that August about the origin of ham acting. I was irritated by the silly derivations being offered and wrote:

"Ham doubtfully has anything to do with the removal of make-up and certainly it has nothing to do with hams which are water meadows not commons, hamlet or 'hamateur'. The last is the most infelicitous suggestion of the lot because the whole point of ham acting is that it is a debasement of professional acting. . . .

"I first heard of ham acting in the U.S.A. in 1912, and like 'highbrow' the expression became current in this country during the decade after the First World War.

"There is a legend that some Elizabethan phrases lost in this country have been preserved in the everyday speech of the Kentucky mountains. If your readers desire an Elizabethan derivation for ham acting I offer them from *Troilus and Cressida* Act I. Scene III:

'And, like a strutting player, whose conceit lies in his hamstring, and doth think it rich.

To hear the wooden dialogue and sound.

'Twixt his stretch'd footing on the scaffoldage!'"

I wish the maddening mental exhibitionists who produce competitive authors for the plays of Shakespeare would get it into their heads, so called, that those plays could have been written only by an actor. However, whatever our fathers suffered from ham tragedians once upon a time we suffer more severely today from the ham comedians of television.

I managed to write my book about the Savoy by the end of July in time to concentrate completely upon the revised proofs of *Eastern Epic*. All through the year Claude Auchinleck had lightened the fatigue of my task by several visits to Denchworth and by letters.

I find one written from the Adelphi Hotel, Liverpool on March 17th when he was leaving for Karachi:

If you are going to have an 'Introduction' or 'Preface' to your book, why not

R

consider Linlithgow to write it? He would, I fancy, do it very well and it might be better than having a soldier or a sailor. After all, he was Viceroy of India for seven years, three of them years of preparation and four of war.

It came into my head last night when thinking of you and the book.

My own idea for an Introduction was for Claude Auchinleck himself to write it, but I was careful to say nothing about that yet.

On June 27th he was writing from Lahore:

If you are thinking of getting anyone to write an Introduction to the book, may I humbly (as always to you!) suggest Alex. (Alexander of Tunis). He is a great friend and admirer of the Indian (old style) soldier and commanded many of them in Burma, Iraq, Africa and Italy. He is I believe still Colonel of the 2nd Punjab Regiment.

When I sent Auchinleck the proof copy in August I sounded him to find out whether he would take the Chair at a lunch which Foyle's were giving when *Eastern Epic* was published in November. He was writing from 5 St James's Street on August 27 to say he had received the revised proof:

I'm starting to read it today. It is very compact and easy to handle. Thank you very much for the suggestion about lunch. I cannot commit myself though—I don't yet know what you have said! ! ! Don't forget please I have no personal official connection with the book. Anyway I hope it will be a tremendous success. . . .

It is very good of you to ask me to stay. I'd like to come. I want to tell you about Pakistan—the outlook is pretty dark.

On September 22nd Claude Auchinleck wrote:

. . . Thank you for a truly delightful weekend . . . it really was a wonderful visit for me and you entertained me right royally. I feel sure the book will 'go'. There will be mugawumps and headshakers of course but it speaks the truth and the truth is what most people want—unless it is about themselves? ! !

Well, anyway here's luck to you and it. This election and the King's health will I suppose make the timing for publication very ticklish? I don't like the bulletins etc., about the King at all. It is bad luck on him because he has tried very hard . . . you are a wonderful tonic. My best wishes to Chrissie. What a curry!

On October 25th Claude wrote:

. . . I will be there (D.V. and Insha Allah) at 6.30 p.m. at the Savile . . . I return Mo Mayne's letter. I am glad he enjoyed Vol. I. I am looking forward to the day. But I am very sorry I shan't be at the lunch.

Those last words were a disappointment. I knew what his reason was for not attending the Foyle's Lunch, and I understood why he felt unable to be present. Nevertheless, I was disappointed that he did not feel able to ignore that reason. Luckily for me Douglas Gracey was back at home again after his Command of the Army of Pakistan, and he took the Chair at the lunch. He had written on June 27th:

. . . on our arrival in England, we found a very pleasant surprise waiting for us in the shape of an invitation from the French Government to go out, both of us, as their guests in Indo-China or Vietnam as it is now called. We flew off on May 18th and got back on June 5th. It was a marvellous experience and, I should say, a unique invitation. . . .

There is a growing inclination nowadays to depreciate the influence of the individual upon public affairs and it is a pity that there have not been a few individuals of Douglas Gracey's quality to visit Vietnam since 1951.

I was away in Wexford before that Foyle's Lunch taking part in its first Festival. I look back to that week in St Luke's little Summer as Alice might have looked back to her adventures in Wonderland. The Mayor and Town Council of Wexford had not yet been persuaded to recognize the Festival. There was not a single lamp illuminated by the municipality. However, *The Rose of Castile* in that old theatre was a great success, and an even greater success was the boundless hospitality of Tom Walsh's wife, Eva. The memory that remains perhaps the most vividly of that first Wexford Festival is of sitting up in a room at White's Hotel with the Franciscan friar who had trained a chorus of local girls for Balfe's melodious opera, and listening with him to . . . who was it that sang to us those Gaelic songs at 4 a.m.?

Owing to the Wexford Festival I had not been able to attend the wedding of young Tony Pollard, that wedding with its tragic sequel when the young bridegroom lost his bride within less than a year. The courage he would show made me realize how wise I had been to make him the ultimate managing director of *The Gramophone*.

The bubble and squeak of a general election was over with Winston Churchill again in Downing Street when the big lunch at the Dorchester was held, with Douglas Gracey in the Chair and a full gathering of appropriate guests. Among them were Lord and Lady Mountbatten, she in uniform, and also Rob Lockhart who kindly found time to attend although he was leaving for Singapore next morning to take over command against the guerrillas in Malaya. Mountbatten made one of his excellent speeches. I was more nervous than I usually am when making a speech because I had to be sure of saying nothing that would offend either India or Pakistan. I was glad to get a letter from Habib Ibrahim Rahimtoola, the High Commissioner for Pakistan, in which he wrote:

"If your book has even a fraction of the feeling and passion of your speech at Foyle's Lunch then it is bound to be a best seller."

Nevertheless, in spite of the success of that lunch I sadly missed Claude Auchinleck. He wrote on December 13th:

My dear Monty,

I have been meaning to write to you for weeks so please believe it!

How is the book going? The reviews I have read were excellent, I thought. There is no doubt that it is a great book, one that will live. I only hope it will be read by many people. Today an otherwise intelligent and decent business-man who knew India and had lived there said to me—of the Hindus—"Of course they can't fight, can they?" Can you beat it? What a nation we are! We deserve to decline and die.

Well, none could have done more than you to help repay our debt to the Sepoy Army. I expect to be off to Pakistan about the 8th January. How I wish you were coming too. Let me know if there is anything I can do for you or the book. . . .

Yours
Claude

To these words of Claude Auchinleck about the Sepoy Army I will add some words of my own in a broadcast.

"Call that old Indian Army an army of mercenaries if you will, but when you do, remember at the same time that in the long long chronicle of humanity at war no army's record of duty, discipline and valour has been less stained by inhumanity. And give a thought to those British officers whose occupation is now gone but whose hearts still beat for that army of mercenaries they loved so wisely and so well. For many months I have spent hour after hour with the glorious records of that army and I have a right with all humility to bid a free India cherish the example of that army of mercenaries. I have a notion that the Roman legions of long ago were wrought out of similar metal, and I do not exaggerate when I assert that I never fully apprehend the reason why Rome was able to rule the western world so long until at home in the quiet of my library I could meditate upon the experience that I had been granted by that passage to India. The moral influence of that old Indian Army today is still magnificently clear. . . .

"If we surrender to the belief that East is East and West is West and accept the incompatibility between them as eternal and insurmountable, then indeed the look out for mankind is dark despair. But we shall not surrender to that belief. We shall learn as we have learned before, though the lesson may seem forgotten in this age of armament and fear, that the day-spring of humanity's hopes has always risen and always will rise in the East."

I was back at work on the second volume of *Eastern Epic* a few days after that Foyle's Lunch at the Dorchester. I was feeling fit and felt hopeful of finishing off my book by next Spring. One night after reading through some faded typewritten reports of military activities I went to bed in the small hours. When Chrissie brought in my coffee next morning she asked me what I had been doing to my eyes.

"There's nothing the matter with my eyes," I said.

"Well, your left eye is all red round the rim."

I asked for my looking-glass and saw that my left eye did look odd. I shut my right eye to look more closely and my face vanished from the mirror. I went up to London and was told by an oculist that my left eye was covered by a retinal haemorrhage. I realized under the examination that the eye was still aware of light, and that to outward appearance the eye looked normal. My left eye was my master eye and when I went to play a game of snooker at the Savile I found that snooker was for me a game of the past. I was naturally worried about the possibility of a retinal haemorrhage over my right eye, and was told that such a mishap was most improbable.

"But not impossible?"

"Not impossible, but *most* improbable."

"But you would have said a retinal haemorrhage right across my left eye was improbable, and it has happened."

I deeply regret now that I did not continue to go on working at volume two of *Eastern Epic*. At that date the cataract in my right eye was only in its infancy. However, that sudden loss of an eye was naturally a shock and I finished with any reading that would tire the eye left to me.

Edward Elgar once told me that the proudest moment of his life was when he received a letter addressed 'Edward Elgar, England'. At the very end of that December I received a letter from Ireland addressed '*Mr Compton Mackenzie, Author, Great Britain*'. Such successful notoriety did not compensate me for the loss of my master eye and my failure to finish the job on which I had set out, a failure which would be reproaching me for many years and still reproaches me.

A WEEK after my birthday I did a broadcast called 'A Week on the way to Seventy'. "I wish I could muster as much respectful emotion," I began, "as once upon a time the prospect of that magical double figure then drawing closer every day evoked in my grateful heart. Never again to contain one's age within a single numeral! Life would then begin at last."

I shall indulge myself at the close of my ninth octave with a few more quotations from that broadcast of eighteen years ago:

"It is a good lesson in the passage of time to count one's age backwards. I cannot feel that 1883 is so very far away from the present. Yet, the other way round, it would mean that I would have had to be born a year before Waterloo if I wanted to talk in 1882 of entering my seventieth year and with that realisation I am immediately awed by Shakespeare's 'dark backward and abysm of time'. Yet why? After all, I can remember sitting on the knees of at least one old pensioner who fought at Waterloo."

As I copy those words I am now, the other way round, back in 1797; I should have been able to fight at Waterloo myself. That old pensioner "brings me to the advantage of a good memory. So many people lose most of the first, and by far the longest decade of their life by failing to preserve a continuous memory. Old men proverbially live in the past, but what a disjointed past it too often is. And because it contains so many gaps, such old men are apt to find themselves out of touch with the present, whereas if, by exercising the memory, they have throughout their lives made the past an eternal present, their minds will not age with their bodies. It seems to me, though I may be wrong, that our present education neglects to promote that reverence for the living memory which is owed to it. Mnemosyne or Memory, the titan daughter of Heaven and Earth, was the mother of the nine Muses, and it is Mnemosyne whom Hesiod, in one of his Homeric hymns, makes Hermes salute first of all the immortals. I cannot believe that Mnemosyne would have been much interested in the snippets of information which contemporary fashion demands from memory. It was with the deliberate intention of honouring Mnemosyne that, except during two years of intensive travel, I have never kept a diary. I suspect that nothing is more destructive of the kind of memory that the Muses inherited from their mother than a diary, unless of course the diarist be a Pepys whose diary is the creative life of his imagination, and therefore as such able to preserve the living past in an eternal present.

"Any man entering his seventieth year, be he townsman or country-man, must ask himself whether the present-day child can retain so sharp an impression of its childhood as he does. That question will have to be answered by somebody broadcasting in 2021. Yet, I will hazard my opinion that in such an unimaginable year of the future all sorts of things which people of my age regard through a distracting blur of noise, colour, height, and speed, will emerge touched by the enchantment of distance as vivid experiences of the youthful mind today. I base this conviction on the sharp impact New York made upon me in my thirtieth year. I daresay New York in 1912 would have seemed just a blur of noise, colour, height, and speed if I had been born in 1843. Of course, it is fantastic for me to walk along Kensington High Street and Hammersmith Road today. . . . Practically nothing is left of my childhood, not even the old milestone that said 'London 4 miles Hounslow 7 miles'. How incredible it seems now that on May Day morning the chimney-sweeps used to dance down the middle of the road in wicker-cages covered with leaves—Jacks-in-the-Green with the centuries behind them to remind us that once there was a Maypole in the Strand. The old cries of London were still heard—'Cherry ripe' in summer's prime . . . or with so sweet a melancholy 'Who'll buy my lavender?' at summer's dusty end. Gypsy caravans as brightly coloured as a bouquet of flowers, with swarthy beauties wearing ostrich-plumed hats, would pass slowly by, returning to pick up the dark man with earrings who sat on the top of the area steps mending a cane-seated chair. Can it be true that at the age of five I was always fearful lest the gypsies in London should steal me away and stain my body with walnut juice?

"And then the beggars! When I hear some of my contemporaries deploring the sins of the welfare state I wonder how clearly they remember the beggars of their youth. Foreigners used to be horrified by what they felt was the brutal indifference of London in the 'eighties to human misery and suffering. No child sees those mutilated or starving spectres of humanity today, but some of us who saw them have not forgotten them, and so we are able to feel less indignant about the expense of social amelioration. . . .

"In my fourteenth year I read. . . . *Cicero De Senectute*—Cicero on Old Age—a good example of the way Latin and Greek were too often spoilt for us by the unimaginative choice of desiccated schoolmasters. Cicero was writing at a time when the prospect for civilisation seemed as menacing and dark as it seems to us, and now, with a greater capacity for understanding his observations about old age than I possessed at thirteen, I find it a tranquil and reassuring thesis, though poor old Cicero himself met a violent end. There is only one notable privilege of old age which he omitted to mention . . . indeed, it is more than a privilege, it is a luxury—that luxury is to escape not from the fevers of love nor from the ache of ambition but from seasickness. Believe me, you bad sailors who are still in middle-age and have to make journeys by sea, that the greatest luxury of old age is freedom from seasickness. When a man in his seventieth year can stand on a reeling deck and survey with surprise the effect that the waves are having upon his fellow-voyagers, then indeed he can say with Sir Thomas Browne: 'In seventy years, a man may have a deep gust of the world; know what it is, what it can afford, and what 'tis to have been a man'."

I had a lot of letters after that broadcast one of which from Willie Erskine[1] brought back that Athens of nearly forty years ago:

I must write you a line to say how much we enjoyed your broadcast on growing old. I seldom listen to such talks. They bore me and I prefer my own thoughts and remembrances, but yours was quite delightful. But seventy years seems to me young. I am over eighty and still enjoy life. You once propounded to me the theory that all who live on islands are or become mad. You seem to be an exception but perhaps you no longer live in the Hebrides. . . . I agree with you that there are many compensations in increasing age. In Athens I enjoyed bounding up Lycabettus before breakfast. . . . Now I enjoy breakfast and newspapers in bed just as much. . . . The only real sad drawback in being eighty is that almost all my contemporary friends are dead or gaga.

I hope you have outgrown those frightful attacks of neuritis you used to have in Greece.

I had last seen Willie Erskine twenty years earlier when he was Ambassador in Warsaw. When I recall figures like him I find the diplomats of today as hard to believe real as the figures in a B.B.C. Wednesday play.

Two days after that broadcast the India League had a demonstration at the Royal Albert Hall. The weather on that Saturday afternoon was vile with an icy east wind, but it was a crowded gathering. The Chairman was Reginald Sorensen, the Labour Member for Leyton. Beside him on the platform were Krishna Menon, the High Commissioner for India, Clement Attlee, the Leader of the Opposition, Walter Monckton, the Minister for Labour in the new Conservative government, Lord Pethick Lawrence, Harriet Cohen and myself. I was sitting between Monckton and Attlee who was on the left of the Chairman. There was a musical programme which went on between the speeches. Those speeches were all very cautious. Krishna Menon spoke first. His personality made an impression on me. At one time he had been a member of the St Pancras Borough Council, that nursery garden of future Labour M.P.'s. He was a member of the English Bar and had just been called to the Irish Bar. I recall asking him why he had not been

[1] The late Hon. Sir W. F. Erskine, K.C.M.G.

called to the Scottish Bar which I reminded him was so much closer to the legal systems of Europe and therefore worthy of an Asian lawyer's attention. I found his ironical, almost sardonic humour attractive. However, he did not allow any of it to flow in his speech. I realized that what was making him so cautious was the imperative necessity of not saying anything that could be used in Pakistan as evidence against India.

Pethick Lawrence spoke with deep sincerity, and in all that great audience, with many Negroes in it, none can have been unaware of what I can only call the saintliness of that aging man.

Attlee was worried by an infernal draught and after his speech sent out for his overcoat. It had been a dull speech, and Attlee sat back with the collar of his overcoat turned up, looking bored. He was only a fortnight nearer to his seventieth birthday than I was but on that chilly January afternoon he seemed to have already reached it.

Walter Monckton spoke next and seemed concentrated on committing himself to nothing. As a member of the new government he could not afford to give too much credit to what the previous government had done for India; at the same time he had to be careful not to say anything to suggest to India that the Conservatives were less sympathetic than their predecessors. When I got up to speak I felt it was time to stir the audience out of what was beginning to seem like apathy. So I let myself go and just before I sat down I made an involuntary sweep of my arms and that emotional gesture knocked over a decanter of water into Attlee's lap.

"You're determined to give him pneumonia before he leaves this Hall," Walter Monckton murmured.

Whatever indignation Attlee may have been feeling against that cold draught he made light of my clumsy gesture.

One of my regrets had been that in the course of the wonderful tour in Asia and Africa Ceylon had been omitted from the itinerary. I regretted it even more when I was the guest of the Association of Ceylon Women in the Commonwealth Lounge of the Imperial Institute soon after that Albert Hall meeting. I never saw so many beautiful women all at once. Moreover, not only were they beautiful; they were also full of humour and of fine intelligence.

The death of King George VI saddened that February. Faith and I lost one of our most intimate friends when Norman Douglas died in that same month.

I find a few words about him in Faith's handwriting which express something of our loss:

We met first in London when he lunched with us 1911 or 1912. Thus began an eternal friendship for me.

He was responsible for Capri in our lives, for on his advice as soon as we were in Italy for the first time we sailed in a small boat from Sorrento to Capri for a week-end. There, enchanted we settled—we thought—forever.

The core of my friendship with Norman was respectful ribaldry, amity and Music. He liked my piano playing and I liked his. He had studied seriously enough in Germany. He gave me a well-worn but not heavily fingered Bote and Bock volume of Chopin's works with his own name spelt with a double 'S' and dated 1886. The favourite Barcarolle which he played so well was not in this volume. But he was playing it one June evening in our Capri salone when he had finished 'South Wind' and brought his manuscript to read to me and for me to type.

He sat at our noisy but controllable Erard Grand and drifted, as often he did, from a beautiful rare Bach Chorale into hymn tunes remembered from early days. Glancing at me, he began Newman's 'Lead Kindly Light'.

I took my cue and sang in my imitation of a choirboy, faintly sharp at times, to the end of the hymn. He played with enormous feeling. There was no mockery. The evening passed as serenely as usual.

Norman Douglas was 83 when he died that February in Capri, and I was able to telephone about him to *The Sunday Times* when we heard the news that Saturday:

"They told me, Heraclitus, they told me you were dead; . . . and for me remains the memory of how often on some terrace above the Mediterranean shaded by ilex and gnarled locust tree, Norman Douglas and I, the wine between us, have 'tired the sun with talking and sent him down the sky'."

I look through old letters and find one of March 1913 in which Douglas advised me to 'go over to Capri and try that. It is a quiet place and sunny and most curious to a student of life like yourself.' Four years later my wife would be typing 'South Wind' for him in that Capri to which he had introduced us.

Immense curiosity, profound laughter, and continuous vitality were the links in our friendship—and dare I add, an absolute freedom from the nightmares of Freud *et hoc genus omne*.

"His mother was Bavarian with a touch of Ruritanian romance about her; his paternal ancestry was pure Scottish. Douglas himself with his florid complexion, small deep-set glittering eyes, and long, tip-tilted, sliced-off pragmatical nose resembled the portrait of almost any eighteenth-century Lowland laird.

"His erudition was large and many-sided; his prose was perfect; he was the last of the European travellers in the Grand Style. Mellow as a pear, astringent as a lemon, sweet and sun-dyed as an apricot, bitter as an almond, crisp as a pippin, ruddy and comfortable as a plum, juicy as an orange, taut as a grape, spicy as a peach, shameless as a fig, assertive as a pineapple—all these he was in turn for he was the fruit of the ages.

"I turn to another letter of Douglas written from Capri in December 1948 on the eve of his eightieth birthday: 'Just finished re-reading Vestal Fire. They are all ghosts now, but very much alive for all that. No freaks nowadays, *not one*, but a considerable lot of bores.'

"And now he, the last left of those Capri characters to whom he introduced me 39 years ago, is himself a ghost; but in the great procession of English literature very much alive for all that."

A portrait of Norman Douglas in the *Times Literary Supplement* that July was a piece of accurate painting. I quote:

"His conversation was fabulous—witty, learned and long. He has been described in thinly veiled fictional terms by Mr Compton Mackenzie, Mr Aldous Huxley and D. H. Lawrence among others, the emphasis varying, of course, with the personality of the novelist: in the first case he is portrayed with joy and wonderment, in the second with a kind of astonishment, and in the third with an envious disapproval which is yet not devoid of affection."

How sad that so many of the people who talk on *Late Night Line Up* have never heard good conversation, as they peck away at words with countless 'y' knows'. The present need not worry; it has Peter Ustinov who as a talker is the equal of any I have known and as a raconteur the best to whom I have listened.

The premature death of Conchita Supervia had been a tragic loss for music. Desmond Shawe-Taylor broadcast a moving and admirable memorial to that great singer. I was able to make a brief allusion to that loss in some broadcast and was much touched to receive a note from her husband, Ben Rubenstein, in which he wrote:

"I happened to be listening to the radio last night when you made your short but complete and moving tribute to my wife, the late Conchita Supervia."

The early part of this year was rather a difficult time. My decision to give up Denchworth and ultimately move to Edinburgh when I found the right house or flat made Faith decide that she must have some retreat in the Mediterranean. The death of Norman Douglas had made Capri too sad a reminder of once upon a time. I was hoping that Christopher Stone would agree to share the Denchworth library with me at any rate until I had finished *Eastern Epic*. He and I would sleep in the bungalow; Chrissie and Nellie could live in the Red Cottage which I had renamed Three Roses after that plaster souvenir of the end of that medieval war. Unfortunately Christopher Stone who had by now recovered from his slight stroke was changing his mind almost daily. I had suggested that if nowhere suitable turned up in the Mediterranean Faith might move to Tenebrae, Christopher's basement flat in The Boltons. This appeared settled when Christopher changed his mind again and decided to stay in Tenebrae.

I was worried because the haemorrhage in the left eye seemed to have settled down as a permanent blanket and now my right eye was growing tiresome. I realized just how tiresome when I went out to salute the new moon and saw two of them.

My income tax case was to come before a judge in April and I had very little hope of getting a verdict in my favour. The prospect made me more worried than ever about the financial future. I was offered what would have been a delicious pot-boiler when Tate and Lyle suggested my writing their history. This would have meant touring the West Indies. However, I felt my first duty was to *Eastern Epic* and that if I went gallivanting off to the West Indies the soldiers, Indian, Pakistani and British might justifiably resent it. So I turned down the suggestion. It is always my habit when I am disappointed to decide that my disappointment was an advantage. So now I told myself that I should probably not have succeeded in writing even as good a book about the West Indies as Kingsley's *At Last*, and that was dull.

What seemed a possible solution of our plans for the future was an advertisement we read of a small villa in Majorca. I wrote to the owner who was over in London and he came down to Denchworth. Today he would not be a conspicuously hairy figure among so many hairy young men; at this date he was unusual. The price he was asking for the villa seemed so small that I supposed it must have many disadvantages. However, apparently there were none. I had always been prejudiced against the Balearic Islands but X made them sound worthy to stand beside even the gems of the Aegean. Finally we decided to acquire this foothold in a place called Fornalutx. Nadegine who was now back in England after some years in Germany volunteered to go to Majorca with Faith, and Christopher planned to go at Easter. In fact he did go, and very nearly went to the Canary Islands instead, having got into the wrong plane at Barcelona.

Of course, nobody knew anything about the various restrictions on buying a property abroad, and a few extracts from letters I was writing after Faith and Nadegine set out in March will show what a fussy business it all was.

March 13.

I was very glad to get your letter this morning though naturally worried by your difficulties. . . . I have no news yet about the Bank of England . . . naturally I am a bit fussed. Nadegine's letter sounded like the description of a thunderstorm. I hope the steps won't be too much. You'll have to get a fast mule.

X had said nothing about those 200 steps leading up to the cottage;

they would ultimately lead Faith to abandon Majorca within a year.

Christopher is full of excitement and talks of being with you by Easter. My own state of mind has not been improved by this bad go of gastric flu, as they call it, though I don't believe it was anything whatever to do with flu. However, I hope to be up tomorrow. I fear this finally makes it impossible for me to play Sir David Carteret in a proposed film of 'Mrs Dane's Defence' because I am now behind with my Buckingham Palace series . . . I am told that all letters abroad are now "unofficially censored by the Customs."

The proposed film of Henry Arthur Jones's play was given up when I had to turn down playing Charles Wyndham's famous part.

On March 18th I wrote to Nadegine:

The Bank of England permit should come through this week. . . . The whole imbroglio could have been avoided if X's solicitors had known that permission from the Bank of England was required to buy a foreign property even if the money is paid over here. I hope by now that everybody has calmed down. One grain of common sense would have prevented all this excitement; there is no finer sedative than common sense. . . .

It is out of the question for me to maintain this place. It means that I have to earn £5,000 a year to do it, and for anyone in his seventieth year with only one eye available for his work to suppose he can count on doing that for another ten years would be madness.

I realized by now that Majorca was a disappointment but hoped that Faith would go on with her experiment for another three months and I was relieved to get a much more optimistic letter.

I wrote on March 20th:

I'm glad things are getting more comfortable. I suggest you give it a try for a few months. Meanwhile, I'll have Three Roses done up in case you decide to abandon the Mediterranean. Christopher will bring out two Lilo's. We ought to have thought of them before. . . . I go to Salisbury tomorrow for that dinner.

That dinner in Salisbury was with the Chamber of Commerce, and I stayed with my old friend Reginald Kennedy-Cox in his medieval house in the Close. We had a great talk about old times after the dinner; it was the golden jubilee of a friendship. I went on from Salisbury to Bristol where I was to take part in a television *Any Questions*. My nephew Nicholas Crocker was in charge of the lights and Freddy Grisewood of the questions. I was asked whether public schools should be abolished.

"Well," I said, "before we discuss that question I should like to know what are the public schools. In the 'fifties or 'sixties of the last century Queen Victoria gave her assent to the introduction of the Public School Latin Primer. It remained in use, dark blue binding with red edges to the contents, until Kennedy's Revised Latin Primer appeared in 1892. But what were the public schools at which the Primer was to be then used. It was in the words of Her Majesty for 'Our Colleges of Eton and Winchester, and our Schools of Harrow, Rugby, Westminster, Charterhouse, Shrewsbury, St Paul's and Merchant Taylor's'."

From all over the country indignant Marlburians, Malvernians, Wellingtonians, Cliftonians and many more old boys from other schools were writing to the B.B.C. or to myself, demanding to know how they or I dared to claim that there were only nine genuine public schools. Presumably once upon a time a public school was defined; I wonder what the definition was that distinguished it from a grammar school. I recall talking with Nye Bevan about what looked like a coming attack on the public schools by the Labour party. I argued that the right reform for the public schools was to insist that all the scholarships founded and endowed originally for the benefit of the poor should be restricted to the children of parents with small means.

"The King's Scholars of Eton, the Queen's Scholars of Westminster, the 153 Scholars of my own school to commemorate the miraculous draft of fishes . . . as things are now one rich man in the stockbroker's belt brags to another rich man that his boy has just won a scholarship at Eton."

I view with pessimism the effect of the new comprehensive schools on the future of our country. Egalitarianism is a laudable aim, and if it be achieved intelligently the world will be the better for it, but the most fanatical egalitarian will never be able to apply his creed to brains, and the brainless tendency today to retard the mental growth of a child to prevent its having an unfair advantage over other children is not merely stupid, it is wicked; the country will ultimately pay the penalty for such wicked stupidity.

I was working hard to finish the book about Buckingham Palace but writing to Faith a little despondently about my eyes. I had decided that I could no longer do the 'one-eyed reading' necessary to pull my weight in the Book Society and regretfully I had to ask for six months off. The weather did not encourage optimism.

March 30

The coldest March day for eighty years, a ferocious north-easter, daffodils destroyed, probably all pear and plum blossom ruined. Quite infernal. And this afternoon it looks like more snow. All roads to the north are blocked. . . .

I'm getting up a lunch to celebrate Martin Secker's 70th birthday next month. Ivor Brown is arranging for a private room at the Garrick. Others will be Frank Swinnerton, Arthur Ransome, Orlo Williams, John Betjeman, Michael Sadleir, Oliver Onions, Ian Parsons, Rupert Hart-Davis and perhaps Jack

Squire. If Christopher is back and Francis Brett Young is in England they could come of course. . . .

That lunch was a complete success. I was particularly glad that Oliver Onions was able to come. He was on the edge of eighty and still writing as well as ever. I have never been able to understand why English critics have failed to grasp his importance to the English novel and short story in the earlier part of the twentieth century. He wrote to me from Aberdover after that lunch:

"This is partly in acknowledgement of our happy little reunion and partly to remind myself that I have not yet paid my whack. I don't think anything so sordid was in anybody's mind when we broke up. . . . We are really indebted to Ivor Brown, but I don't know how much.

"What a happy spontaneous little affair it was. It is a long time since I so enjoyed myself, and Secker has changed very little in all these years. I should have known you too immediately, with or without a beard. . . ."

A warming letter reached me at the end of that icy March; it was from Elizabeth Schnach who had just finished her translation into German of *Whisky Galore;* she wrote:

"It gave me immense pleasure. I suppose people must have found me a bit queer when they heard me laughing quite by myself. . . .

"I thought I should tell you where I translated this novel of yours, where every page is full of whisky! in a kind of Hotel-Kurhaus where Alcohol is strictly forbidden! Not because I am apt to drink too much . . . but this is such a wonderful situation, with a grand view of the woods and meadows and the lake and the Alps. But when I translated Whisky Galore I really felt it was a dry place to live in. (There are some places like that in Switzerland, many Swiss women are against alcohol. I am not. I am German.) It is not even allowed to have alcohol in the rooms, not even with a doctor's recipe! So, after having finished the translation, I went to friends of mine who have a nice bar and whisky, and they did their best to make me forget the hard time. . . .

"With my best regards and many thanks for many smiles and laughter."

Eric Linklater was staying with me at Denchworth for a night and on April 2nd he wrote me from Pitcalzean House a tonic letter, typical of our friendship.

"I can think of no one else who, having so lately lost the sight of an eye, could pass a longish day (and part of the night) without alluding to his loss with some trace of self-pity. . . . I still marvel at your self-control, and even more than that I'm delighted to recall the completely undaunted way in which you were planning to do this, that, and the other for years to come.

"Truly it's the spirit that counts—but it isn't often one sees the spirit burning high in a gale of wind.

"You were speaking, that night, of your early successes, and the jealousies that here and there, they roused . . . you admitted that in your young triumphs there was a little flamboyance—but now you've shown what a stout heart it was that lighted the flamboyance. It was true light and no will o' the wisp.

"Thank you for the example. And may the sun itself shine to illumine all you want to see with the other.

"My love to Chrissie, and many, many thanks to her."

What did worry me about those confounded eyes of mine was having to hold up the second volume of *Eastern Epic*. In spite of being assured by oculists that the likelihood of a retinal haemorrhage failing my right eye was remote, it was impossible not to face up to that possibility, however remote.

I had told the Book Society that I should have to give up extensive reading for six months but that at the end of the six months if my eyes improved I would serve again on the committee. I had refused that very tempting offer from Tate and Lyle. Now came another tempting inquiry, though not from a financial point of view. This was from a friend of King Peter of Serbia in London to ask if I would collaborate with the king in writing his memoirs. Much as I should have enjoyed tackling such a task it was of course impossible.

On April 8th I wrote:

We drove to Winchester for the Foyle lunch between 6-ft drifts of snow. The weather has been indescribably vile. The worst Spring I remember.

It is a disagreeable coincidence that the April of 1969 while I was writing about its predecessor should have been equally unpleasant.

I had a bad fortnight of pain after getting back from Winchester. My income tax appeal was heard and dismissed by Mr Justice Danckwerts in spite of what read like a spirited plea by my counsel, a young barrister called Michael Hughes. Press comment was sympathetic to me and I was urged to appeal. John Moore, Eric Linklater and Alan Herbert all pressed the Society of Authors to finance an appeal by me. I had never expected to get a favourable decision against the Inland Revenue. The fact that they had been represented by Manningham-Buller[1] the Solicitor General seemed to indicate a determination to knock out my claim that what they called income was in fact capital. Manningham-Buller was a Magdalen man of later vintage; I had met him at that dinner in Salisbury and was not deeply impressed by what I thought was a rather mouldy conservatism.

[1] Lord Dilhorne.

When I was in London at the beginning of May doing and preparing various broadcasts I found myself at some public dinner next to Mr Justice Sellers[1] who asked me if I was going to appeal against the Danckwerts decision. I told him I was considering doing so. Thereupon he advised me to take the appeal in person. He said I should infallibly lose if represented by counsel but that there was a faint chance of my getting a favourable decision in equity. He went on to say he did not believe I should get such a decision but perhaps it was just worth trying. The advice of Mr Justice Sellers that evening decided me to go ahead with an Appeal.

A week later back at Denchworth I had the greatest surprise of my life.

When Chrissie brought in my mail, mostly kind letters about various broadcasts of mine, she held one envelope with a puzzled expression.

"It's from Winston Churchill," she said. "He says you're to be made a Knight in the next honours list."

"Nonsense," I exclaimed. "Somebody's trying to be funny."

However, when I read the letter I realized that in fact the Prime Minister had advised the young Queen to make me a Knight, which I was to accept or refuse as soon as possible.

Two years earlier Bob Boothby had said to me one day that it was time I had a knighthood. I had said there was as much chance of my being offered a 'K' as Nye Bevan. The most he could hope was that if I lived to ninety I might be given a C.H."

"That's no good for a popular novelist. The public don't know what a C.H. is."

"But, my dear Bob, even if Attlee did consider a 'K' for me, Whitehall would protest. I've done everything possible to make a K for me ridiculous—official secrets, Windsor Tapestry, Red Tapeworms, Water on the Brain. . . . However, don't worry I shall never suffer from Knight starvation."

And now the incredible had happened; what gave me most pleasure was the thought that I should be one of the knights in the first investiture of our young Queen.

I wrote to Faith on Sunday May 11th:

I'm prostrated by a foul cold, having taken it in my much fatigued condition. I hope to keep it off my chest by staying in bed, but on Wednesday I have to broadcast in Women's Hour and on Thursday record a broadcast about Cunninghame Graham (Centenary) for the Third Programme. I still have one chapter of 'The Queen's House' to finish—gramophone editorial—an introduction to a book about the Stone of Destiny business and one or two other chores. I go to Scotland on May 19. I have to visit Fraserburgh Gramophone Society make

---

[1] Lord Justice Sellers.

S

one or two speeches about C. G. and attend a Directors' Meeting of Albyn Films. . . .

I can't write an intelligent or even intelligible letter. I've just had a letter to say the Prime Minister wants to advise Her Majesty to confer a knighthood on me in the Birthday Honours List if agreeable to me. So I said 'yes' because it will be the first list of the young Queen and I think it's a bit of a triumph to be granted a commission by Queen Victoria and knighted by her great-great-granddaughter. Of course, it's a secret till the announcement early next month. . . .

I'll do my best to fix you up near London if you decide to give up the Majorca experiment next autumn. I shall know more about your ideas when I see Christopher. Head going round and round. I can't write any more.

Robert Bontine Cunninghame Graham died in the Argentine in 1936 when he was attending the birth of a new town to be called Don Roberto. His body was brought back across the two Atlantics to lie beside his wife in the grave that thirty years before he had dug for her on Inchnahome, the isle in the Lake of Mentieth. There on May 24th I was privileged to attend the centenary commemoration of a man whose friendship had been very dear to me. The commemoration was organized by the Young Scots National League. It was a moving occasion with prayers, psalms, pipes, songs and speeches. In my speech I quoted from the speech Don Roberto had made at Stirling on Bannockburn Day, 1938, when he unfurled for the first time the flag of the Scottish National Party.

"I lay upon you as a sacred duty that you agitate until our old Parliament is restored and once again Scotland takes her place as an Independent nationality in the family of nations. . . . We must have Scottish sentiment, we must have that which elevates mankind. I call upon you all here under this flag never to cease agitating until we get that autonomy for Scotland which alone can revive our ancient spirit and make real Scotsmen of us."

Forty years on Don Roberto would have had to say "that autonomy which can revive our local industries under the golden calf rampant".

I was remembering that Bannockburn Day of twenty-two years earlier. Don Roberto and I were driving together in an ancient limousine at the tail of the procession through Stirling. He turned to me and said "You know, we both ought to have ridden to the field instead of crawling along in this abominable motor-car. I suppose it would be damned hot walking up this hill."

"It would, indeed," I said fervently. "And don't forget we have to do a lot of spouting."

"Yes, I suppose we'd better stay where we are, but, *caro amigo*, we do look uncommonly like the tail end of a circus procession."

In a broadcast I said:

"Cunninghame Graham's knowledge of Spanish gave his prose, as it gave W. H. Hudson's prose, that Latin lucidity. I commend to young writers now under the influence of contemporary deliquescent North American prose an intensive study of W. H. Hudson and Cunninghame Graham. . . .

"We may call Don Roberto a happier knight-errant than Don Quixote, for although he did not live to see his dreams for Scotland near to fulfilment he was spared much disillusionment. . . . Yes, he rides now his white steed with the Mexican saddle in Elysium's Rotten Row, a happy warrior."

The other sharp memory I keep of those May days in Scotland was when driving to Sutherland with James Robertson Justice of seeing in Wester Ross a golden eagle being attacked by a peregrine falcon—like a Spitfire attacking a heavy bomber. After a while the eagle gave up and flew away from the peregrine's territory. James Justice had seen once before an eagle get the worst of it. After a crowded week in the North I was writing from Denchworth on June 5th:

The telephone started at 7.15 with a ring from Douglas Gracey who had heard the news at 7 o'clock and wanted to be the first to congratulate Sir Compton and Lady Mackenzie. Since then the telephone has hardly stopped all day. Everybody seems very pleased. . . . I'll write again as soon as possible, but I have to do a personal memory of Max Beerbohm for his 88th birthday and a review of the Gramophone encyclopaedia (for broadcasting) and a synopsis for a thirteen-week strip of Rufus and Flook in the Highlands.

I had been asked when I was in Edinburgh if I would consider taking on the Flook strip cartoon for the Scottish *Daily Mail*. The temptation to discover whether I could do a strip cartoon was too strong. I fell. So when I got back to Denchworth Wally Fawkes, the only begetter of Flook, came to see me. He was an attractive, original and extremely intelligent young Canadian who played the clarinet in Humphrey Lyttleton's Jazz band. Trog, as he called himself, and I clicked. The terms offered at Carmelite House were generous and the first 13-week strip was commissioned.

I discovered that the bubbles for a comic strip must be with the artist always three weeks ahead of publication. The amount one has to write for the bubbles is trifling but it is a severe test for the invention. I recall a party for Flook to meet possible relatives of his at Chessington Zoo where Sir Gerald Kelly made an amusing speech and I met for the first time my young cousin Virginia McKenna. There was another Flook reception where one of Her Majesty's judges admitted to following Flook's adventures every morning before he went to take his seat on the Bench.

As far as I remember I did three or four strips and then I decided

it was time to stop, which I think was a relief both for Trog and the
Daily Mail who were anxious to be more 'with it' than I was prepared
to be. Trog himself has continued to be successfully with it almost
twenty years later. I have not met him for many years, and I was
distressed to see in *The Observer* not so long ago a cheap sneer at the Duke
of Windsor in one of Trog's cartoons. The Flook I used to know would
never have let him draw that cartoon once upon a time.

Two days after the announcement of the Birthday Honours I
received a communication from the Home Office which I give here in
full to illustrate Royal procedure in 1952.

"Sir,
    With reference to the arrangements for conferring upon you the
dignity of knighthood, I am desired by the Home Secretary to say
that he has the honour to convey to you The Queen's Commands to
attend at Buckingham Palace on Tuesday, 8th July, 1952, at 10.15 a.m
to receive the accolade.
    "Dress—Service Dress, Morning Dress or dark Lounge Suit.
    "I shall be glad if you will inform me at your very earliest convenience
whether you are able to attend and by which of your first names you
desire in future to be known.
    "I am, Sir,
        Your Obedient Servant
        Edward Montague Compton Mackenzie, Esq.,"

For the next three weeks I was answering personally well over 500
letters and 120 telegrams I had received from all over the world. I was
much moved by the number of congratulations that came from unknown
friends. Outside Great Britain the largest number of these came from
Australia. One letter from Barra was sent to Wilfred Taylor of *The
Scotsman's Log* which he has been writing daily for so many years, one
of the outstanding journalistic achievements of our time:

"I would like through the medium of your newspaper to express
openly the gratitude of the people of the Island of Barra for the many
services rendered to the Island by Compton Mackenzie, and to say
with what affection we regard Compton the Man.

"He came amongst us in 1932, no doubt with misgivings, for it is
difficult for an outsider into a close-knit community such as Barra. . .
so keen was his appreciation of our island wit and culture, that soon
he became the leading figure on the island

"During his sojourn with us he took upon himself the role of
champion and protector and consistently employed the power of his
pen for the benefit of the Highlands and Islands. Even now, when
ill-health has necessitated his leaving Barra, he springs to our defence

wherever he may be. On no occasion was this more conspicuous than at a Highland concert in St Andrews Hall, Glasgow, two years ago, when he condemned the writings of a certain author who ruthlessly and unjustifiably attacked the isles."

I hesitate to quote the letter but I do so because it shows the amount I owed to the people of Barra, far far more than they owed to me. I am not pretending to modesty; I am stating a simple fact. Readers of previous Octaves will know that I passed through difficult times on Barra, and that I was able to surmount those difficulties was due to the moral and mental support of the people of Barra. John Campbell and I fought a hard battle for the fishing which we lost and a hard battle for the road which we won.

Among the new reign's first knights were Arnold Lunn, Lewis Namier and Carol Reid; I do not recall four figures connected with the Arts in a list of K's since. I had been faintly surprised when I received that letter from the Home Office; I had never supposed that Court affairs had anything to do with the Home Office. I was even more surprised to see the Home Secretary himself checking the various knights-to-be as they lined up in alphabetical order to march round three sides of the great central hall in the Palace, where the orchestra was playing and where on either side were seated the relatives or friends of the various people to be given honours of one degree or another.

As I was passing him Maxwell-Fyffe[1] jumped up and said;

"I must shake hands with you and say how much I've enjoyed all your books about the Highlands. This is most irregular behaviour for a Home Secretary on duty but I simply had to shake your hand."

Some years later Lord Kilmuir succeeded me as the annually elected Chief of the venerable Gaelic Society of Inverness and at the dinner for his inauguration I was able to remind him of that spontaneous gesture and thank him for it.

As we moved along for three-quarters of an hour round the three sides of the hall I was severely affected by the halitosis of a knight-to-be in the line. It was a hot summer's day and I began to wonder if I should make the round without fainting which for years I have been apt to do when air was lacking, and in this case unpleasantly perfumed air. Mercifully as we turned round for the third and final lap of the slow procession the window at the end blew in some fresh air and I felt protected against that disagreeable breath. On the right wall of the last corridor was a large picture of an almost nude Artemis; I had just asked myself what Queen Victoria would have said to such a picture hanging in Buckingham Palace when I read the inscription underneath;

[1] The late Earl of Kilmuir.

"it was one of the young Queen Victoria's wedding presents to Prince Albert."

I was thankful that my leg behaved itself when I knelt for the accolade. I felt that any awkwardness at this moment by the recipients of honours would almost have amounted to high treason. Prince Philip being laid up with jaundice was not there to support that young Queen on what must have been for her a trying experience; I marvelled at the way she handled what to my surprise was a sizeable sword. Somehow I had supposed it would be a kind of miniature weapon to make the business less of a fatigue for the Sovereign. She was gracious enough to say she hoped I would write many more books. I gulped out my thanks and moved on, hoping that my performance had not seemed clumsy.

I wrote to Faith when I got back to the Saville:

A scrawl to thank you for the wire which arrived at exactly the right moment, 20 minutes before I set out to B.P. Rather a tiring business and a K-designate near me had mephitic breath which I had to endure for about ¾ hour.

Bob Boothby is giving a party this afternoon for Lewis Namier and myself in Eaton Square, after which he and I are dining together at the Caprice—nobody else.

The Queen spoke to about one in ten. . . . She looked pale and perhaps she was missing Philip's support for what must have been an ordeal. I was lost in admiration of the way she was going through with it.

Four days later I was writing from Denchworth:

The Appeal to the Lord Justices has been suddenly sprung on us. We expected it in November at earliest but it is to be tomorrow at 10. I am driving up this afternoon and have another experience before me, arguing my own case before Their Lordships. Rather a strain. I don't expect to win but it will do good. I am contemplating resignation from the Society of Authors and forming an Author's Alliance with more fight in them.

When I was preparing my speech for the Appeal a friend of Watson, a solicitor's clerk, checked it for the right legal phraseology. I was deeply indebted to Sydney Newland for his help.

In the Court in which my Appeal was to be heard on that Monday morning, July 14th, I found Lord Justice Somervell was presiding; on his right was Lord Justice Denning, on his left Lord Justice Romer. The Solicitor-General (Sir Reginald Manningham-Buller, Q.C., M.P.) appeared for the Crown prompted and supported by Sir Reginald Hills (instructed by the Solicitor of Inland Revenue). Somervell, Denning, Manningham-Buller and myself were all old Magdalen men.

I should have felt much less nervous if I had been storming the Bastille on another fourteenth of July than I felt as I rose to make my speech the script of which was fluttering in my shaky wrist. This was a novel experience for me. I had never before felt nervous when making a speech. However, after about five minutes, my wrist was steady, but simultaneously my only eye began to misbehave and it seemed a long time before I got it back into focus.

"I trust your Lordships will not think that I am in any way disappointed with the services of learned counsel on my behalf in the Court below, on the contrary, but there are other reasons for my appearing with some trepidation on my own behalf."

Thus I began, but when I had finished reading my preliminary speech and was arguing impromptu trepidation had completely vanished. I think the exact moment of speaking off the cuff was when, as I was saying "In 1924 I was tenant of the Treasury in possession of the Island of Jethou in the Bailliwick of Guernsey", the Solicitor-General bounced up to splutter:

"I do not know to what this is leading, but there is nothing relating to this tenancy in the case. It may be a very interesting matter of history and very entertaining to hear, but it can hardly be advanced, in my submission, in support of the case."

"I think, Mr Solicitor, you will find it extremely to the point in one moment," I said and Lord Justice Somervell supported me.

"At the time there was an agitation in the popular press about authors living on the Riviera and not paying tax. There was a starry-eyed disregard of fact. It was estimated that a million pounds were lost annually to the Treasury. Mr Churchill announced in his 1925 Budget that income tax at the current rate would be deducted at source. . . . I was told by the Treasury that an outright sale of a book was capital but not subject to income tax. . . . When in 1938 I became resident in Scotland the Inspector of Taxes in Inverness told me such a sale was not a capital transaction in Great Britain. Although this seemed contrary to the old axiom of Euclid which declared that things equal to the same thing were equal to one another, so much of Euclid had been disposed of by the Theory of Relativity by then that I accepted the ruling. . . .

"The number of authors likely to sell at the age of sixty any books written in their twenties is infinitesimal; and yet stress was laid on the fact that those twenty books of mine, some of them written over thirty years earlier, were a part of the normal reward I might annually expect as an author carrying on my profession."

The argument went on with occasional interventions by one or other Lord Justice, always in the kindliest way. At one point I paid a tribute to Income Tax Inspectors which nearly twenty years later I can stress.

"I have always found the Inspectors helpful, as indeed the Inspector here has been in this particular case. Nobody could have been more considerate or patient. I want to make that perfectly clear. The precedents Mr Justice Danckwerts had found for his judgment included among others a dispute over the profit on the sale of a public house in 1876, and development of the Vallombrosa rubber company in Malaya.

"Surely", I argued, "the author is being treated as if he was a kind of crop, spring wheat, winter wheat, or potatoes. The analogy is imperfect, the parallel is incomplete. You may reasonably expect, unless winter or a summer drought comes, to go on producing, but you have no reasonable expectation as an author what you will produce next year. . . . Mr Justice Lawrence once said, 'An author's capital is his brain'—he cannot get any allowance for depreciation, and he certainly cannot buy a new brain as he can buy a new typewriter. . . . It is a pity that all these analogies should be so remote from the position of an author today. . . . To me it seems irrelevant that the books I wrote between 1907 and 1931 should be regarded as immature rubber trees."

After further arguments from me for not assessing the tax on an author's earnings in the year of a book's publication but of spreading such an assessment over the time taken in preparing and writing the book I wound up:

"The future of authors in this world of mechanization is threatening. We are reducing them to rubber trees and public houses. I am thinking about the authors of the future. I do ask your Lordships to reconsider this matter most carefully. I cannot quote precedents; I have not the legal knowledge; but I trust you will find in my favour. . . . I could wish my words were not merely more autumnal leaves to strew the brooks of the Vallombrosa rubber company."

Their Lordships now retired to confer. When they returned the Solicitor-General to his obvious astonishment was asked by Lord Justice Somervell whether an author normally living on royalties ought not to have different treatment for an abnormal sale of copyrights. Mr Solicitor seemed fussed by feeling that their Lordships were not being as sympathetic as they should be with the Inland Revenue, and in the course of a long speech kept turning to Sir Reginald Hills for help in the references to be quoted. All three of the Lord Justices kept interrupting him with questions. One of these he was unable to answer and Sir Reginald Hills came to his rescue.

"At the risk of Sir Compton Mackenzie reminding your Lordships that he is not a colliery company. . . . I must refer to the case of the Glamorgan Coal Company Limited versus the Commissioners of Inland Revenue," said Sir Reginald Hills.

By this time I was tired of what I thought were the irrelevant arguments of Mr Solicitor and Sir Reginald Hills. I was also irritated by what I considered Mr Solicitor's fatuous rhetoric in asking what guarantee there was that I would not sell all my existing copyrights again next year.

"Do you wish to add anything?" Lord Somervell asked.

I said that I did not want to go on arguing with Mr Solicitor about what seemed to be irrelevant words. He was evidently content with the planting of rubber trees as an argument over author's royalties, but I ventured to remind him that rubber trees are not planted on Parnassus.

"I explained clearly why I sold those twenty copyrights. The suggestion that I am always doing it and might do it again I find rather offensive."

When their Lordships returned Lord Justice Somervell decided that the Appeal must fail. They made it obvious that they would have liked it to succeed, but they were up against the drafting of the Finance Act of 1944 when Sir John Anderson as he then was laid down that any sale of copyright was taxable.

Lord Justice Somervell began by saying that the clarity with which I had presented my case had been of great help, and Lord Justice Romer put in "And I should like to add eloquence to that." At the end of the judgment the Solicitor-General rose and barked:

"The Appeal will be dismissed with costs?"

Lord Justice Somervell replied with a sigh:

"I suppose so, yes."

Gilbert Harding had wandered off after my speech was finished to another Court of Appeal. He came back now and said:

"I've just been listening to the most horrifying case I ever heard or read of."

"A murder case?"

"Much more horrible than any murder case. Some solicitor was appealing against a sentence of eight years for compelling his unhappy wife to copulate with his dog. The details were ghastly, and thank God the Lord Justices in dismissing his appeal added two years to his sentence."

The comments of the Press on my Appeal were unanimously sympathetic. I have already recorded my gratitude for the goodwill of the Press through over sixty years, but I record it once more.

Three letters all written on July 18th, 1952, made me feel that the strain of that appeal had been worthwhile.

The first was from H. R. Watson who was in charge of my financial affairs:

"You conducted the Appeal in a first-class manner, and to have got the Solicitor-General on his feet to reply was a feat in the circumstances of this case—which no counsel could have achieved."

The second letter was from Harold Raymond:

"We all feel miserable, and more than a trifle bitter, over the results of your case. Never mind. It was a sporting and gallant effort on your part, and it would take more than a loss like that to get you down.

"When Norah and Ian and I were discussing we came to a unanimous decision that we should like to contribute our mite to what I am sure was a costly business. Our living as publishers is dependent on authors having a will to work. If, through unfair or excessive taxation, they are disincentivated into silence, it would be a sad day for the reading public and goodbye to Chatto and Windus. (I make you a present of that word 'disincentivate'; indeed, I'd be glad to get rid of it.) So here is a something towards a fight which we know you took up for authors as a whole and not merely on your own behalf. And even if it had been solely a personal tussle of your own, there is no author on our list whom we would more gladly help. You have broken all records of warm and generous treatment from author to publisher. You spoil us outrageously, but how pleasant it is to be spoiled!"

Norah Smallwood and Ian Parsons had both been in Court during the Appeal, and it can easily be realized how much I was moved by those generous words.

The third letter was from Osbert Sitwell,[1] the Chairman of the Society's Committee of Management:

"My dear Monty,

At their meeting on Wednesday the members of the Society's Committee of Management voiced their very real sympathy with you over the outcome of your battle with the Revenue authorities.

"The fact that the law being what it is, it was inevitable that judgment should go against you, only served to heighten everyone's regard for the gallant perseverance with which you pursued the enemy.

"One very valuable effect of your action and of the publicity it has received is to win over public opinion to a sense of the need for the reforms which the Society has been urging on the Treasury by every direct and indirect means in its power.

"With best wishes
Yours ever
Osbert Sitwell"

I had been angry at what I considered the pusillanimity the Society in doing nothing to support me, and so Osbert Sitwell's letter was most welcome. A. A. Milne had written a letter to the *Daily Telegraph* in which he had wondered what authors who sold twenty copyrights for £10,000 had to grumble about; he was as happy as Christopher Robin himself.

---

[1] The late Sir Osbert Sitwell, Bt., C.H.

I wrote to Osbert Sitwell:

"I was glad to get your letter. I shall be frank and say that I think the Society has taken a defeatist line for some years now. No protest, for instance, was made in 1925 when Churchill as Chancellor of the Exchequer announced that in future all authors living abroad would have full income tax deducted from their royalties at source, and that publishers would be responsible to the Revenue for doing this. This was a monstrous piece of penalization done to win a little cheap popularity, and from that time onwards a pusillanimous attitude was taken steadily by the Society. My case has shown the way to influence public opinion, but I received no kind of moral support from the Society in the course of arguing it. I could not even manage to persuade the Secretary to find time to discuss the matter with me. When Alan Herbert was fighting in the columns of *The Times* Alan Milne was allowed to behave like what genuine Unions call a scab without any protest.

"That I have not resigned from the Society is due to John Moore's persuasion, for he assures me that he believes that a fighting policy is to be adopted, and your very welcome letter today gives me some hope that such is to be the case. If in the end I do feel driven into resigning it will mean that I shall try to form another Society or Union or Alliance of authors prepared to fight for their rights. Bureaucracy not publishers or agents is the threat nowadays, and if Alan Milne wants to wrap himself and his pen in cotton wool I don't see why the rest of us should. You have always been such a doughty fighter yourself that I feel you'll understand my indignation at the moment."

Hardly a week after I wrote those words Osbert Sitwell died. I read again that private and confidential letter written in his own hand already shaken by that Parkinson's disease which he suffered with such bravery. That letter which cost him such a physical effort to write displays Osbert's courage, wisdom and generosity:

Personal and Confidential.

July 22.1952.

My dear Monty,

    Thank you so much for your letter. I hope, in the meantime, that you will hear from John Moore, asking you to dine either with him or me, early in September to discuss the whole matter.

    I was beside myself when A. A. Milne wrote what I consider his disgraceful letter. I wanted to write a scorching answer, but as we were then in touch with the Chancellor, I did not want to set off a whole trail of fireworks on one side, and Christopher Robin damp squibs on the other.

    The difficulty so far with the Society hasn't been lack of fight, but the divergence of views held by leading authors; for it is vital that the Society should have a united backing for any case it presents, as we had in the long campaign against the B.B.C., in which we won a rewarding victory. I think that we are now on the verge of a fresh advance in the direction of victory with the tax problem. I feel very strongly on the matter, as I not only object to the vicious system that exists on theory, but in practice am being ruined by it: so the spur is there.

I greatly value the tone of your letter.

> *With warmest regards*
> *Yours ever*
> *Osbert Sitwell*

P.S. I must apologise for my appalling handwriting but it is in part the result of illness.

I am glad to remember that I was always an admirer of the Sitwells. I had hoped that Edith would live to be the first woman Poet Laureate. I salute the memory of two of the richest personalities I have been privileged to know.

John Moore wrote:

"I talked to Kilham Roberts and it may be in consequence that Osbert wrote to you. . . . In the evening I got hold of Alan Herbert and we drank a lot of wine over it. I find him, if possible, even more belligerent than you, and very anxious to start a break-away union. However, I persuaded him to take no steps until he returns from Venice at the end of August.

"By then I imagine the Society will have hammered out a definite and strong policy regarding taxation in the framing of which I think they should consult yourself and A.P.H., or co-opt you both on to a sub-committee. . . . Incidentally, Alan Herbert has never been invited to serve on either the Society's Council or on its Committee of Management. So he tells me. This seems extraordinary. How about yourself? . . . .

"Are these suggestions agreeable (about a sub-committee)? Frankly I don't want you and Alan to form a break-away Union, as I think this would demonstrate our weakness to the politicians; but I do want to wake up the Society, if necessary into a charge of gunpowder.

"Finally, let me say that, as I think you know, I have throughout been entirely on your side at all the meetings, but unfortunately I have been in a small minority."

When I read again that old letter of John Moore's I am more glad than ever that Alan Herbert is now President of the Society of Authors.

To John Moore Denys Kilham Roberts wrote:

"I think it is important that Monty should be given his head over this business and take the corresponding responsibility for putting forward practical proposals which have at least some chance of finding favour with the Chancellor."

If any reader is sufficiently interested in that sub-committee's work he can read of it in Appendix E.

In the previous autumn I had been unable to attend Tony Pollard's wedding to a beautiful girl. Hardly eight months later I was attending the funeral of that beautiful girl at the Golders Green Crematorium. Young Tony's courage was something I shall always be grateful to have witnessed. When I am tempted to deplore the self-pity in which so many young men indulge themselves today and which is so foolishly indulged by plays on television I remember that funeral and am reassured. Tony Pollard was rewarded for that courage by marrying Margaret the closest friend of his lost Ann and this has been a marriage of perfect happiness, a happiness that was truly deserved.

At the end of that July I was asked to take part in a brains' trust at Canterbury where the quatercentenary of The King's School was being celebrated. Gilbert Harding was also taking part but not as quiz master. I sounded Canon Shirley, the headmaster, to find out if he would give me back the manuscript of the first volume of *Sinister Street* which had been presented to his old school (for a term and a half) by Hugh Walpole, who had bought it when I had to sell manuscripts to pay some of the costs of my trial at the Old Bailey which I described in Octave Seven. I offered to give four manuscripts in exchange but Canon Shirley was not tempted.

The hall in which the Brains' Trust was held was packed. Some tactless question concerned Anglican Orders; as a Papist I naturally kept silent and so did another Papist. Not so Gilbert Harding, who denounced Anglican Orders. From the back of the hall an elderly Canon of Canterbury rose to argue with Gilbert Harding whereupon the blue pulse beside his temple started to throb and he began to abuse the poor old Canon until I managed to drag him down into his chair.

By the time I set out in August for Edinburgh I was tired by broadcasting, trying to go on with *Eastern Epic*, writing articles for *Illustrated* and with saying 'yes' too often. I had a go of pain just before we started but it succumbed to aspirin, and off we set with Kenny MacCormick driving.

I quote from a letter of Chrissie to Faith:
"Denchworth Manor, August 23.

"Here we are back after a not very successful Scottish trip ... our first mishap was with the windscreen when a stone hit it and the whole crystallized into one cloudy mess in front of our eyes. Kenny was doing 70 miles per hour at the time and passing another car on a long stretch of straight Roman road, but with his superb quickness in such emergencies he drove into the side of the road quite safely. After that he had to drive for fifteen miles with his head stuck out of the side until

we came to an AA box where he and the attendant took the whole
windscreen out because it was dangerous and small bits could get into
our eyes. We drove for fifty miles without any windscreen at all until
we reached Wetherby where we put up at an uncomfortable little inn.

"C.M. was feeling better by now, but at 2.30 a.m. he woke with
violent pain and we couldn't get a doctor till morning. He could do
nothing to stop the pain and we drove on to Edinburgh with C.M. in
agony all the way. Kenny had managed to get the windscreen patched
up in the Wetherby garage and it did keep the rain out.

"We stayed at the Scotia Hotel in Great King Street where C.M.
went to bed at once. Luckily Moray McLaren was able to deputize
for him at some conference and even more luckily was able to get hold
of a really first-class doctor who immediately did all he could to stop
the pain with morphine without argument or supposing that C.M.
was an addict!"

That 'really first class doctor' was Gilbert MacNaughtan who has
looked after my health ever since he was called in on that August day
in 1952. To him and his dear wife I have dedicated this Octave.

"The Scotia was packed with Festival people and we could only
be given two tiny bedrooms right at the top of the house. There were
no telephones in these rooms, and I spent the whole time running up
and down to answer the damned thing, for as you can imagine everyone
—press and private—kept ringing up to ask how he was or whether he
could talk here or dine there. By the end of the week I was like a piece
of chewed string. . . . We spent the weekend at North Berwick with the
Thomsons. . . . I was allowed to spend nearly a day in bed without
feeling I was a nuisance as the girls looked after me beautifully. By
this time C.M. was really better, and I enclose for your amusement the
comments which were provoked by his talk to the Film Guild. . . .

"I looked at lots of flats most of them pretty frightful. . . ."

In the course of my talk to the Film Guild I said how lucky we had
been with *Whisky Galore* to have 'extras' who were natural actors. Such
extras could never have been found in the south of England. I went on
to say that when one came to think of it the English never had produced
a great actor. All the great 'English' actors had had Highland, Irish,
Welsh, Cornish, Jewish or foreign blood.

The *News Chronicle* reporter brought this assertion of mine back to
the Editorial office, where orders were given to ring up well-known
actors and actresses to comment on my observation. I shall charitably
refrain from putting what they said over the telephone into a book,
and shall content myself with the reply I sent to the *News Chronicle*
on August 23rd:

"My contention that all the greatest 'English' actors have had in
their veins Highland, Jewish, Irish, Welsh, Cornish or foreign blood

has been reinforced by the instances brought forward to confound me.

"Mr Alec Clunes (himself presumably like myself, of ultimate Easter Ross origin) asks what about Sir Laurence Olivier and Mr John Gielgud. I presume that Olivier is Norman-French by way of the Channel Islands. Gielgud is certainly Baltic, and to that may be added the Welsh and Scottish of his maternal ancestry.

"Dame Sybil Thorndyke thinks 'it is all tactless and silly' and with a glow of generosity produces Dame Edith Evans to refute me. I shall remind Dame Sybil that I was talking about actors not actresses and that whatever Dame Edith's immediate forbears may have been she must enjoy a Welsh ancestry.

"Mr MacQueen Pope quotes a string of names which he does not believe I had forgotten. I had not. Garrick had a French father and mother (and wife!). Mrs Siddons was half Irish, Kean was almost certainly Irish, Lewis Waller partly Jewish, and Ellen Terry's mother was Scottish. I should hesitate to call Hawtrey, Wyndham, Cyril Maude, and Bancroft great actors in spite of all their immense accomplishment within a narrow range. As for Nell Gwynn she was not even a good actress, and therefore I shall not speculate about her Welsh origin. My sister Fay reveals a depth of un-intelligent comment which fraternally I deplore: I hope she has read the intelligent comments of Sir Godfrey Tearle and Miss Hermione Gingold.

"Mr Michael Redgrave is evidently quite ignorant of what I did in fact say and therefore it is hardly worthwhile arguing with him.

"It is the reporter's job to extract from a speech lasting nearly an hour as many provocative assertions as possible, but it is wiser to know the context of such assertions and the full extent of what was actually argued before rushing to the rescue of one's contemporaries over the telephone.

"I recommend Sir Godfrey Tearle's observations to the rest of his confrères: he had the imagination to grasp what I was getting at without hearing my argument, and therefore did not give the impression of wounded vanity."

Faith was going to spend the autumn at Bagni di Lucca, gathering material for the book she was planning about the English colony there once upon a time with plenty of eccentric figures. It was by now clear that the Spanish experiment had been a failure and it was imperative to find a suitable place of abode for Faith somewhere in the south of England. What seemed the answer to the problem was a suggestion by Molly MacCarthy[1] that Faith should take half of the flat in Garrick's Villa at Twickenham which after Desmond's death had been too much for her. She and Faith had been friends in girlhood; Desmond himself

---

[1] Lady MacCarthy.

with the late Lochiel had been the favourite juniors at Stonehouse, the private school started by Faith's father when he gave up his house at Eton. Over forty years ago my father had played for a time with the idea of buying Garrick's Villa. I interviewed the present proprietor who lived in Devonshire. At first Christopher was taken with the notion of Garrick's Villa which would have given him space for his books but as he was changing his mind daily about the destination of his books when Denchworth was sold I did not count on his cooperation. In the end after interminable correspondence and numerous visits to Garrick's Villa the plan had to be given up because the owner would not agree to the way it was proposed to divide the MacCarthy flat.

I hoped I should be rewarded for going down to Devon to discuss the future of Garrick's Villa with its owner by staying with Magdalen and Jack Eldon[1] at Rackenford Manor, near Tiverton. I was rewarded and spent an all too brief time with them. Magdalen had been captivated by Flook. She had written:

I have been asked to do a strip cartoon for the Weekly Universe. A melancholy paper but still a small beginning. I need your and Trog's expert advice as I don't think I can resist taking it on. Could you help me?

Now when I was still dealing with the Garrick's Villa problem Magdalen wrote:

Trog, Mrs Trog and Baby Flook are coming to stay on Friday for the weekend. . . . This is to beg you from both of us to come too. . . .
Flooks waving from every window. . . .

Alas, I was fetched back for some broadcast in London and missed that weekend.

When Osbert Sitwell returned from Italy that September it was decided to form the committee for which John Moore had argued and of which I was made Chairman. It was also decided that every effort should be made to persuade Rab Butler[2] to ask the heads of the Revenue at Somerset House to receive a deputation from the Society to plead for a spread of income tax for authors. It was considered that it might be tactful to consult Lord Maugham. He answered my request to see him:

I am afraid I shall be wasting your time, as I am no longer an expert on Income Tax law, but I shall be delighted to see you here on the 10th anytime between 10 and 12.

We talked about the memoirs he was engaged in writing and about old days in the Savile at 107 Piccadilly.

"Willie is lunching with me at the club tomorrow," I told him.

[1] The Earl and Countess of Eldon.
[2] Lord Butler of Saffron Walden.

"If Willie had died when he was seventy," said the elder brother, "he'd have been forgotten by now."

I demurred to this.

"Oh, yes, it's only because he's on the edge of eighty that he's still in the public eye."

Next day at lunch I told Willie that I'd been talking to the ex-Lord Chancellor in Cadogan Square yesterday.

"Freddie's a very stupid chap," said Willie. "Last year I gave him some p-port which the P-Portugese drink themselves and do you know what Freddie said when he tasted it. 'This isn't p-p-port at all'. I suppose he knows a good deal about law but he's very ignorant and often very stupid about anything else."

I recall once going into the billiards room at the Savile and finding Lord Maugham sitting by himself looking down at the table where the balls were set out for snooker.

"Why do all the young members rush out of this room as soon as they see me," demanded Lord Maugham irritably.

"Well, if I had not known you since before you were a K.C. I would have been out of this room too by now. You frighten them."

In that September The Dickens Fellowship held a Golden Jubilee banquet at the Dorchester with Gerald Barry, the current President in the Chair. It was typical of Leslie Staples' modesty that he should have put himself at one of the three dozen other tables instead of at the top table. He had done more than anybody in the Fellowship to maintain its vitality, a vitality which consoles me with the thought that there are still plenty of sensible people left, after I have been looking at some hairy fairy talking on T.V. about the difficulty of writing a book or acting a part.

I was writing towards the end of that month about the fearful increase in my correspondence owing to the cold September which had kept people indoors. A good deal of that correspondence was from our *Gramophone* members, some of whom were accusing me of hopeless conservatism because we were not being as enthusiastic about the new long-playing records as they felt we ought to be. The fact was that as once upon a time when electric recording began we had to take a kind of a 'wait and see' attitude for the sake of the dealers still loaded with 78's. However, we were soon able to abandon this 'wait and see' attitude, and the circulation of *The Gramophone* rose steadily every month.

I was going over to Wexford for the Festival at the end of October and remembering that I had not been able to attend Tony Pollard's wedding because I had been going to Wexford I wrote to tell him of my sorrow that now instead of sending my congratulations on his first wedding anniversary I should have to write to sympathize with his tragic loss of a young bride. At the same time I was able to praise

T

his courage and I received from him a very moving letter, a letter which made me grateful for the decision I had made to hand over my shares to him in trust. I knew after reading his letter that the future of *The Gramophone* was set fair and that the part I had played in keeping it going with Cecil Pollard during the last war would not be forgotten. Our circulation had now reached over 36,000 and during the two decades would rise to over 70,000.

The opera that year was Donizetti's *L'Elisir d'Amore*. After 1952 two operas were performed annually until 1968 when three operas would be performed. The Town Council of Wexford had been sufficiently impressed by the first Festival to indulge in the extravagance of lighting up one street with coloured lights. Today the illumination of the whole town and the seaport shows how the Festival's brightness has steadily grown in brightness. The other sensible contribution that the Town Council made to the Festival spirit was to extend the licence for drinking to 3 a.m.

This visit to Wexford was short and sweet because I had to be back in London to take part with Christopher Sykes in preparing an hour-long broadcast about Queen Mary. At this moment there was anxiety about her health and the broadcast had to be made for what might be an obituary. However, that anxiety mercifully passed.

The B.B.C. were also planning a series of broadcasts for early in the new year called 'Throne and People' about the five monarchs who had preceded our young Queen. I had been booked for George V.

Christopher Sykes wrote:

"Here is my draft for the conclusion of the 'Throne and People' preceding yours. Whatever changes I make I promise not to depart from this in mood and subject. I had thought of introducing George V so as to give you a convenient point of departure, but whereas my predecessor is obliged to mention Edward VII quite a lot, I am under no necessity to say anything at all about George V, and it has occurred to me in studying the subject that George was so remarkably dim at that time that the great point—the renascence of George V—is probably best made if I leave everything, including his dimness as Prince of Wales, to you. For the one listener in a million who listened it might make an interesting contrast. What do you think?"

Presently Ted Liveing was letting me know that the Directors of the Chartered Bank of India, Australia and China were considering inviting me to write a history of the Bank to celebrate its centenary. At the end of November Ted and I lunched with the Chairman and the chief General Manager in the Bank parlour at 38 Bishopsgate. Just a month later Chrissie had gone up to Edinburgh to look at one more possible house. By an encouraging coincidence I was offered a fee to write what I proposed to call *Realms of Silver* which exactly covered the price asked for 31 Drummond Place, Edinburgh. I decided that the research would involve less of a strain on my eyes than the mass of faded papers for the second volume of *Eastern Epic* besides providing the money for the Edinburgh house and I accepted the job. The oculists were more optimistic about my eyes than I was and told me that if I rested them from strain I should probably be able to tackle the completion of *Eastern Epic* by the end of the following year.

In that same November Charles Eade of the *Sunday Dispatch* asked me to contribute to a book he was compiling to celebrate Winston Churchill's 80th birthday in the following November. Some of his contemporaries were to write about his various aspects. I was to write of Churchill the novelist after reading *Savrola*, his only novel. I did not find *Savrola* a great novel but I did find a fascinating adumbration of the Churchill to come.

I was fortunate enough to be blessed with a perfect conclusion of what had been such a stressful year. Magdalen Eldon wrote from Rackenford Manor early in November:

When are you coming to stay?. . . . The Indian Generals are panting for your arrival—treating their curries—polishing their buttons. . . . We both long for you to come West.

I wrote back to say how much I was longing to stay again at Rackenford but that there was no chance of my coming west before the beginning of December. Magdalen wrote from Sandringham:

. . . . I suggest the best of all that you come down any time in the Christmas holidays that suits you . . . from the 18th onwards . . . and Indian colonels go so well with snapdragon and nuts and port, and we will have them over in shoals to please you—and the house is really cosy and warm. . . .

So Please darling Monty just save a date and come bouncing west into our little grey home. What a lovely plan. Please, please come.

Finally the only time I was able to propose myself was for Christmas when I suggested going down to the west with Kenny.

That will be perfect, Magdalen wrote. *There is plenty of room for your chauffer and the household are delighted at the thought of a visiting Scotsman.*

You will be able to rest—or decorate the house Christmas tree all Christmas Eve. . . . No one else is coming except Father Angus Macdonell who is 82! and I don't know but who went to Canada for my Father and whom Jack loved as a little boy. He is over for 3 months and Jack has invited him down. He says he's a darling and full of Highland ghost stories.

The Chapel where Father Macdonell was saying midnight Mass was packed with Poles who had arrived from all round. Half way through Mass I disgraced myself by having one of my fainting fits and poor Magdalen had to get me somehow or other to my bedroom where I lay down and passed out for a while. We decided next day when I was completely myself again that the Poles chilled by their long walk had drunk up all the warm air of the chapel.

What an enchanting visit that was and I did meet one of the Indian Generals—Reggie Savory whom we have met earlier in this Octave. All too soon I had to be back at Denchworth to deal with the problem of a meeting with the Chancellor of the Exchequer before we tackled the heads of the Inland Revenue.

Denys Kilham Roberts had written to me from the Society of Authors on November 19th:

"I enclose a copy of a letter which Osbert has had from the Chancellor, and a copy of Osbert's reply.

"As Osbert is just off to America he left it to me to pass over to you with his blessings and good wishes the finalizing of arrangements for the meeting with Butler. He thinks that, in the light of what Butler says, it would be unprofitable to press him for a luncheon date this side of Christmas, but he feels that it might, perhaps, be worth while to proffer dinner as a possible alternative on the off chance of Butler's having a free evening during the next week or two. Obviously it would be far more satisfactory from our point of view if the meeting could take place before the Revenue people have their plans more or less cut and dried.

"Perhaps in the first instance the best plan would be for you to review the situation with Alan Herbert, and to make sure that whatever date you finally agree with Butler, whether for luncheon or dinner, is a date on which A.P.H. is available. . . .

"Meanwhile Masefield has been in consultation with Osbert and me, and has concocted a letter which will reach the Chancellor at the weekend and should serve as a helpful preface to your talk. I shall be receiving the letter in its final form within the next day or two, and will at once send you a copy. . . .

"Yours ever
Denys Kilham Roberts"

That lunch with the Chancellor of the Exchequer was becoming as elusive as Puck when I wrote to Alan Herbert a day or two after the New Year:

"I thought I had secured an informal meeting with the Chancellor through Thelma Cazalet, when I hoped to pin him down to a date for our lunch, but he evaded this. I now suggest writing to ask him to meet you and me and John Moore at lunch on January 29 . . . I rather feel that he is trying to put off this lunch until he is in a position to say that this year's budget is already fixed up. Meanwhile, I understand from Kilham Roberts that the Revenue officials have been tactfully approached, but so far I have had no bulletin."

SEVENTY YEARS OLD: 1953

JUST after the New Year I gave two broadcasts—one on old omnibuses and the other on old sweets. When I suggested the subjects for the talks the B.B.C. Home Service was not enthusiastic and I think it was only because I hinted Overseas might be interested that Home Service took them on. There was a ridiculous amount of jealousy between the two services at this time. I recall a half-hour brains' trust in which Bertland Russell, Aneurin Bevan, Lord Byres and I took part at 15 guineas a piece. It had been a great success and Home Service was offered it as a repeat at half-price (£7, 17s. 6d. a piece). Home Service was not interested in the bargain.

The broadcasts about omnibuses and sweets were two of the biggest successes I have had, and I received many letters, especially about the old omnibuses, which made me realize how much I had still to learn. There was, for instance, an Omnibus Society in existence which brought out a monthly paper. People sent me pictures of old omnibuses, and even old bus tickets. Both broadcasts were printed in *The Listener* and later on would appear in the collection of my broadcasts called *Echoes* which was published by Chatto and Windus a year or two later.

I shall quote from only two of those many letters. The first was written from The Pantiles, Tunbridge Wells by an old lady of 75:

I wish to thank you for your broadcast about old sweets. I was lying in bed and listened to what you had to say. You cannot realize what a great pleasure you gave me in taking me back to my childhood days. I went to school again and bought some of the sweets you mentioned. 'Satin Pralines' were my greatest joy. . . .
Thanking you for giving me back a vivid day of my childhood. . . .
Your Grateful Listener
A Back Number aged 75 years.

I expect that when I wrote to thank her for that letter I told her the address from which she wrote gave me back a vivid day of my childhood in that wet summer of 1888 when she was ten and I was five years old.

The second letter came from Tweedmouth Road, Plaistow, E.13 and I have kept the one or two slips of spelling. I feel proud to have elicited such a letter:

Dear Sir,
I being an old Road Car Omnibus Driver with the old Horses, thought your talk was very good and very sorry their was not many records kept of them or not

many people who remember riding on them I had to put my wits about me when you spoke of the Green Bus up Regent St then it came to me quite well it was Thames Tillings which run from Peckham to Oxford Circuss their first journey up in the morning they used to have four Horses on them and in their green panel it was call Times, I thought you would have spoken about when they took our Horses away for the Boer War, all they left us was grey ones because they said that colour would show up on the Velt in Africa. well there is a lot of old times comes in my memory sometimes which I could make you laugh some of them are very funny, all the Best from an old Driver.

T. Barrett.

Did I ever drive beside him when a Road Car was galloping ahead of a General up the Hammersmith road, which as I copy that letter is 77 years ago?

The British Federation of Wholesale Confectioners found my talk so "extremely interesting and especially topical at this time in view of the derationing of confectionery" that they asked permission to reprint it in their monthly house organ 'The Wholesale Confectioner'.

How many of those old sweets were derationed? Alas, hardly one was still being made.

The late Hubert Clifford, that accomplished Australian musician, suggested that I should do with him a series of broadcasts to be called Beaux and Belles in which I would interview at the old Avenue Theatre some musical comedy stars of the past. He suggested Ellaline Terris, Ada Reeve, Phyllis Monckman, and Muriel George. By an encouraging coincidence on the day after I had been talking to Hubert Clifford about this series I received a letter from Ellaline Terriss who as I write these words is still with us and not at all a little bit of string but an adorable nonagenarian on the edge of her century:

My dear old friend Sir Compton,

I did so enjoy your Omnibus talk, and a lot of it brought tears to my eyes.

I am longing to hear the next and I am wondering if you will talk about the old Lowther Arcade. I remember being taken there by my mother when she bought me a life size doll (8/11d) and we took it home—I was unable to carry it—and dressed it in my own baby clothes. It eventually became a target for my brothers.

Then I remember the 'sweet' shop near the Arcade—the whole windows from top to bottom with twisted barley sugar, pink and white sugar mice with string tails, alphabet sweets and then, much to my disgust, grey paragoric "cough no more" tablets. Again thank you for the nice things you said of my Seymour in your speech at the Dorchester.

I do hope I haven't bored you with my reminiscences.

Yours always sincerely
Ellaline Terriss Hicks

That series planned by Hubert Clifford was done later on this year and had a great success, particularly overseas where repeats were frequent. I found those interviews one of the most enjoyable experiences I have had in broadcasting.

I shall indulge myself by quoting one letter which reached me on the morning of my birthday from General Kaiser who until lately had been representing Nepal in Great Britain:

> *Kaiser Mahal*
> *Katmandu*
> *7th January 1953*

My dear Sir Compton,

I have been All Over the Place with you and thank you for the exhilarating company. Your portrait of Nepal is not only vivid but accurate. That tall scraggy hydrangea with rosey-buff flowers of the paniculata type is, I think, Luculia gratissima.

This letter will reach you on about your seventieth birthday. Please accept my congratulations and best wishes for many happy returns of the day.

> *With high regards*
> *Yours sincerely*
> *Kaiser*

It was reassuring to find that old letter and know that what I have included in this Octave from *All Over the Place* had been approved in Katmandu.

Three days after that seventieth birthday I was given a wonderful occasion by my beloved friends of the Savile Club. I have a dearly cherished keepsake of that occasion in a tiny booklet:

> SODADITAS CONVIVIUM
> TO MONTY
> As a memento
> of the dinner to celebrate
> your seventieth birthday
> these pages have been signed
> in affectionate admiration
> by your friends of
> the Savile
>
> 20th January 1953

David Keir with the support of Doyne Bell, the Club's chairman, was the organizer of that dinner and he arranged that the speeches should be made in turn by people who could talk about me at different periods. The only two non-Savilans at the dinner were Bob Boothby and Ian Parsons, both of whom spoke. The opening speech was by Dick Graves[1]

---

[1] The late R. M. Graves, C.B.E.

and as he spoke I could see that good-looking third-year man in the Magdalen Lodge 51 years ago standing next to Johnny Bramston, an old Wykehamist, who in that summer of 1901 had been runner-up for the Amateur Championship of golf and who would die of consumption before he was 25. Johnny Bramston was the son of the Reverend Trant Bramston of whose House at Winchester I have written in Octave Three.

I read now through the seventy-six names who signed that keepsake. Not half a dozen of their owners were older than myself; yet of those seventy-six signatures over twenty are no longer alive. Alas, since writing those words my dearly loved David Keir himself has left us.

When I was making my speech of thanks for so much generous friendship the Club staff came in and I was able to express my gratitude for what the Club staff had always done for me through the forty years of my membership.

Charles Eade wrote to tell me that Winston Churchill had got to hear about the book. "He seems to be rather elderly and touchy these days, so I think you should avoid any substantial quotes from 'Savrola' or he might start grumbling about infringing his copyright . . . as you probably know he guards his own literary work very jealously." A week or two later I was able to send Charles Eade my contribution of 'Winston Churchill the Novelist' without causing Charles Eade any anxiety.

By good luck the problem of Faith's residence seemed likely to be solved in this last week of January when Chrissie went to look at a flat in Sheffield Terrace, Campden Hill which seemed exactly right for Faith who was finding the wind and snow of Majorca at this time of the year not something she was prepared to face for another winter. She had finished her novel *The Crooked Wall* and was evidently looking forward to being in London when it was published. The flat in Sheffield Terrace would not be available until June, but Spring in Majorca would be as pleasant as winter there was being unpleasant. I was writing to her on January 28th:

Unless there's an abrupt clearance here through somebody's buying Denchworth in the next month or two (most unlikely) you can be here until you go to Campden Hill. I expect you will be able to sell the Fornalutx cottage much more easily than Denchworth Manor. . . . Eyes are bad. The haemhorrage in the left eye covers all but the extreme outside of it, but the cataract in the right eye appears to be ripening. My mother's first operation was at 72. I have had to postpone Eastern Epic for a while. The papers are beyond me. So I shall write 'Ben Nevis Goes East' for publication in the autumn.

I did forty letters yesterday and still have a lot to answer. My talks about omnibuses and sweets were a bit too successful for convenience.

Three days after writing that letter the lunch at the Savoy with the Chancellor of the Exchequer took place. I felt that Butler was more likely than most Chancellors to grasp the problem of the author's fluctuating income and he had already asked the Inland Revenue authorities at Somerset House to receive the deputation from the Society of Authors which I was leading next day.

Nobody could have listened more patiently than 'Rab' Butler listened during that lunch. I recall one remark of his,

"The people I am most sorry for are those with incomes from £2,000 to £4,000, but imagine how they would groan on the other side of the House if I said that from the Front Bench."

One thing I do remember from that lunch. When one of us asked for caviare the Savoy found that they had to open a new tin and for the first and last time in my life I was able to eat as much caviare as I wanted.

On the morning after this Alan Herbert, John Moore, Denys Kilham Roberts and myself met at the Savile, whence we proceeded to the United Universities Club in Suffolk Street for lunch before proceeding to Somerset House. The United Universities was famous for its champagne cocktails, the best I ever drank. Fortified by these we arrived at Somerset House and were shown up to the judgment seat of the Inland Revenue. There were about half a dozen high officials who sat at a long table with their backs to the big window looking across to the Thames. The deputation had the disadvantage of facing the light. Alan Herbert sat on my right, John Moore and Kilham Roberts on my left.

In the middle of my argument I was interrupted by one of the officials.

"But surely, Sir Compton, what you are arguing about the fluctuating income of an author applies to the fluctuating income of a barrister?"

"Ah, yes", I agreed. "But with this slight difference. The fluctuating income of a barrister depends on human misery, anxiety and crime whereas the fluctuating income of an author depends on human entertainment. Otherwise, it is, of course, a parallel example of fluctuating incomes."

We heard no more about the fluctuating incomes of barristers.

When the various questions had been answered and the hearing was over Alan Herbert, who had been doodling while the argument was going on, suddenly said to those magnates of the Inland Revenue as he offered them a sheet of paper.

"Would you like to buy my doodle and help me to pay my Income Tax?"

The Chancellor presumably found that Somerset House was not hostile to the idea of spreading an author's earnings because that was allowed for in the 1953 Budget. I had argued also that painters and sculptors should have the same consideration but it was not until the Budget of 1969 that this was granted to them.

With that deputation to Somerset House at the end of January I shall bring this Octave to a close and I pray that my eyes will hold out and allow me to finish the last Octave to which I hope to add a Coda up to 1970.

APPENDIX A

So far as the SIKH Regt goes I have had it Sir. I belong to the WESTERN PUNJAB and being a MUSLIM have no choice but to serve in PAKISTAN. I am a most disappointed person today. The INDIAN ARMY is systematically being destroyed, a fine machine being disintegrated to satisfy some of the so called politicians who till now called us "mercenary soldiers". We are watching a 'TRAGEDY' being performed in front of us.

I love my SIKHS, Sir, and for the last 8 years I had only two months leave. I went all out for the name of this fine Regt. now to be told I cannot stay in it any more.

What luck!

We hope to be back by the first week of October and then I will come and see you, Sir.

CONFIDENTIAL

British Forces in Iraq.
21 Sep 47.

A tragedy had befallen us but it seemed inevitable in view of the BRITISH Govt announcement of the 3rd June 47.

Today, I am commanding this Bn. . . . Tomorrow when I give up the command I will be a foreigner to most of those who are my own men today. Then I would belong to a different nationality.

This incredible, impracticable notion of those who have NO idea at all of the strength and the worth of the INDIAN Army had been put to practice and as we are the first victims of this experiment in this Regt, I thought I would let you know so that you get the correct picture as to the future of the SIKH.

We were to embark from BASRA on the 22 of Sep. Everybody was very happy and pleased to leave this country and all had great hopes for the future. We all were determined to set an example of mutual trust and good-will once we were in INDIA and to prove to the World that there are still some of us who respect and honour DUTY much more than the petty sentimentality of communal favouritism. We wanted to prove that we were completely impartial when dealing with the communal bickering.

But it was NOT to happen like this.

On 17th Sep we received an order from the Supreme Commander's HQs telling me to split up the Bn before leaving IRAQ. You can well imagine our feelings. It was a great blow, but it seemed inevitable.

The two P.M. Coys will embark on the 22 Sep for KARACHI. Their final destination is LAHORE where they will join F.F.Rif. The rest of the Bn will embark on the 7 Oct for Bombay and their final destination is DEOLALI where they will become POONA Sub Area troops.

On the eve of my departure, I most sincerely wish you all those who have served and are serving this fine Regt the very best of luck.

I leave with heavy heart and with prayers on my lips that GOD willing we will unite once again.

Good-bye to you all.

GOD bless you all.

Extract from a letter dated 18 October 47

"The Paltan, in spite of everything, has done very well indeed. A week ago, when we came off train escorts, we had escorted 250 trains with not one incident, except when a badmash threw a rock into a carriage at Beas and killed two women.

"Since a few days ago we have been transferred to escorting Muslim foot kafilas towards Pakistan.

"We are now all Muslim. Our two Muslim Coys—from—Sikh—arrived three days ago and two days before that our Sikhs and Dogras left. It was a sad moment. We had a combined parade and bara khana before they left, in the greatest friendship, and the senior Sikh VCO wept in my office as he was about to go. In spite of all this I think everyone felt that it was time to part for the compulsion of outside events was too great for the individual."

Army H.Q. (Pakistan)
RAWALPINDI.

31.10.47

Respected Sir,

I regret to inform you that the communal disturbances in the Punjab have touched me and my family very heavily. I belonged to Amritsar and with all other Muslims who called Amritsar home, lost all that I had then. We bore this patiently.

We had extensive holdings of land in the Gurdaspur district of which also we stand deprived. An elder brother fighting in protection of hearth and home was killed. This too we bore patiently.

A younger brother was working as Telegraphic master in the G.T.O. Chamba when this trouble started. A Hindu officer relieved him early in September and he left Chamba to join the Refugee Camp at Dalhousie. He was waylaid and butchered with wife, aged mother, four children on Sept. 12th. One boy 8/9 years old was stabbed and thrown on the roadside as dead. Friends from Dalhousie who came to bury the dead on the following day, found the boy alive and carried him to Dalhousie where his physical wounds healed. Thank God he has been restored to me since.

But still our cup was not full. A daughter of our martyred brother, a comely girl of 13/14 years was abducted. She has a fair complexion, a round face and sharp features. This tragedy took place near a village BATRI on the Chamba to Dalhousie road, and this poor girl is said to be in that village.

The C.O. of the Refugee Camp at Dalhousie, an English officer, touched by the immensity of the disaster, is said to have made an unsuccessful attempt at her rescue.

I humbly request your help for the rescue of this poor girl, for which I and all other members of my family, will for ever, remain grateful.

From:— Lieut.-General Sir Reginald Savory,
    K.C.I.E., C.B., D.S.O., M.C.

NEW DELHI
29th November 1947

Thank you for your letter of 16 November in which you express all your views on Regimmental Silver.

I know exactly how you feel. I feel very like that myself; we all do. I think, however, we must realise that whatever the situation in India and Pakistan may become in the future, the situation as it stands at present is that these two countries are members of the British Commonwealth. For us to have allowed or even connived at any Mess Silver or other regimental property being sent out of the country would have been just not worth it. For your information, I know there are one or two regiments who have sent either all or a big proportion of their regimental Silver to England. I know of this unofficially. I also know how extremely strongly the Indian members of those Messes feel on the subject. It has given rise to resentment which will take a long time to live down. The whole essence of our transfer of power to India has been and still is to do it in such a way as to leave behind us good-will and willingness to co-operate in the future. That is a very big thing and something I suppose for which it is worth while making some kind of sacrifice, and it is possible that Mess Silver may form part of that sacrifice.

India and Pakistan are now two separate "Independent" countries and what they decide as to the future of Messes in their respective Armies is a matter for them and them only to decide. We (i.e. the Supreme Commander's Headquarters) have no longer any say in the matter whatever.

If either or both of the new Dominions decide to abolish Messes and sell the Silver or bury it, or destroy it, or return it to its original donors, or put it in a Museum or, in fact, do anything with it which they choose, it is entirely their own affair. That is the brutal truth and there is no use trying to blink it. You may cry to high heaven and write to as many members of Parliament as you choose including the Prime Minister if you like, but it will not have the slightest effect, and might well make more difficult the relationship between the U.K. and the two new Dominions.

So far I have been pretty frank as I think it is only right that we should know where we stand. I must, however, point out to you that certain regiments have taken action with regard to their Mess Silver, etc., which is within the policy laid down by the Commander-in-Chief (as he then was).

I know of one regiment, as the result of a Mess meeting, has sent certain pieces of Silver home in order that they may be used at the Regimental dinner. I gather that the Mahrattas have done something of the same kind.

I know of another regiment which has sent certain articles of the Mess which had a particular family connection, back to the descendants of the persons with whom those particular objects originated.

I know of another regiment which, as the result of a Mess meeting, resolved that if at any time that regiment ceased to run a Mess, the articles of Mess

Silver and other things should be specially disposed of in some way which was laid down. I forget exactly what they proposed to do as I only got this information in a demi-official letter. So you see that the remedy lies with the regiments themselves and has done so all the time. I gave one or two fairly broad hints of this in some "Durbar Notes" which I issued about a year ago. You will, of course, appreciate that as Adjutant General in those days it was not possible for me to do more than give a hint. Had I done so, I would quite rightly have been accused of merely pointing out how British Officers could avoid the spirit of the letter which I sent round on behalf of the Commander-in-Chief.

You also raised in your letter the question of some kind of acknowledgment of the services of British Officers in the Indian Army, in particular from the British themselves. It may interest you to know that nearly a year ago when the trend of events was becoming pretty clear, we had arranged for a statement to be made in the House of Commons acknowledging the services of British Officers. The Minister of Defence (A. V. Alexander) did get up in the House and started to make this particular acknowledgement. He had hardly spoken a couple of sentences before he was interrupted by Winston Churchill on some minor point which really missed the main point and the result was that this acknowledgment was never finished. It is a curious thing that the person who was responsible for torpedoing this acknowledgment should have been unwittingly the one person who probably would have been more pleased than anyone else to have made such a statement himself. However, things sometimes happen like this.

There was also an acknowledgment of the services of British Officers made during a debate on the Indian Independence Act early last August.

We have been trying also for some time to get a real acknowledgment of the services of British Officers from the Political leaders of India and Pakistan but without success. The probable reason is that they have been themselves unable to say publicly what they were quite prepared to say privately. I think the two letters by Jinnah and Nehru which have recently been published asking for British Officers to volunteer to serve after 31 December 1947 in their respective Dominions is as near as we could ever get to an acknowledgment of the type that you require.

I write, of course, in my private capacity and not as Adjutant General, as appointment, incidentally, which I only continue to hold for only another day.

(Sd) R. A. Savory.

Brigadier S. A. H. Hungerford,
Club of Western India,
Poona.

APPENDIX B

Southampton,
Dec. 9 '82.

My dear Dyer,

I visited the Museum at Kew, and saw the specimen of the *Lodoicea Seychellarum* you have there. I am sorry to see that the Museum has not been better supplied from Seychelles with a better set of specimens of this most curious palm, and I am still very sorry to think that the palm itself, unless some very stringent orders are given, may become extinct. The constant change of Governors of these Isles requires continual reiteration of orders respecting the conservation of this palm. I am aware of the very strong way the authorities of the Royal Botanical Gardens have presented the subject to the Colonial Office.

I think that the appointment of Mr C. Button of Mahé, Seychelles, to look after these palms should be a permanent one, and one not subject to the change of Governors. Mr Button is perhaps the only man who knows the palm and its proper cultivation.

In order to rouse some degree of interest in the palm, allow me to make a few remarks which, though known to you are not so generally to the Colonial Office.

The Palm is unique to one island (Praslin)—(actually a few grow in Mahé also, probably planted there by some former Governor as they are in the Governor's Grounds—5 miles by 2 miles in size. It takes 20 years to form its skull-like bole, 47 years ere it bears its fruit, weighing 40 to 50 lbs. in weight, takes 7 years to ripen, and grows to a height of 120 feet. There is no other Palm like it, its mode of propagation is entirely different from the ordinary coconut.

As we generally believe that there was a Tree of Knowledge of Good and Evil and a Tree of Life, actual trees, set aside for a time to be imbued with mystic powers, there is no reason why these trees should not exist now. They, having fulfilled their purpose, are relegated back to ordinary trees. Now any man who has ever examined this Palm must have been struck with it in a way that he would not have been with any other tree.

Its fruit is shaped like the human heart, the bed or stem which attaches it to the branch like the male organ of generation. When the husk is taken off, the inner double nut is like the belly and thighs of a woman. The male baba and the branch spring from between the thigh-like division of the huge leaf stem in a striking way. It is not buried in order to sprout, it is usually placed on the ground where it shoots out a long round rod which splits into the plumule and radicle some 10 or 12 feet from the seed and this forms the bole.

In a word, its fruit are those of the male and female organs of generation, and it is a fruit which cannot fail to attract attention by any one seeing it.

It is taken to India for the Harems, its shell is used at the Well of Knowledge at Benares.

There are comparatively few trees now to what there were, and the continual depredation of the natives who cut out the heart of the Palm is much to be found and will end in its extinction.

It is only found on Praslin Isle and does not seem to thrive elsewhere.

It has been urged that if this is the tree which was used to test our mother Eve, then this Isle should be in the Garden of Eden. On this subject I will say a few words.

1. Water floods do not change materially the ranges of mountains, therefore the sources of the Tigris and Euphrates, which are separated by ranges of 10,000 feet, must be where they were from Adam's time.

2. The usual reading of Genesis, "A river flowed out of Eden and watered the garden; thence it was divided into four heads," is that the four rivers flowed out from the great river not *into it* as I think the term four heads would imply, and the position of the sources of Euphrates and Tigris is against this supposition that they flowed out, for then the River of Eden would be somewhere near their sources, which the nature of the country they are in is against. I say, therefore, they flowed into the Great River. The Tigris meets the Euphrates and goes into the Persian Gulf. If the water is taken off the Indian Ocean there will be seen a deep cleft running down to near Socotra, where it meets a deep cleft from the Red Sea, and there the deep ravine or cleft runs down to near Seychelles where is the greatest depth of the Indian Ocean, and where there is a circular plot 2,600 fathoms deep.

The theory of the Indian Ocean being once a continent is old. We have the Euphrates and Tigris flowing into this central lake or basin, while from the Red Sea we have the cleft which joins the Persian Gulf gully near Socotra, and we have to account for the other two rivers Pison and Gihon.

'Pison' means 'overflowing', a feature of the Nile. 'Pison' is said to encompass Havilah, a land of gold. Havilah was son of Tochtar's grandson then, brother to Sheba and Ophir, names connected with gold and with Abyssinia. The Blue Nile encompasses Gojam where there is gold and I think the Blue Nile is the 'Pison', encompassing Gojam or Havilah and flowing before the flood into the Red Sea—the Gihon. South of Jerusalem is a deep ravine called 'Gihon, Grehennea, Irphat, Vale of Hismurur'. Irphat is joined to the Kadren and the ravine, which is of great depth, goes by the Valley of Fire to the Dead Sea. This deep depression of the Valley of Aqaba leads to the Gulf of Aqaba in the Red Sea.

This letter seems rather discursive, but if it will save the Coco de Mer species from extinction or go some way towards it you will pardon it.

Believe me,
Yours sincerely,
C. G. Gordon.

P.S. Oddly enough there is a species of serpent at Praslin, none on any of the other islands in these seas. It is some 3 or 4 feet long.

The Seychelles Islands are granite, all the stones are volcanic.

The *Artecarpus incisa*, or Bread fruit tree, is to my mind, the tree which was set apart at the time of the fall as the Tree of Life.

APPENDIX C

If you agree with the contentions in the enclosed draft of a proposed letter to the Chancellor of the Exchequer will you be good enough to let me know that you will sign the final copy and if possible accompany the proposed deputation?

I should welcome any suggestions for improving the text.

You will accept my assurance that I should not have ventured to trouble you unless I were aware of the gravity of the situation and I earnestly hope you will be able to associate yourself with this effort before the next Budget to obtain for music the exemption from tax granted to literature.

SENT TO

Sir Arnold Bax, D.Mus.,
White Horse Inn,
STORRINGTON, Sussex.

Dr Arthur Bliss, Mus.Doc.,
15 Cottismore Gardens,
LONDON, W.8.

Sir Adrian Boult, D.Mus.,
Northlands,
Landford, SALISBURY.

Sir George Dyson, Mus.D.,
Royal College of Music,
LONDON, S.W.7.

T. S. Eliot, Esq., O.M., Litt.D.,
19, Carlyle Mansions,
Cheyne Walk, S.W.3

Sir Stanley Marchant, C.V.O., D.Mus.,
Royal Academy of Music,
Marylebone Road, N.W.1.

Dr Boyd Neel,
Cherry Tree Cottage,
Stoke Row,
HENLEY-ON-THAMES, Oxon.

Dr William Walton, Mus.D.,
10 Hallyberry Lane,
HAMPSTEAD, N.W.3.

John Masefield, Esq., O.M., D.Litt.,
c/o Heinemann, Ltd.,
99, Great Russell Street, W.C.

Ernest Newman, Esq.,
"Polperro",
Epsom Lane,
TADWORTH, Surrey.

Dr R. Vaughan Williams,
O.M., Mus.Doc.,
The White Gates,
DORKING, Surrey.

The Right Honble. Sir Stafford Cripps, P.C., K.C., J.P., M.P.,
Sir,

We have the honour to request that you will receive a deputation from the undersigned representatives of music and literature in order that we may hear

U

from you whether you will consider sympathetically our reasons for venturing to suggest that the freedom from taxation allowed to books since the Purchase Tax was first imposed on October 21st 1940 should now be extended to gramophone records. Our arguments are embodied below:

1. The first fifty years of the gramophone record which will very shortly be completed display a steady advance in artistic worth for which there is no parallel since the invention of printing. The treasury of recorded music already rich in masterpieces becomes richer with every month that passes, and to these may be added the recordings of poetry and drama both past and present, of folk songs and dances, and of many language records of powerful educational value. To this treasury the contribution made by the British Gramophone Industry is recognised throughout the world as the largest and the best.

2. The record has diffused a knowledge of the work of British composers and orchestras abroad, and the British Council has recognised this by associating itself with the Recording Companies in making that work available in other countries. There seems to be something anomalous in asking the taxpayer to contribute toward such occasional subsidies and then to tax him twice over for supporting the products they assist. He would presumably not be asked to pay entertainment tax for supporting a National Theatre built and endowed by his own taxation.

3. The Record Catalogues of the British Companies have enabled the British Broadcasting Corporation to build up a library of over 250,000 records without which the variety of present programmes could not be sustained either financially or artistically.

4. The record has become as necessary as the printed book to Educational Authorities, Community Centres, Discussion Groups, Youth Clubs, Summer Schools, and Colleges of Music. The fact that all over the country Municipal Libraries are beginning to add records to their books is significant of the place the record has won. This development is of recent date and had not begun when the Purchase Tax was first imposed.

5. The programmes of "Music While You Work" in factories all over the country which began in time of war and still continue depended and still depend principally on records.

6. It was recognised from the start that a Purchase Tax on books, magazines and periodicals would be a tax on culture, and no doubt the exemption of sheet music was granted for the same reason. Surely the logic of such an exemption should not be imperilled by refusing it to the record, which for the vast majority of people represents the printing of music. The growth of musical taste during the last quarter of a century has been truly astonishing, and what would have seemed a miracle to an earlier generation has been achieved by broadcasting and the gramophone record. Great music is now to be found in the humblest homes, but the cost is high and the record is now as expensive as the book was formerly. It was the desire to make the book available to all that prompted our ancestors to confiscate the products of an author's work after his death. We dread the effect of raising the standard of living of the poor and at the same time cramping

their spiritual and mental standard, in raising which music plays so vital a part.

The occasional appearances of great artists and orchestras are confined to London, Edinburgh, and a few of the larger provincial cities and towns. The larger part of the population has no certainty of hearing such artists and orchestras except on the gramophone record. There is no doubt that the prospect of being recorded in this country is one of the major inducements to great artists and orchestras to come here because to be recorded in London is the hallmark of reputation. The lowering of purchase power today combined with the heavy taxation on records and instruments may lead to great artists and orchestras seeking from America what hitherto they have so eagerly sought from Great Britain.

7. Furthermore, the definite advance made recently in the technique of British recording has demanded a corresponding advance in reproduction of which all too many are unable to avail themselves owing to the Purchase Tax on both records and instruments. This must restrict the ability of the Companies to record the work of young British composers because the public will not experiment with novelty when it has to pay so high for it. Furthermore still, so long as the Purchase Tax on records remains in force any possibility of issuing cheap reissues of the musical classics must be ruled out.

8. Ever since the Purchase Tax was first imposed the gramophone record and the instrument upon which it is reproduced have been subjected to variable but always heavy rates.

	On and from		*Rate*
October	21st 1940		$33\frac{1}{3}\%$
April	15th 1942		$66\frac{2}{3}\%$
April	13th 1943		100 %
April	10th 1946		$33\frac{1}{3}\%$
November	11th 1947		50 %
April	9th 1948		$66\frac{2}{3}\%$

9. When Purchase Tax was introduced during the war it was understood that the radical purpose of it was the discouragement of unnecessary spending. $33\frac{1}{3}\%$ was then considered enough for this. Are we to understand that today it is considered so desirable to discourage unnecessary expenditure upon music that the rate of taxation has to be double what it was originally?

10. Since the introduction of Purchase Tax £7,750,000 (seven and three quarter million pounds) on records and £5,250,000 (five and a quarter million pounds) on record-playing devices—a total of £13,000,000 (thirteen million pounds) has passed to the National Exchequer. For the year 1948 the corresponding figures were £1,500,000 (one and a half million pounds) on records and £2,500,000 (two and a half million pounds) for record-playing devices.

11. We recognise that the taxation of records and instruments has provided and still provides a substantial annual sum to the Exchequer, but we wish

to stress that it is in effect as much a severe tax on music as a similar tax on books would be upon literature and education.

We hope that the considerable export trade of the Gramophone Industry will compensate for the loss of revenue by exempting it from Purchase Tax. That trade has been won entirely by the superiority of the British product over any other in the world, a fact which is freely admitted even in America where the Gramophone Industry has developed on parallel lines. That superiority can be maintained only if the Gramophone Industry, already threatened by rising costs of production, can at least escape the handicap imposed on it by a Purchase Tax which, we repeat, is fundamentally a tax upon music and to a lesser degree upon poetry.

If after perusal of these eleven points you will be good enough to receive our deputation, may we ask that you will name a date and an hour convenient to yourself?

We have the honour, Sir,
to remain in all regard,
Your obedient Servants,

APPENDIX D

CONFESSIONS AND IMPRESSIONS

The following twelve questions, which have gone to persons eminent in various walks of life, have been drawn up by the editor of 'The Saturday Book'. He hopes very much that you will be able to provide replies for inclusion in his book. These answers may be as long or as short as you please. It would be a great help to him if he had your reply some time within the next fortnight.

1. Is there any other profession you might have been good at?
2. What has been your greatest personal deficiency in life? (e.g. shyness, self-assertiveness, etc.)
3. What century or period is your spiritual home, and why?
4. On what occasion have you been most frightened in your life?
5. What was the most momentous interview of your life?
6. Where and when did you have the most memorable holiday of your life?
7. Where and when did you have the most memorable meal of your life?
8. Have you any pet reforms?
9. Are you urban or rural by temperament, and what is your conception of the ideal house or flat?
10. Are you a host or a guest?
11. To what do you attribute your success?
12. What lessons has life taught you?

To LEONARD RUSSELL
for *The Saturday Book*   MARCH 1949

1. The only other profession in which I could have felt sure of being as successful as I have had the good fortune to be in my own would have been the stage.
2. A dislike of saying 'no'.
3. The present, because I can add to the present so much of the past.
4. Hearing the Jack the Ripper murders being shouted by hoarse throated paper-sellers at night.
5. Probably when I told the High Master of St Paul's School that I did not intend to win a scholarship at Oxford and thus secured myself from any possibility of entering the Civil Service. I was fifteen years old at the time.
6. I have not had a holiday in the strict sense of the word since I left Oxford, but if I may count as the equivalent of a holiday the enjoyment of a job of work I should say either my time at Gallipoli or the year I spent recently following in the tracks of the Indian Army over three continents.
7. In Paris, July 1938, when as a Member of the Saintsbury Club I was guest of the greatest Society of Epicures in the world—*The Club Des Cent*.
8. The equalization of the rates for travel and freight on the lines of the Post Office. In other words the same fare whether you travel from London

to Brighton or to Wick, and the same charge for a ton of goods irrespective of distance. Such a reform would distribute the population of Britain equitably and ultimately, when extended, the population of the world.

9. I am rural by temperament. Apart from believing that no flat can be ideal I cannot answer the second part of this question.

10. I suffer from the delusion that I am a host, but I am informed by all those who ought to know that I am always a guest.

11. Vitality, brains, sympathy and hard work.

12. This is the kind of Brains Trust Question I deplore, and I shall have to reply, the discovery by personal experience that the copy book maxims of youth are true. Too many cooks do spoil the broth, stitches in time do save nine, and birds of a feather do flock together, and one of them in the hand is worth two of them in the bush.

APPENDIX E

Denchworth Manor,
Near Wantage, Berkshire.
August 8th 1949.

A.   The payment was actually £10,000 less 10 per cent agent's commission
to Raymond Savage making it £9,000 nett. The original offer by Messrs
Macdonald was for £1,000 advance on royalties for the republication of 20 of
my earliest books. Of these 13 had originally been published by Martin Secker
and had passed to Messrs Secker and Warburg when Martin Secker's business
was taken over by them. The titles were then allowed to go out of print and
therefore by the terms of the original contract reverted to me. Six of the other
seven titles were bought outright by Messrs Cassell and Co and these were given
back to me in 1943 as a gift. I replied to Messrs Macdonald's offer by saying
that I should prefer to capitalize any royalties I might hope to receive from
the 20 titles in the future by selling them all outright for £10,000. Originally I
reserved the rights above a certain price in view of a possible definitive edition
at any time in the future, but presently the economic conditions of publishing
made this so improbable that for a further £1,000 I sold the 20 titles without
any reservation, even of film rights. My reason for capitalizing my royalties was
principally my desire to pay off immediately a loan of £3,500 from the Scottish
Equitable Insurance Company on my house in Barra. On the interest I was
paying for this the Income Tax authorities were of course allowing me relief
and therefore in paying off this loan and finally reinvesting the money in
buying a house in England (Denchworth Manor, Wantage) I was and am
paying Income Tax on the Income accruing from my capitalization. I submit
that a transaction cannot possibly be considered Income from an author's work
because it is an unique transaction and can never be repeated. If I had supposed
that it would be treated as Income I should never have made it at a time when
Income Tax stood at the rate it then did. I must point out further that if I had
accepted Messrs Macdonalds original offer the money accruing to me from
royalties would have been spread out over at least ten years and that the amount
of £10,000 could hardly have been expected to accrue in under twenty or even
thirty and the Revenue would have had to wait as long for any Income Tax
on them.

B.   The books involved in this transaction were all written when I was domiciled, first in Italy and then in The Channel Islands, with the exception of
The Passionate Elopement, and therefore I submit that being non-assessable at
the time they were written and originally published a later capitalization of
them cannot be considered an assessable transaction.

C.   If on the other hand if it is ruled that they are assessable as Income I must
observe that in that case I am entitled to claim an allowance for expenses in
connection with the writing of them. In the case of the first title *The Passionate
Elopement* which was written and published before I was domiciled abroad,

every farthing I made out of the book in royalties was spent in advertising it, and Mr Martin Secker the publisher will be able to testify this. He at the same time spent all his profits in the same way by mutual agreement. At the time of writing *The Passionate Elopement* I was in receipt of an annual allowance from my father on which Income Tax had already been paid, and therefore my Income was not assessable outside my own work. If my expenses in connection with writing books from 1912 until I was domiciled in Great Britain in 1931 be considered in comparison with expenses allowed me by the Income Tax authorities from 1931 to the present day it will be clear that such expenses would considerably exceed the assessment on £9,000 as Income. I submit that the question of expenses incurred can only be excluded if this transaction be treated as a capital transaction. If it is Income then no matter when the expenses were incurred they must be allowed.

D.   Furthermore six of the titles involved in this transaction were a gift to me from Messrs Cassell, having been sold outright to them when I was domiciled in The Channel Islands and should, I submit, in any case be excluded from the assessment.

I desire to add that so firmly am I convinced that this payment of £9,000 nett plus £1,000 later to cover even film rights is a capital receipt that it is my intention to carry this matter up to the House of Lords because it is essential for literary men to have an unequivocal ruling from the highest legal authority in the land.

  1. Sinister Street
  2. Sylvia Scarlett
  3. Sylvia and Michael
  4. Guy and Pauline
  5. Carnival   The Vanity Girl
  6. Poor Relations
  7. Rich Relatives
  8. Extraordinary Women
  9. The Passionate Elopement
 10. Seven Ages of Women
 11. Unconsidered Trifles
 12. Reaped and Bound
 13. Kensington Rhymes.

Books bought outright by Cassell
Coral
Rogues and Vagabonds
The Altar Steps
The Heavenly Ladder
The Parson's Progress
Fairy Gold

18th December 1952.

The Secretary
The Board of Inland Revenue,
Somerset House,
LONDON, W.C.2.

Dear Sir,

The Society of Authors has, during the past few months, again had under active consideration the question of the taxation of the income of authors, especially of lump sum payments received from film companies for the purchase of copyright and of large amounts received from royalties shortly after the publication of books that have taken many years in preparation. There have been several cases in which sur-tax in its highest ranges has become chargeable and, as was stated in the Millard Tucker Report made last year to the Chancellor of the Exchequer, "Sur-tax in its highest ranges is virtually confiscatory."

2. It seems highly probable that virtual confiscation of earned income so far as from being the intention of Parliament is an unforeseen and unintended by-product of a policy designed to impose high taxation on the wealthy members of the community, a description which, partly by reason of irrational taxation, can rarely, if ever, be applied to authors.

3. Although cases of "virtual confiscation" may be proportionately few, they are catastrophic in their effect and there are many other instances of authors, including dramatists, being so heavily taxed as the consequence of producing an unusually successful book or play that they are allowed to retain only quite a small proportion of their earnings from that source.

4. That the position of authors is exceptional in this respect, and that a remedy was required was recognized by the legislation in the Finance Act of 1944, but this first and tentative attempt to give relief has not proved to be very effective, and the case for a more radical reconsideration of the basis of assessment of authors appeared to the Society to be a very strong one.

5. They therefore appointed a sub-committee in August last to consider the question of Authors and Taxation. This sub-committee has reported, its report has been adopted and a copy is enclosed.

6. It will be observed that the sub-committee has limited its proposals to income-tax assessment and that no specific reference is made in its report to give, on application by the taxpayer, some relief from sur-tax by applying the "spreading" provisions contained in paragraphs 84 to 93 of the Millard Tucker Report. The Chancellor of the Exchequer in the debate in the House of Commons on the 1952 Finance Bill relied to such an extent on this part of the Report and the case for granting at the earliest opportunity of this relief is so strong on its merits that we feel that it would be reasonable to assume that legal effect to the recommendation will be given in the next Finance Act. We claim that the present basis of assessment of authors is unique in regard to—

(a) the taxation of *Capital*, e.g. the sale of a right to receive annual income from royalties, etc.

(b) the inadequacy of the recognition of the length of the period during which the work that produces the income has taken in preparation.

and (c) the extent of the resulting deprivation of the author of the fruits of his labours.

7. We are conscious that the sub-committee's proposals in regard to spreading for purposes of income tax assessment might present administrative difficulties if these were adopted without modification. We are confident, however, that it is within the capacity of the Inland Revenue Department to make any modification necessary to meet such difficulties and to bring the proposals into a form suitable for consideration of the Chancellor, and, if appropriate, the Royal Commission on Taxation.

It would, we think, be helpful if an informal discussion could be arranged between the Society of Authors (which has the support of the League of Dramatists) and the Board of Inland Revenue, and we should be very glad to send representatives to Somerset House to meet the Board. We hope that it may be found practicable to arrange such a meeting before the close of the year.

Yours faithfully,

Secretary-General.

REPORT OF THE *Ad hoc* COMMITTEE SET UP UNDER THE AUSPICES OF THE SOCIETY OF AUTHORS TO CONSIDER THE QUESTION OF "AUTHORS AND TAXATION"

Your committee consisted of Sir Compton Mackenzie (Chairman), Sir Alan Herbert, Messrs H. E. Bates, John Moore, Raymond Postgate, John Pudney and E. P. Smith. Mr Balleny of Messrs Chalmers, Wade & Co., Chartered Accountants, attended meetings of the committee so that the Committee could have the benefit of his professional advice.

We assumed that by our implied terms of reference we were concerned only with the taxation of authors, playwrights and composers though we have a natural and special sympathy with artists and sculptors. It may be that some other sections of the community with fluctuating incomes have a good case for ax relief; if so, it is for them to bring it forward through their own organizations.

I. There is no question of asking for special "privileges"; but there should be no fear of pressing for special arrangements. Section 24 of the Finance Act 1944 (now section 471 of the consolidating Income Tax Act, 1952) by instituting within severe limits a 3 years' backward "spread" for authors, playwrights and composers, has already recognised their special conditions, and made them a special class of tax payer. But—

II. The relief is too strictly limited to have much effect, and does not even, it is believed, do all that Sir John Anderson, then Chancellor of the Exchequer, intended and desired. It allows the author, in certain conditions, to "spread back" for tax purposes a "lump sum" payment.

The lump sum may be an advance on royalties, or the sale-price of full copyright (or some part of it).

But (1) (a) the spread applies only to the period in which the work was written and (b) the maximum spread allowed in three years, even if the work

APPENDIX E   315

took much longer, e.g. Trevelyan's *Social History*, Harold Nicolson's *Life of King George*, Chester Wilmot's *Struggle for Europe*, and if it took less than one there is no spread at all.

(2) there is no spread at all for royalties accruing in the ordinary way (i.e. not by way of an "advance"), from a sudden and perhaps unrepeatable success, e.g. *The Cruel Sea, Bless the Bride, Edward my Son*.

III.   There are two main points:

(*A*) taxation of royalties [1] (and lump sums in advance of royalties)
(*B*) taxation of lump sums on a sale of copyright (or part of it)

Section 471 touches confusingly two different kinds of "lump sum", and the committee proposes that the two should be differently treated. It would probably be better, therefore, not to attempt to amend Section 471 but to repeal it and begin again. That is a matter of drafting. Meanwhile, separating the two points, the committee proposes as follows:

(*A*) (1) The "time in which the work was done", in most cases, is not in fact provable or ascertainable. The collection of material, the germination and growth of ideas and plan begins long before "Chapter One" or "Act One" is written. This limitation is rejected by the committee and should not be included in any draft amendment.

(2) The period should be extended from three years to five: but the relief should not be by way of "spread"[2] but "average."

A five-year's backward "spread", we were advised, would be open to practical objections. For one thing, it would mean that no income tax assessment could become final and complete for any year more recent than six years back. It is suggested, therefore, that the assessment over any year should (at the option of the taxpayer) be based on the average earnings over the preceding five years. This should not have the same practical objections and is supportable in logic, because it is no different in principle from the existing arrangement whereby the assessment is based on the earnings of the previous year, or from the old arrangement, abandoned in 1926 whereby all assessments were based on average. Moreover, the amount of the assessment for any year could be settled once and for all during that year.

This arrangement would not be advantageous in the case of individuals who have a high starting average, and whose earnings are likely to fall. It also imposes the necessity of making, out of the earnings of fat years, provision for lean years which may follow. Consequently, individuals should have an option as to whether they will adopt the new basis or remain on the existing basis. No doubt, once exercised, such an option could not be withdrawn.

(*B*) A new Clause (2) should cover any capital sum being a payment for the release of (i) full copyright or (ii) any portion of the copyright, e.g. stage-rights,

---

[1] NOTE—We are concerned with "royalties" and nothing else—not, for example, with payments for journalistic work, or other sources of income.

[2] NOTE.—As proposed in the amendment of Mr Woodrow Wyatt, M.P., in 1952.

film-rights, foreign-rights, amateur performing rights, etc., accepted by the author in lieu of royalties which would otherwise have been earned over a long period, not only by the author but by his heirs for fifty years after his death.

The committee here proposes what they dare to believe to be a concession of principle. They will maintain that, in principle, these are capital transactions and gains, and that it should not be beyond the wit of man to recognise that principle without injuring the Revenue. But, for the sake of simplicity and goodwill, the committee are willing to make a surrender of principle, that is, to accept liability for income tax on these capital gains, upon special terms; that is, a "spread" of at least six years forward.

In this case a "spread" forward is logical, because the effect of a sale of copyright is to dispense with the payment of royalties in the future. A separate arrangement would, no doubt, be necessary to cover the case of the death of the taxpayer within the period of the spread. In such a case the sum could, no doubt, be adjusted to cover the period from the date of sale to the date of death, with a corresponding adjustment to income tax assessment during that period. Any additional tax liability thereby arising would, of course, be a deduction from the Estate for Estate Duty purposes.

NOTE.—Some of what that Sub-Committee was granted in the Finance Act of 1953. What we ventured to recommend for painters and sculptors has just been granted in the Finance Act of 1969.

APPENDIX F

London Letter by John Connell
NORTH AMERICAN SERVICE
Wednesday, 31st August 1949

This is John Connell from the BBC in London. "I was thinking of the pettiness of youthful tragedies" said Michael. "There is only one tragedy for youth." "And what is?" "Age" said the stranger. "And that is the tragedy of age?" "There is no tragedy of age," said the stranger.

Those are the last sentences of a famous English novel. It was first published 36 years ago this week; and to commemorate the anniversary a new edition has just been put out here in Britain. I found a review copy lying on my desk a few days ago. I opened it; and I was at once transported back to my own youth—to a time whose joys and sorrows, aspirations and despairs I thought I'd long since forgotten and could not for an instant recapture.

The novel is called *Sinister Street*. Its author, Compton Mackenzie, is enjoying at present a remarkable Indian summer so far as public esteem and reputation are concerned. Thirty-six years is quite a sizeable chunk out of anyone's life; it's certainly time enough for a book to reach and maintain a position as a classic in its own kind from which it's probably never likely to be dislodged. The first wave of popular favour and the inevitable backwash of critical contempt, have both passed. And it's possible with a reissue like this to talk dispassionately about the book and its background. But in those thirty-six years since *Sinister Street* was first published, what a huge gulf of suffering, sorrow and disappointment and hardship the world and the society which Mackenzie there described has traversed.

I wonder if the book's at all familiar to you. Here in England its influence on a whole generation of sensitive and intelligent young people was profound and pervasive. It's the story of a romantic education. It's set in the last decade of the nineteenth century and the first decade of the twentieth. An upper middle-class boy—a clever, moody, attractive boy—grows up, goes to a big day school in London, makes friends, goes to Oxford, falls in love, suffers, makes an ass of himself, stumbles into manhood. The story is told in a lovely, evocative, rippling prose, sensuous and multi-coloured and suffused with romantic melancholy and romantic zest. The style grows up as the boy grows up; the reader experiences the whole of a boyhood, through the eyes, intelligence and spirit of the chief character, Michael Fane. In the story of one intensely felt youth, it is the pattern and symbol of everybody's youth.

That I think is the particular and abiding magic of *Sinister Street*. To what extent it can similarly affect people who've grown up, not only in a different epoch but in a totally different social universe, I don't know. Is it only an English romantic education that is here so exquisitely and so nostalgically mirrored?

I only know that for me *Sinister Street* is inextricably woven into the texture and fabric of my own past. I first read it when I was seventeen; I didn't read it—I drenched myself in it. Just three years later I had my own first novel published—it was romantic, autobiographical and extremely sentimental and my publisher thought it would help if it if I had an introduction by some eminent older author. Very timidly I asked Compton Mackenzie. He read my book and then he wrote a sane, wise, astringent introduction to it for which, as the years went by, I grew more and more grateful as I grew to understand it better.

My novel has long since gone into that curious hazy limbo in which repose the promising first novels of promising and sentimental young men. But Compton Mackenzie made one observation in his introduction which at twenty I found very baffling; now, at forty, I see how penetrating it was. "Within another five years," he remarked, "Mr Connell may be wondering why he once committed his book to an introduction by the author of *Sinister Street*. But perhaps he will be able to find a place on his bookshelves both for his own book and for *Sinister Street*, for he shows more signs of wanting to look at the world, than of wanting the world to look at him. So he may not be so much ashamed of his first book as to disown it in the near future with all its literary accomplices."

In my middle twenties I naturally thought myself very tough, very mature, very cynical; and I was convinced that I had far outgrown the fresh, naïve, sentimental romantic outlook of an ignorant lad in his teens. But . . . I didn't disown my first book; I didn't disown my affection for *Sinister Street*. I kept them both on my shelves, as Mackenzie had shrewdly suggested I would. And from time to time I would reread a quotation from John Keats's letters, which is on the fly leaf of my own copy of *Sinister Street*: "The imagination of a boy is healthy, and the mature imagination of a man is healthy; but there is a space of life between in which the soul is in a ferment, the character undecided, the way of life uncertain, the ambition thick-sighted". And I would think how profound and true that was. I looked for it on the fly leaf of this new commemorative edition; and it isn't there; and that seems to me a pity.

Twenty years have gone by; the way of life and the order of society, out of which my first novel flowered quite naturally, have been subjected to vast, remorseless tides of change. I can look back at it, as at *Sinister Street*, to a distant, vanished world. And I believe about *Sinister Street* that it can and will stand as an almost matchless picture of the youth of the generation of Englishmen who fought and won the First World War. It's a picture of a class, of course; of a leisured, intelligent, ardent, self-conscious, conscientious, ruling class—a class and a generation which had evolved, smoothly and inevitably, out of more than a century of prosperity, increasing security and peace, and a material and spiritual serenity which we, in our time, can but dimly comprehend.

Of that golden epoch Compton Mackenzie is an articulate, vigorous, sensitive and highly civilized survivor. He's well over sixty now; he's passed through that period of disparagement and neglect which seems inevitable for any serious creative artist in this country; he's bustling with activity, yet he's very gentle, very urbane, very mellow.

In fact he's a very remarkable person, enjoying the full afternoon sunlight of a varied and distinguished and exciting career. He's an eminent public figure; but he's an eminent public figure with a very lively quirk of difference about him. As I expect you know, he comes of a very long-established family of actors; his sister, Fay Compton, has been for years one of London's best-known leading ladies; and I think if Compton Mackenzie himself hadn't been a novelist, he'd have been one of the best and most polished actors of his time. And he brings to everything he does and says a very sure, quick touch of the dramatic.

In recent years he's grown a short, trim white beard; and it gives to his appearance the most enchanting swagger—a hint of the Italian Renaissance, and a hint too of the Spanish Main and fierce, freebooting buccaneers. He was born in an age and a society in which conversation was still a significant art; and he remains one of the great conversationalists and raconteurs of our time. He has worked and travelled and written prodigiously. No fewer than seventy books stand to his name; and that surely is a most astonishing record. A prodigality of energy and talent is indeed one of his most persistent characteristics.

He's written books for children; he's written a study of the Gas industry; he's been Lord Rector of Glasgow University; he's been an ardent Scottish nationalist; he's regarded in Greece, where he soldiered in the 1914-18 war, with a veneration and an affection second only to that given to Lord Byron; he's stood in the dock at the Central Criminal Court in London, charged with an offence against the Official Secrets Act, because in a book of memoirs he disclosed certain facts about the conduct of the 1914-18 war. A movie was made not long ago of one of his recent light novels called "Tight Little Island"—all about some strange goings on in the Outer Hebrides in the 1939-45 War; and there he is, in the movie playing the part of a merchant skipper with the utmost confidence and dash.

He remains a person of dazzling ability, and still—at nearly 70—of promise. In a short time he'll be publishing another book which, I believe, is quite likely to rank—along with *Sinister Street*—as one of his main claims to enduring recognition. Four years ago this autumn he was extremely ill, in St Mary's Hospital here in London. He received a letter from the Historical Section of the Defence Department of the Government of India asking him if he'd write a history of India's part and contribution to victory in the Second World War. He was going to turn it down. He was well over sixty, he was tired, he was ill, he knew nothing about India. While he was pondering the terms of his rejection a visitor came to his bedside—an old friend, General Sir Ian Hamilton, who was then ninety-two. They had been friends ever since the first World War, when the General commanded the British and Dominion attack on Gallipoli and the novelist was an Intelligence officer on his staff. Mackenzie told his visitor how sad he was at having to turn down the India offer. "You've got to go," said the General. "You've got to round off your career by learning something about India."

And a year later Mackenzie was sufficiently recovered to set out on what he's since called "the most enthralling job" of his life. He determined to see and walk over on foot every battlefield in every theatre of war where the Indians fought. He determined to get to know and understand the elaborate, highly-disciplined spiritual and physical machinery which was the old Indian Army. He had ten months of concentrated research. He went all over India—as it happened during that period of extreme political drama and tension which

culminated in the emergence of the two new sovereign states of India and
Pakistan. He got to know people and Army at breathless speed. He was trying
to retrieve historical memories of tremendous importance; and all round him
as he worked even more important history was being made in raw, violent
splashes of political and emotional colour.

Then outside India—because Indian units fought with great bravery and
distinction in every major theatre of War except North West Europe and the
Russian Front—outside India he had to travel thousands of miles by land, sea
and air. He had to go across those serrated ridges of country in Burma which
the maps mark "impassable jungle", but where in 1944 the 14th Army, which
was made up of British and Indian troops, gave the Japs the first big licking
they had on land. He had to go to Malaya and Hong-Kong, and to small
remote islands in the Indian Ocean; he had to go, too, to the Western Desert
and Syria and Tunisia, and to the Italian mountains north of Florence. He had
to go to East Africa to interview a retired general or two, and to reconnoitre
Keren, the unassailable fortress out of which in 1941 the 4th Indian Division
dislodged a host of extremely surprised Italians. All that was pretty arduous
work for a man of over sixty, lately recovered from a grave illness, and by no
means free from twinges and jabs of sharp pain.

Now for many months he's been at home, working on the history. For much
of his life Mackenzie was a passionate lover of islands; he lived in Capri, and
then he owned Jethou, one of the smallest of the Channel Islands, and then he
owned an island off the coast of Scotland. But now he's settled down deep in
the English country, not far from Oxford. You couldn't imagine a more
profound contrast than the one between the place where he's working and the
scenes and the deeds he's got to describe; the deep, sleepy peace of the one;
the violent and heroic strangeness and fierceness of Kohima or Cassino or the
Sangro crossing. He says his book won't pull any punches; but I hope and believe
it'll be something more than combative and energetic. I believe it can have an
epic quality, this final bugle-call of the old Indian Army which I—because
I served alongside it—know to have been, in those years of its zenith, an
incomparable corporate achievement of men of diverse creeds and races.
That Army was unique. It deserves an epic to do it justice. And Compton
Mackenzie's got the opportunity of writing that epic. That's why I say there's
still promise ahead for this adventurous, gay, courageous, superbly talented
man of letters who's nearing seventy. "There is no tragedy of age" he wrote,
long ago, when he himself was young. How right he was—or rather how right,
in his own life, he has proved himself . . . and this is John Connell signing off
in London.

Twenty years later I read that broadcast with a pang. John Connell left us
before he was able to finish his life of Lord Wavell; he had already published
an admirable book about F.M. Auckinleck.

As I write these words *Sinister Street* is being presented by BBC2.

APPENDIX G

5, Lower George Street,
Wexford,
Ireland.
9th Oct. 1950.

Dear Sir,

Enclosed you will find a letter of introduction from Father Sydney MacEwan.

I am an amateur of opera endeavouring to revive an interest in the art, traditional to our town up to the year 1938, since when the old touring opera companies have ceased to visit us.

Since we cannot have actual opera performances (at least for the present) I am making a start by arranging a number of lectures illustrated by gramophone records during the coming winter.

I understand that you are to speak to the Irish Book Association in Dublin early next month and I am venturing to ask if you would be kind enough to consider delivering the opening lecture to what I expect will be known as the Wexford Opera Circle during this visit to Ireland.

Wexford I should add is just two hours journey by car from Dublin, and I should, of course, make all arrangements for your journeys.

The subject of your lecture would be entirely a matter for yourself. To illustrate it I have a rather extensive collection of records ranging from the earliest Berliners to the latest L.P's.

Might I say that to have you speak at Wexford would be the culmination of many years of great pleasure derived from your novels and Gramophone editorials, and at the same time give me an opportunity to thank you personally for your enduring friendship and loyalty to our country's cause.

Yours very truly,

T. J. Walsh.

5, Lower George Street,
Wexford.
13th November 1950.

Dear Mr Mackenzie,

I am today sending you the books by registered post. I have included a copy of "Sinister Street" which I bought in Dublin for His Lordship. I am sure it would give him great pleasure if it were autographed by you, and consequently, if it would not give you too much bother to return it, perhaps you would be kind enough to do this. His full name is James Staunton, D.D., and his bishopric is Fearns.

Once more may I thank you from the bottom of my heart for the great pleasure you gave to me, and to all of us who heard you speak. I think you really have revived an interest in opera in Wexford, for our preliminary meeting some nights ago was most enthusiastic. I will write you from time to time to let you know how we are progressing.

5, Lower George Street,
Wexford.
28th November 1950.

My dear Compton Mackenzie,

Many thanks indeed for your letter. Through an oversight of mine the books were not sent out for about a week, but I feel sure they will have reached you by now. I feel highly honoured to learn that I am to be quoted in the editorial of "The Gramophone", and I am now rather anxiously waiting to read what I actually did write!

I am very happy to know that you enjoyed your brief visit in Wexford. May I point out that we are only a very short distance from Berkshire via Fishguard and Rosslare, and that any time you should care to have an Irish holiday, we will be honoured if you should choose us as your hosts.

We had our first gramophone lecture on last Friday night commencing with about 40 odd members. Of these 40, I should say that 25 are sufficiently interested to stick at it. I am enclosing the programme, and I shall send you on the others as they occur.

I understand you were speaking over the wireless about ten days ago, but unfortunately I missed you. I am keeping a very close watch in the *Radio Times* for future talks.

With every good wish from my wife and myself, and hoping that you *will* visit us soon.

Yours

Tom Walsh.

APPENDIX H

RAYANT PICTURES LIMITED,

13th February 1951

Here is an outline of the writers' Quiz Session to be filmed at Wembley Studios on the 21st.

You will see that it is in fact an "outline", and that the dialogue and commentary are put in merely as suggestions and as a guide to those taking part.

In fact, in each case I have used the words "to this effect", the whole thing being the result of conversations I have had with the four writers.

We propose to film the first part of your scene in the chair on the morning of the 21st, so perhaps you could let me know the place and time where I could call for you in a car to take you to the studio. As we are simply racing against time to complete the whole scene in a day, could we make a really early start from London at, say, 8.45 or 9.0 a.m.?

Would you be so kind as to remember to bring with you a nearly completed "blotting-paper doodle" which will play a big part in the close-up?

RAYANT PICTURES LIMITED

Appendix to Sequence 5 of Final Treatment

of

"SPOTLIGHT ON THE BEST-SELLER"

Scene 1:

The interviewer introduces all four writers, and asks Compton Mackenzie to start. He puts a perfectly straightforward request, for example.

"PERHAPS COMPTON MACKENZIE WILL TELL US ABOUT HIS METHOD OF WRITING A BOOK?"

Scene 2:

Compton Mackenzie replies on his method of writing, and starts to doodle on the blotting paper. After the first few words, for example,

"MOST OF THE WORK ON MY PLOTS IS DONE WHILE I'M ASLEEP. OF COURSE, I HAVE TO PLAN MY CHARACTERS AND THE SETTING IN WHICH THE STORY WILL TAKE PLACE."

dissolve over C/S of doodle to

Scene 3:

Compton Mackenzie in his armchair, at work on a nearly completed doodle. The voice of the commentator takes over to this effect—

"AT ONE TIME MR COMPTON MACKENZIE MIGHT HAVE BECOME AN ACTOR AND USED HIS VERSATILITY IN INTERPRETING OTHER PEOPLE'S WORK. BUT,

IN HIS OWN WORDS, HE FELT THAT AFTER GENERATIONS OF FAMILY CONNEC-
TIONS WITH THE STAGE, HE REQUIRED A NEW MEDIUM OF EXPRESSION . . .
AND . . . WELL, HE BECAME A WRITER INSTEAD."

At this point Compton Mackenzie leans back in his chair and falls asleep.
Camera now tracks in to C/U of his sleeping face. Commentary continues
to this effect—

"IT IS THROUGH THE SUBCONSCIOUS THAT COMPTON MACKENZIE'S PLOTS ARE
WORKED OUT. IN THAT STRANGE BORDERLAND OF THE MIND OF WHICH WE
KNOW SO LITTLE . . ."

Here we bring up in super-imposition dimly-seen marionette figures, as if
moving about in his head.

". . . AND IT IS THROUGH THE THEATRE AND HIS LONG ASSOCIATION WITH IT
THAT HE WORKS, LIVING AND ACTING HIMSELF IN TURN THE PARTS OF HIS
OWN CHARACTERS."

(NOTE.—This whole scene should be treated with an air of romance, and
it is suggested that appropriate music should underlie the whole scene and
thereby form a contrast to the following scene.)

Scene 4:

Main Quiz scene. Gilbert Frankau comes in immediately with a comment
appropriate to the preceding scene, thus stressing the assumption that the
writers round the table have also seen the dream sequence. Gilbert Frankau's
remark is to this effect—

"MY DEAR MONTY, YOU CAN'T POSSIBLY WRITE BOOKS LIKE THAT. THE
TROUBLE WITH YOU IS THAT YOU HAVE NO POETRY IN YOUR SOUL!"

Then follows a brief exchange between Compton Mackenzie and Gilbert
Frankau, and the Quiz Master picks on Gilbert Frankau as the next victim.

Scene 5:

Gilbert Frankau starts to explain his method of writing to this effect—

"TO START WITH, I CAN'T STAND MUSIC OF ANY SORT. MUSIC FOR ME KILLS
EVERYTHING STONE DEAD. I LOATHE THE THEATRE, ACTORS, THE CINEMA
AND EVERYTHING TO DO WITH IT. I HAVE NOT THE LEAST DESIRE TO WRITE
A PLAY. I AM ESSENTIALLY A POET."

Dissolve to

Scene 6:

Gilbert Frankau at home, preparing card-index for a new book and working
to a time schedule. Voice of the commentator describes Gilbert Frankau's
method of working.

Scene 7:

Back to the Quiz table again, where the others are again presumed to have
seen the behind-the-scenes working of Gilbert Frankau.
Miss Ruby M. Ayres immediately starts an exchange with Gilbert Frankau
to this effect—

"ALL THIS NONSENSE ABOUT DISLIKING THE THEATRE AND BEING A POET. I THINK IT'S ALL A POSE. I THOUGHT YOU'D BEEN TRYING HARD TO GET A PLAY ACCEPTED."

Further exchange by Gilbert Frankau.

The Quiz Master interrupts again to question Miss Ayres on her method of writing.

Miss Ayres starts to explain to this effect—

"I HAVE NO INHIBITIONS AT ALL. I WRITE PURELY TO ORDER. FOR ME IT'S A BUSINESS. I FIRST THINK OF A TITLE AND WRITE A BOOK ROUND IT. I TYPE EVERYTHING OF COURSE, AND WHEN I SIT DOWN TO START I HAVEN'T THE FAINTEST IDEA WHAT I'M GOING TO WRITE NEXT. FOR ME THE BOOK WRITES ITSELF . . ."

Scene 8:

Here we dissolve to Miss Ayres at home showing her background and method of work. Her collection of china and porcelain, her parrot and cat and a book-case completely filled with her own works.

Scene 9:

Back at the Quiz table, Margaret Kennedy picks on Miss Ayres' remark about writing spontaneously, to this effect—

"NOW I'M JUST THE OPPOSITE. I HAVE BLUE PRINTS FOR STORIES PUT AWAY FOR YEARS BEFORE I ACTUALLY COME TO WRITE THEM. WHAT'S MORE, AS A YOUNG WRITER I WAS AN ARDENT ADMIRER OF COMPTON MACKENZIE'S TECHNIQUE . . . FOR ME, ANYTHING I SEE OF AN UNUSUAL NATURE IMMEDIATELY SUGGESTS A STORY . . ."

Dissolve to

Scene 10:

Reconstructed scene of Margaret Kennedy in which to amplify her remark "Any odd occurrence suggests a story."

Scene 11:

Back to the Quiz table, where the Quiz Master sums up after brief exchange between authors.